THE AFRICAN ECONOMY

In the wake of economic crisis and civil war, it is tempting to take a pessimistic view of Africa's future. However, recent policy reforms, accompanied by improved growth, suggest a more optimistic prospect for the next decade.

This collection of essays outlines and discusses the multiple challenges that Africa faces as it is entering the new millennium. How should it transform its demonstrated resilience into the virtues of sustained growth, poverty reduction and the building of democratic institutions? How will individual countries respond to the exigencies of the world market economy?

Steve Kayizzi-Mugerwa has assembled an impressive team of international experts who analyse in depth the current state of the African economy and make constructive suggestions about its future direction. The contributors argue that, despite enduring challenges such as food security and employment creation, Africa faces a brighter future in sustainable growth provided that governance and policy-making are effectively employed to maintain peace, achieve greater regional collaboration and encourage private sector competitiveness.

Steve Kayizzi-Mugerwa is Associate Professor of development economics at Göteborg University, Sweden and has worked for the African Development Bank. His current research focuses on privatisation and market development.

Contributors: Wilfred Aboum-Ongaro, Renato Aguilar, Arne Bigsten, Margaret Chitiga, John Ddumba-Ssentamu, Göte Hansson, Peter Kimuyu, Charles Leyeka Lufumpa, Jörgen Levin, Mats Lundahl, Ramos Mabugu, Kupukile Mlambo, Victor Murinde, Abraham Mwenda, Manenga Ndulo, Temitope W. Oshikoya, Mariam S. Pal, Thomas Sterner and Howard White.

ROUTLEDGE STUDIES IN DEVELOPMENT ECONOMICS

THE AFRICAN ECONOMY

Policy, institutions and the future

edited by

Steve Kayizzi-Mugerwa

London and New York

First published 1999
by Routledge
11 New Fetter Lane, London EC4P 4EE

Simultaneously published in the USA and Canada
by Routledge
29 West 35th Street, New York, NY 10001

© 1999 Steve Kayizzi-Mugerwa, editorial matter and selection; the
contributors, individual chapters.

Typeset in Garamond by PureTech India Ltd, Pondicherry
http://www.puretech.com

Printed and bound in Great Britain by
Biddles Ltd, Guildford and King's Lynn

British Library Cataloguing in Publication Data
A catalogue record for this book is available from the British Library

Library of Congress Cataloging in Publication Data
The African economy: policy, institutions and the future / [edited by]
Steve Kayizzi-Mugerwa.
(Routledge studies in development economics; 13) Includes
bibliographical references and index.
1. Africa, Sub-Saharan—Economic conditions—1960—Case studies.
2. Africa, Sub-Saharan—Economic policy—Case studies.   I. Kayizzi-
Mugerwa, Steve.   II. Series.
HC800.A5675   1999
338.967—dc21 98—15338

ISBN 0–415–18323–5

FOR ARNE BIGSTEN

CONTENTS

CONTENTS

FIGURES

TABLES

CONTRIBUTORS

Wilfred Aboum-Ongaro is agricultural economist, Economic and Social Policy Division, United Nations Economic Commission for Africa, Addis Ababa.

Renato Aguilar is associate professor in economics, School of Economics, Göteborg University

Arne Bigsten is professor of development economics, School of Economics, Göteborg University

Margaret Chitiga is lecturer, Department of Economics, University of Zimbabwe.

John Ddumba-Ssentamu is head, Department of Economics, Makerere University, Kampala.

Göte Hansson is professor of international economics, Lund University.

Steve Kayizzi-Mugerwa is associate professor of development economics, School of Economics, Göteborg University

Peter Kimuyu is associate professor of economics, University of Nairobi, and fellow, Institute of Policy Analysis and Research, Nairobi.

Charles Leyeka Lufumpa is acting division manager (Statistics), African Development Bank, Abidjan.

Jörgen Levin is research fellow, School of Economics, Göteborg University.

Mats Lundahl is professor of development economics, Stockholm School of Economics.

Ramos Mabugu is lecturer, Department of Economics, University of Zimbabwe.

Kupukile Mlambo is senior economist, Research Division, African Development Bank, Abidjan.

Victor Murinde is director of Development Finance Programmes, Birmingham Business School, University of Birmingham.

Abraham Mwenda is Deputy Governor (Operations), Bank of Zambia, Lusaka.

Manenga Ndulo is head, Department of Economics, University of Zambia, Lusaka.

Temitope W. Oshikoya is division manager, Research Division, African Development Bank, Abidjan.

Mariam S. Pal is economist (Social Sector), Programs West Department, Asian Development Bank, Manila.

Thomas Sterner is professor of environmental economics, Department of Economics, Göteborg University.

Howard White is senior lecturer, Institute of Social Studies, The Hague.

PREFACE

This book is the product of a broad international collaboration. For many it is the realisation of a long-held wish to contribute to a volume on the African economy. However, writing a book on Africa at the end of the century, and for that matter the millennium, is not entirely without risk, with the temptation to prophesise great. To avoid this, two constraining features were suggested: first that contributions should be based on syntheses of research and practical experience and, second, that the book be accessible to African policy-makers, with a focus on policy formulation, institutional constraints and future prospects.

I would like to thank individual contributors for their collaboration and Sida/SAREC for financial assistance towards the book's dissemination. Dr Mario Zejan and Professor Mats Lundahl provided useful advice at the beginning of the project while Karen Lindberg provided editorial assistance.

Finally, offshore academic interest in Africa is mainly thanks to individuals who have dedicated their professional lives to research on the various aspects of the continent. Our colleague, teacher and fellow traveller Professor Arne Bigsten is a good example. We dedicate this book to him in the hope that it will propel him towards new research horizons.

Göteborg, February 1998
S. Kayizzi-Mugerwa

1

INTRODUCTION

Steve Kayizzi-Mugerwa

Africa at the end of the twentieth century is in some ways quite different from when the century began or when, half-way through it, the struggles for independence were embarked on in the various countries. Its cities have expanded, modern communications have speeded up the acquisition of knowledge and conducting of business, and a sizeable elite enjoys a standard of living at par with any in the richer world. However, in terms of poverty, gross inequalities in resource distribution and disease, things have changed very little, and seem to have worsened in comparison with other regions. The century will thus have a mixed review: Africa achieved its independence from colonial powers, but its new leadership was often inadequate. Its poverty worsened even as more of its people acquired better education. Civil wars displaced vast populations, while diseases continued to ravage the rural areas and the cities. These plus a heavy debt burden and the policy conditionalities of the multilateral donor agencies have led to loss of economic and political self-determination.

Still, a number of evaluations concur on one issue, namely that the 1990s have witnessed a convergence of factors bound to have important implications for Africa's future. The end of the Cold War reduced Africa's strategic interest to the West, and seemed at first to unleash conflicts all over the continent, with some fearing the demise of the African nation state. This has also compelled African countries to seek their own solutions to economic and political problems in an unprecedented burst of activity referred to in some circles as an 'African renaissance'. Countries seem to be on their way to transcending the era of structural adjustment, putting in place long-term strategies for development. Moreover, in the rapidly changing global economy, even developed countries are looking for new modes of co-operation with Africa based on mutual partnerships (African Development Bank 1997, Kifle *et al.* 1997, Kayizzi-Mugerwa 1998, Kayizzi-Mugerwa *et al.* 1998, Swedish Ministry of Foreign Affairs 1997).

What then are Africa's economic policy priorities at the end of the decade? A statement made by twelve African leaders at the end of a regional meeting in Kampala, January 1998, to discuss economic development made the

1

following list: 'education and professional training, rural transformation, private sector development, the development of infrastructure, conflict prevention and resolution and public sector reform and good governance' (*PANA News*, 26 January 1998).

The study is divided into three parts: Part I concentrates on policy issues, with a focus on credibility, reputation and learning. Part II looks at institutions in the broader sense, including the performance of the evolving social, political and macroeconomic structures. Part III looks at the future, in terms of political economy, the performance of agriculture, the environment–development nexus, and the implications of private sector expansion.

POLICY

Until recently, with the emergence of economic crisis, East Asia's spectacularly rapid pace of development, with average growth rates of close to 10 per cent, made Africa's modest recovery inconsequential by comparison. In the 1950s, Africa's level of development was at par with those of countries like Malaysia, Indonesia and Taiwan. Today the two regions are in most respects incomparable. How do countries become tigers? That is, how do they sustain growth rates of 6–10 per cent? In Chapter 2, 'Looking for African tigers', written before the Asian economic crisis, Arne Bigsten highlights some of the salient features of economic success.

Recent experience has shown, Bigsten argues, that many poor countries and regions have been able to close the gap between them and the rich countries, indicating a growth advantage to being relatively poor. The question then is why have the forces of convergence eluded Africa, even though it is capital-scarce, implying potentially high returns on investment? Three factors are identified: a high level of risk, including that related to policy reversal; high levels of aid inflows which have distorted the governments' ability to signal their intentions; and the relatively poor human capital endowment that holds down the efficiency of investment.

Changing the policy stance is also important. Bigsten argues that inward orientation, characterised by trade restrictions, has been a major impediment to growth. More recently, however, countries that have pursued a more open stance have experienced rapid rates of growth. On the subject of governance, Bigsten argues that governments need to care about the incentive structures they put in place. The policies of price and exchange rate controls tilted incentives in favour of powerful groups in urban areas, and generally against the farmers in the countryside. Sidelining the majority explains the paucity of growth to a large extent.

Bigsten concludes that Africa's problems are not immutable. Many countries are now importing much more than they export, thanks partly to the repatriation of flight capital. He also notes that the public in Africa is more vocal than before, while civil society has a real meaning in a growing number of countries. If these changes are supported by parallel ones in the political sphere, then Africa could embark on sustainable growth. This might not be at the speed of the tigers, but certainly at the more indigenous and steadier pace of the African elephant.

In Chapter 3, 'Investment, macroeconomic policies and growth', Kupukile Mlambo and Temitope Oshikoya develop further the themes introduced by Bigsten by looking more explicitly at factors influencing private investment in Africa. They show that while explanations advanced by the endogenous growth literature are persuasive, capital accumulation is of cardinal import-ance to growth. The general fragility of the growth process in Africa is blamed on the continent's low rates of capital accumulation. Though compar-able with those of East Asia in the 1960s and early 1970s, at about 20 per cent, African savings rates were less than 20 per cent in the 1990s, while those of East Asia were above 30 per cent. The evolution of investment rates has been largely similar. Failure to attract private foreign investment is especially marked. In the mid-1990s, Africa was able to attract only 5 per cent of the global capital inflows to developing countries.

Mlambo and Oshikoya then survey the empirical evidence. They argue that studies that have tried to establish a quantitative relationship between invest-ment and output growth in Africa have yielded conflicting results. Mlambo and Oshikoya concur with Bigsten with regard to the important role of the policy environment. They argue that policy uncertainty is bad for investment. Since most investment is irreversible, investors will avoid making long-term commitments. Africa's large foreign debt is also seen as a serious impediment to credibility. It constitutes a claim on the countries' future income, and thus reduces the funds available for investment.

Mlambo and Oshikoya conclude that although earlier policy reforms lay the foundation for long-term growth, they do not constitute a sufficient con-dition for increased investment. It is important that African countries pursue a strategy that emphasises the pivotal role of the private sector in develop-ment, one supported by the public sector's provision of an enabling business environment. This includes an adequate supply of infrastructure services, functioning legal institutions and an efficient financial sector.

In Chapter 4, 'Aid and economic reform', Howard White identifies the links between aid and the pace and extent of economic adjustment. He departs from the double paradox identified by Streeten (1987): if reforms are so beneficial why aren't they carried out anyway, and why should countries be paid for implementing them? White argues that Streeten's paradox is resolved if it is accepted that there are important mechanisms by which aid can facilitate the reform process.

White notes, however, that the fact of the failure of conditionality is not the same thing as saying donors should not finance reform. That the relative neglect of how it is that aid can support reform is one possible factor behind the general failure to do so. Evidence from the aid literature suggests that aid has a number of positive impacts on the reform process. For example, aid to support government expenditures is important in the early stages of reform, since the reform programme may require restraint of non-aid-financed expenditures. In the macroeconomic area, aid was crucial in bringing inflation down in countries like Zambia and Uganda, since it enabled an increased supply of imports. In Ghana, aid helped the country build up its foreign exchange reserves before the opening up of the foreign exchange market. It was also necessary for financing the poverty alleviation programme that helped reduce domestic discontent. White concludes that while aid is not sufficient to ensure reform, it is a necessary ingredient of the reform process.

In Chapter 5, 'Aid-constrained trade reform in Kenya', Jörgen Levin analyses the impact of trade reforms undertaken under donor conditionality. Though the Kenyan economy dominates the region, it has become increasingly difficult for it to make inroads in international markets. Trade policy reforms were initially resisted, but became inevitable following external shocks and an aid embargo in the early 1990s. A general equilibrium model is used to conduct policy and external shock experiments, under the assumption of a 50 per cent tariff reduction. The experiments include the impact of aid compensation of the revenue shortfall arising from the tariff reduction, terms of trade shocks with and without aid, and the impacts of increasing government expenditure with or without aid.

Levin argues that while the efficiency gains of lowering tariffs might appear small, there are a number of associated dynamic effects. Notably, important incentives are created for producers of tradables. Still, the increase in economic activity is not able to compensate fully for the loss of tariff revenue. Kenya's example shows that while foreign aid inflows enabled a more gradual implementation of the new tariff structures, it had, via the appreciation of the exchange rate, serious costs in terms of delays to the reallocation of resources to tradable sectors.

Chapter 6, 'Monetary policy effectiveness in Zambia', by Abraham Mwenda, looks at the conduct of macroeconomic policy in Zambia in a period of economic liberalisation. From an insular and controlled economy, the country has in recent years made one of the more dramatic policy transformations in Africa. A key reform has been the switch from direct monetary instruments such as credit and interest rate controls to indirect ones, including open market operations. The current and capital accounts were liberalised and the Bank of Zambia became the key player in monetary policy, with the prime objective of inflation control.

In an empirical investigation, Mwenda analyses the impact that switching to indirect instruments has had on monetary policy effectiveness in reducing and stabilising the growth of money supply and inflation. This is done by checking for structural breaks in money supply behaviour and by trying to determine whether the change resulted in significant reductions in the growth and stability of broad money supply and inflation.

Mwenda concludes that indirect monetary control brought about significant reductions in inflation, accompanied by a reduction in the variability of both money supply and inflation. However, there was a general failure to meet targets. This was due to weak fiscal controls, especially failure to implement a cash budget. Other demands, including the need to service foreign debt and to accumulate reserves, negatively affected the value of the kwacha. To succeed, indirect monetary control must be accompanied by well designed measures to address problems related to slow learning and system inefficiencies.

Chapter 7, 'Minimum wages and trade regimes: CGE results for Zimbabwe', by Ramos Mabugu and Margaret Chitiga, looks at the impact of minimum-wage legislation under changing trade regimes. The authors conduct simulations by assuming a 5 per cent increase in the minimum wage under foreign exchange controls and a liberalised regime, representing roughly the experience of the country. Not unexpectedly, this reduces the employment of unskilled workers across the board, as sectoral production costs go up. The decline is compensated somewhat by higher demand for food and services, sectors which are relatively low skill intensive. However, higher unskilled wages are partly at the expense of skilled wages. The impact on the tradable sector is also negative. In the liberalised regime, the sectoral impacts, though negative, are milder.

Mabugu and Chitiga conclude that while trade reforms are expected to benefit export-oriented sectors, by reallocating labour from the importable sector, this outcome has not materialised in Zimbabwe. Except for mining, all sectors have seen reductions in employment levels. It may well be that labour market distortions have been more serious than anticipated.

INSTITUTIONS

Part II of the book focuses on the economic and political aspects of African institutions. African institutions range from the Pan-African and regional institutions that governments have tried to set up over the decades to rural based non-government organisations with a fairly limited and localised development agenda such as savings clubs. Among the lessons of structural adjustment are that policy efforts undertaken within a weak institutional framework are bound to achieve very little and that economic policies cannot make much headway if they neglect politics.

In Chapter 8 Victor Murinde discusses 'Financial institutions and the mobilisation of resources for development'. He argues that there is considerable scope for capital mobilisation within domestic markets but that this has not been easy to do in the past owing to the excessive controls under which the financial sector has had to operate. Central banks became mere appendages of government, failed to innovate, and their regulation and supervision of the banking system and the rest of the financial sector remained poor.

Murinde notes further that in addition to commercial banks, there is a need for the development of several other types of banks in order to expand services to areas such as merchant and investment banking, as well as venture capital financing. He also argues that financial dualism should be reduced by extending banking services to the countryside and helping to upgrade the informal services offered in the rural and urban areas. Looking at the development of financial institutions, Murinde expresses some pessimism regarding the efficacy of stock markets in delivering long-term financing for development. Still, he sees them as important in the revitalisation of the African economies, especially if done at the regional level. Similarly, the creation of supranational institutions such as regional central banks with a mandate to effect policy will be important in establishing credibility.

In Chapter 9, 'Institutions and rural development in Uganda', John Ddumba-Ssentamu focuses on rural institutions. Many African governments have identified rural development as their main policy concern. However, many years after independence the rural areas in Uganda remain undeveloped, with a critical shortage of modern services. Ddumba-Ssentamu argues that the slow progress is to be blamed on the lack of an adequate institutional framework. The long years of economic chaos in Uganda aggravated the situation by destroying infrastructure and rural markets, interrupting the introduction of new techniques.

Non-governmental organisations have increased activities to fill the gap left by the public sector. However, NGOs have sometimes been unable to meet the farmers' requirements, partly owing to shortage of resources and partly owing to poor knowledge transfer. Ddumba-Ssentamu concludes that it is important for rural dwellers to take part in the policies that influence them.

In Chapter 10, 'Building African institutions: learning from South Asia', Mariam S. Pal discusses the important issue of whether Africa can learn from the successful grass-roots institutions for credit lending and development pioneered in Bangladesh. She argues that a south–south transfer of knowledge and ideas might be far superior to the more traditional north–south transfer of ideas for development.

Pal argues that since much of the Grameen Bank's approach is steeped in Bangladeshi culture, it is necessary to identify an 'essential Grameen', that is, the basic elements of the model which could be replicated. This includes a strict focus on low-income groups, compulsory regular savings, strong emphasis on training for members and bank staff, homogeneous group formation and integration of a socio-economic development agenda with banking for the poor. Pal then provides examples of the application of the Grameen model in Malawi and Burkina Faso. Pal concludes that, to succeed, the Grameen approach should be targeted to the poor, credit non-availability must be serious, and women must constitute an important proportion of the beneficiaries. Furthermore, financial sustainability must be a declared objective of the lending effort.

In Chapter 11, 'Market power and productivity in Zimbabwean manufacturing', Kupukile Mlambo and Thomas Sterner analyse the evolution of factor productivity in the presence of market power. In the course of a long international embargo, Zimbabwean industry acquired a degree of diversity via policies of import substitution. Indeed by 1982 the country was said to be on the road to industrialisation, with manufacturing accounting for 25 per cent of GDP. However, the resulting industrial structures were both monopolistic and oligopolistic. This continued to be the case well into the late 1980s.

Using a translog function to model variable costs and thereby calculate price–cost mark-ups, Mlambo and Sterner argue that the latter are significant across the sub-sectors of manufacturing. Total factor productivity was decomposed into the technical change effect, the returns to scale effect, and the price–cost margin effect. It was found that the productivity increases in some sectors were highly illusory since they were merely the effects of increased concentration. There are bound to be sharp profit declines as the cutting edge of competition sharpens.

In Chapter 12, 'Regionalism in African development', Peter Kimuyu looks at the rationale for regional co-operation in Africa and looks at reasons why outcomes have fallen short of expectations. In the expanding global economy, there is a fear that African countries may fail to benefit from the emerging configurations. Since they are individually weak, it is important that they establish viable regional co-operation to help them meet the challenges ahead.

Kimuyu argues that while theory predicts substantial benefits from regional co-operation, African attempts have failed because political motives have tended to override economic ones. There was thus a tendency to overcommit, since there was no serious mechanism for enforcement. Looking at the integration record, Kimuyu argues that structural adjustment policies helped introduce a uniform set of policies among African countries. This has made it possible to pursue more successful forms of economic collaboration. As policy credibility is established at the national level, regional institutions will become stronger and more relevant.

In Chapter 13, 'Transforming economic and political structures for growth: the Zambian experience', Manenga Ndulo surveys Zambia's transformation from a one-party state, with a controlled economy dominated by parastatals, to a multi-party system of government that has adopted a market-based economic system.

Manenga argues that in spite of adjustment efforts during the late 1980s, the mainstream political views and the general ideological inclination of the country opposed market forces as a means of resource allocation and as a tool of economic management. Part of the problem seemed to be that economic policy was being run increasingly by technocrats, while government was blamed for the unfavourable outcomes. Market-oriented policies would not be pursued consistently until a government not burdened by the control legacy was elected.

Manenga argues that in spite of broad economic reforms under the Movement for Multi-party Democracy government, a high and stable growth rate remains elusive. Part of the difficulty seems to be the lingering problems of governance and slow institutional reform. The liberalisation of the economy has since been accompanied by a noticeable reticence in the political arena. The political inertia has led to an increased threat of policy reversal, dampening in turn the investment and growth prospects of the economy. Manenga concludes that commitment to sound macroeconomic policies is ultimately a political decision. It is thus imperative to strengthen all aspects of good governance as the best way of enhancing policy credibility and ensuring irreversibility.

In Chapter 14, 'The other Africa: economic development in Lusophone countries', Renato Aguilar looks at aspects of development that differentiate Portuguese-speaking Africa from the French- and English-speaking countries.

Aguilar argues that the failure of the West to support liberation movements in Portuguese Africa pushed them to the Soviet bloc and led to the adoption of socialist systems of government. Looking specifically at Angola, Mozambique and Guinea-Bissau, Aguilar notes that economic reforms have been far more difficult to undertake than in other African countries. This is because the command type of economy that the Lusophone countries adopted was much more resistant to change than those of their neighbours. Furthermore, most countries had gone through a long civil war.

Aguilar concludes that since Portuguese-speaking countries in Africa do not share borders with each other, they need to work more closely with their immediate neighbours. This is already happening in southern Africa, where both Angola and Mozambique are members of the Southern African Development Community. Guinea-Bissau on the other hand has joined the CFA franc zone. For countries where stability was tenuous in the past, these new alliances will help create guarantees of a more stable future.

THE FUTURE

Part III takes a look at aspects of Africa's future. In Chapter 15, 'The new South Africa: growth or stagnation?', Mats Lundahl looks at South Africa's development prospects in the next decade. With the end of apartheid in South Africa, many analysts saw the country as the economic engine that the continent was looking for. Yet the country has had innumerable obstacles to overcome on the home front. Lundahl argues that if South Africa fails to resolve its growth equation and create the jobs that the black constituency is demanding, it will be extremely difficult for the country to play the role of locomotive to the rest of Africa.

In analysing constraints on growth, Lundahl sees investment as the most serious. Though high rates of private investment are assumed by the government, it is difficult to see how it will ensure them, given that they are determined entirely by the private sector's own estimation of returns on investment. Another relates to employment. How will the authorities be able to create the labour market flexibility that is so important for the working of a modern economy? Lundahl also sees some built-in policy brakes, especially with regard to fiscal balance. The choice between higher taxation and expenditure cuts will be difficult to make. Lundahl concludes that the redistribution debate will become stronger as the economy fails to meet growth targets. Ultimately politicians will have to devise methods of meeting the demands of their constituency or be prepared to face political retribution.

In Chapter 16, 'The political economy of the Horn', Göte Hansson looks at the feasibility of economic development in the absence of 'agents of stability' in the Horn. During the Cold War the countries of the Horn of Africa were deemed important in the eyes of the superpowers. This brought considerable rivalry, but also benefits to countries that were able to manipulate events in their favour. Above all, conflicts were not allowed to escalate. Since the end of the Cold War, the countries of the Horn have been left to fend for themselves.

Hansson looks at a number of regional challenges in the Horn. The first relates to the question of regional integration, both as a way of strengthening the economies and of reducing the conflicts and political tensions in the region. The second issue relates to the concept of ethnonationalism and economic development. Hansson notes that, owing to the ethnic diversity of the Horn and the porous borders, national cohesion is weak. The third issue relates to emerging geopolitical tensions. Among these is the issue of water, especially relating to the control of the waters of the Nile. Religious fundamentalism and related civil wars are also seen as seeds of future conflict in the region.

Hansson concludes that in the absence of strong economic and political institutions, and with instability continuing to afflict the region, the Horn of Africa will not be able to overcome its marginalisation. International assistance thus needs to focus on strengthening the region's socio-economic institutions.

In Chapter 17, 'Agriculture, policy impacts and the road ahead', Wilfred Aboum-Ongaro reviews the evolution of agricultural policies in Africa, their impact and what should be expected in the future. He argues that three issues are frequently raised in policy-related discussions of African agriculture. The first relates to the continent's poor capacity to grow food, leading to serious food insecurity, the second to poor incentives and inadequate levels of technology adoption that have lowered agricultural productivity, and the third to population pressures and the resultant impact on resource husbandry.

In looking at the future of agriculture, Aboum-Ongaro argues that the most important issue is research and its dissemination to end users, the farming community. In the past the bulk of funding for agricultural research has come from the donor community. This has in turn set the national research agenda. To make research a central feature of agricultural output, national universities need to be incorporated in the on-going effort. There is also scope for collaboration and the pooling of research resources among the various countries in Africa. Aboum-Ongaro concludes that a fast-growing agricultural sector is a prerequisite for the growth of modern industry. It will create the spur, in terms of demand for inputs, that industry needs in order to take off. There is thus also need to support the development of dynamic linkages between agriculture and non-agriculture.

Expanding on the above, Charles Leyeka Lufumpa looks in Chapter 18, 'Towards sustainable development: the poverty–environment nexus', at poverty and the environment within the scope of Africa's search for sustainable development. Africa's rapid population growth, inadequate food production, poor access to social services, and increasing degradation of the environment may create a vicious circle of poverty, especially in the rural areas, that will be difficult to tackle in the future. He thus argues that, for a poverty-reducing development strategy to be feasible, it must also address environmental concerns.

Lufumpa identifies strategies for combining efficient natural resource management with poverty reduction. Policymakers need to improve their knowledge of the factors influencing the changes in the environment and how to manage them. There is also need for an institutional framework to ensure that the long-term goals of sustainable development are achieved. This relates in turn to adequate legal and land tenure systems. Lufumpa concludes that economic policies which increase overall efficiency are beneficial to the environment. The removal of distortions and improvement of people's access to productive resources enhance growth and reduce poverty. The main goal of policymakers should be to avoid irreversible use or destruction of natural resources.

In Chapter 19, 'Privatisation and market development', Steve Kayizzi-Mugerwa dwells on the subject of private sector development, the focus of considerable debate in the past decade. He notes that, though initially assumed to be politically extremely sensitive, privatisation became common in Africa at the end of the 1990s. Many countries, irrespective of earlier ideology, have divested from the parastatal sectors and market-oriented policies have been adopted. Kayizzi-Mugerwa reviews the debate by discussing the indigenous question, the dynamics of privatisation, the support structures needed for an expanding private sector, and a number of privatisation experiences. He concludes that the success of privatisation will be judged by the extent to which it contributes to sustainable economic growth, via the fostering of institutions for market development and improved corporate governance.

REFERENCES

African Development Bank (1997) *African Development Report*, Oxford: Oxford University Press.

Kayizzi-Mugerwa, S. (1998) 'Africa and the donor community: from conditionality to partnership', *Journal of International Development*, 10(2): 219–25.

Kayizzi-Mugerwa, S., Olukoshi, A.D. and Wohlgemuth, L. (eds) (1998) *A New Partnership for African Development: Issues and Parameters* II, Uppsala: Scandinavian Institute of African Studies.

Kifle, E., Olukoshi, A.D. and Wohlgemuth, L. (eds) (1997) *Towards a New Partnership with Africa – Challenges and Opportunities*, Uppsala: Scandinavian Institute of African Studies.

Streeten, P. (1987) 'Structural adjustment: a survey of the issues and options', *World Development*, 15 (12): 1469–82.

Swedish Ministry of Foreign Affairs (1997), *Partnership with Africa: Proposals for a New Swedish Policy towards sub-Saharan Africa*, Stockholm: UD.

Part I

POLICY

2

LOOKING FOR AFRICAN TIGERS

Arne Bigsten

Coming to Africa for the first time close on twenty-five years ago, I found poverty more widespread than I had imagined. What excited me most, however, was the mood of self-confidence and optimism then still common among most groups. Most of the newly independent states had experienced radical social and economic changes in the previous decade, and growth had been buoyant. However, as the effects of the first oil crisis hit the continent and the countries began to run out of easy import-substitution options, the fortunes, and the mood, started to change. Economies stagnated and sub-Saharan Africa's *per capita* incomes fell unceasingly for a good part of two decades. While on the other side of the Indian Ocean the countries of East Asia had lifted themselves from poverty to prosperity, no economies in Africa have been anywhere as successful, although some have performed relatively better than others. The successful exceptions have been Botswana and Mauritius. Both had reached *per capita* incomes of over US$3,000 per year by the 1990s. There is also the special case of South Africa, which has had high average income levels throughout, but where incomes are very unevenly distributed. During the last few years a few other countries, such as Uganda and Ethiopia, have seen higher growth rates, but from a very low base.

The question raised in this chapter is whether it is possible for African countries to become tiger economies, with sustained growth rates in the range of 6–10 per cent. I argue that although Africans are generally poorer today than they were two decades ago, a change for the better is not only possible but seems to be taking place in a number of countries. As in the early 1970s, there is again guarded optimism. The determination of Africans to take control of their own destiny is unmistakable. There is a realisation that strategies once broadly acclaimed were non-starters, and that difficult choices have to be made. Those choices are by now rather obvious, but the question is whether decision-makers will find it in their interest to make them.

15

THE GROWTH RECORD

In spite of some recovery in 1995 and 1996, with *per capita* incomes increasing by 0.3 per cent and 2.1 per cent respectively (African Development Bank 1997), Africa still stands out as the worst performing region of the world. During the 1980s and the first half of the 1990s *per capita* incomes in sub-Saharan Africa fell by 1.3 per cent per year (see Table 2.1). The low level of income led to poor access to education and health.

Since World War II the world economy has grown rapidly, and many countries have closed or reduced the income gap relative to the most developed countries. This indicates that there may be advantages in being a latecomer or that there is a growth advantage in being relatively poor. Since Africa is a poor continent, it should have a conditional advantage, although the forces of convergence have so far not been effective there. It is estimated that about a third of the gap between Africa and the rest of the LDCs, in terms of growth rates, may be explained by the lower investment rates, while the remaining two-thirds are due to slower productivity growth (Collier and Gunning 1997). As shown in Table 2.1, the investment rate in East Asia is twice that of Africa, where, since 1979, the amount of capital per worker has fallen by a fifth. However, in spite of this apparent capital scarcity, the return on capital stock is low. *Per capita* net private capital inflow is three times higher in East Asia than in Africa. There is also evidence (Claessens and Naude 1993) that in the face of poor economic returns, African wealth holders have chosen to transfer a substantial part of their capital elsewhere. It is estimated that people ordinarily resident in Africa hold 37 per cent of their wealth outside the continent. Africa thus seems to be a region which investors, including its own citizens, have tended to avoid. Lack of private capital inflow has partly been compensated by large inflows of foreign aid. Thus while aid, as a share of GDP, is between 1 per cent and 2 per cent in the other developing regions, it is more than 16 per cent in Africa.

Why are rates of return on investment in Africa so low? Inadequacies in standard policy variables such as exchange rates and trade policy, fiscal and monetary policy, and public service provision explain a sizeable part of the low productivity level, and measures included in structural adjustment programmes to change policies have had some positive impact. Countries which have enjoyed peace and avoided high macroeconomic instability and large allocative inefficiencies have indeed seen improved growth rates. However, overall the African response to reforms has been worse than expected.

So what could account for this outcome? The high level of risk is certainly a crucial factor. When risks are high, we would expect high returns to coexist with low investment. However, in Africa returns on domestic investment are low. This suggests that in spite of the high outflow noted above there are still restrictions on capital movements. With regard to foreign direct investment, this does not matter. Foreign investors do in fact recognise high risk as the

16

Table 2.1 African, Asian and Latin American development indicators

Region	GDP per capita 1995 (US$)	GDP per capita growth 1980–90 (%)	GDP per capita growth 1990–95 (%)	Life expectancy (years)	Adult illiteracy (%)	Growth of exports 1980–90 (%)	Growth of exports 1990–95 (%)	Gross domestic investment (% of GDP)	External debt (% of GDP)	Aid (% of GDP)
Sub-Saharan Africa	490 (285)[a]	−1.3	−1.2	52	43	0.9	0.9	19	81.3	16.3
East Asia and Pacific	800	6.0	9.0	68	17	9.3	17.8	39	32.9	1.1
South Asia	350	3.5	2.7	61	51	6.6	8.6	23	30.5	1.9
Latin America and Caribbean	3,320	−0.3	1.5	69	13	5.2	6.6	20	41.0	1.7

Source: World Bank (1997).

Note
[a] Excluding South Africa.

major obstacle to investment in Africa. Indeed, here we do find the expected combination of high risk/high returns/low investment. The continent has grown slowly because it has been an unusually capital-hostile environment. One of the fears of investors is the high risk of policy reversal. It has also been noted that the high aid inflows may have reduced the ability of genuinely reforming governments to signal their intentions (Rodrik 1992).

In spite of dramatic improvements in human resource development since independence, Africa still has relatively low levels of human capital. It has a much lower life expectancy, and higher adult illiteracy rates than comparable regions. Poor health and education are holding down the efficiency of investment.

Thus the economic environment in Africa seems to cause both slow productivity growth and low investment. This is also reflected in Africa's poor export performance relative to other developing regions.[1] The continent has not been able to upgrade its productive capacities to keep up with the demands of the world market. The issues looked at are the following: first, what specific characteristics of the African environment cause slow growth? Second, how can they be changed?

RISKY ENVIRONMENT

Agriculture remains the most important sector in Africa. However, Africa's rural sector is a high-risk environment without formal insurance and credit markets. Agents in the traditional economy operate in this risky environment with few liquid assets, and have to devise costly mechanisms to protect themselves. Typically this is done through diversification, the accumulation of assets for consumption smoothing and via informal insurance arrangements. To establish workable insurance mechanisms, attempts have to be made to address moral hazard and adverse selection problems. Traditional institutions have dealt with these problems through village or kinship groups. Since there is more social intimacy in the village, moral hazard problems are reduced, while membership of kinship groups, being based on birth, eliminates the problem of adverse selection. While lineage rules of inheritance enforce inter-generational transfers of assets, the kinship groups can ensure adherence to other rules by the threat of exclusion. However, all risk reduction-related measures have costs with regard to growth.

Social capital, that is the combination of social, legal and political factors necessary for a well functioning economy, is crucial for development. It is also important with regard to learning, e.g. the adoption of innovations. It increases investment and generates inter-household externalities such as the diffusion of techniques, the efficient use of credit, and raises the scope for collective action, e.g. with regard to local schools or roads. Lack of social capital has constrained growth in two respects. First, land rights have not evolved enough to facilitate the scale of transactions necessary to achieve allocative efficiency. Rural households, for example, are faced with the trade-off between size and intensity. Owing to high transport costs, in agriculture for example, and low population densities generally, small intensive networks are preferred. An insurance system based on almost complete information from participants also tends to favour small firms. Thus land-specific investments are insufficiently liquid and are therefore discouraged.

Another form of risk is that associated with the difficulty of enforcing contracts. Traditional and informal institutions become increasingly unable to cope with the problems arising from lack of contract compliance. Institutions that reduce the costs of contract enforcement and other transaction costs (North 1990) are important for a dynamic business environment.

African credit markets are quite underdeveloped. This is partly due to lack of collateral. Substitutes for collateral may be interlinked contracts or high observability. The former have been constrained by the low level of activity in those markets. Informal credit is possible when there is no asymmetric information, that is, when the borrower and lender know each other well. Poor households may also be constrained from entering into high-return activities, even relatively safe ones, if they require large, indivisible investments. Households are thus often constrained in their ability to reach their desired capital stock.

In a high-risk environment financial markets should have a large role to play. They should facilitate portfolio diversification, and help smooth consumption during shocks via credit, and by enabling hedging schemes of various types. However, in the financially repressed African economies, credit markets have rarely served these functions. Although economic reforms have started to change the picture, there is still little financial deepening and the micro efficiency of the banking system remains poor.

The situation in industry is similar to that in agriculture in many ways. African firms are less diversified and thus relatively more exposed to large shocks, which they are ill equipped to address. Few of the risks are insurable because of asymmetric information. Poor financial accounts in small firms as well as generally poor accounting practices worsen these risks. Data collected by the World Bank in the course of an enterprise development project (RPED) for manufacturing industry in half a dozen African countries suggest that net investment has been negative, and that efficiency has been low. Causes of this poor record are, for example, lack of financial depth, high risk, lack of openness and extensive use of foreign exchange controls and licensing, lack of social capital and weak contract enforcement and learning, and finally poor public services. Risks are increased by the low level of contract enforcement, inadequate infrastructure, and the vagaries of the macroeconomic environment. Investments are unusually illiquid, largely because of trade and licensing restrictions. Coping strategies for firms include holding large inventories and erecting generators to guard against power interruptions. Entrepreneurs often have to restrict business dealings to known firms.

CHANGING POLICY STANCE

There have in recent years been a number of studies trying to explain inter-country growth differences with the help of cross-country regressions.[2] A crucial factor behind the poor performance of African economies has been their inward orientation.[3] The lack of openness in Africa is partly due to natural barriers to trade, but the major explanation is the severity of trade restrictions. Given the small size of African economies, the effects of protectionism are bound to be severe. Trade restrictions reduce investment levels and alter the composition of investment, and in both cases there are costs arising from distortions. It may be hard to establish a causal link between exports and growth, but the degree of distortionary intervention certainly matters (Easterly 1993). However, although the economy may lose in the aggregate from these distortions, there will still be some groups that benefit (at least in the short run), notably those that have traditionally controlled the government. However, the forces of change have been strengthened in recent years, African countries are opening up, and the results in countries like Uganda are encouraging. It is hard to believe that the trend will see a reversal. Open economies will be more attractive to foreign investors.

Africa has had a high incidence of shocks, some from the natural environment and some from policy. Real exchange rates have fluctuated more in Africa than elsewhere, and volatile real exchange rates have a negative effect on both domestic and foreign direct investment. The high concentration on primary exports has made Africa particularly vulnerable to terms of trade shocks. The concentration has not been reduced significantly over time, and this is partly due to policy. The anti-export bias has hindered new export activities. Apart from being in a volatile economic environment, African economies have seen an extended period of falling terms of trade. The latter deteriorated by about 23 per cent between 1980 and 1992. Deaton and Miller (1996) find that the effect of terms of trade decline on growth was very negative. The strongest effects were through the impact on investment. Terms of trade declines may also have been particularly severe because the policy regime in place was bad. By opening up their economies, African countries can start to diversify, and reduce their vulnerability to external shocks. While the earlier inward-looking strategies tended to reduce flexibility and the scope for adjustment, opening up will lead to diversification and a richer menu of international links, making it easier to deal with the volatility of the world economy.

A controversial issue in current development debate concerns the extent to which selective, non-neutral, market interventions played a positive role in the Asian 'miracle'. The answer given by the World Bank (1993) is a qualified 'no', while, for example, Amsden (1994) argues that the evidence is misread and Rodrik (1994) that the World Bank has taken too simplistic a view. One area where the experience of the Asian NICs suggests that there may be scope for non-neutral interventions is export support. For such interventions to work, however, it is essential that they be based on performance criteria, and that the bureaucracies that handle them are not corrupt. African experience of selective interventions is mostly bad. The complaints about the old-fashioned system of intervention were not primarily that it was extensive, complicated and expensive, but that it was applied in a biased and unpredictable fashion. An example of such intervention in Kenya was the pre-shipment export financing facility, through which an exporter could get credit on the basis of an export order. However, this system was so much abused that it had to be discontinued in 1993 (see Bigsten 1993). The policy regime in Kenya has since shifted towards market-based allocation of both foreign exchange and investment resources, and this more neutral stance has definitely been to the liking of the business community (Departments of Economics 1994).

The quality of the socio-economic infrastructure is another serious impediment. In spite of the fact that Africa's level of public expenditure to GDP is generally higher than in comparable regions, the continent has poor infrastructure. Provision of railways, telephones and electricity has grown more slowly in Africa than in other LDCs and the quality of services has been generally lower. Public utilities have performed badly, and as a result electricity costs are higher than elsewhere, while water supplies are unreliable. Projects in education have not performed well, while public institutions supporting the rural household have been weak. This is true with regard to research, extension and education. Only with regard to roads have growth and quality been comparable (Pradhan 1996). Yet transport costs are higher in Africa than in other regions. However, Oshikoya (1994) shows that investment in infrastructure increases growth, while other public investments do not. He also finds that infrastructural investments have a positive impact on private investment; the latter may well be the most crucial variable for African economic recovery. One way of improving the infrastructure is to open it up to competition, and this is now happening on a fairly broad front.

Africa is seen as a continent characterised by political disturbances, and undoubtedly one of the most negative factors for economic development in recent years has been the spate of civil wars in such countries as Somalia, Rwanda, Sierra Leone and Liberia. The effects of this kind of shock are felt beyond the countries directly affected, since they undermine investor confidence. There are, however, hopeful signs in the region, with countries disposing of dictators and moving towards democratic government. The move to majority rule in South Africa could be a tremendous boost to development in the whole of southern Africa, where apartheid overshadowed economic development for decades.

As noted above, Africa receives more aid than any other region. Aid augments investment and could help change the policy environment, but could also have Dutch Disease effects which counteract efforts at opening up the economy. Boone (1994, 1996) found no significant effect, while Burnside and Dollar (1996) found that aid significantly increased growth in good policy environments (measured by a composite measure of macroeconomic policies), had no effect in average environments and was actually damaging in bad policy environments. A similar conclusion was reached in reviews of Swedish aid to Tanzania and Zambia (Bigsten *et al.* 1994a, b), two cases of ambitious but irrational and distorted development strategies. In the two countries, aid probably prolonged the period of counterproductive policies. In the 1980s the donors reacted to poor economic policies by combining their aid with strict conditionality. This meant that some sound policy changes were forced upon African economies, but their credibility was often limited by the lack of ownership and commitment. There is now a trend away from detailed conditionality towards a relationship that may be described as a partnership. Here the recipients assume greater control over policy-making, making it possible for them to learn and to honour commitments, thereby gaining credibility. This should make it more likely that policies are systematically implemented and sustained. Uganda is one country where it is felt that the government has really been behind the reforms, and it is also one of the recent success stories. One hopes that the impact of aid in the future will be more decidedly stimulating for growth.

Finally, there has been a general increase in market orientation in African economies. The newly independent governments tried to Africanise the markets through state ownership and control and to transfer income to favoured groups. These interventions reduced efficiency and growth. The weakening of product markets increased risks. The reliance on market mechanisms for resource allocation will be beneficial, especially since market failures in Africa have generally been less of a problem than government failures.

AFRICAN GOVERNMENTS AND CIVIL SOCIETY

Governments set the incentive regime and provide services. On both counts, African governments have performed poorly. At independence a large portion of the modern sector was owned by ethnic minorities. To wrest control from them, governments chose to nationalise private property or to expand parastatal activities. They also chose to tax export agriculture in order to finance industrial expansion. Governments increased public employment at the same time as they endeavoured to ensure cheap labour to industry, via a policy of food price controls and subsidies. Again, this required taxation of exports. The banking system was controlled and interest rates were kept low, and the bulk of credit was allocated to industry. Agriculture was again the main victim. Since remoteness helped insulate African leaders from pressure from the rural population, the system could prevail for a long time. Government was under some pressure from its own urban supporters, but external pressure for change was weak. Instead aid flows contributed to this insulation from pressure for change. In the end it was the accumulating failures of the policy stance that forced change. Still, in many instances, the belated reforms led to urban protests and to policy reversals. The latter are what investors dread and what keep them on the sidelines. Governments should try to find domestic or external restraints on policy relapse. However, given the weakness of the legal framework and the dominance of the incumbent rulers, the use of domestic restraints has proved difficult in Africa. The only domestic measure that has had some success is the introduction of cash budgets. To broaden their capacity for policy commitment, governments could use some of the provisions of the World Trade Organisation to bind tariffs at low levels or reach some arrangement with the European Union whereby reforms would be sustained by some form of reciprocal threat, such as a loss of trade favours in the case of policy reversals (Collier and Gunning 1997).

Recent research has emphasised the importance of civil society for growth (Putnam 1993, Bigsten and Moene 1996). A plural society enables a broad sector of the population to influence politics. It enables the governed to have a stake in the political outcomes. A quickly evolving social structure may affect outcomes either by affecting politics directly and thus policies and service delivery, or by affecting the level of trust in government and other economic actors and thus the costs of economic transactions. One indicator used to capture relevant aspects of social structure is the degree of ethnic fractionalisation, since it reduces the ability of society to generate co-operative outcomes and lowers the level of trust. In regression analyses on African economies, fractionalism seems to worsen policy and to reduce productivity directly. Its most serious consequence, however, is the prevalence of civil war (Mauro 1995).

Assuming that people are utility maximisers, they can choose between becoming entrepreneurs or becoming rent-seekers involved in activities that reduce growth. When markets are small, the size of the firm that can be effectively managed is limited. Owing to poor property rights the entrepreneur is uncertain about whether the surplus generated can be appropriated without hindrance. If this is doubtful, it is likely that many of the talented people will become rent-seekers. This leads to lower growth rates. In Kenya, for example, there are relatively few African entrepreneurs engaged in large-scale private businesses (Departments of Economics 1994). On the other hand, there are many wealthy individuals who have built up large asset portfolios via the political route. So why does a potential entrepreneur choose the political route? We have already noted that markets are quite limited. Although this can sometimes be compensated for by various forms of government protection, it seems easier to capture a large share of a small market via political connections than via competition. Similarly, in a small credit market loans are easier to get if one is well connected. The insecurity of property rights also means that it may be wiser to start by establishing a political base. It is thus very plausible to argue that it is the relative attractiveness of the different options, plus an assessment of risks, that determines the choices made by potential African entrepreneurs. There is no lack of entrepreneurial skills as such, but the question is, to what uses are they put?

Why does the public sector perform poorly? The reasons are partly the same as for the private sector, that is, the inadequate policy environment, including trade restrictions, and a large fiscal deficit. All those contribute to lower returns on public projects. Second, since there is no scope for public debate and protest, expenditure priorities are dictated by the needs of the elite. Third, the public sector is often used largely to generate employment. Finally, Collier and Gunning (1997) point to the fact that, as a result of strong kinship groups, corruption in Africa is highly decentralised – uncoordinated and competitive, making it more extensive and difficult to eradicate. Moreover, the incentive system in the public sector is characterised by high rewards for social contacts. It is, therefore, hard for managers to motivate their staff to achieve higher levels of productivity.

The issues of shared growth and equal social opportunities have featured prominently in the Asian development debate. Campos and Root (1996) note that although some of the successful tigers had authoritarian regimes, they realised the need to devise institutions and rules that gave individuals and firms confidence that they would be able to share in the proceeds of economic growth. Private investments, it is argued, are stimulated by political stability, which, in turn, derives from shared growth. Dreze and Sen (1995) argue that the failure of India to increase the welfare of large segments of the population is partly due to the neglect of social issues by both policy-makers and the public at large. Thus, to change the attitudes and perceptions of the population, illiteracy has to be eradicated. Broader public awareness in turn increases popular pressure on politicians. They thus argue that the role of the state should not be reduced, but instead should be increased in the areas of human capital development, that is, health and education, and in developing systems that guarantee access to these services, as well as their quality.

These insights are also relevant to Africa. The government has a special responsibility in equalising social opportunities by providing education and health services to the population. This may directly improve productivity, but it will also be part of a virtuous circle between the better-educated electorate and the government. The latter is already more open to pressure from the electorate and civil society because of the democratic reforms which are under way, although the impact of rural opinion still remains weak. There has emerged a civil society, including organised groups and associations, which argues the case for democracy, justice, and protection of the interests of various minority groups. All these factors make it harder for governments to ignore the interests of the population. Since the policy needs are by now fairly well identified, it is the political decision-making process and the character of the bureaucracies that implement the reforms that will determine whether we will see tigers in Africa.

CONCLUSION

Is there a basis for optimism? Will tigers emerge? The main reason for my optimism has not been touched upon above, but derives from the lesson of history. The industrial revolution, which started in England, engulfed a larger and larger share of the world economy. Change has essentially been unidirectional, continuously shifting the frontier between developed and underdeveloped countries towards the 'south'. Although we have identified an extensive list of problems, there is no reason to believe that they are immutable in Africa while they have been solved elsewhere. There are no obvious reasons why Africa should not eventually be absorbed into the group of developed countries. The dating of this is harder, but I think that Africa may be in the early phases of growth acceleration.

So is there reason to believe that African economies can come out of this morass of growth constraints?[4] It is certainly possible to undertake the reforms required for rapid growth, and I am hopeful that the necessary changes will be implemented. The prospects now look better than they have done for decades. First, the economic reform programmes have eliminated or at least reduced the most blatant policy distortions at the macro level. The economies are vastly more open than they were before the reforms. That will help to develop social and economic networks, and it may help reduce risks by improving access to the world market. There may even be repatriation of flight capital, and we have already seen a beginning in some countries. Micro reforms are less advanced, but here too there has been progress. Public services and infrastructure may be improved, once they can function in a more competitive and less distorted environment. Inefficient parastatals have been closed down or sold off. Hopefully, under the new environment the judicial system may become more successful in enforcing the law impartially. To what extent governments will bring these changes about will depend on the pressure brought to bear by civil society. The public is definitely more observant and vocal than before, and a social infrastructure outside the control of the government is being built up. Development of the latter is a vital ingredient in the evolution of a growth-enhancing environment.

A final issue concerns the degree to which the process of political reform can be continued, without endangering peace and stability. There is now freer debate in most countries, and there has been partial democratisation, which has empowered broader interest groups. Yet in many countries there have been setbacks, the ultimate failure being relapse into civil war. Strategies for growth based on an open society, with predictability and trust, will ultimately fail in such a situation, while it takes a long time to restore growth and stability once the earlier trust has been lost. Development may ultimately depend on whether tolerance and a democratic spirit can prevail.

NOTES

1 Ng and Yeats (1997) point out that Africa's slump in world markets is due to its loss of competitiveness. Had it retained the share of world trade it had in 1962–64, exports would now be 75 per cent higher. This pattern of development cannot be explained by increasing protection in developed countries, either. On the contrary, African countries have had preferential access.
2 Collier and Gunning (1997) provide a good review of the evidence with regard to Africa.
3 There are a number of estimates of the impact of this on growth (Fischer 1993, Sachs and Warner 1996, Easterly and Levine 1995, Elbadawi and Ndulu 1996).
4 Collier and Gunning (1997: 65) sum up their review as follows: 'Africa stagnated because its governments were captured by a narrow elite which undermined markets and used public services to deliver patronage. These policies reduced the returns to assets and increased the already high risks which private agents faced. To cope, private agents moved assets abroad and diverted their social capital into risk-reduction and risk-bearing mechanisms at the expense of social learning.'

REFERENCES

African Development Bank (1997) *African Development Report*, Oxford: Oxford University Press.

Amsden, A.H. (1994) 'Why Isn't the Whole World Experimenting with the East Asian Model to Develop? Review of the East Asian Miracle', *World Development*, 22: 627–34.

Bigsten, A. (1993) 'Regulation versus Price Reforms in Crisis Management: The Case of Kenya', in M. Blomström and M. Lundahl (eds) *Economic Crisis in Africa: Perspectives on Policy Responses*, London: Routledge.

Bigsten, A., Adam, C., Collier, P., Julin, E. and O'Connell, S. (1994a) *Evaluation of Swedish Development Cooperation with Tanzania*, Stockholm: Secretariat for Analysis of Swedish Assistance, Ministry of Foreign Affairs.

Bigsten, A., Adam, C., Andersson, P.A. Collier, P. and O'Connell, S. (1994b) *Evaluation of Swedish Development Cooperation with Zambia*, Stockholm: Secretariat for Analysis of Swedish Assistance, Ministry of Foreign Affairs.

Bigsten, A. and Moene, K.O. (1996) 'Growth and Rent Dissipation – The Case of Kenya', *Journal of African Economies*, 5 (2): 177–98.

Boone, P. (1994) 'The Impact of Foreign Aid on Savings and Growth', mimeo, London School of Economics.

Boone, P. (1996) 'Politics and the Effectiveness of Foreign Aid', *European Economic Review*, 40 (2): 289–330.

Burnside, C. and Dollar, D. (1996) 'Aid, Policies and Growth', mimeo, Policy Research Department, Washington DC: World Bank.

Campos, J.E. and Root, H.L. (1996) *The Key to the Asian Miracle: Making Shared Growth Credible*, Washington DC: Brookings Institution.

Claessens, S. and Naude, D. (1993) 'Recent Estimates of Capital Flight', Policy Research Working Paper 1186, Washington DC: World Bank.

Collier, P. and Gunning, J.W. (1997) 'Explaining African Economic Performance', mimeo, Oxford: Centre for the Study of African Economies.

Deaton, A. and Miller, R. (1996) 'International Commodity Prices, Macroeconomic Performance and Politics in sub-Saharan Africa', *Journal of African Economies*, 5 (supplement).

Departments of Economics, Universities of Göteborg and Nairobi (1994) *Limitations and Rewards in Kenya's Manufacturing Sector: A Study of Enterprise Development*, Washington DC: World Bank.

Dreze, J. and Sen, A. (1995) *India: Economic Development and Social Opportunity*, Oxford and New York: Oxford University Press.

Easterly, W. (1993) 'How Much do Distortions affect Growth?', *Journal of Monetary Economics*, 32 (2): 187–212.

Easterly, W. and Levine, R. (1995) 'Africa's Growth Tragedy: a Retrospective 1960–89', Policy Research Working Paper 1503, Washington DC: World Bank.

Elbadawi, I. and Ndulu, B. (1996) 'Long-run Development and Sustainable Growth in sub-Saharan Africa', in M. Lundahl and B. Ndulu (eds) *New Directions in Development Economics*, London: Routledge.

Fischer, S. (1993) 'The Role of Macroeconomic Factors in Growth', *Journal of Monetary Economics*, 32 (3): 485–512.

Mauro, P. (1995) 'Corruption and Growth', *Quarterly Journal of Economics*, 110 (3): 681–712.

Ng, F. and Yeats, A. (1997) 'Open Economies Work Better! Did Africa's Protectionist Policies cause its Marginalization in World Trade?', *World Development*, 25 (6): 889–904.

North, D.C. (1990) *Institutions, Institutional Change and Economic Performance*, Cambridge: Cambridge University Press.

Oshikoya, T. (1994) 'Macroeconomic Determinants of Domestic Private Investment in Africa', *Economic Development and Cultural Change*, 42 (3): 573–96.

Pradhan, S. (1996) 'Evaluating Public Spending', World Bank Discussion Paper 323, Washington DC: World Bank.

Putnam, R.D. (1993) *Making Democracy Work: Civic Traditions in Modern Italy*, Princeton NJ: Princeton University Press.

Rodrik, D. (1992) 'Conceptual Issues in the Design of Trade Policy for Industrialization', *World Development*, 20 (3): 309–20.

Rodrik, D. (1994) 'King Kong meets Godzilla: The World Bank and the East Asian Miracle', Discussion Paper 994, London: CPER.

Sachs, J.D. and Warner, M. (1996) 'Sources of Slow Growth in African Economies', Development Discussion Paper 545, Cambridge MA: Harvard Institute of International Development.

World Bank (1993) *The East Asian Miracle: Economic Growth and Public Policy*, Oxford: Oxford University Press.

World Bank (1997) *World Development Report 1997*, Washington DC: World Bank.

3

INVESTMENT, MACROECONOMIC POLICIES AND GROWTH

Kupukile Mlambo and Temitope W. Oshikoya

Traditional growth theory looks at capital accumulation as the most important determinant of economic growth. Globally the return on capital will be high in countries with low levels of capital per worker, such that capital moves to poorer countries, inducing them to grow at a higher rate. High saving and investment rates, combined with low initial levels of capital per worker, are the key to achieving high and sustained growth rates. This theory would have predicted relatively higher growth rates for Africa, which has some of the lowest levels of capital per worker in the world, and developing countries in general. This has, however, on the whole not been the case. The expanding endogenous growth literature has sought alternative explanations based on the role of human capital and institutions in the growth process (see, for example, Barro 1991, Barro and Lee 1993, Fischer 1993, Levine and Renelt 1992). While these cross-country studies portray economic growth as a complex process whose causes are still highly contentious, it can be safely concluded that poorer countries are unlikely to catch up with richer ones in the absence of an institutional set-up that supports successful innovation.

Still, though alternative explanations are persuasive, empirical studies have demonstrated the cardinal importance of capital accumulation for economic growth. In a study covering 119 countries, Levine and Renelt (1992) found that the relationship between growth and investment was both positive and robust. Using data for ninety-five developing countries, Khan and Kumar (1994) found that, for the period 1970 to 1990, a 1 per cent increase in the investment ratio was associated with a 0.75 per cent increase in *per capita* GDP. Decomposing investment into private and public components, they found that although both types have a positive impact on *per capita* GDP, private investment had a quantitatively larger impact. However, they noted that it was not until the 1980s that the impact of private investment outstripped that of public investment, indicating a structural shift in investment

28

behaviour in recent decades. De Long and Summers (1991) decomposed investment into equipment and other components, and found that, relative to others at the same level of development, countries which invested heavily in equipment enjoyed faster growth between 1960 and 1985. In a cross-section study of African countries, Ojo and Oshikoya (1995) found that growth in *per capita* GDP was robustly related to investment, with a 10 per cent rise in the share of investment to GDP increasing long-term *per capita* growth by 2 per cent.

On the whole, a number of issues remain unresolved. Africa's recent economic experience has demonstrated that the link between economic growth and investment is sometimes weak. For example, in a number of adjusting countries, investment has responded slowly to renewed growth.

This chapter summarises empirical work on the determinants of private investment in Africa, highlighting the role played by the macroeconomic environment. The chapter thus contributes to the current debate on Africa's transition from stabilisation to long-term growth. The question addressed is: what more should African countries be doing to ensure sustained investment and growth?

INVESTMENT AND MACROECONOMIC PERFORMANCE

Africa's growth performance in the past two and a half decades has been disappointing indeed: for the continent as a whole the 1980s were labelled outright as a 'lost decade'. Average annual *per capita* growth declined from about 1 per cent in the second half of the 1970s to negative growth for much of the 1980s and early 1990s (see Table 3.1). Only a few countries have been able to sustain positive real *per capita* GDP growth rates in the past two decades,

Table 3.1 Africa: basic macroeconomic indicators, 1965–96 (ratios and averages, %)

Indicator	1965–73	1974–9	1980–5	1986–90	1991–5	1996
GDP growth	5.7	3.5	2.1	2.8	1.7	4.8
Per capita growth	3.0	0.7	−0.8	−0.1	−1.2	2.0
Agriculture	2.7	3.0	1.9	4.0	1.9	6.9
Manufacturing	7.3	6.7	3.6	3.4	0.5	3.2
Investment/GDP	20.2	26.8	23.4	20.7	20.2	19.6
Saving/GDP	19.9	26.2	19.3	16.4	17.4	17.0
Export growth	8.2	2.6	1.0	6.2	1.1	10.1
Import growth	7.4	6.2	2.5	6.8	6.1	7.1
Fiscal deficit/GDP	–	5.4	5.9	6.7	5.9	2.9
Inflation	5.8	13.8	15.8	16.3	30.7	27.3
CA deficit/GDP	6.7	14.4	–	3.7	2.5	2.8

Source: African Development Bank (various years).

indicating for the rest a rapidly declining welfare. Between 1970 and 1995, *per capita* growth rates in Botswana, Lesotho and Mauritius were between 3 per cent and 6 per cent while Africa's large countries, Egypt, South Africa and Nigeria, registered *per capita* growth rates of hardly more than 2 per cent. These countries had an even poorer record during the debt crisis, between 1982 and 1989, with average *per capita* growth rates of −0.12 per cent for Egypt, −6.6 for Nigeria and 1.5 for South Africa. Africa's performance over the past two decades is thus in sharp contrast to that of other developing regions, such as East Asia, which achieved *per capita* growth rates in excess of 5 per cent, and Latin America, which grew at an average rate of almost 2 per cent *per capita* and year.

In the 1990s, Africa's economic performance has shown signs of recovery, with *per capita* GDP growth estimated at 2 per cent in 1996 compared with 0.1 per cent in 1995 and −1.2 per cent between 1991 and 1995. The recent recovery has also encompassed more countries than in previous years. Still, it is the smaller African countries that seem to have registered the best performance (see Appendix 3.1). In 1996 Botswana, Lesotho and Mauritius had *per capita* growth rates of 2.9 per cent, 10.3 per cent and 3.4 per cent, respectively. Other countries recording positive real *per capita* growth rates included Morocco, with 8.1 per cent, Zimbabwe, with 5.3 per cent, and Uganda, with 4.4 per cent. Still, among the continent's large countries, performance remained sluggish, Egypt recorded a *per capita* GDP growth rate of 2 per cent, while South Africa's real *per capita* GDP growth increased by 0.7 per cent and that of Nigeria by 0.4 per cent. The economic motor effect expected of these large economies has been lacking.

This general fragility of growth in Africa is a result of the continent's low rates of capital accumulation. From the 1960s, and up to the mid-1970s, Africa and East Asia had comparable rates of saving, only slightly less than 20 per cent. However, following the energy crises in the early 1970s this pattern began to change, with the savings gap widening in the 1980s, during the debt crisis. Thus while Africa's gross domestic saving as a share of GDP averaged 22.6 per cent between 1974 and 1980, and about 25 per cent in Asia, the two regions had diverged dramatically between the beginning of the 1980s and the mid-1990s. By then average saving as a ratio of GDP was 36 per cent in East Asia, while it fell to less than 20 per cent in Africa.

The evolution of investment has been largely similar. Thus, while in the decade before the energy crisis Africa had an average gross domestic investment to GDP ratio of 20 per cent, compared with 21.8 per cent in East Asia, the latter's investment rates had increased to an average of 36.2 per cent between 1981 and 1994. Africa's investment rates remained largely stagnant at 21.5 per cent. Still, simple averages disguise significant differences in performance between African countries. Smaller countries had generally high investment rates compared with large ones. Between 1980 and 1995, for example, the ratio of domestic investment to GDP was 29 per cent in Botswana, 30.5 per cent in Gabon, 59.3 per cent in Lesotho (this exceptionally large investment ratio was partly due to sanctions imposed on South Africa, forcing firms to set up shop next door) and 26 per cent in Mauritius. Among the larger African countries, only Algeria recorded a higher investment to GDP ratio, 31.7 per cent, over the period. Sizeable economies like Egypt, Nigeria and South Africa recorded fairly average investment rates, between 19 per cent and 23 per cent. Owing to more than a decade of economic disruption the Democratic Republic of the Congo recorded one of the lowest average rates of investment, only 9 per cent.

Africa's poor growth performance is partly to be blamed on inadequate private investment and stagnation in public investment. In sub-Saharan Africa, private investment as a share of the GDP fell from 12.2 per cent in 1970–79 to 9.8 per cent in 1980–89, recovering marginally to 10 per cent in 1990–94. In North Africa it remained constant at about 12 per cent over the period. In comparison, private investment in East Asia increased from 18 per cent of GDP in 1970–79 to 19 per cent in 1980–89, and 25.5 per cent in 1990–94. In many African countries, public investment has tended to dominate fixed capital formation, exceeding, for example, private investment in Egypt, Ghana, Malawi, Nigeria and Zambia between 1980 and 1994.

Following structural adjustment programmes, some countries have seen a reduction in the ratio of public investment to total investment. Thus, in the Côte d'Ivoire and Tunisia, public investment exceeded private investment in earlier periods, but fell below private investment in 1990–94. However, in countries such as Malawi, Morocco, Nigeria, South Africa and Zambia the performance of private investment weakened between 1990 and 1994.

Another feature of Africa's growth process has been the widening gap between saving and investment. Between 1974 and 1980 the saving–investment gap stood at 0.6 per cent, but it increased to 1 per cent between 1991 and 1994, and in 1995 to 2.9 per cent. The widening savings–investment gap has been covered by the increasing role of aid flows in total investment in Africa. For example, concessional aid flows to Africa averaged 14.8 per cent of GDP in 1994, exceeding 50 per cent of GDP in countries such as Mozambique and Rwanda. However, increased dependence on aid has negative implications, notably the impact of aid on macroeconomic policy. Moreover, under prevailing conditions in developed countries, the prospects of increased official development finance are poor. At the same time, Africa has failed to attract a significant amount of private foreign capital. In 1996 Africa's share of global private capital inflows to developing countries was just 5 per cent, compared with 49 per cent for Asia and 31 per cent for Latin America (see World Bank 1997). Within Africa, South Africa has received the bulk of portfolio investment, while Nigeria and Egypt have received a large share of foreign direct investment as well.

This overview suggests that the bulk of African countries run the risk of being trapped in a situation of low growth, low saving and low investment. Action is needed to raise investment rates in order to ensure higher and sustainable economic growth.

DETERMINANTS OF INVESTMENT

Applied work on investment in Africa is rooted in the neoclassical tradition, assuming that intertemporal changes in investment are influenced by differences between the desired level of investment in the current period and actual investment in the previous period:

$$\Delta K_t = \alpha[K^* - K_{t-1}] \tag{1}$$

where K^* is the optimal or desired stock of capital, and K is actual capital. The coefficient α refers to the speed with which firms adjust to the desired level of capital stock. Given the difficulty of measuring the actual capital stock in Africa, this model is usually transformed to the following expression in empirical studies:

$$IP_t = \alpha[(1 - (1 - \sigma)L)]K^* + (1 - \sigma)IP_{t-1} \tag{2}$$

where IP refers to private investment, L the lag operator, and σ the rate of depreciation. Investment thus depends on the desired level of capital and the amount of investment in the previous period. In turn, the optimal or desired capital stock is hypothesised to be a function of expected profits (E_π) which are also in turn determined by output (Y), costs (R) and autonomous shocks (A):

$$K^* = f(E_\pi) = f(Y, R, A) \tag{3}$$

Output measures the accelerator effects, while costs, such as the user cost of capital, inflation and exchange rates, capture the substitution effects. Autonomous shocks include such factors as terms of trade, external debt and other structural factors that impact on private investment decisions. In the rest of this section we examine some of the main determinants of investment in Africa.

Output-accelerator effects

Traditional investment behaviour theory assumes that investment in a given year is induced by the level of output (or more appropriately the rate of change in output) in that or the previous year. Rapid growth raises the rate of saving, which in turn releases resources for investment. While strong and persistent in studies, the relationship between output growth and investment is nevertheless quite puzzling. Because most of the observed fluctuation in output appears transitory, it should not be expected to affect investment, since the latter takes time to accumulate and is largely irreversible. Although the puzzle remains unresolved, its existence may be due to the fact that investors have a short planning horizon, making even short-term fluctuations in output have impacts on their decisions (see Serven and Solimano 1993). On the whole, empirical studies that have tried to establish a quantitative relationship between investment and output growth in Africa have yielded conflicting results. Serven (1997), Elbadawi et al. (1997) and Oshikoya (1994) for low-income African countries found the output growth coefficient to be both positive and significant. On the other hand Kumar and Mlambo (1995), Hadjimichael and Ghura (1995), Oshikoya (1994) for middle-income African countries, and Mlambo and Elhiraika (1997) for countries belonging to the Southern African Development Community, found that output growth had no significant impact on investment.

In Appendix 3.1 we present figures for GDP growth and gross domestic investment for individual African countries between 1980 and 1997. Countries are divided into those with high growth, medium growth and low growth. As expected, high growth is concentrated among countries with high investment ratios. Between 1980 and 1997 countries with high growth rates had, on average, investment ratios of 23.6 per cent of GDP, compared with 21 per cent in medium growth countries and 16.5 per cent in low growth ones. Still, among high growth countries there are a number of cases with low investment rates, notably Uganda and Ethiopia, indicated in the high returns to peace and infrastructure rehabilitation. However, on the whole countries with a longer history of high growth rates also had higher investment rates, while those that have failed to sustain growth in the past also had low rates of investment. Thus a revival of capital accumulation is critical for achieving high rates of GDP growth.

Impact of macroeconomic policies

To reverse the poor investment performance, policy-makers need to implement policies that will help free countries from the cycle of low investment and low growth (Elbadawi and Ndulu 1995). A number of recent studies have highlighted the role of sound macroeconomic policies in reducing uncertainty, one of the most serious deterrents to investment. Our focus here is on fiscal, monetary and financial as well as exchange rate policies.

Two basic indicators of fiscal policy used in investment studies are public investment and the fiscal deficit. Effects of the latter on private capital formation are usually analysed within the framework of neoclassical models of monetary growth, which emphasise the 'crowding-out' effects of government spending. Rising government deficits push interest rates up and reduce the amount of credit available to private investors. Thus financing government purchases by money creation lowers real money balances and raises the real interest rate; on the other hand, financing deficits via taxes increases production costs, and introduces distortions in the economy, adversely affecting private investment.

The size of the fiscal deficit also has a strong bearing on the credibility of government policy, with large fiscal deficits viewed as indicating an unstable macroeconomic policy stance. In the case of public capital formation, the discussion has concentrated on whether it complements or competes with private capital. The complementarity hypothesis suggests that public capital, referred to by Meade (1952) as an 'unpaid for' factor of production, has a positive impact on private sector decisions. By making available to firms intermediate services such as roads, education and health, public service provision reduces private production costs and thus raises the marginal productivity of private capital. The role of publicly owned companies has been questioned, however. It has been argued that not all public investment complements private investment, with investment in non-infrastructural activities directly competing with private investment.

Empirical studies that have attempted to differentiate the two types of capital have found public investment to be complementary to private investment, while fiscal deficits have a negative impact. Most studies found the coefficients of the fiscal deficit variable to be negative and significant. On the other hand, the public investment variable has a positive and significant coefficient. The coefficient also tends to be relatively large, in some cases indicating that a 1 per cent increase in the ratio of public investment leads to a 0.5 per cent increase in private investment. The exception to the above is the study by Kumar and Mlambo (1995), which found fiscal deficits to have a negative but insignificant impact on private investment.

Studies that have broken public investment down into infrastructural and non-infrastructural investment have found the former to have a greater impact on private investment than the latter. In the study by Oshikoya (1994), in particular, investment in infrastructure was found to have a positive impact on private investment, while the effect of non-infrastructural investment was negative.

These results indicate that fiscal reforms have an important bearing on Africa's prospects of investment recovery. In Table 3.2 we illustrate aspects of Africa's fiscal stance over the period 1980 to 1995. The fiscal deficit (excluding grants) increased from an average of 6.5 per cent in the early 1980s to 7.1 per cent in the latter half of the 1980s, rising further to 8.5 per cent during 1991–95. With grants included, to account for the government's net financing requirements, the fiscal deficit remained relatively constant, averaging about 5.9 per cent between 1980 and 1994. The rather large difference between the two measures of fiscal imbalance reflects the

Table 3.2 Macroeconomic policy stance in Africa, 1980–95

Policy variable	1980–85	1986–90	1991–95
Fiscal policy			
Central govt revenue (% GDP)	25.5	27.1	24.5
Central govt expend. (% GDP)	31.4	33.8	30.4
Capital spending (% total expend.)	20.0	18.2	17.5
Budget deficit (% of GDP)			
Including grants	5.1	5.9	5.9
Excluding grants	6.5	7.1	8.5
Monetary policy outcomes			
Growth in money supply (M1) %	15.8	15.9	28.7
Inflation rate (%)	15.8	16.3	30.7
Nominal interest rate (%)			
Commercial bank lending rate	13.0	14.8	17.9
Commercial bank deposit rate	6.9	7.9	9.1
Discount rate	9.5	9.9	12.4
Real effective exchange rate index (1987 = 100)	118.3	98.1	84.3

Sources: African Development Bank (1997), World Bank (1997).

importance of net official grants in many countries. Between the second half of the 1980s and the early 1990s, foreign grants as a ratio of GDP increased to 2.5 per cent in Egypt, 0.1–0.4 per cent in South Africa, 0.4–0.5 per cent in Tunisia, fourfold in Zambia to 3.2 per cent, and from 1.3 to 1.8 per cent in Zimbabwe.

In this context, fiscal adjustment remains a big challenge for most African countries. Government revenues are already a high proportion of GDP in many countries, and while efficiency in tax collection could be improved in some countries, it is difficult to see fiscal adjustment in terms of increased revenue. The difficulty of achieving an increase in revenues is particularly serious in countries with already high rates of taxation such as Zimbabwe and South Africa. Thus, instead, a greater part of the adjustment will have to involve a significant reduction in government spending. Table 3.2 shows that though total government spending as a proportion of GDP has been falling, government revenues have been falling as well.

However, cuts in government spending have implications for private investment, especially if they affect infrastructure and basic social services, such as health and education. In striving to effect fiscal adjustment, the policy challenge lies in ensuring that spending on physical infrastructure and social services that contribute directly to long-term growth and human and social development are not unduly affected. However, it should be noted that while public investment in infrastructure is important, historically this type of investment has not been undertaken efficiently.

In many countries non-economic considerations have been important in reaching decisions affecting the implementation of such investments. There is a strong implication in the literature that what matters for sustained growth is not necessarily the size of public spending itself, but its quality, that is, the efficiency with which the public sector delivers services to the private sector.

Monetary and financial policy

One of the main goals of monetary policy is to maintain macroeconomic stability. The interest rate, which measures the opportunity cost of capital, and is a principal indicator of the monetary policy stance, also forms a large part of the rental cost of capital. An increase in the rate of interest is, therefore, expected to affect investment negatively, while low interest encourages firms to increase borrowing for investment purposes. Such an outcome presupposes functioning financial markets. However, in many African countries credit and financial markets have been performing poorly. Until recently, monetary policies were characterised by repression, a result of the government's need to finance its budget deficits. Firms were thus constrained more by general lack of resources for investment resources than by the cost of capital itself. To reach the level of real money balances required for investment, real interest rates had to rise. Thus, in such countries, real interest rates and private investment are positively related.

After more than a decade of adjustment, what is the current state of financial and monetary policy in Africa, and what does it imply for the recovery of investment? Though there has been improvement in recent years, African countries are still characterised by rapid growth of the money supply, high inflation and the persistence of negative real interest rates (see Table 3.2). A rapid increase in the money supply between 1980 and 1995 was accompanied by increases in inflation, while real interest rates were negative. Most recently, however, monetary and financial policies have improved significantly. In 1996, for example, average inflation declined to 27.3 per cent from an average of 36 per cent in the previous two years. Moreover, the median inflation rate was even lower, about 9 per cent, suggesting that the relatively higher mean inflation rate was heavily influenced by the poor performance of countries such as the Democratic Republic of the Congo and Angola, both of which had triple-digit inflation rates for most of the 1990s. In the CFA franc zone countries, inflation, which had increased sharply following the devaluation of the CFA franc in 1994, declined rapidly as economies returned to growth.

Low inflation rates, accompanied by financial sector reforms (mostly interest-rate liberalisation), have led to positive real interest rates in many African countries. This has helped arrest the earlier decline in capital accumulation and to improve the productivity of investment.

Exchange rate policy

An important policy discussion in recent years regards the impact of changes in exchange rates on capital accumulation and macroeconomic performance. Table 3.2 shows that since the introduction of economic reforms in the 1980s, real exchange rates have depreciated considerably in Africa, falling by 14.2 per cent between 1975–84 and 1985–89, and depreciating by a further 16.4 per cent in 1990–94. Exchange rate depreciation has been accompanied by other improvements in the foreign trade regime, including the elimination of import licensing and price controls. The removal of foreign exchange controls has been a key policy change. Since the mid-1980s a number of countries, from all regions, among them Ghana, Mozambique, Tanzania, Uganda and Zimbabwe, have introduced market exchange rates, resulting in a substantial reduction (in some instances, the virtual elimination) of parallel market premiums. Partly in response to progress made in correcting exchange rate overvaluation, but also partly owing to terms of trade improvements, there has been a marked improvement in export performance, with exports increasing in real terms by 8.3 per cent in 1995 and 10.1 per cent in 1996. With regard to trade liberalisation, quantitative restrictions have been reduced, while the number of tariff schedules as well as their levels has been lowered. By the mid-1990s more than half the countries had average tariff rates of between 15 per cent and 20 per cent.

However, the impact of exchange rate reforms on private investment has been ambiguous. With African countries importing most of their capital stock, currency devaluation increases the cost of capital, leading to a fall in the demand for investment goods. In addition, devaluation affects private investment through its impact on the interest rate. It may well be that the impact of devaluation works in the opposite direction. Currency depreciation increases the profitability of export production and result in higher growth and private investment. Moreover, if devaluation is accompanied by the removal of import restrictions, firms may reach a more efficient combination of capital goods. Thus the benefits of devaluation come from the removal of distortions in the foreign exchange markets, enabling firms and other actors to make more market-determined decisions.

To a large extent, these opposing effects of exchange rate policy on investment reflect the timing of devaluation. In the short run, contractionary demand effects and increases in the cost of imported inputs are dominant, while in the long run, expansionary effects, through higher export and, therefore, output growth, dominate.

Empirical studies of investment behaviour in Africa have highlighted these short-run impacts of devaluation. Kumar and Mlambo (1995) and Mlambo and Elhiraika (1997), for instance, found the exchange rate variable to have a negative and significant impact on private investment, while Hadjimichael and Ghura (1995) found the impact of devaluation to be positive but insignificant. For low income African countries, Oshikoya (1994) found the exchange rate variable to have a negative but insignificant coefficient, while for middle income countries it was positive and significant. Serven (1997) used changes in the size of the black market premium to study the impact of exchange rate policy on private investment in Africa. It was found to have a negative and significant impact on private investment. Thus one can surmise that a reduction of the black market premium following a devaluation has a positive impact on private investment.

IRREVERSIBILITY, UNCERTAINTY AND INVESTMENT

The slow private investment response to economic reforms has reverted attention to the issue of uncertainty. Its importance derives from two main features of investment decisions which were generally ignored in the traditional neoclassical framework. First, that investment is partially or completely irreversible. Second, that it takes time to build. The two features imply that if producers are faced with an uncertain future, the time-consuming and irreversible nature of investment increases risk. Firms will then defer taking irreversible investment decisions until the uncertainty is resolved. Under conditions of uncertainty, investment demand will thus tend to fall.

Macroeconomic uncertainty

How risky is investment in Africa? Table 3.3 presents three indicators of macroeconomic stability in selected regions of developing countries. In Africa, two major sources of uncertainty have been macroeconomic policy incredibility and the debt overhang. First, uncertainty in Africa appears to be tied to the initial slow pace of adjustment. Table 3.3 shows that compared to East and South Asia, the macroeconomic environment in Africa has been more volatile. With regard to inflation, for example, the median inflation variability, which reflects variability in a 'typical' African country, is much higher than that of East and South Asia. The mean inflation variability index increased from 5.98 in 1970–79 to 9.55 in 1980–90 in Africa, while it declined from 6.43 to 2.38 in South Asia, and from 6.35 to 2.59 in East Asia. High and variable inflation distorts the information content of relative prices, and increases the variability of expected returns on investment and hence the risk of investment. Firms will be reluctant to expand capacity; as a result, realised or current investment will be low.

The period 1980–90 was also characterised by high volatility of exchange rates. The mean volatility of the black market premium in Africa increased from 19.8 in 1970–79 to 53.8 in 1980–90, while that of the real exchange rate increased from 7.96 to 9.89 over the same period. In comparison, both

Table 3.3 Indicators of macroeconomic instability (variability, by region)

Region	Inflation		Black market		Real exchange rate	
	Mean	Median	Mean	Median	Mean	Median
1970–79						
Africa	5.98	5.46	19.81	7.96	6.40	5.95
Latin America	16.04	5.74	17.30	4.76	5.40	4.33
South Asia	6.39	6.43	25.20	22.45	7.15	7.44
East Asia	6.42	6.35	4.95	1.88	5.16	4.71
1980–90						
Africa	9.55	5.38	53.80	9.89	10.45	11.02
Latin America	153.96	9.09	40.72	25.10	9.13	8.64
South Asia	3.49	2.38	16.11	13.54	4.22	4.42
East Asia	7.84	2.59	4.46	3.56	4.94	5.05

Source: Serven (1997).

the mean variability and median variability of the real exchange rate in other regions were lower between 1980 and 1990.

Africa's relatively large external debt has been another important source of instability in the macroeconomic environment (see Borensztein, 1990). It constitutes a claim on a country's future income, and thus reduces the amount of funds available for investment. The size of debt repayment also depends on factors such as world interest rates, the purchasing power of exports, and the terms of trade, which are outside the control of policy-makers in individual countries. Failure to service debt has reflected badly on Africa's creditworthiness, and on policy credibility generally. Table 3.4 compares the evolution of

Table 3.4 Comparative debt indicators, sub-Saharan Africa/Latin America and the Caribbean, 1980–96 (ratios of exports and GNP)

Year	Sub-Saharan Africa		Latin America and the Caribbean	
	% of exports	% of GNP	% of exports	% of GNP
1980	91.7	30.6	201.8	36.0
1989	238.9	69.3	273.1	49.9
1990	226.6	71.1	255.9	46.5
1991	239.7	74.1	261.1	45.5
1992	236.1	71.5	252.9	42.6
1993	249.3	76.1	255.3	41.4
1994	262.3	82.2	233.4	38.6
1995	241.7	81.3	212.0	41.0
1996	236.9	76.2	202.8	41.4

Source: World Bank (1997).

the debt situation in Africa and Latin America, a once extremely indebted region. Latin America had much higher debt ratios in 1980 than Africa, and saw a rapid deterioration in the 1980s, reaching a peak at the end of the decade. However, by 1996 the situation had been reversed, with Latin America managing to return debt ratios to the levels of the early 1980s. However, in Africa the debt burden had worsened and many countries had defaulted. As many as thirty-one African countries (more than 50 per cent) were classified as highly indebted.

Political instability

Related to macroeconomic uncertainty is the problem of political instability. As Collier (1997: 3) puts it, 'Africa is a difficult environment in terms both of what might be thought of as macro security, the threat of civil war to the survival of the state, and micro security, the threat to an individual from weak property rights.' In general, Africa has experienced more political instability than other regions. It has one of the highest levels of corruption, has higher levels of ethnic fractionalisation, and suffers frequent occurrences of civil wars. The latter destroy private property, and thus present a serious risk to potential investors. Although little theoretical work has been done on the impact of these indices on investment, empirical studies show that their variations alter the basic 'rules of the game', increasing the value of waiting.

There is, on the other hand, strong empirical evidence that political instability is harmful to private investment in Africa. Serven (1997), for instance, uses civil liberties as a proxy for political instability, while Kumar and Mlambo (1995) use both civil liberties and political rights as proxies. Both studies conclude that political instability has a negative and significant impact on private investment. This suggests that the state of security is an important determinant of the desired capital stock. Using a probit equation, Azam and Calipel (1997) derive an index of political risk as a function of various components of public expenditure such as the level of public spending on health and defence, and school enrolment rates. This index measures the probability of a major negative political event taking place in a particular country. In the investment regression the authors include both the political risk variable and the actual occurrence of a major negative political event. Although the political risk variable turns out insignificant, its coefficient is nevertheless negative. However, the coefficient of a major political upheaval is negative and significant, suggesting that it impacts negatively on investments.

In most African countries, pressures for democratic change have led to multi-party elections, ending the one-party regimes of the past thirty years. More than twenty-seven multi-party presidential elections were held between 1990 and 1996, three-quarters of them for the first time. Further, by 1996, thirty-one countries had legalised their opposition parties (see UNDP 1996).

These are dramatic changes in a continent that just a decade ago was ruled largely by autocratic military or one-party regimes. Still, the democratic project in Africa is imperfect and incomplete. To what extent, then, has the resurgence of movements for greater democracy in African countries affected private investment?

Collier and Gunning (1997) and Collier and Pattillo (1997) have argued that the challenge faced by many democratising African countries, or those making the transition from war to peace, is that of building credible reputations for political and social stability that will be maintained. Countries that have experienced political or social upheaval in the past are considered more risky by investors, that is, they face time inconsistency problems. This is demonstrated by a country like Uganda, which, despite having performed better than Kenya in the last few years, is still assigned higher risk by investors (see Collier and Pattillo 1997). Thus, while 'getting security right' is a necessary condition for economic recovery, it may not be sufficient to ensure credibility since investors take earlier episodes of instability into consideration in their risk assessment. Such credibility problems can be addressed only by the establishment of 'agencies of restraint', or the creation of 'lock-in' mechanisms which bind countries to sustainable peace and prevent policy reversal. These agencies could be domestic, such as the Office of the Ombudsman in Namibia or the Inspector General of Government in Uganda, or foreign, such the World Trade Organisation, the Multilateral Investment Guarantee Agency (MIGA) or a results-oriented trade agreement with the European Union.

POLICY IMPLICATIONS

While the strategy for encouraging private sector investment must of necessity be country-specific, varying in content and speed of implementation according to domestic circumstances, there are three thematic areas that provide a general framework for strategic intervention. First, private investments thrive best in a market-oriented business environment. Second, adequate infrastructure services are essential to sustain such an environment. Third, it is necesary to accelerate financial sector reform by restructuring the banking system, ensuring prudential regulation and supervision, as well as deepening capital markets. We shall look at these issues in turn.

Improving the environment for private investment demands that attention be paid to three key policy areas: the legal and judicial system, the regulatory framework and promotion of private–public sector dialogue. A legal and judicial framework that is able to enforce private property rights and laws relating to business contracts, collateral and debt recovery, and to adjudicate disputes is essential for private sector activity. In many countries, law enforcement has been difficult for lack of legal institutions, standardised procedures and qualified personnel. There is thus a need for greater investment in judicial systems and personnel if the desired legal framework to ensure a credible environment for investment is to be created (Biggs and Srivastava 1996)

Regulatory reforms must focus on rationalising tax and customs administration, and business licensing and registration requirements. Labour market reforms are also necessary to allow firms more flexibility in responding to changing competition. The slow response of the private sector to reforms has been blamed on the low level of private participation in both programme design and implementation. Poor consultation has thus limited the level of domestic support for the reform process. A conclusion is that policy-makers must reach out to the new breed of entrepreneurs who believe in the benefits of liberalisation and competition.

The importance of an efficient infrastructure in creating an environment suitable for private investment cannot be overemphasised. It facilitates the production and distribution of goods and services as well as the flow of information. However, the poor state of the public infrastructure in Africa has imposed high transaction costs on economic actors and has restricted access to both domestic and international markets. In a number of countries, greater efficiency in the delivery of infrastructural services has been achieved via the use of cost recovery programmes, user charges and the removal of price controls. Further, in a bid to supplement limited government resources, management contracts and leases to private companies have also been used.

To improve access to the infrastructure, new ways of attracting private participation and investment should be explored, including public guarantees and insurance schemes, and the co-financing of projects between public and private sectors. Special privatisation facilities could act as a catalyst in mobilising capital for infrastructure projects.

In a bid to improve the business environment, privatisation has become a key component of economic reform. Still, implementation has been slow, with considerable domestic opposition. Thus public enterprises continue to make substantial claims on public resources. Most intractable has been the process of privatising the parastatals responsible for the provision of public services and infrastructure, including electricity, telecommunications, water and financial services. Among the obstacles to privatisation are poor domestic competition in product markets, thin capital markets, as well as generally poor government commitment (Levy 1993).

Last, strengthening the financial sector is an important element in the mobilisation of resources for long-term growth. The primary role of an effective financial sector is to mobilise savings and efficiently channel them to the most productive investments. Building an efficient financial sector will require the establishment of sound payment and settlement systems, reliable accounting and auditing procedures and better trained banking personnel, as well as effective supervision of the banking system. An efficient system of banking supervision will ensure a high standard of banking praxis, with low level of non-performing assets, adequate capitalisation and sound management.

The banking system of many African countries has been poor at financial intermediation. Many banking institutions, especially public ones, remain insolvent. There is thus a need for recapitalisation, restructuring, privatisation or even liquidation. However, recapitalisation and restructuring without changes in the incentive framework have often been accompanied by serious banking crises. Outright privatisation is seen as one way of increasing bank sector performance. However, without allowing for increased competition, privatisation of public banks may simply result in ownership transfer without improved financial intermediation. With increased globalisation, more broadly based financial systems that include money and capital markets, non-bank intermediaries and financial instruments are bound to emerge. Non-bank financial schemes such as venture capital, bonds and equity funds, pension funds, insurance underwriting, leasing and mortgage finance would also expand. There is, thus, a need to create a suitable infrastructure in which these new firms can operate efficiently. Deepening and broadening domestic capital markets will require an effective institutional framework to regulate and monitor market operations, and encourage the development of private brokerage, underwriting and credit rating institutions.

While emerging domestic markets are bound to attract increasing numbers of foreign investors, micro-enterprises will remain a major part of the private sector in Africa, and effective means of meeting their financial requirements should be explored. The informal financial arrangements on which these firms have traditionally relied have been incapable of meeting expanding demand. Efforts should initially concentrate on upgrading informal financial firms and on strengthening their links with formal institutions such as savings and credit cooperatives, rural and community banks, etc., in order to ensure that they can continue to provide financial support to large numbers of clients on a sustainable basis.

CONCLUSION

This chapter has focused on the determinants of private investment in Africa. We have argued that while the continent is showing signs of economic recovery, the still low levels of capital accumulation imply that the prospects of sustained growth remain poor. There is thus a need for policy-makers to undertake measures that stimulate domestic private investment and attract foreign capital.

A stable macroeconomic environment is a prerequisite. Africa is a high risk and low investment region, and needs to establish a reputation by improving its macroeconomic performance. Policies aimed at maintaining low levels of inflation, promoting financial deepening, keeping fiscal deficits manageable and exchange rates correctly valued, have significant and positive effects on private investment. Owing to its political implications, fiscal adjustment has been one of the most problematic policies to implement in Africa. Over half the countries had fiscal deficit to GDP ratios that exceeded 6 per cent between 1994 and 1996. This directly contributed to the variability of other macroeconomic indicators such as inflation and real exchange rates. However, while keeping fiscal balances at sustainable levels will contribute to the recovery of investment, achieving it by reducing government investment, especially in the physical and social infrastructure, may have the opposite effect.

Further, although policy reforms have laid the foundations of long-term growth, they do not, in themselves, constitute a sufficient condition for increased investment. It is important for African countries to pursue a strategy that emphasises the pivotal role of the private sector in development, one supported by the public sector's provision of an enabling business environment, including a functioning institutional and legal framework, a good socio-economic infrastructure and efficient banking and capital market institutions.

APPENDIX 3.1 Average real GDP growth and investment ratios in Africa

Table 3.5 Average real GDP growth rates, 1980–97: high growth countries (%)

Country	1980–84	1985–89	1990–94	1995–97
Average HGC	6.6	4.0	2.7	4.7
Botswana	11.8	10.4	4.9	5.5
Cape Verde	13.0	5.2	3.7	4.4
Equ. Guinea	−1.1	1.7	6.5	24.5
Swaziland	3.9	9.1	3.9	2.7
Lesotho	0.5	7.2	4.9	8.8
Uganda	2.0	4.1	6.8	8.0
Mauritius	1.3	7.6	5.4	5.0
Gambia	8.8	3.4	4.1	0.1
Egypt	7.9	3.8	1.6	4.2
Benin	5.9	2.1	3.9	5.4
Tunisia	4.6	2.9	4.9	4.4
Chad	3.6	6.0	1.3	4.1
Ethiopia	4.9	2.8	1.8	6.2

Source: All Tables 3.5–10, Statistics Division, African Development Bank, Abidjan.

Note: HGC, high growth countries. High growth is defined as growth above the mean plus half the standard deviation for 1980–97. Low growth is defined as growth below the mean plus half the standard deviation for 1980–97.

Table 3.6 Gross domestic investment/GDP ratio, 1980–95: high growth countries (%)

Country	1980–97	1980–85	1986–89	1990–95	1980–95
Average HGC	4.5	23.1	22.3	25.5	23.6
Botswana	8.4	33.4	24.0	26.8	28.1
Cape Verde	6.8	52.8	30.7	30.3	37.9
Equ. Guinea	6.1	n/a	16.7	25.9	14.2
Swaziland	5.1	30.6	20.5	22.3	24.5
Lesotho	5.0	43.5	57.7	76.8	59.3
Uganda	4.9	7.2	11.4	16.8	11.8
Mauritius	4.8	21.1	27.3	29.6	26.0
Gambia	4.6	21.5	17.7	19.1	19.4
Egypt	4.4	28.2	22.2	17.5	22.6
Benin	4.2	16.3	13.6	15.8	15.2
Tunisia	4.2	30.3	22.9	26.6	26.6
Chad	3.7	5.1	9.1	11.7	8.6
Ethiopia	3.7	10.3	15.8	12.0	12.7

Note: HGC, high growth countries. See Table 3.5.

Table 3.7 Average real GDP growth rates, 1980–97: medium growth countries (%)

Country	1980–84	1985–89	1990–94	1995–97
Average MGC	2.4	3.8	2.0	3.6
Guinea-Bissau	2.0	4.4	3.7	4.9
Zimbabwe	5.1	4.7	1.5	2.7
Kenya	3.2	5.7	1.6	4.0
Congo (Brazzaville)	14.0	−0.9	−0.3	−0.2
Burkina Faso	2.8	4.9	1.6	4.8
Morocco	2.9	5.0	3.5	0.4
Ghana	−1.2	5.2	4.3	4.9
Guinea	−0.6	4.5	4.1	4.6
Seychelles	−1.0	6.3	4.2	1.6
Nigeria	−1.8	5.7	4.0	3.3
Algeria	5.5	2.4	−0.6	4.0
Malawi	1.4	1.8	1.3	8.3
Senegal	1.8	3.2	1.3	4.8
Sudan	2.6	0.6	3.4	4.3
Mauritania	0.4	3.4	2.5	4.7
Mali	0.1	4.2	1.5	5.4
Tanzania	1.0	3.1	2.5	3.8
Comoros	5.8	1.4	1.3	−1.0
Côte d'Ivoire	1.6	2.2	0.1	6.5
Namibia	−1.2	2.4	3.5	4.3
Angola	1.1	3.2	−3.0	9.7
Gabon	2.9	−0.1	1.7	3.3

Note: MGC, medium growth countries. See Table 3.5.

Table 3.8 Gross domestic investment/GDP ratio, 1980–95: medium growth countries (%)

Country	1980–97	1980–85	1986–89	1990–95	1980–95
Average MGC	2.9	21.6	20.5	20.1	20.7
Guinea-Bissau	3.6	33.0	33.9	31.2	32.7
Zimbabwe	3.6	19.6	19.9	21.9	20.5
Kenya	3.6	24.3	24.1	20.2	22.9
Congo (Brazzaville)	3.5	40.8	19.1	30.3	30.1
Burkina Faso	3.4	18.8	20.9	21.0	20.2
Morocco	3.2	25.8	22.8	21.9	23.5
Ghana	3.1	5.6	13.4	15.6	11.5
Guinea	3.0	n/a	16.6	15.5	10.7
Seychelles	2.9	28.1	24.0	23.6	25.2
Nigeria	2.7	17.3	17.6	21.8	18.9
Algeria	2.7	36.9	28.7	29.6	31.7
Malawi	2.6	19.7	17.5	15.8	17.7
Senegal	2.6	12.1	12.5	13.7	12.8
Sudan	2.5	14.4	10.9	n/a	8.4
Mauritania	2.5	32.0	24.0	16.7	24.2
Mali	2.5	16.4	21.3	23.8	20.5
Tanzania	2.5	21.6	27.7	31.6	27.0
Comoros	2.2	33.3	21.7	18.1	24.4
Côte d'Ivoire	2.2	19.9	10.5	9.2	13.2
Namibia	2.0	21.0	17.2	20.9	19.7
Angola	2.0	n/a	12.9	17.6	10.2
Gabon	1.8	35.4	33.6	22.5	30.5

Note: MGC, medium growth countries. See Table 3.5.

Table 3.9 Average real GDP growth rates, 1980–97: low growth countries (%)

Country	1980–84	1985–89	1990–94	1995–97
Average LGC	1.3	2.0	0.3	3.0
Burundi	7.1	0.4	−3.9	4.4
South Africa	3.0	1.5	0.1	2.9
Rwanda	3.9	2.9	−11.0	16.9
Mozambique	−9.8	5.6	6.0	4.6
Zambia	0.8	2.1	0.1	1.9
São Tomé and Príncipe	−0.9	2.6	0.9	2.1
Somalia	−0.7	3.3	−1.5	3.8
Togo	−1.6	3.0	−2.2	6.3
Libya	−4.6	2.4	4.4	1.0
Central African Republic	0.7	1.5	0.5	0.2
Niger	−2.7	1.8	1.3	3.5
Madagascar	−1.3	2.4	0	2.3
Djibouti	4.5	−2.0	−0.4	−1.4
Liberia	−2.5	0.8	−0.3	2.8
Sierra Leone	2.1	2.4	−4.3	−4.5
Congo (Kinshasa)	1.7	1.4	−8.8	0.4

Note: LGC, low growth countries. See Table 3.5.

Table 3.10 Gross domestic investment/GDP ratio, 1980–95: low growth countries (%)

Country	1980–97	1980–85	1986–89	1990–95	1980–95
Average LGC	1.5	18.9	16.5	15.7	16.5
Burundi	1.8	30.5	21.2	15.8	22.5
South Africa	1.8	16.7	16.1	14.0	15.6
Rwanda	1.7	27.1	19.5	17.1	21.2
Mozambique	1.6	15.6	14.3	12.1	14.0
Zambia	1.3	17.7	38.9	55.5	37.4
São Tomé and Príncipe	1.1	37.3	20.7	41.1	33.3
Somalia	0.9	29.3	25.6	13.7	22.9
Togo	0.8	24.5	17.7	11.5	17.9
Libya	0.8	26.5	n/a	n/a	n/a
Central African Republic	0.8	9.9	13.1	13.1	12.0
Niger	0.7	17.3	12.8	7.6	12.6
Madagascar	0.7	10.1	12.6	10.7	11.1
Djibouti	0.4	n/a	15.2	15.1	10.1
Liberia	−0.1	15.4	12.1	11.8	13.1
Sierra Leone	−0.7	14.3	9.8	11.4	11.8
Congo (Kinshasa)	−1.5	10.1	13.0	3.9	9.0

Note: LGC, low growth countries. See Table 3.5.

NOTE

The authors are responsible for the text, whose content should not be ascribed to the African Development Bank.

REFERENCES

African Development Bank (1996) *African Development Report 1996*, Abidjan: African Development Bank.

African Development Bank (1997) *African Development Report 1997*, Oxford: Oxford University Press.

Azam, J.P. and Calipel, S. (1997) 'Political Risk, Investment and Growth in Africa', paper presented at the tenth anniversary conference of the CSAE, Oxford University.

Barro, R.J. (1991) 'Economic Growth in a Cross-section of Countries', *Quarterly Journal of Economics*, 106: 407–44.

Barro, R.J. and Lee, J-W. (1993) 'Losers and Winners in Economic Growth', *Proceedings of the Annual World Bank Conference on Development Economics*, pp. 267–97.

Biggs, T. and Srivastava, P. (1996), *Structural Aspects of Manufacturing in sub-Saharan Africa*, World Bank Discussion Paper 346, Washington DC: Africa Technical Department, World Bank.

Borensztein, E. (1990) 'Debt Overhang, Credit Rationing, and Investment', *Journal of Development Economics*, 32 (1): 315–35.

Collier, P. (1997) 'The Role of the State in Economic Development: Cross-regional Experiences', *Journal of African Economies*, 6 (supplement).

Collier, P. and Gunning, J. (1997) 'Explaining African Economic Performance', mimeo., University of Oxford: Centre for the Study of African Economies.

Collier, P. and Pattillo, C. (1997) *Private Investment, Risk and the Policy Environment in Africa*, Economic Research Paper 29, Abidjan: African Development Bank.

De Long, J. and Summers, L.H. (1991) 'Equipment Investment and Economic Growth', *Quarterly Journal of Economics*, 106 (2): 445–502.

Elbadawi, I., Ndulu, B.J. and Ndung'u, N.S. (1997) 'Risks, Uncertainties and Debt Overhang as Determinants of Private Investment in sub-Saharan Africa', paper presented at the tenth anniversary conference of the CSAE, Oxford University.

Elbadawi, I. and Ndulu, B.J. (1995) 'Growth and Development in sub-Saharan Africa', paper presented at the eleventh World Congress of the International Economic Association, Tunis, December.

Fischer, S. (1993) 'The Role of Macroeconomic Factors in Growth', *Journal of Monetary Economics*, 32 (3): 458–512.

Hadjimichael, M.T. and Ghura, D. (1995) *Public Policies and Private Saving and Investment in sub-Saharan Africa: an Empirical Investigation*, IMF Working Papers 95 (19).

Khan, M.S. and Kumar, M. (1993) *Public and Private Investment and the Convergence of Per Capita Incomes in Developing Countries*, IMF Working Papers, 193 (51).

Kumar, M. and Mlambo, K. (1995) 'Determinants of Private Investment in sub-Saharan Africa: an Empirical Analysis', paper presented at the eleventh World Congress of the International Economic Association, Tunis, December.

Levine, R. and D. Renelt (1992) 'A Sensitivity Analysis of Cross-country Growth Regressions', *American Economic Review*, 82: 942–63.

Levy, B. (1993) 'Obstacles to Developing Indigenous Small and Medium Enterprises: an Empirical Assessment', *World Bank Economic Review*, 7 (1): 65–83.

Meade, J.E. (1952) 'External Economies and Diseconomies in a Competitive Situation', *Economic Journal*, 62 (1): 54–67.

Mlambo, K. and Elhiraika, A.B. (1997) *Macroeconomic Policies and Private Saving and Investment in SADC Countries*, Economic Research Papers 33, Abidjan: African Development Bank.

Ojo, O. and Oshikoya, T. (1995) 'Determinants of Long-term Growth: Some African Results', *Journal of African Economies*, 4 (2): 163–91.

Oshikoya, T. (1994) 'Macroeconomic Determinants of Domestic Private Investment in Africa: an Empirical Analysis', *Economic Development and Cultural Change*, 42 (3): 573–96.

Serven, L. (1997) 'Irreversibility, Uncertainty and Private Investment: Analytical Issues and some Lessons for Africa', *Journal of African Economies*, Supplement to vol. 6 (3): 229–68.

Serven, L. and Solimano, A. (eds) (1993) *Striving for Growth after Adjustment: The Role of Capital Formation*, Washington DC: World Bank.

UNDP (1996), *Human Development Report*, New York: Oxford University Press.

World Bank (1997) *Global Development Finance 1997*, Washington DC: World Bank.

World Bank (1996) *African Development Indicators*, Washington DC: World Bank.

4

AID AND ECONOMIC REFORM

Howard White

During the 1980s an increasing share of World Bank lending has been conditional upon implementing Bank-approved adjustment policies; by 1987 such loans accounted for 47 per cent of all World Bank loans to Africa (World Bank 1993: 21). Within the last ten to fifteen years most bilateral donors have gone down the same path (see Hewitt and Killick 1996 for a discussion of bilateral conditionality). But why should reform require conditional aid? Streeten questioned the rationale for conditional aid by suggesting there was a double paradox:

> There is, on the face of it, a double paradox, in an international lending agency imposing conditions for loans that are in the interest of the borrowing country. If they are truly in the interest of the receiving country, why are they not pursued by the policy makers? If they can be convinced of their correctness, why do they have to get money? You would expect to pay for good advice, not to be financially rewarded for following it.
>
> (Streeten 1987: 1480)

Streeten proposed ten resolutions to this paradox, which can be classified as (1) differences in knowledge, opinion or objectives (including attitudes to distribution, uncertainty and time horizon) between donor and recipient, (2) a desire by the recipient government to make the donor a scapegoat for unpopular policies, and (3) the short-run costs of the policies are too high to be borne without external assistance.

The last of these was claimed by Streeten to be the most plausible explanation. But, if this is so, we may expect that countries which have received conditional aid will by now, more than ten years after Streeten was writing, have successfully implemented reform programmes. Yet a consistent message from many World Bank publications is that many African countries still have some way to go down the road toward adjustment. The 1994 report, *Adjustment in Africa*, commented that 'none of the countries in the region has yet achieved a good macroeconomic stance' (World Bank 1994: 44). Whilst the World Bank has responded to this situation by seeking new ways to put pressure on recipients, the general feeling amongst academic observers (e.g. Collier and Gunning 1996, Killick 1997 and forthcoming, Mosley and Hudson 1996) is that the design of conditionality is inherently prone to failure; this position is reviewed below. However, this view does not mean that donors should not support reform. The main point of this chapter, elaborated in the following section, is to examine the relatively neglected topic of how it is that external support may be necessary to facilitate the reform process. Finally some conclusions are offered.

THE FAILURE OF CONDITIONALITY

The debate over adjustment has mostly been concerned with the content of adjustment programmes. This is true of both the World Bank and its critics. All three of the Bank's Reports on Adjustment Lending (World Bank 1988, 1990, 1992a) focus on this issue, as does the controversial report *Adjustment in Africa* (World Bank 1994). World Bank evaluations of the impact of adjustment policies focus on the impact of the policies themselves. But there is an implicit assumption here that the policies are the result of the lending (otherwise an evaluation of the policies is irrelevant to the impact of the funds).[1]

But it is far from clear that adjustment loans do result in better policies. Figure 4.1 summarises the possible impacts of conditional aid. Using a reform/no reform dichotomy, the combination of the factual (what actually happened) and the counterfactual leads to four possible outcomes. In only one of these cases – in which there would have been no reform in the absence of aid (the counterfactual) but with it reform has taken place – can conditional aid be said to have worked. In two other cases the factual and counterfactual

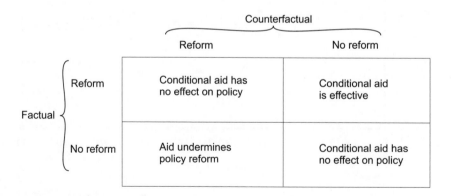

Figure 4.1 Possible impacts of conditional aid on policy

are the same, so that the aid has no effect. Some may argue that the successful reformers in sub-Saharan Africa (most notably Ghana and Uganda) are instances of the reform/reform outcome. Many other countries, in which the reform effort has been sluggish, may be placed in the no reform/no reform category. In the final possible scenario (a counterfactual of reform with an actual outcome of no reform) the aid inflow actually impedes the reform effort. Tanzania, particularly in recent years, may provide an example of this case.

Whilst there has been a feeling for some time that aid may in fact postpone reform, it is only recently that attention has shifted to focus on the nature of conditionality. The results have not been encouraging. Theoretical models presented in, for example, Mosley *et al.* (1991: I, chapter 3) and White and Morrissey (1997) suggest that the structure of conditionality is likely both to produce slippage (since recipients are encouraged to sign up to policies they do not intend to implement) and to result in donors condoning bad policies (since they want to disburse the funds anyway).

Empirical analysis has tended to confirm this pessimistic view. For example, Collier and Gunning (1996) state that 'the present form of conditionality cannot be effective'. Mosley and Hudson (1996) present data from sixteen

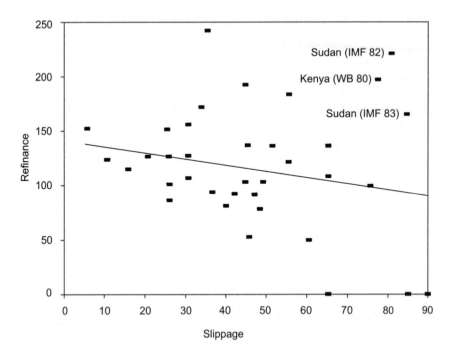

Figure 4.2 Relationship between slippage and refinance, Kenya and Sudan
Source: Mosley and Hudson (1996).

countries which have been subject to World Bank conditionality. They find, at best, a weak relationship between slippage (the proportion of agreed policy measures not implemented in the five years following the adjustment loan) and refinance (the value of programme finance in the two years following the programme as a percentage of programme finance in two years before implementation), since there are several cases of countries with high slippage being refinanced (most notably Kenya and Sudan, see Figure 4.2).[2] There is at least a weak relationship, since there are no countries which have low slippage which have not been refinanced. A country's debt burden appears to also affect the probability of refinance, indeed for countries with a debt service ratio of above 40 per cent no apparent relationship exists between slippage and refinance (ibid.: 17).

Killick (1997 and forthcoming) analyses World Bank adjustment programmes in twenty-one countries in a principal–agent framework, and comes to the conclusion that

> in the general case, conditionality is not an effective means of improving economic policies in recipient countries. The incentive system, most notably the absence of a credible threat of punishment of non-implementation, is usually inadequate in the face of donor–government differences in objectives and priorities, and other factors contributing to governments' participation constraints.
>
> (Killick forthcoming)

Finally, a widely cited study by Burnside and Dollar, from the World Bank's research department, found that 'aid has not systematically affected policy' (Burnside and Dollar 1996: 30).

There is, therefore, fairly overwhelming evidence that conditionality as currently constituted has not been a success, and reforms are afoot. One change already implemented by the Bank has been to break programmes down into smaller chunks so that tranche releases are not held up by delay in implementing one or two measures, as has happened before in many countries (e.g. Ghana and Zambia). However, to most observers, this change is a move in the wrong direction. There is a growing feeling in favour of *ex post* performance-based conditionality, in preference to the current *ex ante* conditionality. A related concern is current discussion in donor circles about selectivity, i.e. only giving aid to countries whose governments are really serious about reform.[3] It is not the point of this chapter to contest these trends. However, it is important to realise that *the fact of the failure of conditionality is not the same thing as saying that donors should not finance reform.* Rather to the contrary, the relative neglect of how it is that aid can support reform is one possible factor behind the general failure to in fact do so. The next section thus examines the mechanisms by which aid may facilitate adjustment.

HOW CAN AID SUPPORT ECONOMIC REFORM?

Existing views

Despite the large volume of resources channelled in support of the reform effort, there has been surprisingly little analysis of how this support is meant to work. There are three literatures that may offer insight into this topic: (1) the method of calculating how much aid is required by adjusting countries; (2) the Bank's occasional attempts to provide a rationale for conditional lending; and (3) the debate in Ghana as to whether aid helped or hindered reform.

The Revised Minimum Standards Model (RMSM)

Regular Consultative Group (CG) meetings are held between a recipient and the major donors at which policy performance is discussed, the World Bank presents forecasts of the country's financing requirements and donor pledges are made. These forecasts are based on the World Bank's Revised Minimum Standards Model (RMSM), which is a one gap model in the tradition of Chenery and Strout (1966).[4] The RMSM model is sometimes taken to be the analytical foundations of the stabilisation and adjustment policies (Mills and Nallari 1992, Tarp 1993). Although adjustment is placed in the context of RMSM it is in fact difficult to make such a link. A contrast may be made with the financial programming model of the IMF. This model has its theoretical basis in the Polak model, and is indeed the analytical underpinnings of the IMF's policies, yielding information on both policy targets and financing. The same cannot be said about RMSM and adjustment lending. RMSM is a foreign exchange-constrained gap model with no role for the changes in relative prices which are a major part of how adjustment policies are intended to work. Actual projections made with these models often assume an improving incremental capital–output ratio over time; whilst such improvements are to be hoped for from adjustment, the model itself tells us nothing about how they are to be achieved, or even if they are achievable. Hence RMSM can offer no insight as to how aid may facilitate the reform process. As Tarp concludes:

> The RMSM does not provide a quantitative structure linking economic policy actions with macroeconomic performance. Consequently it cannot provide the detailed resource allocation analyses needed in the design and appraisal of structural adjustment packages.
>
> (Tarp 1993: 95)

World Bank views

The third World Bank report on adjustment lending (RAL III) challenged the view that conditionality was 'buying reform'. The report explicitly posed the two questions raised in Streeten's paradox, but said that 'both questions miss the point of adjustment lending' (World Bank 1992a: 9). It was argued that good policies can achieve growth, but that it takes capital. In time, private international finance will become available, but in the meantime the growing economy will experience a balance of payments gap, which adjustment lending can fill. However, no further detail is provided on how the inflow will affect the economy beyond filling the foreign exchange gap. Given the rather extensive literature on aid's macroeconomic effects (discussed below), such a position leaves several questions unanswered.

Another answer to be found in World Bank publications is that there are 'short-run costs of adjustment'. The benefits will appear in the medium to long term, and in the meantime adjustment finance will help support the transitional costs. These 'costs' may be in terms of lower consumption or from a temporarily tightened foreign exchange constraint (in line with the traditional *J* curve effect from a devaluation). However, with the possible exception of programmes for what are rather euphemistically called the 'social costs' of adjustment, the level and nature of adjustment finance are not related to these considerations (being based on projections of a forex gap, not consumption levels), and the World Bank's analysis of adjustment finance pays no attention to whether the funds have played the role which is their supposed rationale.

The Ghana case

Finally we consider the case of Ghana. Having carried out a consistent programme since 1983, and been hailed by the World Bank (prior to 1992) as one of Africa's success stories, the Ghanaian case has spawned a voluminous literature. A small part of this literature considers the role that aid has played in the reform process, and all points to positive effects. First is the positive assessment by Kwesi Botchey, the Minister of Finance during much of the reform effort:

> It does not take the imagination of a genius to see that without those [IMF] inflows, our national situation and the state of poverty of the majority of our people would have been much weaker...

Two other documents have elaborated on why this may be so. An evaluation of programme aid carried out on behalf of CIDA argues strongly that the reforms would not have been possible without the programme aid: 'the donor contributions were essential to the structural adjustment effort' (Asante *et al.* 1994: 28). Their main argument is as follows:

> it would have been much more difficult for the government to maintain adequate public support for the reform programme if

the full impact of declining terms of trade [in the later 1980s] had been absorbed by a compression of consumption and living standards.

(Asante *et al.* 1994: 28)

But they also say that

The introduction of the auction system and the subsequent foreign exchange reforms in particular required the build-up of foreign exchange reserves in order to be credible. The reform would clearly have been impossible without these resources and technical assistance from the IMF... [T]he need for domestic firms to rebuild capacity in the face of increasing foreign competition necessitated access to resources that had to be financed with foreign resources.

(Asante *et al.* 1994: 28)

A similar conclusion is reached by Aryeetey, who states that:

There is no doubt about the fact that reform would hardly have been possible without foreign aid. At best reform would have been marginal, with only limited scope.

(Aryeetey 1996: 31)

The main reasons that he gives for this position are the use of programme aid to support consumption and the role of PAMSCAD.

So from these studies we start to get some idea of the positive role aid may play in the reform process. The rest of this section draws on these ideas, and the literature on the macroeconomics of aid, to develop a more systematic story.

A view from the aid literature[5]

Aid may potentially support the adjustment process by strengthening economic performance and social welfare during the adjustment period, through support to the government budget and more explicitly by enabling an anti-inflationary policy, tariff reduction and liberalisation of the market for foreign exchange. In this sub-section these various effects are described. It must be emphasised that the mechanisms described here are possibilities based on an optimistic view of aid's role. If aid does not have these positive effects then of course the support to the reform process is correspondingly diminished. The extent of support is ultimately an empirical matter. A further caveat is that the analysis remains within the realm of economics, ignoring the important political constraints on the adjustment process (see, for example, Haggard and Kaufman 1992).

Table 4.1 Aid and economic reform: a summary of channels

Channel by which aid supports reform	Mechanism	Ghanaian experience
Output and income		
Support consumption	Increased government expenditure	Government expenditure rose during reform period in response to both higher aid inflows and increased tax effort
	Increased foreign exchange availability	Imports rose by more than value of aid flow given export growth and higher remittances
Promote output growth	Increase capacity utilisation in manufacturing	Double-digit growth in the manufacturing sector 1984–88, partly as capacity utilisation increased
	Input supply and incentive goods effects in agriculture	No strong evidence of these effects, and agricultural growth has been weak (2.7% p.a. 1983–95)
	Government investment in infrastructure	Government investment rose faster than overall government expenditure, though with some urban bias
Encourage higher private investment	Crowding-in through government expenditure/ investment	Some effect for cocoa and extractive industries
	Reduce debt overhang	Debt overhang has not been a problem in Ghana
Fiscal effects		
Support government expenditure	Project aid and countervalue	Aid appears to have had both these effects – government expenditure has been increased, but government balance has also improved
Reduce need for deficit financing	Countervalue with no incremental expenditures	See previous row
Facilitate public sector reform and restructuring of parastatals	Financing restructuring (including retrenchment) and technical assistance	Aid does not seem to have been used in this way: privatisation only took place recently and financial performance of some parastatals remains problematic
Macroeconomic policy		
Help control inflation	Reduce deficit financing	Yes (see above)

Table 4.1 (Contd.)

	Demand reduction (or counteracting effects from demand increase or non-tradables)	Supply-increasing effects appear to have dominated
Tariff reform	Provides alternative source of government finance	Tariff reform achieved in context of growing tax effort, so does not appear to have been a major issue in Ghana
Support foreign exchange liberalisation	Makes forex available for auction	The large inflows to Ghana have clearly allowed both these mechanisms to operate
Technical assistance	Reduces extent of devaluation required	See previous row
Social welfare		
Protect the poor	Targeted programmes	PAMSCAD, though data suggest not a great success
Improve quality and targeting of social services	Support government social expenditures	Government has increased social expenditures by both level and their share of total expenditures

Output and income-related effects

One of the original rationales for adjustment finance given by the World Bank was that the funds would support consumption, which might otherwise decline temporarily if the policies had a recessionary impact. It was not, however, made clear by what mechanisms the funds would be used in support of consumption. Moreover, the design of adjustment programmes changed from the mid-1980s to be less likely to have deflationary impact. None the less, this channel may be important, especially if the country is subject to adverse external shocks at the time the policies are being implemented. Under these circumstances adjustment finance can support consumption through government expenditure and preserve foreign exchange availability.

Adjustment finance can also support consumption indirectly through enabling increases in output. A major rationale for programme aid is that the tight foreign exchange constraints in many countries resulted in very low rates of capacity utilisation in the manufacturing sector. There is little point in disbursing investment aid to further expand capacity under such circumstances. Rather import support will allow the importation of machinery, spare parts and intermediates, enabling better utilisation of existing capacity. Where these funds are available at favourable rates (which was the case in the 1980s rather than the 1990s) in theory the subsidy may facilitate restructuring – though it is also possible that the funds will delay the need for such restructuring (as has indeed been the case in Tanzania).[6]

In the agricultural sector the increased availability of fertiliser (which will require imported inputs even if it is domestically produced) and other inputs may have some stimulating effect on output. But an important effect is argued to come from the increased availability of consumer goods (incentive goods) as domestic output revives and imports increase. These goods provide the incentive for farmers to produce, which they had become reluctant to do in the absence of goods to buy with any cash from the sale of crops. The agricultural supply response may also be facilitated if aid allows government to engage in the maintenance and construction of roads and other infrastructure.

In the longer run, sustained growth requires higher investment and the aid may also contribute in this respect. Government investment may be supported directly from the aid funds, and indirectly as the tax base is strengthened through growth. Private investment may be encouraged by improved incentives, crowding in from government expenditure and the elimination of the debt overhang.

As mentioned above, the effects depend on a 'best outcome' scenario. If aid funds do not have the positive impacts on output described here then of course the mechanism by which aid supports adjustment is undermined. Empirical analysis of these issues must therefore try to gauge the strength of these effects.

Fiscal effects

Adjustment finance may support the government budget, both through additional project funds and through the countervalue raised from the sale of the forex (or commodities) made available as programme aid. These funds may be used either to increase expenditures or to offset the need for deficit financing (and so counter inflation). In the case of project aid, deficit reduction would be an example of fungibility. If donors refrain from earmarking their programme aid, less deficit financing is one intended result. Debt relief may also have these effects, as it reduces pressure on government expenditure (provided of course that government planned to pay the debt in the absence of the support).

Aid to support government expenditure is important in the early stages of reform, since the reform programme may require restraint of non-aid financed expenditures. The fact that Sahn found that fiscal contraction had occurred in only one of nine countries in a series of case studies illustrates that aid has indeed played a part in maintaining government expenditures (Sahn 1994: 16). The need for such support is reinforced if trade taxes are reduced, as is often the case, thus undermining government's revenue base. In the longer run, the higher growth delivered by the aid and reforms will increase taxes.

Of course, government may increase expenditures on non-developmental items or reduce tax effort rather than deficit financing. In such cases the beneficial effects of aid for reform are undermined, though with two important exceptions. Lower taxes or non-developmental expenditures may be necessary to 'buy off' opposition to reforms. One example of 'buying off' would be support to the retrenchment process, including the restructuring or privatisation of parastatals. More generally aid may support public sector reform and privatisation through technical assistance, though it is doubtful that lack of expertise is the binding constraint on such reforms.

Macro policy effects

Two macro policy effects have already been mentioned. First, aid may help counter inflation by offsetting the need for deficit finance. Second, adjustment finance may facilitate trade reform by providing an alternative source of government income. A third effect is support to exchange rate liberalisation. Before elaborating on the last of these a word more needs to be said about inflation.

The 'aid as Dutch Disease' story operates through the spending effect pushing up the price of non-tradables, i.e. an inflationary effect. Whilst there may be such pressure from aid-financed expenditures there are two counteracting forces which mean that the net aid–inflation relationship is ambiguous. One of them is the use of the countervalue from programme aid to reduce deficit financing, and there are cases where this channel has been perhaps the main factor in bringing inflation down. The case studies in White (1998) examine this effect, which is found to have been a major factor in bringing inflation down in Nicaragua and to have been of some importance in Zambia. It has been less important in Tanzania and Guinea-Bissau, particularly in the latter, as the collection of countervalue was weak.

The second anti-inflationary effect of aid comes from its demand reduction effect (as imports displace domestic production; Bhaduri and Skarstein 1996), though such an effect will occur only if the marginal impact of aid on absorption is less than unity.[7]

If the net effect of aid is not inflationary then the real exchange rate appreciation that aid is supposed to induce may disappear. However, in a liberalised foreign exchange market it is of course to be expected that additional foreign exchange will reduce the price of that foreign exchange (i.e. cause the exchange rate to appreciate). But there are still good grounds to argue that the net effect of aid is to allow a depreciation. The argument is illustrated in Figure 4.3.

Suppose that there is a free market in foreign exchange. The demand for foreign currency is given by the import demand function and the supply by the export function. The higher the exchange rate the more foreign exchange exporters will supply but the less importers will demand, so that equilibrium

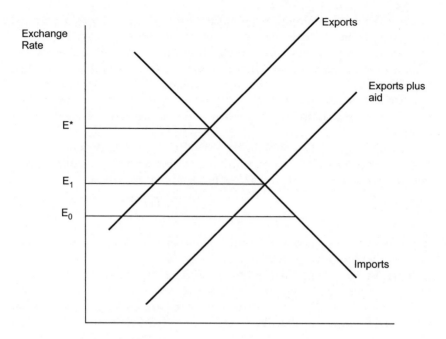

Figure 4.3 Aid and depreciation

in the foreign exchange market may be established at E^*. If there is an aid inflow, the extra foreign exchange will shift the supply curve to the right (the availability of foreign exchange at each exchange rate increases by the amount of aid). A new market equilibrium is at E_1. Hence the exchange rate has fallen (appreciated), bringing down exports. Imports increase, but not by the full amount of the aid inflow, as the appreciation has caused an export displacement effect.

But this story assumes that the country started at E^*. In fact, most developing countries embarked on adjustment from fixed exchange rate regimes. For example, the exchange rate was fixed at a level such as E_0. Foreign exchange was 'too cheap' (the domestic currency was overvalued) so that there is excess demand (many more people want foreign exchange to import than exporters are willing to provide), so that the government must ration the available forex. If aid is now made available, conditional upon liberalisation of the foreign exchange market, the combined effect of aid monies and aid-supported policies is a move of the exchange rate from E_0 to E_1 – that is, a depreciation (and an increase in both exports and imports).

In fact the liberalisation may not be possible in the absence of the aid monies. In the first instance, government can hardly institute a foreign exchange auction if there is no forex to auction. Donor funds have been a major source of the forex sold in this way, as the available forex was just sufficient to meet minimum requirements (such as oil and basic foodstuffs) met through official channels. Moreover, it can be seen from Figure 4.3 that an attempt to liberalise in the absence of the aid inflow would require a much larger depreciation in order to achieve equilibrium. Given the opposition in most countries to depreciation, the fact that aid provides a buffer against the full extent of depreciation necessary for liberalisation is an important way in which aid may support the political feasibility of reform.

In each of these policy areas donors may also support reforms through the provision of technical assistance, which may be necessary for, say, new legislation and procedures for the liberalised foreign exchange market.

Social welfare effects

Aid to adjusting countries can help to cushion the poor from the claimed adverse effects. Assisting the poor may sometimes be important for domestic political support, though it is more likely to be important for international support for the reform programme. The support comes direct if there are programmes explicitly designed for the purpose, or less directly if consumption is supported in the way described above.

CONCLUSION

It has long been been thought by critics that conditionality may be ineffective, or even harmful if it allows the recipient to postpone reforms. Recent evidence indeed confirms the view that many countries have received conditional aid without implementing substantial programmes of adjustment. The correctness of these findings should not obscure the fact that external finance can have a legitimate role in facilitating economic reform. This chapter has described the various channels by which well managed aid inflows can increase both the pace and the extent of reform. Table 4.1 summarises these effects, with some reflections from the Ghanaian case.

However, aid can only ever be at best a necessary ingredient of the reform process. Aid is not sufficient to ensure reform, a fact which should be obvious from the numerous cases of highly aided non-reformers. The case of Ghana, which has managed to sustain real *per capita* GDP growth through nearly fifteen years of reform, is an illustration of this point. Aid has played a role here, but the success is not solely attributable to the aid. The government's commitment to reform has been of vital importance; Ghana was a good case of ownership long before the term became fashionable.[8] It is under such circumstances that aid can work to support policy and, together, aid and reform can deliver a return to rising living standards.

NOTES

Prepared for the Policy Seminar on External Finance and Macroeconomic Policy in Eastern and Southern Africa, Cape Town, 16–18 July 1997, and presented at the Development Economics Seminar, Copenhagen, 20 October 1997. The author thanks participants at those events, and is also grateful to Robert Lensink for useful comments on an earlier incarnation of this chapter. The usual disclaimer applies.

1 The reports of OED are a partial exception, since they have been more concerned with analysing when reform programmes seem to work better, which has led them to stress the importance of ownership (e.g. World Bank 1992b, 1993).
2 The R^2 from the simple regression of refinance on slippage is only 0.05, and the corresponding t statistic is -1.36.
3 This position, which is not in itself new, has been given considerable impetus by the Burnside and Dollar (1996) finding that aid affects growth only when policies are right.
4 Of course, Chenery and Strout presented a two gap model. The RMSM model, is a one gap model since the foreign exchange gap is assumed to be binding.
5 Recent reviews of the literature may be found in White and Luttik (1994) and White (1998).
6 A further, and very real, adverse effect is that the additional foreign exchange may support imports which undermine the market for domestic output. The impact of imports of second-hand clothes on garment manufacturers is a case in point.
7 Of course, if income is demand-constrained, then a demand displacement effect from aid will reduce domestic output.
8 The extent of domestic ownership is in fact debated. See Ahiakpor (1991) for the view that Rawlings has a genuine commitment to reform.

REFERENCES

Ahiakpor, J.A. (1991) 'Rawlings, Economic Policy Reform, and the Poor: Consistency or Betrayal?', *Journal of Modern African Studies*, 28 (4): 583–600.
Aryeetey, E. (1996) *Structural Adjustment and Aid in Ghana*, Accra: Friedrich Ebert Stiftung.
Asante, K., Hood, R. and Parent, Y. (1994) *CIDA Balance of Payments Support for Ghana*, Ottawa: CIDA.
Bhaduri, A. and Skarstein, R. (1996) 'The short-run macroeconomic effects of aid', *Cambridge Journal of Economics*, 20 (2): 195–206.
Burnside, C. and Dollar, D. (1996) 'Aid, Policies and Growth', mimeo, Washington DC: World Bank.
Chenery, H.B. and Strout, W. (1966) 'Foreign Assistance and Economic Development', *American Economic Review*, 56: 679–733.
Collier, P. and Gunning, J.W. (1996) 'Rethinking Donor Conditionality', mimeo, University of Oxford and Free University, Amsterdam.
Haggard, S. and Kaufman, R. (eds) (1992) *The Politics of Economic Adjustment*, Princeton NJ: Princeton University Press.

Hewitt, A. and Killick, T. (1996) 'Bilateral Aid Conditionality and Policy Leverage' in Olav Stokke (ed.) *Foreign Aid towards the Year 2000: Experiences and Challenges*, London: Frank Cass.

Killick, T. (1997) 'Principals and Agents and the Failings of Conditionality', *Journal of International Development*, 9 (4): 483–95.

Killick, T. (forthcoming) *Conditionality: the Political Economy of Policy Reform in Developing Countries*, London: Routledge.

Mills, C.A. and Nallari, R. (1992) *Analytical Approaches to Stabilisation and Adjustment Programmes*, Washington DC: World Bank.

Mosley, P., Harrigan, J. and Toye, J. (1991) *Aid and Power*, London: Routledge.

Mosley, P. and Hudson, J. (1996) 'Aid, Conditionality and Moral Hazard', mimeo, Universities of Reading and Bath.

Sahn, D. (ed.) (1994) *Adjusting to Policy Failure in African Economies*, Ithaca NY and London: Cornell University Press.

Streeten, P. (1987) 'Structural Adjustment: a Survey of the Issues and Options', *World Development*, 15 (12): 1469–82.

Tarp, Finn (1993) *Stabilization and Structural Adjustment*, London: Routledge.

White, Howard (ed.) (1998) *The Macroeconomic Impact of Aid: Theory, Evidence and Case Studies from Four Countries*, London: Macmillan.

White, Howard and Joke Luttik (1994) 'The Country-wide Effects of Aid', PPR Working Paper 1336, Washington DC: World Bank.

White, H. and Morrissey, O. (1997) 'Tailoring Conditionality to Donor–Recipient Relationships' *Journal of International Development* 9 (4): 497–505.

World Bank (1988) *Adjustment Lending: an Evaluation of ten years' experience* (RAL I), Washington DC: World Bank (Country Economics Department).

World Bank (1990) *Adjustment Lending Policies for Sustainable Growth* (RAL I), Washington DC: World Bank (Country Economics Department).

World Bank (1992a) *Adjustment Lending and Mobilization of Private and Public Resources for Growth* (RAL III), Washington DC: World Bank (Country Economics Department).

World Bank (1992b) *World Bank Structural and Sectoral Adjustment Operations: the Second OED Overview*, No. 10870, Washington DC: World Bank (Operations Evaluation Department).

World Bank (1993) *Adjustment in sub-Saharan Africa: Selected Findings from OED*, No. 12155, Washington DC: World Bank (Operations Evaluation Department).

World Bank (1994) *Adjustment in Africa*, Washington DC: World Bank.

Younger, S. (1992) 'Aid and the Dutch Disease: Macroeconomic Management when everybody loves you', *World Development*, 20 (11): 15 87–97.

5

AID-CONSTRAINED TRADE
REFORM IN KENYA

Jörgen Levin

The Kenyan economy is fairly well developed, with a sizeable manufacturing sector. Though promising, especially with regard to the regional markets, Kenyan manufactures were unable to compete successfully in international markets. This was blamed on the low level of efficiency in industry, a result of the tariff walls under which it operated. When neighbouring countries pursued even more insular economic policies, Kenya was able to command a large export share in regional trade. The rents arising from tariff structures, both as government revenue and as profits to individuals positioned to capture them, created powerful political forces for their preservation. Still, a series of negative external shocks, the effects of the aid embargo of the early 1990s and pressure from donor agencies to undertake trade reform forced Kenya to speed up the adjustment process. Part of the donor strategy has been to ameliorate the revenue loss with aid inflows. In the 1990s trade policy reform became a key component of Kenya's adjustment programme.

Countries undertaking trade reforms normally go through four distinct phases (World Bank 1994). First, government controls and mechanisms for import rationing are dismantled. Second, most non-tariff measures for protectionist purposes are eliminated. Third, there is a movement towards exclusively tariff-based protection. Fourth, free trade or low uniform tariffs become the norm. However, trade policy reform is often based on theoretical prerequisites that have had little empirical support, especially in developing countries. For example, it is often claimed, without qualification, that lowering tariffs increases exports, that reducing tariff dispersion increases efficiency, and that moving towards uniform tariffs implies uniform effective rates of protection. There are at least four factors that may cause these standard prescriptions to fail (Devarajan *et al*. 1990). Tariffs may be an important source of government revenue, while increasing income taxes could anger the vocal middle class. There may be other domestic taxes in place. Further, not all goods may be traded, and imports and domestically produced goods in the same sector may not be perfect substitutes.

In undertaking trade reforms two important issues have to be considered: one is the impact on the balance of payments and the other is that on fiscal compatibility (Bevan *et al.* 1990). From the donors' point of view, a policy option is to support trade policy reform with increased foreign aid. Aid inflows would cover the revenue shortfall caused by reduced tariff revenues while at the same time supporting the balance of payments. What are the implications of this at the macro and sectoral levels? Terms-of-trade shocks often derail trade policy reform or delay it considerably. What has been Kenya's experience in this regard? As is well known, aid is often attached to a set of performance criteria or conditionalities, such as limits on government expenditure or its distribution. Conditionalities notwithstanding, fiscal balance has been difficult to achieve in Kenya, and more aid has been necessary to balance the budget. How is an aid-supported trade reform strategy affected by weak implementation? The issue is explored in this chapter.

OUTPUT, TRADE AND TARIFF STRUCTURE

In a number of respects, Kenya's production structure is typical of that of a low-income country. Agriculture dominates, with tea and coffee and food production as the main activities. Service sectors, including transport, storage and communications, public services as well as restaurant and hotel services, are also important. Rapid development of the hotel industry has been a result of the expansion of the tourism sector. Its contribution to national output and foreign exchange earnings has increased markedly in past decades. The manufacturing sector accounts for about 40 per cent of total output and the most important sub-sectors are food, petroleum, metal, beverage/tobacco, transport equipment and textiles. In a traditionally import-substituting industry, cost and the availability of intermediate inputs are important factors in production. Table 5.1 shows the importance of intermediate inputs for production in each sector, given by the price ratio PV/PX, the ratio of per-unit net price to the price of domestic output, inclusive of value added tax.

Primary goods-producing sectors are least dependent on intermediate inputs, while sectors within manufacturing are most dependent. Service sectors lie between the two earlier sectors in their dependence on intermediate inputs. In terms of total value added, the two agriculture sectors account for about 28 per cent, the manufacturing sectors for 18 per cent, public services and administration for 16 per cent, and tourism for 11 per cent. The rest of value added derives from construction, electricity and other service-oriented sectors.

The last three columns in Table 5.1 indicate the sector's trade orientation, that is, share of exports in sectoral output, the share of imports of the sector's description in total demand, and its level of dependence on imported

Table 5.1 Kenya: production and trade (%)

Sector	X	PV/PX	V	E/X	RMC	RMI
Agriculture	11.2	86.0	19.9	5.5	1.6	33.9
Bakery	1.7	39.8	1.5	0.6	0.0	2.5
Beverages and tobacco	3.5	17.5	3.6	2.1	0.4	8.8
Construction	5.4	39.2	4.4	0.0	0.0	13.4
Fish and forestry	0.4	89.2	0.8	6.7	0.3	18.4
Food	10.7	5.1	1.6	3.8	7.7	11.3
Footwear and leather	0.4	17.7	0.2	2.1	0.7	17.6
Metallic products	5.0	12.7	2.7	5.3	81.9	24.9
Mining	0.3	29.5	0.2	98.7	0.0	11.6
Non-metallic mineral products	1.0	16.1	0.4	12.0	9.4	9.8
Other chemicals	0.9	14.9	0.4	27.4	31.7	32.5
Other private services	8.0	58.9	10.4	1.9	0.0	7.2
Paint	0.4	20.4	0.3	12.1	3.6	17.5
Paper products	1.4	24.6	0.8	2.9	85.5	19.4
Petroleum	7.2	7.1	1.9	11.0	7.1	48.6
Public services	10.9	73.4	16.5	0.0	0.0	20.1
Restaurant and hotel services	10.3	52.3	11.4	28.3	3.3	6.5
Rubber	0.7	30.8	0.6	1.1	5.8	21.6
Tea and coffee	4.5	87.1	8.0	97.0	0.0	40.8
Textile and garments	2.2	15.6	1.5	2.4	4.8	20.4
Textile raw materials	0.5	26.9	0.3	0.8	0.5	14.4
Traditional sector	3.1	76.9	4.9	0.0	0.0	9.1
Transport and equipment	3.1	14.2	1.8	0.6	77.2	13.3
Transport, storage and communications	6.7	39.6	5.5	20.5	0.0	7.1
Wood products	0.6	27.6	0.4	4.7	1.8	14.2

Source: Damus (1990).

Notes: X sectoral shares in gross output. PV/PX sectoral value added as a percentage of domestic price. V sectoral value-added shares. E/X ratio of exports to domestic output. RMC ratio of final imports to total domestic demand. RMI ratio of intermediate imports to total sectoral intermediate use.

intermediates. With export shares of 97 per cent and 98.7 per cent, respectively, tea and coffee and mining are the most export-oriented sectors. Sectors producing intermediate goods, such as chemicals, paint and petroleum, have high export shares as well. Service-oriented industries, including transport, communication and services and tourism, have export shares of above 20 per cent. This is a result of Kenya's importance as a transit route to Uganda and other landlocked countries and as a major tourist destination. The relatively high shares of imports in aggregate expenditure are typical of a low-income country, with capital goods mostly imported. Other goods, with high import shares, include paper products and chemicals.

Use of imported intermediate inputs is shown in the last column of Table 5.1. Almost half the inputs used in the petroleum sector are imported. The imported fertiliser and insecticides used in coffee and tea production account for about 40 per cent of total intermediates. The food, bakery and beverage and tobacco sectors demand low amounts of imported inputs, a situation similar to tourism. The non-traded sectors in the economy are building and construction, public services and the traditional sector. However, they still depend to some extent on imported intermediates in their production. For example, the share of imports in total intermediate demand in building and construction and the public service sector is about 13 per cent and 20 per cent, respectively.

With the deepening of economic reforms, the import tariff structure began to change at the end of the 1980s. Table 5.2 shows that tariff dispersion was lowered as the number of tariff bands was reduced. Thus, while the tariff band 11–30 per cent had accounted for 30 per cent of all goods in the 1987/88 financial year, it was accounting for over 70 per cent by 1995/96. Moreover, tariff rates were then confined to 50 per cent. The 71–100 tariff band was removed in 1992 and the 51–60 one in 1993.

Table 5.3 shows that average tariff rates, both weighted and unweighted, have fallen in the 1990s. Average tariffs reached their highest levels in 1989/90; this was a result of replacing quotas with equivalent tariffs. The downward trend was, however, disrupted by the need for crisis management, with a temporary increase in tariff rates in 1993/94.

A recent study (UNDP/World Bank, 1993) calculated effective rates of protection for 1990–92, shown in Table 5.4. Average effective protection fell over the period from 1990 to 1992, but by less than the fall in nominal protection. Tariffs were reduced on both final and intermediate goods, which means that average protection fell more than average effective protection. Sectors with highest protection were garments, finished textiles, rubber products and food processing, in that order.

Table 5.2 Kenya: distribution of goods, by tariff band, 1987–96 (%)

Tariff rate	1987/88	1988/89	1989/90	1990/91	1991/92	1992/93	1993/94	1994/95	1995/96
0	6.9	7.0	5.8	6.1	3.7	2.9	3.1	3.2	3.3
1–10	0.3	0.9	1.6	1.6	4.0	4.6	5.2	4.9	1.8
11–30	30.7	29.6	37.6	37.4	47.6	47.6	56.5	67.8	71.8
31–50	45.4	43.7	23.8	21.6	17.7	20.9	35.2	24.1	23.1
51–60	3.9	5.6	6.0	6.3	3.0	24.0			
61–70	3.8	4.1			24.0				
71–	9.0	9.1	25.2	27.0					
Total	100.0	100.0	100.0	100.0	100.0	100.0	100.0	100.0	100.0

Source: Based on data from the Ministry of Finance, Nairobi.

Table 5.3 Kenya: average tariff rates, 1987–95 (%)

Tariff	1987/88	1988/89	1989/90	1990/91	1991/92	1992/93	1993/94	1994/95
Average tariffs								
Excluding duty-free goods	42.8	44.4	49.2	47.2	39.4	36.6	40.5	27.3
Including duty-free goods	39.9	41.3	46.3	44.3	37.9	35.5	39.2	26.4
Average weighted tariffs								
Excluding duty-free goods	–	–	–	31.8	27.2	27.2	30.9	22.2
Including duty-free goods	–	–	–	25.6	23.5	23.2	26.3	18.9

Source: Based on data from the Ministry of Finance, Nairobi.

Table 5.4 Kenya: effective rates of protection in manufacturing, 1990–92 (%)

Sector	1990	1991	1992
Food processing	51.0	50.6	44.1
Bakery products	42.9	40.7	30.9
Beverages and tobacco	40.9	39.7	36.8
Raw textiles	41.1	41.1	35.9
Finished textiles	60.0	60.3	57.5
Garments	77.1	79.9	99.7
Leather and footwear	43.0	43.3	40.5
Wood products	48.2	47.3	43.4
Paper products	46.3	46.4	40.9
Rubber products	47.1	47.6	45.2
Paint detergents	43.7	44.3	37.5
Other chemicals	44.8	45.9	39.3
Non-metals	36.5	34.9	30.9
Metallic products	46.9	46.1	40.4
Mean	47.9	47.7	44.5
Coefficient of variation	20.3	22.1	37.2

Source: UNDP/World Bank (1993).

As in many other developing countries indirect taxes have been and still are an important source of tax revenue in Kenya (Table 5.5). In the fiscal year 1985/86 indirect tax revenue accounted for approximately 58 per cent while the share of import duties was around 17 per cent of the total.[1] The remaining part consists of direct taxes and other revenue.

The trend over the years is that direct taxes have become more important while the share of indirect taxes has fallen. Since the late 1980s broadening

Table 5.5 Kenya: composition of government current revenue, 1985–95 (%)

Source	1985	1986	1987	1988	1989	1990	1991	1992	1993	1994	1995
Direct taxes	29.5	27.8	28.1	26.7	28.7	29.3	30.5	28.7	36.4	35.5	34.9
Import duties	17.5	17.8	16.9	15.7	16.7	13.7	9.2	13.2	14.6	15.1	16.4
Excise duties	7.3	7.6	7.6	7.2	7.2	7.6	12.2	12.0	11.0	15.7	14.8
Sales tax on domestic manufacturing	15.8	17.4	18.6	18.3	15.5	17.3	12.0	11.7	12.9	11.0	10.3
Sales tax on imports	9.3	11.2	13.5	12.4	15.2	14.1	21.2	20.2	15.8	8.9	8.6
Other indirect taxes	8.6	7.5	5.1	5.5	4.5	4.3	3.6	2.5	2.4	1.9	2.0
Other revenue	12.0	10.7	10.2	14.2	12.2	13.7	11.3	11.7	6.9	11.9	13.0
Total	100.0	100.0	100.0	100.0	100.0	100.0	100.0	100.0	100.0	100.0	100.0

Source: Republic of Kenya (various issues).

the tax base and increasing efficiency in tax collection have been important components of the reform programme. However, poor administrative capacity has slowed the process down. Complexity of tax schedules, with variability across goods and services, increases discretionary practices, leading to tax evasion. To cushion the revenue impact of the tariff reform increased financial inflows from abroad have been necessary. They ensure that the programme is compatible in both fiscal and balance of payments terms.

MODEL PRESENTATION

The analysis in this chapter is based on a computable general equilibrium (CGE) model. With a view to analysing structural adjustment issues, a number of CGE models with well developed trade components have been constructed.[2] The model used here is a variation of the approach popularised by Dervis *et al.* (1982).[3] The trade and production structure of the model is specified as a multi-level nest of functional forms. Specification of export and import functions is different from the standard neoclassical trade model, which tends to yield specialisation in production and one-to-one correspondence between domestic relative prices and changes in trade policy or world prices.[4] Elements of imperfect substitution, and thus incomplete specialisation, are allowed for in our model. At the highest level of aggregation, the Armington (1969) specification is used to define a composite commodity for each sector as a constant elasticity of substitution (CES) function of commodities produced domestically and imported from abroad. Similarly a composite intermediate output is produced, using domestically produced goods and imported inputs. Output in each sector is either sold to the domestic market or exported. A constant elasticity of transformation (CET) framework allocates domestic output between exports and domestic sales. This implies that there are product differentiation or market penetration costs involved in reallocation of output between domestic markets and foreign markets (Robinson *et al.*, 1990).

Sectoral output is derived from fixed proportions of real value added and composite intermediate inputs. Value added is a Cobb–Douglas function of labour and composite capital. In the two agricultural sectors, the latter is a combination of capital and land. Assuming profit-maximising industries, the demand for primary factors increases up to the point where market wages, inclusive of sector-specific differentials, equal the marginal value products of the specific factors.[5]

Incomes in each sector are distributed to the wage bill, to the government and to firms as retained earnings. Government revenue is the sum of tariff revenue, direct taxes on the corporate sector and a single household, indirect taxes, and transfers from abroad, here assumed to be exclusively foreign aid. It is assumed that a fixed proportion of household income accrues to government as tax, corporate taxes are imposed on capital income net of depreciation, while indirect taxes are a fixed proportion of the value of output.

In the model, private savings are a fixed proportion of both household disposable income and profits from firms. Government savings are equal to total revenue net of current expenditures on goods and services, transfers and interest payments on foreign loans. The sum of foreign savings and total domestic savings equals (exogenously fixed) aggregate investment. The demand for goods for investment purposes is derived with the help of a capital coefficient matrix. Analogously, fixed expenditure shares are used to determine government and household demand for consumption goods.

Given the behavioural and institutional constraints outlined above, there is a set of prices that ensure market equilibrium. Domestic prices for imported and exported goods are products of world prices and the exchange rate, adjusted for tariffs and indirect taxes. The prices of the two composite goods are derived by dividing their monetary with their real values. Similarly, the price of output in each sector is defined as the monetary value of domestic deliveries and exports divided by the sector's real output. The price of value added or the net producer price is equal to the output price minus indirect taxes and the cost of intermediate inputs. The price of a unit of capital is a weighted average of capital prices by sector of origin. The aggregate price index, defined as the numeraire in the model, is computed as the ratio of nominal to real GDP.

POLICY AND EXTERNAL SHOCK EXPERIMENTS

The model outlined above was used to conduct six policy and external shock experiments, patterned on Kenya's recent experience. In all cases the overall tariff was reduced by 50 per cent. Thus the different experiments relate to the government's attempt to bridge the revenue shortfall, under various assumptions about the external environment. The following experiments were conducted:

E1   Apart from tariff reduction, government undertakes no other measures. Aid inflows remain unaltered, and the terms of trade unchanged.

E2   The revenue shortfall arising from the tariff reduction is compensated by increased aid inflows.

E3   This experiment looks at the impact of terms of trade shocks (a 20 per cent decline in coffee prices), in the absence of a compensating mechanism.

E4   Combines compensatory aid inflows with adverse terms-of-trade movements.

E5   This experiment adds increased government expenditure to the combination of aid inflows and decline in coffee prices conducted in the fourth experiment.

E6   The last experiment looks at the impact of adverse terms-of-trade shocks combined with increased government expenditures.

Tariff reduction with and without aid

Results from the above experiments are presented in Tables 5.6–9, while the elasticities used are presented in Appendix 5.1. A 50 per cent reduction of tariffs on final and intermediate goods increases real GDP by 0.47 per cent. Household incomes improve by 2.5 per cent, which in turn increase private consumption, savings and taxes. But although this way government receives additional revenue, it falls short of bridging the shortfall caused by lowering tariffs. With no adjustment in real expenditures the budget deficit deteriorates, from 1.7 per cent to 3.3 per cent of GDP.[6] In the absence of foreign borrowing or aid, and given increased demand for importables following tariff reduction, exports have to increase to maintain external balance.

In the second experiment (E2) aid flows in to ensure that the fiscal deficit remains at the same level as before the tariff reduction. The macroeconomic outcomes show that additional foreign resources, in the form of aid, bridge the trade deficit and reduce some of the pressure in the foreign exchange market (Tables 5.6 and 5.7). The inflow of resources raises the overall income in the economy, which in turn raises private consumption. However, the inflow of foreign capital also affects the real exchange rate. Thus, although the budget deficit is now under control, the real exchange rate appreciates, owing to the increased aid inflows. Compared with the 'no aid' scenario, this not only reduces domestic prices for imported goods but also reduces incentives to the export-oriented sectors. Thus with increased aid inflows tradable sectors would be negatively affected, while non-tradable sectors would gain. Aid inflows would thus have Dutch Disease impacts, such as have often been remarked in the literature.[7] However, comparing scenarios E1 and E2 shows that the impacts are by no means uniform across export sectors. Almost all sectors with export shares above 10 per cent in the base run experience reduced output when aid is used to compensate tariff revenue losses.

Producers of non-metallic mineral and paint products are the exception, while both sectors experience a decline in exports, sales in the domestic market increase, and output rises above the no-aid scenario. In the case of the non-metallic sector, this is partly due to the production requirements. Up to 45 per cent of the sector's intermediate inputs originate from the petroleum sector, where prices are reduced substantially by lower tariffs and the appreciation of the exchange rate. Moreover, the sector's low import share implies that even if prices on competing imports were reduced substantially, the effect on domestic sales would be limited. With regard to the sector producing paint, production of final goods is more dominant than that of intermediate goods and the import share is low with regard to final products. This implies, as above, that the sector is relatively insulated from competition. Further, input prices are reduced on its two major inputs: food products and other products.

Sectors producing importables are negatively affected by reduced protection, though transport and equipment is an interesting exception. Here domestic sales increase quite substantially. This is partly due to the low elasticity of substitution, which differentiates imported from domestically produced products. Second, major inputs also experience price reductions, making the sector competitive in the domestic market. Other private services, though less tradable, are also negatively affected by the overall tariff reduction. This is because their production is geared towards intermediate goods. Mining, petroleum and the tourism sectors are extensive users of private service inputs and, since all experience reductions in output, the demand for private services is reduced.

With a few exceptions, the impact of an aid-compensated tariff reduction is that the less traded sectors gain while traded sectors lose. There are two main factors behind this. First, aid increases the overall demand in the economy, with positive effects on all sectors. Second, the appreciation of the exchange rate puts producers of tradables at a disadvantage; since less traded sectors are more insulated, compared with traded ones, from competition, they are able to increase prices and expand output. It can be concluded, therefore, that tariff reform, accompanied by aid inflows, could alter production incentives in favour of non-tradables. A result not intended by policy-makers.

Tariff reform, aid inflows and terms-of-trade shocks

Kenya, like many other developing countries, has been extremely vulnerable to external shocks in past decades. Experiment E3 looks at how the economy is affected by a combination of tariff reform and terms-of-trade shocks. In the

Table 5.6 Kenya: macroeconomic indicators, by experiment (K£ million, and index)

Indicator	Base	E1	E2	E3	E4	E5	E6
Real exchange rate	1.00	1.05	0.96	1.17	1.07	1.06	1.16
RGDP	5983.66	6011.91	6013.51	5998.67	6001.06	6185.43	6183.07
Foreign savings	44.70	44.70	44.70	44.70	44.70	44.70	44.70
Enterprises' savings	95.98	98.81	101.23	97.72	100.23	98.86	96.42
Government's savings	−104.54	−199.38	−104.54	−212.06	−106.29	−369.81	−472.67
Households' savings	763.82	856.46	779.32	840.16	755.37	1023.29	1104.92
Total savings	1169.00	1169.00	1169.00	1169.00	1169.00	1169.00	1169.00
Government revenue	1498.36	1427.69	1513.59	1451.11	1545.82	1600.25	1506.47
Household tax	211.98	217.26	218.12	215.34	216.38	222.81	221.77
Indirect tax	532.19	536.16	534.43	548.84	545.88	539.97	543.35
Tariff revenue	220.47	122.56	118.22	129.19	124.21	123.15	128.24
Households' income	4540.51	4653.60	4672.04	4612.60	4634.81	4772.59	4750.31

Notes:

E1 Overall tariff reduction by 50%.

E2 Overall tariff reduction by 50% + aid compensation.

E3 Overall tariff reduction by 50% + adverse terms-of-trade shock (20% drop in world market price of coffee).

E4 Overall tariff reduction by 50% + aid + adverse terms-of-trade shock (20% drop in world market price of coffee).

E5 Overall tariff reduction by 50% + aid + adverse terms-of-trade shock (20% drop in world market price of coffee) + increased government expenditure.

E6 Overall tariff reduction by 50% + adverse terms-of-trade shock (20% drop in world market price of coffee) + increased government expenditure.

latter case, a 20 per cent reduction in the world prices for coffee. The result is that the real exchange rate depreciates further, in comparison with the tariff-reform-only case (Table 5.6).[8] The latter is necessary to recapture forgone export revenue and to overcome the structural rigidities in the economy that make it difficult to substitute domestically produced goods with imports. Adverse external shocks also have the effect of reducing overall income in the economy, wiping out or delaying the benefits of tariff reform. The government deficit deteriorates, partly owing to lower tax revenues but also to increases in public expenditures, following price increases resulting from the depreciation. If fiscal compatibility is considered to be one of the objectives of the reform programme, a terms-of-trade shock makes it even more important to supplement a policy of tariff reduction with aid.

Adding aid to a scenario of tariff reduction and a terms-of-trade shock (E4), some of the income loss is restored. Consumption and investment shares, as a percentage of GDP, as well as the budget deficit return to their pre-shock levels (Tables 5.6 and 5.7). Further, though aid inflows remove some of the pressure on the foreign exchange market, the exchange rate still depreciates, although to a smaller extent than in the scenario without aid (E3). Compared with the no-aid scenario the real depreciation is here 7 per cent, compared with 17 per cent.

Tariff reform, external and fiscal constraints

In the best of circumstances maintaining fiscal balance has been difficult in Kenya. The task has not been made easier by persistent external shocks, and domestic demand for increased public expenditures. In the last two experiments (E5 and E6), the impact of increasing government expenditures during the process of tariff reform, with and without aid, is investigated. Increased public expenditure has two main effects. First, expansion of public sector activity has Keynesian multiplier effects which lead to increases in GDP (Table 5.6). Second, the fiscal position of the government deteriorates, with a switch from private to public consumption (Table 5.7). This implies that the increase in GDP growth is at best only temporary. However, compared with a scenario without increased public expenditures, there is no major impact on the exchange rate. When private consumption is reduced, demand for domestic and imported goods is lowered. Since the public sector's share of imports is less than that of the private sector, less depreciation is required to balance the foreign exchange market. At the sectoral level increased public sector activity has a positive impact on food, petroleum, other services and construction, while sectors with high export shares, except the special case of petroleum,[9] register a reduction in output (Table 5.8). When aid is excluded from the package, the scenario of tariff reform, adverse terms-of-trade shock and increased government expenditure leads to a substantial depreciation, with a serious fiscal deterioration.

Table 5.7 Kenya: resource use and balance of payments, by experiment (K£ million)

Use	Base	E1	E2	E3	E4	E5	E6
Private consumption	3564.7	3579.9	3674.6	3557.1	3663.1	3526.5	3423.6
Public consumption	1275.4	1289.8	1298.2	1302.4	1311.6	1631.3	1620.1
Investment	1169.0	1169.0	1169.0	1169.0	1169.0	1169.0	1169.0
Exports	1400.4	1493.9	1325.0	1588.2	1398.2	1385.3	1575.7
Imports	1425.9	1520.7	1453.4	1618.0	1540.7	1526.6	1605.3
Trade balance	−25.5	−26.8	−128.3	−29.9	−142.6	−141.4	−29.6
Foreign aid	126.7	133.1	225.6	148.5	250.6	248.5	147.4
Factor payments abroad	−193.5	−203.3	−185.9	−226.8	−206.5	−204.8	−225.1
Remittances	47.6	50.0	45.7	55.7	50.8	50.3	55.3
Current account	−44.7	−47.0	−42.9	−52.4	−47.7	−47.3	−52.0
Capital account	44.7	47.0	42.9	52.4	47.7	47.3	52.0
As % of GDP							
Private consumption	59.6	59.5	61.1	59.3	61.0	57.0	55.4
Public consumption	21.3	21.5	21.6	21.7	21.9	26.4	26.2
Investment	19.5	19.4	19.4	19.5	19.5	18.9	18.9
Trade balance	−0.4	−0.4	−2.1	−0.5	−2.4	−2.3	−0.5
Foreign aid	2.1	2.2	3.8	2.5	4.2	4.0	2.4
Factor payments abroad	−3.2	−3.4	−3.1	−3.8	−3.4	−3.3	−3.6
Remittances	0.8	0.8	0.8	0.9	0.8	0.8	0.9
Current account	−0.7	−0.8	−0.7	−0.9	−0.8	−0.8	−0.8
Capital account	0.7	0.8	0.7	0.9	0.8	0.8	0.8

Table 5.8 Kenya: changes in sector output, by experiment (% change over base level)

Sector	Base	E1	E2	E3	E4	E5	E6
Agriculture	1319.9	0.0	0.0	0.0	0.0	-0.2	-0.2
Bakery	197.1	-0.2	1.0	-1.3	0.1	-1.3	-2.7
Beverage and tobacco	414.8	0.1	1.4	-1.1	0.4	-1.2	-2.7
Construction	641.5	0.1	1.7	-2.6	-0.9	0.2	-1.6
Fish and forestry	50.4	-0.1	0.0	0.1	0.2	-1.3	-1.4
Food	1258.6	0.5	1.5	-0.3	0.7	0.8	-0.2
Footwear and leather	46.9	0.4	3.3	-2.4	0.8	-1.5	-4.6
Metallic products	584.8	0.5	0.4	0.3	0.1	0.7	0.8
Mining	38.8	6.6	-4.2	18.9	6.5	5.5	18.0
Non-metallic mineral products	114.2	1.1	1.3	0.7	0.9	0.4	0.2
Other chemicals	106.8	1.8	0.8	3.1	1.9	0.9	2.3
Other private services	939.4	0.5	0.0	1.1	0.5	1.9	2.6
Paint	50.0	0.8	2.1	-0.3	1.1	-0.6	-1.9
Paper products	162.6	-0.4	-1.7	1.1	-0.3	0.8	2.3
Petroleum	844.1	-0.7	-1.0	-0.4	-0.7	-0.3	0.1
Public services	1291.5	0.0	0.0	0.0	0.0	19.7	19.7
Restaurant and hotel services	1210.5	1.0	-0.4	2.8	1.0	0.3	2.1
Rubber	79.6	0.3	1.5	-0.9	0.5	0.5	-0.8
Tea and coffee	530.9	0.4	-0.6	-0.8	-1.8	-1.8	-0.8
Textile and garments	257.9	0.7	3.9	-2.2	1.2	-1.3	-4.7
Textile raw materials	60.6	-1.2	-2.0	-0.3	-1.2	-2.2	-1.4
Traditional	366.7	0.0	0.0	0.0	0.0	-0.1	-0.1
Transport and equipment	370.7	0.4	1.8	-1.1	0.2	1.0	-0.3
Transport, storage and communications	789.7	1.4	0.1	3.2	1.6	1.5	3.1
Wood products	69.4	0.5	2.0	-1.4	0.3	-0.6	-2.2

Table 5.9 Kenya: changes in sector exports (% change over base level)

Sector	Base	E1	E2	E3	E4	E5	E6
Agriculture	72.5	4.0	−5.9	14.8	3.4	5.4	17.1
Bakery	1.2	4.3	−5.3	15.0	4.0	4.7	15.9
Beverage and tobacco	8.9	4.5	−4.2	14.0	4.3	4.4	14.2
Fish and forestry	3.4	3.9	−5.8	15.0	3.8	3.8	15.1
Food products	47.4	4.8	−3.2	13.6	4.6	5.2	14.4
Footwear and leather	1.0	6.0	−2.9	15.8	5.9	5.4	15.3
Metallic products	31.1	6.7	−1.0	15.1	6.7	6.1	14.6
Mining	38.3	6.7	−4.3	19.2	6.6	5.6	18.2
Non-metallic mineral products	13.7	6.3	−1.9	15.3	6.2	5.3	14.4
Other chemicals	29.3	6.3	−2.1	15.6	6.2	5.9	15.3
Other private services	17.7	3.5	−5.8	14.1	3.4	2.2	12.8
Paint	6.0	5.5	−3.9	15.9	5.3	5.4	16.1
Paper	4.7	6.3	−2.5	16.1	6.2	5.3	15.1
Petroleum	92.8	4.0	−1.9	10.3	4.0	3.5	9.8
Rubber products	0.9	6.0	−3.8	16.9	5.8	5.3	16.4
Tea and coffee	514.8	0.5	−0.7	−1.0	−2.2	−2.2	−0.9
Textile and garments	6.3	6.9	−1.2	15.8	6.9	5.9	14.8
Textile raw materials	0.5	5.7	−4.2	16.8	5.4	5.5	17.0
Transport equipment	2.2	7.5	−1.2	17.0	7.4	6.7	16.4
Transport, storage and communication	161.8	4.9	−3.9	14.8	4.8	4.2	14.2
Restaurant and hotel services	342.6	3.8	−5.2	14.0	3.7	3.4	13.7
Wood products	3.3	5.9	−3.1	15.8	5.8	5.1	15.1

Finally, let us evaluate the impact on exports of the various experiments with the help of Table 5.9. In E1, the experiment without shocks or increased government expenditure, exports increase by 4–7 per cent, in response to the tariff reduction. When aid is introduced as a compensating mechanism (E2), exports are reduced across the board. The most seriously affected sectors are those with high shares of exports in total production, such as agriculture and tourism.

In the two scenarios (E3 and E6) where terms-of-trade shocks are introduced, the results show dramatic increases in exports for all sectors, except coffee and tea (from where the shocks emanate in the first place). The interpretation is that, if the full impact of the shocks is allowed to pass through the economy, the exchange rate would depreciate, leading to increases in exports. Still, the amount of imports would remain high in these scenarios, since imported intermediates play such a key role in Kenyan production. What is important is that the trade deficit would remain relatively small. The above scenarios contrast markedly with the two (E4 and E5) where aid is introduced, with E5 assuming increased government expenditure while E4 does not. In both cases, the exchange rate depreciates less compared with the scenarios without aid, halting the intended structural shifts in the economy. Moreover, aid flows, in tandem with increased government expenditure further discourage sectors with high export shares.

CONCLUSION

In this chapter we have discussed trade reform in relation to foreign aid, terms-of-trade shocks and government expenditures. It was found that efficiency gains from lowering tariffs were small. However, most sectors gain from a tariff reduction and important incentives are created for producers of tradable goods. Although the resulting increase in economic activity has a positive impact on government revenue, it fails to compensate entirely for loss of tariff revenue. The government deficit widens as a result and foreign inflows are necessary to close the gap. However, trade policy reform that is supported by revenue-compensating aid inflows has a cost in terms of appreciating the real exchange rate. With a few exceptions, this puts producers of tradables at a disadvantage compared with those in non-traded sectors.

Reducing tariffs in the wake of an adverse external shock, such as a sharp decline in coffee prices, wipes out or delays the benefits of tariff reform. The government deficit deteriorates and, if fiscal compatibility is a programme objective, compensating inflows are needed. But even here there is a trade-off between fiscal balance and production incentives. Although exports increase to close the trade gap, they would have grown even faster in the absence of aid.

In the period 1986–90 Kenya made attempts to lower tariffs and restructure the economy while at the same time relaxing its fiscal and monetary policy stance. While foreign aid helped provide a more gradual implementation of the new tariff structures, it had serious costs in that it delayed resource reallocation to tradable sectors via an unfavourable impact on the real exchange rate. A relaxed fiscal policy stance worsened the situation further. Thus the ultimate goal of increasing incentives to the export sector was not achieved.

Appendix 5.1 Substitution and transformation elasticities

Sector	Rhoci	Rhoc	Rhot	Eta
Agriculture	2.00	2.00	2.00	2.00
Bakery	0.75	0.75	2.00	2.00
Beverage and tobacco	0.75	0.75	2.00	2.00
Construction	0.25	0.25		
Fish and forestry	0.50	0.50	2.00	2.00
Food	0.75	0.75	2.00	2.00
Footwear and leather	0.75	0.75	3.00	2.00
Metallic products	0.33	0.33	3.00	2.00
Mining	0.33	0.33	2.00	2.00
Non-metallic mineral products	0.33	0.33	3.00	2.00
Other chemicals	0.33	0.33	3.00	2.00
Other private services	0.25	0.25	2.00	2.00
Paint products	0.33	0.33	3.00	2.00
Paper products	0.75	0.75	3.00	2.00
Petroleum products	1.20	1.20	3.00	2.00
Public services	0.25	0.25		
Restaurant and hotel services	0.25	0.25	2.00	2.00
Rubber products	0.33	0.33	3.00	2.00
Tea and coffee	2.00	2.00	2.00	4.00
Textile and garments	0.75	0.75	3.00	2.00
Textile raw materials	0.75	0.75	3.00	2.00
Traditional	0.25	0.25		
Transport and equipment	0.25	0.25	3.00	2.00
Transport, storage and communication	0.25	0.25	2.00	2.00
Wood products	0.75	0.75	3.00	2.00

Notes: Rhoci: trade substitution elasticity between final imports and domestically produced goods. Rhoc: trade substitution elasticity between intermediate imports and domestically produced intermediate goods. Rhot: transformation elasticity between goods produced for the export market and the domestic market. Eta: price elasticity of export demand.

NOTES

This chapter is based on the author's doctoral dissertation.

1 In Kenya import duties have been less important than in other African economies. In sub-Saharan Africa the share of import duties in government revenue was about 26 per cent in 1985 (Weiss 1996).
2 See, for example, de Melo and Robinson (1989), Shoven and Whalley (1992) and Devarajan *et al.* (1990). A survey of trade-focused models can be found in de Melo (1988).
3 The full model is presented in Levin (1998).
4 There is no distinction between tradable and non-tradable sectors in the model; tradability among sectors is defined by degree. Substitution and transformation elasticities and export and import shares in the model determine how closely the domestic price is linked to the world price.
5 Capital is assumed fixed across sectors, hence the model incorporates short-run aspects only.
6 The model is run under the assumption of exogenously determined real government expenditures, fixed real investment and fixed savings. The exchange rate and government savings adjust to achieve equilibrium in the foreign exchange and the loanable funds market.
7 On the Dutch Disease impacts of aid see Younger (1992), Collier and Gunning (1992), White (1992) and Devarajan *et al.* (1990).
8 See Devarajan *et al.* (1990) for a discussion of the terms of trade shocks and exchange rate policy. Given that imported and domestically produced goods are imperfect substitutes, the rule of thumb is to depreciate the real exchange rate in the event of an adverse terms-of-trade shock. However, if foreign and domestic goods are close substitutes, a likely outcome in developed economies, the policy stance should be an appreciation.
9 Kenya processes oil products for export to Uganda, Rwanda and southern Sudan.

REFERENCES

Armington, P.S. (1969) 'A Theory of Demand for Products Distinguished by Place of Production', *IMF Staff Papers*, 16 (1): 159–78.

Bevan, D., Collier, P. and Gunning, J.W. with Bigsten, A. and Horsnell, P. (1990) *Controlled Open Economies: A Neoclassical Approach to Structuralism,* Oxford: Oxford University Press.

Collier, P. and Gunning, J.W. (1992) 'Aid and Exchange Rate Adjustment in African Trade Liberalisations', *Economic Journal*, 102: 925–39.

Damus, S. (1990) 'A Social Accounting Matrix and CGE Model Data Base for 1986', Technical Paper 90–05, Nairobi: Long Range Planning Unit of the Ministry of Planning and National Development.

de Melo, J. (1988) 'Computable General Equilibrium Models for Trade Policy Analysis in Developing Countries: a Survey', *Journal of Policy Modelling*, 10: 469–503.

de Melo, J. and Robinson, S. (1989) 'Product Differentiation and the Treatment of Foreign Trade in Computable General Equilibrium Models of Small Economies', *Journal of International Economics,* 27: 47–67.

Dervis, K., de Melo, J. and Robinson, S. (1982) *General Equilibrium Models for Development Policy,* Washington DC: World Bank.

Devarajan, S., Lewis, J.D. and Robinson, S. (1990) 'Policy Lessons from Trade-focused, Two-sector Models', *Journal of Policy Modelling,* 12: 625–57.

Greenaway, D. and Milner, C. (1993) *Trade and Industrial Policy in Developing Countries,* London: Macmillan.

Levin, J. (1998) 'Structural Adjustment and Poverty: The Case of Kenya', Ph.D. thesis, Göteborg: Department of Economics, Göteborg University.

Republic of Kenya (various issues) *Economic Survey,* Nairobi: Central Bureau of Statistics, Office of the Vice-President and Ministry of Planning and National Development.

Robinson, S., Kilkenny, M. and Hanson, K. (1990) 'The USDA/ERS Computable General Equilibrium Model of the United States', *Staff Report,* AGES 9049, Washington: Agriculture and Rural Economy Research Service, US Department of Agriculture.

Shoven, J.B. and Whalley, J. (1992) *Applying General Equilibrium,* Cambridge: Cambridge University Press.

UNDP/World Bank (1993) 'Kenya – the Challenge of Promoting Exports', Trade Policy Division Policy Research Department, Washington, DC: World Bank.

White, H. (1992) 'The Macroeconomic Impact of Development Aid: Critical Survey', *Journal of Development Studies,* 28: 163–240.

Weiss, J. (1996) *Economic Policy in Developing Countries – The Reform Agenda,* New York and Hemel Hempstead: Prentice Hall/Harvester Wheatsheaf.

World Bank (1994) *Adjustment in Africa: Reforms, Results and the Road Ahead,* Washington DC: World Bank.

Younger, S.D. (1992) 'Aid and the Dutch Disease: Macroeconomic Management when Everybody Loves You', *World Development,* 20: 1587–97.

6

MONETARY POLICY EFFECTIVENESS IN ZAMBIA

Abraham Mwenda

In the past decade, Zambia has seen one of the more dramatic switches in policy in Africa. From an insular, heavily controlled economy, based on a large parastatal sector and the encashment of rents from copper mining, to one where free markets determine the economic thrust. To stay on course, the emerging economic framework clearly demands another set of policy tools. An area where developments have been rapid, and sometimes dramatic, has been that of monetary policy. Controls of the past had effectively eradicated the power of the monetary authorities to intervene effectively in the financial markets. Today, the Bank of Zambia enjoys considerable autonomy, making it a key player in the emerging economic structure.

In the 1970s developed countries switched from direct monetary policy instruments such as credit and interest rate controls to indirect ones, including open market operations, rediscount facilities and reserve requirements (Alexander *et al.* 1995). Developing countries have only recently begun to move in a similar direction, in relation to adjustment programmes supported by the World Bank and the IMF. Indirect monetary policy instruments have two main advantages over the more traditional approach. First, market-based instruments, being effective in stabilising money supply growth and inflation in the short run and the long run, as opposed to the short run only for direct instruments, enhance policy credibility.[1] Second, since indirect instruments (with the exception of reserve requirements) are market-based, they encourage competitive financial intermediation, which fosters the development of efficiently functioning money and capital markets.

Zambia made the switch to indirect instruments towards the end of 1992 and this chapter evaluates whether the change to market-based monetary instruments has enhanced policy effectiveness, in reducing and stabilising the growth of broad money supply and inflation.

INDIRECT MONETARY CONTROL

Traditionally the Bank of Zambia relied heavily on direct instruments, including interest and credit regulations, to control the money supply and inflation (see Mwenda 1993, UNCTAD 1996). There were ceilings on lending rates and floors on deposit and savings rates. The goal of the control regime was partly to enable policy-makers to channel funds into 'priority' activities such as public administration, agriculture and mining. They were supplemented by special deposit requirements.

It was not until the end of 1992 that the Bank of Zambia switched to indirect instruments. First, interest rates were liberalised, with wages and prices freed soon afterwards. Other measures included the liberalising of exchange rates, and the gradual liberalisation of the balance of payments (Mwenda 1995, 1996). The current account was liberalised during 1992–93 and the capital account in 1994 with the revocation of the Foreign Exchange Control Act.[2]

Following these changes, the prime objective of monetary policy became that of inflation control. This was emphasised in all policy statements and was eventually incorporated in the revised Bank of Zambia Act of 1995. Other macroeconomic objectives became subservient to this overriding goal.

Open market-type operations involving the auctioning of treasury bills and bonds were introduced during 1993–94.[3] Weekly treasury bill tender committee meetings of the Bank of Zambia and the Ministry of Finance and Economic Development determined the amount of funds to be raised at each auction, although the amount of treasury bills for sterilisation purposes is set by the central bank alone. Initially treasury bills were auctioned on the basis of a multiple price or Dutch auction system. Later, this was replaced by a marginal pricing system where successful bidders received the weighted average of the yields they had bid for, also called the cut-off yield rate. Further, one-year coupon bonds, also Dutch-auctioned, were introduced, issued every four to six weeks and/or when special tenders were deemed necessary.

The second indirect instrument was the daily auction of credit and deposits to commercial banks, beginning in 1995, on the basis of a Dutch auction. Successful commercial banks receive credit from or offer deposits to the Bank of Zambia at bid or offer interest rates, respectively. The amount of liquidity to be injected into or withdrawn from the money market by credit and debit auctions, respectively, is determined through liquidity programming. The process starts with a forecast of primary commercial bank balances at the Bank of Zambia to establish the trends in money market liquidity over a period ranging from a day to a full week. Comparing the estimated net change in liquidity with a predetermined upper limit establishes, in turn, the expected excess or shortfall in liquidity supply to the money market.[4]

However, pure open market operations where the Bank of Zambia buys and sells treasury bills on the basis of its portfolio, to influence money market liquidity, have proved difficult, owing to the unwillingness of the commercial banks to take part. There is thus a serious problem of credibility, especially since an active and deep secondary market that guarantees trade in government debt, and thus policy irreversibility, is absent. The central bank has thus supplemented open market operations with rediscount facilities and reserve requirements. The former have included adjustments to the rediscount penalty rate, which affects commercial bank borrowing at the Bank of Zambia, and limits the value of treasury bills that a bank can rediscount. Beginning in 1996, banks cannot rediscount treasury bills worth more than 15 per cent of their capital as opposed to no limits earlier. In addition, the Bank of Zambia has in recent years regularly extended overdraft facilities, often unsecured, to commercial banks, notably those unable to borrow on the interbank market.[5]

As already noted, reserve requirements have been used occasionally. For example, core liquid assets and statutory reserve ratios were raised in 1993 and 1994, to help deal with the liquidity overhang inherited from earlier. However, again indicating the discretionary element of policy, funds acquired in this way bear no interest, so an indirect tax is imposed on commercial banks. A wedge thus develops between lending and deposit interest rates which, in turn, distorts the monetary transmission mechanism. Lingering control and distortionary measures, in a supposedly liberalised system, have meant that the problem of lack of confidence has largely remained.

Recognising the counterproductive nature of these problems in a liberalising regime, the Bank of Zambia substantially reduced the commercial banks' asset and reserve ratios in 1995. However, to avoid the potentially large and disruptive liquidity injections that would follow, the ratios were converted into statutory bonds that earned market interest rates, with maturities staggered over four years. Still, the liquidity implications of a difficult fiscal situation and the need to accumulate reserves, coupled with high interest rates, forced the Bank of Zambia to raise the assets and reserve ratios of the commercial banks twice during 1996–97.

A CONCEPTUAL FRAMEWORK

In a market economy, a two-tier banking system is necessary for the control of the money supply. The first tier relates to the reserve money market, accessible to commercial banks, with the central bank contracting or expanding reserve money, using indirect instruments. The second tier relates to the broad money market. Here commercial banks respond to changes in the cost and availability of reserve money by either contracting or expanding credit and broad money supply.

The indirect monetary transmission mechanism operates via instruments, operational targets, intermediate targets and ultimate targets (see Callier

1990). Monetary policy affects these ultimate targets through other financial variables. The assumption is thus that monetary policy has little immediate effect on the ultimate objectives. The ultimate effects of monetary policy are therefore uncertain.

There are generally three types of indirect instruments. The first are open market operations, which may be either outright or repurchase order sales and purchases of securities (usually treasury bills or central bank notes), foreign exchange, credits and deposits. The second set of instruments relates to rediscount facilities. The third set incorporates reserve requirements, i.e. uniform or differential core liquid assets and statutory reserve ratios. With the exception of reserve requirements, which are implemented by regulation, the rest of the instruments are market-based, that is, they are implemented through trading on capital markets.

Variables that monetary authorities can control directly with policy instruments are called operational targets. These include reserve money, net domestic assets, and money market interest rates. Variables comprising intermediate targets have a stable and predictable relationship with the ultimate targets of monetary policy. They are, therefore, variables the monetary authorities influence through the manipulation of operational targets. Examples include broad money and credit supply aggregates, commercial bank lending rates and retail exchange rates.

Ultimate targets are the desired monetary policy objectives. These have traditionally included positive *per capita* GDP growth, a sustainable balance of payments, a high level of employment, and low and stable inflation. Recently, however, a low and stable inflation rate has become the prime objective of monetary policy, turning others into subsidiary objectives. The focus on inflation has been prompted by empirical evidence suggesting that, while monetary policy changes only have temporary effects on real variables, they have lasting effects on the growth and stability of prices. In addition, low and stable inflation has been found to be a prerequisite of achieving other macroeconomic objectives.

While theorists have advanced several alternative channels of monetary transmission (Mishkin 1995), Zambia's indirect monetary control framework is based on the traditional money supply and interest rate channel. This model has three main ingredients: aggregate demand, and broad money demand; broad money and reserve money demand, and reserve money and its sources (the central bank balance sheet). This is also the model used by the IMF in its programming (see, for instance, Bolnik and Hussein 1995, Palmisani 1994).

Aggregate demand, money demand and supply

The relationship between broad money demand and aggregate demand is given by the following exchange equation:

$$MV = PY \tag{1}$$

where M is broad money demand, equal to the sum of currency (notes and coins) in circulation plus demand, time and savings deposits, V the velocity of money, P the price level and Y real GDP. V is assumed to be constant, so that a given ultimate target growth rate for PY requires the same intermediate target growth rate for M.

The equilibrium condition in the first-tier money market is given as

$$RM = RMD = C + RR + ER + VC = RMS \tag{2}$$

where RMD is reserve money demand, C currency in circulation, RR required reserves, ER, excess reserves (normally equal to commercial banks' current accounts held at the central bank), and VC, commercial banks' vault cash. Currency demand is positively related to real income but negatively related to deposit interest rates. Required reserves are a positive function of deposits and the statutory reserve ratio. Among factors impacting on interbank lending interest rates are the ease with which banks clear their deficits and surpluses with the central bank, the nature of the reserve requirements and payments systems, and the central bank's interest rates on bank deposits relative to those of the interbank system. Commercial banks will, for example, demand large excess reserves if interbank rates are high, when the payments system is volatile or if it is based on gross settlement.

Equilibrium in the second-tier money market is given by the following money multiplier equation

$$M = MS = sRM \tag{3}$$

where M is defined as in equation 1 above and MS is broad money supply determined as equilibrium reserve money, RM, times the money multiplier, s, equal to $(c + 1)/(c + rr)$, where c is the currency to deposit ratio, assumed to be stable, and rr is the statutory reserve ratio set by the monetary authorities. The multiplier indicates that broad money supply is positively related to reserve money and the currency to deposit ratio, and negatively related to the statutory reserve ratio.

The main sources of reserve money supply are net domestic assets and net foreign assets. This is represented by the central bank balance sheet equation

$$RMS = NDA + NFA \tag{4}$$

where RMS is defined as above, NDA is net domestic assets, which include net credits extended to government and the private sector – these increase the supply of reserve money through debits to commercial banks' current accounts at the central bank – and NFA is net foreign assets. Net purchases of foreign assets increase reserve money through increases in the banks' current accounts.

Monetary programming

A multi-step monetary programming system is used to ensure that the growth path of the money supply is consistent with the ultimate targets. First, ultimate targets for inflation and real GDP growth are set (Rajcoomar and Bell 1996). Second, the intermediate target for broad money demand is determined, using the exchange equation (that is, $M = PY/V$). The velocity of broad money demand is calculated as $Y/M2$, where Y is the previous period's nominal GDP level. Third, the operating target for reserve money demand is derived as the sum of its estimated components. Fourth, the target for net foreign assets is determined after taking into account the limits on foreign borrowing and external debt service requirements. Fifth, the operating target for net domestic assets is determined as the difference between the estimated targets for reserve money demand and net foreign assets. Sixth, autonomous sources of net domestic assets, that is, those beyond the central bank's control, are projected. They include items such as credit to government, credit supplied to banks at their discretion, and automatic overdrafts to banks arising from negative clearings (in a gross settlements system). Finally, estimated autonomous net domestic assets are subtracted from the estimated operating target level for reserve money demand. This provides an indication of the discretionary monetary policy measures the central bank requires to realise the operational targets for net domestic assets and reserve money, intermediate targets for broad money supply, and an ultimate target for inflation.

EVALUATION METHOD

To evaluate the impact that switching to indirect instruments has on monetary policy effectiveness in reducing and stabilising the growth of the money supply and inflation, a two-step method is used. First, an autoregressive broad money supply equation is estimated and a Chow test is used to check for structural breaks in money supply behaviour. Second, Z and F tests are used to determine whether the change resulted in significant reductions in the growth and stability of broad money supply and inflation. In our analysis, the period January 1988 to October 1992 represents the era of a direct monetary control system. It was a period of mounting fiscal pressure during which the Bank of Zambia intensified its use of direct controls while fiscal pressures mounted. Though there was no sudden break, the periods of indirect monetary control started towards the end of 1992, when interest rates were liberalised. In our sample the latter period spans the period November 1992 to July 1997.

The auto-regressive broad money supply equation to be estimated is specified as follows:[6]

$$\ln M_t = \beta_0 + \sum_{i=1}^{n} \beta_{t-i} \ln M_{t-i} + u_t \tag{5}$$

where M is the broad money supply ($M2$), equal to the sum of currency (notes and coins in the public hands), demand, savings, and time deposits, t is time, equal to a month, n the lag length, and u an error term, assumed to be normally distributed with zero variance. Ordinary least squares (OLS) are used to estimate the auto-regressive equation, beginning with a general equation with twelve lags. Using the Schwartz criterion, insignificant lags were eliminated, to arrive at a more efficient estimation (see Charemza and Deadman 1992).

Two tests are used in the analysis. First, a Z test is used to determine whether the shift to indirect monetary control has resulted in significant reductions in the growth of the broad money supply and inflation, implying effective monetary policy. Let the Z test statistic be denoted by d, which is determined according to the formula:

$$d = \bar{x}_2 - \bar{x}_i \tag{6}$$

where $x_i (i = 1, 2)$ with a bar refers to average growth rates of broad money and inflation corresponding to the periods of direct and indirect monetary control, respectively. The critical value for the test statistic denoted by d^* is given as

$$d^* = z_\alpha \sqrt{\frac{S_1^2}{n_1} + \frac{S_2^2}{n_2}} \tag{7}$$

where n_1 and n_2 are sample groups one and two, corresponding to the direct and indirect monetary control periods respectively, s_1 and s_2 are the standard deviations of the first and second samples, z is the normal deviate corresponding to a lower-tail area equal to α. The significance level is determined as d^*/S_d, where S_d is the standard deviation of d derived as follows:

$$S_d = \sqrt{\frac{S_1^2}{n_1} + \frac{S_2^2}{n_2}} \tag{8}$$

The null (H_0) hypothesis states that the switch to indirect monetary control has not been effective in reducing the broad money supply and inflation. That is, that d is greater than or equal to d^*. The alternative hypothesis (H_1) states that the switch to indirect monetary control has enhanced monetary policy effectiveness, that is, that d is less than d^*. The decision rule is to accept the null hypothesis if d is greater than or equal to d^* and to reject it or fail to reject the alternative hypothesis if d is less than d^*.

Second, an F test is used to determine whether the shift to indirect monetary control has resulted in a significant reduction in the instability of broad money supply and inflation growth. A significant reduction in variances indicates policy effectiveness in the stabilisation of broad money growth and inflation. The test statistic is calculated as follows:

$$F = \frac{S_2^2}{S_1^2} \tag{8}$$

where the variables are defined as in the Z test. The null hypothesis (H_0) states that indirect monetary control has not stabilised the growth of broad money supply and inflation, that is, that $(s_2)^2$ is equal to $(s_1)^2$. There are two alternative hypotheses. First (H_1) that indirect monetary control has stabilised the growth of broad money and inflation, that is, that $(s_2)^2$ is less than $(s_1)^2$. Second (H_2) that indirect monetary control has weakened the effectiveness of monetary policy in stabilising broad money supply growth and inflation, that is, that $(s_2)^2$ is greater than $(s_1)^2$. The decision rules are to accept the null hypothesis if the F test statistic is equal to the F critical value; we cannot reject the first alternative hypothesis if the calculated F test statistic is less than the critical value nor the second alternative hypothesis if the calculated F test statistic is greater than the F critical value.

RESULTS

Deseasonalised monthly data for broad money ($M2$) and inflation rates for the period January 1988 to July 1997 are used for the empirical evaluation.[7] Results of the autoregressive broad money supply equation are presented in Table 6.1. Diagnostic tests indicated the absence of both heteroscedasticity and autocorrelation in the residuals, while the linearity assumptions were not violated. Both short (one-month) and long (six, nine, and twelve-month) lags of broad money supply growth have significant effects on the current growth rate of the broad money supply. They explain 87 per cent of the changes in the current growth of the broad money supply.

However, the Chow break point test for the model's forecast stability indicates a structural break in the behaviour of the broad money supply during 1992. Further, the plot of the residuals from the recursive least square estimation presented in Figure 6.1, rejects the null hypothesis of stationary residuals. The switch to indirect monetary control thus caused a structural shift in the behaviour of the broad money supply.

Table 6.1 Estimated results of the auto-regressive M2 equation

Variable	Coefficient	T *statistic*
Constant	0.33	1.86
$\ln M_{t-1}$	0.80	14.34
$\ln M_{t-6}$	0.23	3.16
$\ln M_{t-9}$	0.20	2.74
$\ln M_{t-12}$	−0.31	−4.73

Adjusted $R^2 = 87\%$ SE $= 0.15$ F statistic $= 258$ Schwartz criterion $= -3.527$

Diagnostic tests		
Test	*Calculated F value*	*Probability*
Arch test	0.415	0.734
White heteroscedasticity	0.727	0.706
Reset test	0.065	0.799
Serial-correlation test	0.015	0.902

Structural shift test		
Chow break point test	$F = 2.89$	0.017

Note: All test statistics are significant at the 5 per cent confidence level.

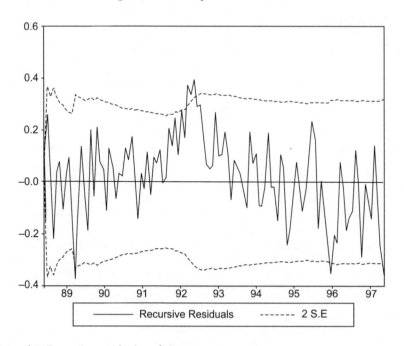

Figure 6.1 Recursive residuals stability test

ABRAHAM MWENDA

Table 6.2 Z test results

	N_2	X_1	X_2	s_1	s_2	D	d^*
M2	57.00	4.70	3.60	5.00	4.00	−1.10	−1.40
CPI	57.00	6.70	3.90	5.03	4.04	−2.90	−1.30

Z test results are presented in Table 6.2. The calculated test statistic for the broad money supply is greater than the critical value. Thus the null hypothesis that indirect instruments have no impact on monetary growth cannot be rejected. In other words, although there has been some reduction in the average monthly growth rate of the money supply after the shift to indirect monetary control, it is statistically insignificant. For inflation, the hypothesis that the decrease in monthly inflation during the indirect monetary control system is significant cannot be rejected. Thus the shift to indirect control of the money supply enhanced monetary policy effectiveness in reducing inflation. However, since the reduction in broad money supply growth is insignificant, monetary policy has contributed to lowering inflation through another channel, explained below.

F test results are presented in Table 6.3. The calculated F test statistics for both the broad money supply and inflation are less than the critical value and significant at the 5 per cent confidence level. Consequently we cannot reject the first alternative hypothesis (H_1) that there have been significant reductions in the variability of broad money supply growth and inflation. The switch to indirect monetary control has thus stabilised broad money supply growth and inflation. In this regard, it has been via increases in the stability of broad money supply growth that indirect monetary policy has contributed to reducing inflation.

Table 6.3 F test results

	s_1	s_2	F statistic	F critical
M2	5.00	4.00	0.64	0.67
CPI	5.03	4.04	0.64	0.67

Table 6.4 Zambia: selected macroeconomic indicators, 1992–97 (growth, %)

Indicator	1992	1993	1994	1995	1996	1997
GDP	−2.60	6.50	−3.10	−3.90	6.40	5.50
K/US$	166.00	168.00	48.00	24.00	22.00	3.00
Def/GDP	4.80	3.70	2.20	−0.80	−2.50	−2.70

Note: Data for 1997 are based on Bank of Zambia estimates.

Table 6.4 shows changes in real output (GDP), in the nominal kwacha/dollar (K/$US) exchange rate, and in the ratio of the fiscal deficit to GDP (Def/GDP). Growth of real GDP was high in 1993, but fell in the following two years, picking up in 1996–97. The recovery in real output and the marked reduction and stabilisation of the exchange rate gave a boost to consumer and business confidence, and have been important factors in reducing inflation. It would seem, therefore, that the contribution of indirect instruments has been mainly to smooth money supply fluctuations. However, while indirect controls have been effective in smooth money supply fluctuations, they have been decidedly less effective in sterilising excess money supply, thus failing to maintain its target growth path. This was largely due to the general lack of credibility. The government failed to overcome the legacy of controls; its attempts were characterised by repeated backtracking in the middle of liberalisation.

Last, we look at the targets for monetary supply and inflation during 1995–97, a period when economic reforms were pursued with increased intensity. Table 6.5 indicates that although the growth of the broad

Table 6.5 Zambia: money and inflation, targets and actual, 1995–97 (kwacha million and %)

	1995	1996	1997
	Reserve money		
Target	88,929.25	99,085.00	182,666.67
Actual	92,003.60	136,029.95	191,818.50
	Net domestic assets		
Target	822,976.50	99,085.00	1,148,399.30
Actual	905,023.45	136,029.95	1,255,661.40
	Net foreign assets		
Target	$-734,047.25$	$-1,050,314.3$	$-1,362,666.6$
Actual	$-813,019.85$	$-1,119,631.5$	$-1,373,229.6$
	Net claims on government		
Target	98,968.25	94,136.45	85,200.00
Actual	94,150.50	125,435.68	168,325.00
	Interest costs (%)		
	13.30	16.70	12.60
	M2 %		
Target	37.00	10.00	17.00
Actual	40.00	28.00	24.00
	Open market operations Losses		
Actual	940.20	328.50	2314.40
	CPI		
Target	35.00	27.00	15.00
Actual	46.00	35.00	23.00

Source: Bank of Zambia; those for 1997 are estimates.

money supply and inflation has been reduced over time, there has been persistent failure to meet the reform programme's monetary and inflation targets.

None the less, it must be pointed out that even after switching to indirect monetary policy instruments a number of serious economic and financial constraints remained, inhibiting the effective control of money supply growth and inflation. For example, the cash budget, supposed to be the nominal anchor of the system, has failed. The government had deficits in the early 1990s and it was not until 1995 and 1996 that real improvements were made (see Table 6.4). Yet the government has continued to experience frequent budget deficits, financed by borrowing from the Bank of Zambia and the banking system as a whole. Indeed as Table 6.5 indicates, the government's domestic borrowing requirement (net claims on government) has been on the increase in recent years. A small tax base, combined with considerable tax evasion, and poor monitoring and control of expenditures have undermined the Bank of Zambia's ability to control the growth of the money supply and inflation.

Further, rather ambitious reform programme targets for reserves accumulation, coupled with tough external debt service obligations, amid reduced foreign exchange inflows, have compelled the Bank of Zambia to purchase foreign exchange for government use instead of for stabilisation of markets. Moreover, droughts have led to poor harvests and large maize (the country's staple) deficits, necessitating credit to private merchants for importing the grain. Not unexpectedly, the cost of government borrowing has risen as the prices at which institutions and private individuals are willing to engage in the Bank of Zambia's open market operations have gone up. Table 6.5 shows that interest costs on treasury bills have been rising in recent years as well as losses due to open market operations. Until all these problems are addressed, keeping money supply growth as well as inflation close to the targets prescribed in the structural adjustment programme will remain elusive.

Contrary to assumptions, the money multiplier and velocity of money, vital relationships in the indirect monetary control framework, have been very unstable. The money multiplier (S) trend depicted in Figure 6.2 shows that the instability was due to an unstable cash/deposit ratio (CDR) and frequent changes in the statutory reserves ratio. Figure 6.3 shows that money velocity (V) rose sharply over the 1991–93 period before declining (Mutoti 1997). It has been difficult, under these conditions, to undertake the kind of monetary programming that ensures effective control of money supply and inflation.

Slow growth of the money and capital markets has also made it difficult for the system to perform properly. The most serious constraint is the absence of an active secondary market for government paper with over six-months' maturity. The Bank of Zambia has thus been unable to use the treasury and

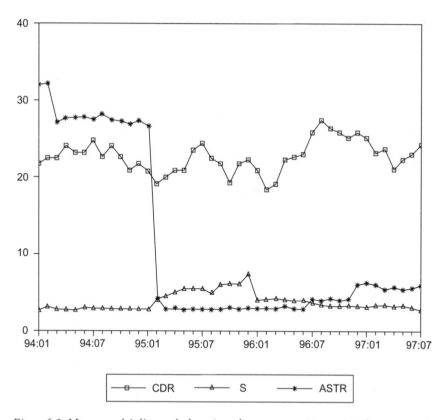

Figure 6.2 Money multiplier, cash deposit and statutory reserve ratios. *S* money multiplier, *CDR* cash/deposit ratio, ASTR statutory reserves ratio

bond market to control the money supply. Second, the interbank market is highly segmented, so that, even when forecasts indicate good liquidity, the central bank is forced to intervene in various ways, such as extending credit to distressed banks or those not able to borrow from other banks. In turn the implied increase in liquidity makes monetary control difficult. Third, high operating costs and non-performing loans put upward pressure on interest rates. The implied poor response to monetary policy impulses weakened indirect monetary control.

Further, Zambian inflation has exhibited considerable inertia, even during periods of very tight monetary conditions, implying that monetary conditions *per se* have not been the only causes of inflation. Indeed it would seem that factors, including loss of consumer and business confidence, depreciation of the kwacha, as well as imported inflation have also played significant roles.

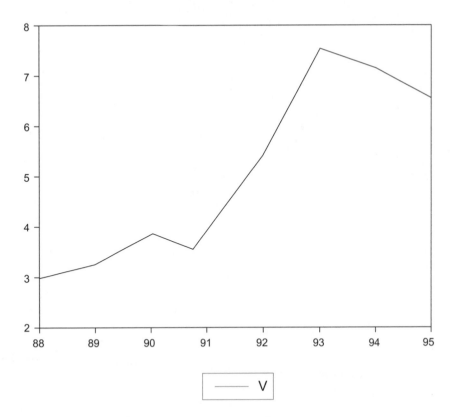

Figure 6.3 Velocity of broad money. *V* velocity of money

POLICY IMPLICATIONS

This chapter has sought to evaluate the effectiveness of monetary policy in Zambia, notably the impact of the recently introduced indirect monetary policy instruments. The results indicate that while the reduction in the growth of money was small, the introduction of indirect monetary controls brought about significant reductions in inflation, accompanied by a reduction in variability of both the money supply and inflation. That the new approach has only been able to stabilise broad money supply growth and not to reduce it suggests that the importance of indirect monetary control has been mainly in smoothing money supply fluctuations. It is via this that the new approach has contributed to reducing inflation. Other factors contributing to the fall in inflation have been the recovery of real output, a reduction in and the stabilisation of the nominal exchange rate and the improvement in consumer and business confidence.

The failure to meet targets is mainly due to weak fiscal controls, especially failure to implement a cash budget. The need to finance borrowing via open market operations led to high interest rates, thus raising the cost of financing government debt. On the other hand, substantial purchases of foreign exchange to meet the ambitious reserves accumulation targets and to service huge external debts, given reduced capital and export inflows, led to rapid depreciation of the kwacha.

The following policy implications emerge from our investigation. To succeed, indirect monetary control must be accompanied by well designed measures to address problems related to slow learning and system inefficiencies. Fiscal deficits will be eliminated only when budgetary practices are improved. For indirect monetary controls to work, well developed and efficient money and capital markets are needed. However, they do not just emerge. Monetary authorities must play an active role in their development by helping to eliminate imperfections, by offering incentives, and by developing new financial instruments and institutions.

NOTES

The author wishes to acknowledge assistance from Noah Mutoti, Isaac Mhanga, Nancy Mwilwa-Malulu, Mwiza Mbewe and Alex Chakufyali. The views expressed here are not necessarily those of the Bank of Zambia.

1 In the long run commercial banks devise ways, such as the creation of non-bank subsidiaries, that enable them to transact outside these controls. Time is, however, expended in looking for alternatives and controls are, therefore, costly from the efficiency point of view.

2 To promote a fully fledged market-based foreign exchange system, the 100 per cent export revenue retention scheme for non-traditional exporters was restored in 1992, while the Zambia Consolidated Copper Mining Company (ZCCM) was allowed to retain all its export revenues in 1996. The Bank of Zambia would, however, intervene at its own discretion to influence the exchange rate and money supply.

3 Treasury bills have three maturities, twenty-eight, ninety-six, or 128 days. However, 10 per cent of tender issues were sold on the 'off-tender window' to cater for individual investors. This ended in 1996.

4 Excess liquidity calls for deposit auctions, while deficits are removed by credit auctions. The upper or lower limit which the commercial banks must not exceed or fall below was initially set at 1 billion kwacha (K), later raised to K 1.5 billion. These limits were determined on the basis of liquidity levels previously maintained by the banks.

5 A two-tier, large and small, value clearing system, where negative large positions will be financed by overnight repurchase order arrangements, is in the process of being established. It will, among other things, reduce automatic overdrafts, whether secured or not.

6 Lack of monthly GDP data made it impossible to estimate a fully specified behavioural equation for the broad money supply.
7 Monetary data are from the Bank of Zambia, while inflation data are derived from the composite consumer price index (CPI) of the Central Statistical Office, Lusaka.

REFERENCES

Alexander, W.E., Balino, T.J.T. and Enock, C. (1995) *The Adoption of Indirect Instruments of Monetary Policy*, Occasional Paper 126, Washington DC: IMF.

Bolnik, B.R. and Hussein, M. (1995) 'Financial Programming: a Case Study of Zambia', HIID Macroeconomic Policy and Management Working Paper, Cambridge, MA: Harvard University.

Callier, P. (ed.) (1990) 'Financial Systems and Development in Africa', EDI Policy Seminar, Washington DC: World Bank.

Charemza, W.W. and Deadman, D.F. (1992) *New Directions in Econometric Practice*, Aldershot: Edward Elgar.

Mishkin, F.S. (1995) 'The Monetary Transmission Mechanism', *Journal of Economic Perspectives*, 9 (4): 3–10.

Mutoti, N. (1997) 'Demand for Money and Monetary Policy in Zambia', working paper, Lusaka: Economics Department, Bank of Zambia.

Mwenda, A. (1993) 'Credit Rationing and Investment Behaviour under Market Imperfections: Evidence from Commercial Agriculture in Zambia', Ph.D. dissertation, Göteborg University.

Mwenda, A. (1995) 'Inflation Formation under Economic Liberalization and Implications for Stabilization Policy', working paper, Lusaka: Financial Markets Department, Bank of Zambia.

Mwenda, A. (1996) 'Foreign Exchange Liberalization in Zambia: Nature, Performance and Prospects', paper presented at a conference on Economic Liberalization: Experiences and the Way Forward, Mulungushi International Conference Hall, 21–3, August Lusaka.

Palmisani, F. (1994) 'Demand and Supply of Central Bank Liabilities', paper presented at a workshop on Monetary Operations, St Petersburg, 18–23 September.

Rajcoomar, S. and Bell, M. (1996) 'Financial Programming and Policy: the Case of Sri Lanka', Washington DC: IMF Institute, International Monetary Fund.

UNCTAD (1996) 'Financial Repression and Financial Sector Reforms in Zambia', project on Financial Sector Reforms in Least Developed Countries, Lusaka: UNIDO.

7

MINIMUM WAGES AND TRADE REGIMES

CGE results for Zimbabwe

Ramos Mabugu and Margaret Chitiga

Zimbabwe provides an interesting case for the study of African labour market behaviour under changing trade orientation. Since a major trade policy reform was embarked on in 1991, the gap between the earnings of skilled and unskilled workers has widened. There has also been a notable relocation of labour from previously import-substituting sectors to export and service-oriented ones. Meanwhile, urban unemployment and under-employment have increased. This outcome has been explained, as in Harris and Todaro (1970), by the existence of a binding nominal wage in the urban sector. To a large extent, this analysis focuses on the internal workings of the domestic factor markets although in a partial equilibrium framework. However, partial analysis abstracts from the induced effects of shocks on relative prices, income and wealth and assumes that the demand curve for labour, especially in the non-traded goods sector, is flat. Prescriptions for addressing wage and employment issues from such a partial analysis would be inadequate.

In this chapter, a computable general equilibrium model (CGE) of Zimbabwe is used to shed light on the wage and labour market behaviour under different trade regimes. The model incorporates a labour market module, while goods are differentiated into tradables and non-tradables to allow for analysis of issues related to trade orientation.

THE ECONOMY SINCE 1980: AN OVERVIEW

During the decade that followed independence in 1980, Zimbabwe followed a broadly regulated, inward-looking strategy, with controls on prices and wages, and on foreign trade. Though a number of piecemeal reforms were undertaken with the aim of conserving foreign exchange, the impacts were often negative socially. Income and asset redistribution were key goals, and the government intervened extensively in labour markets and raised taxes on incomes. Although falling short of the extent hoped for by potential beneficiaries, land allocation has probably been the most important wealth redistribution measure undertaken in Zimbabwe since independence. The government also undertook major labour market legislation in a bid to reverse the policies of racial discrimination pursued before 1980. Inequalities between skilled (mainly white) and unskilled (mainly black) workers were especially focused on.

Among the changes introduced, minimum-wage legislation (for unskilled workers) was perhaps the most far-reaching measure. Policy-makers hoped that this would have two important effects: a reduction in income inequalities in the country as a whole and an increase in the incomes of unskilled workers, also among the poorest in the country (see, for example, Fallon and Lucas 1991). However, as Table 7.1 indicates, while minimum-wage legislation during this period helped preserve the real wages of unskilled workers in agriculture and industry, increases fell short of expectations. Thus while minimum wages had risen sharply in 1982, they could hardly keep pace with inflation afterwards. It is also possible that minimum wage legislation could have slowed down the pace of job creation in the private sector.

Though erratic, partly as a result of poor weather, growth in GDP over this period was quite reasonable, averaging 2.9 per cent. Zimbabwe was one of the few African countries whose economy did not decline in the course of the 1980s. Commentators have used structural and neo-Keynesian arguments to explain this relatively good performance. It was a period when the government combined deficit financing and foreign exchange allocation to strategic sectors with some effort at redistribution to achieve growth-compatible outcomes. However, as social expenditure got out of hand, and inflation

Table 7.1 Zimbabwe: minimum wages in agriculture and industry, 1980–88 (Z$ per month in 1980 prices)

Year	Agriculture	Industry
1980	30	70
1981	29	83
1982	43	90
1883	32	68
1984	35	68
1985	33	73
1986	37	68
1987	36	65
1988	35	63

Source: Quarterly Digest of Statistics (various issues), Central Statistical Office, Harare.

increased, the fiscal deficits were unsustainable. The foreign credit constraint on the economy became binding.

With increased opportunities for education, and following the removal of controls on rural–urban migration, unemployment became a big problem in the cities. Between 1980 and 1990, for example, the labour force grew by close on 4.6 per cent per year to 3.8 million, while formal sector employment grew by only 1.7 per cent to 1.19 million. In 1991 the government launched a structural adjustment programme supported by the IMF and World Bank. It would seem that economic stagnation, increasing unemployment and rising fiscal deficits were crucial factors in the decision. However, though considerable reform has taken place since then, performance in the 1990s has been mixed (see Table 7.2). The two years 1989–90 registered high growth rates, with moderate inflation. There followed a sharp economic contraction as structural adjustment reforms were implemented. In 1992 the economy declined by over 8 per cent, stagnating the following year. In 1996, however, the economy registered a substantial recovery. Average real wages have been declining for much of the 1990s, so that by the mid-1990s they were close to half those in the early 1980s.

During the first years of the reform there was a rapid deterioration in the trade balance, the result of a real appreciation in the early 1990s, but also due to currency speculation as economic actors adjusted their positions with the opening up of the economy. However, though there was subsequently a terms-of-trade improvement, and a positive export response, recent reforms have been unable to close the trade deficit. This is partly to be blamed on a still too large fiscal deficit, and an overvalued exchange rate in the early 1990s. However, following further devaluation and other trade liberalisation measures, the trade deficit started to fall in the mid-1990s.

In the labour market, the ratio of skilled to unskilled workers rose, which indicates that reforms have favoured skill-intensive production techniques. However, increases in labour productivity, measured as output per factor input, have been negligible in the reform period. Table 7.2 shows that average earnings were stagnant during the late 1980s, reflecting the failure of minimum wage legislation to raise earnings. Average earnings fell steeply following the reforms of 1991, and continued to decline thereafter.

Table 7.2 Zimbabwe: growth of GDP, inflation and wages, 1989–96 (%)

Variable	1989	1990	1991	1992	1993	1994	1995	1996
GDP	5.3	11.2	0.6	−8.2	0.8	5.5	−0.2	7.0
Inflation	13.0	15.0	28.0	42.0	32.0	30.0	26.0	24.0
Real wages	−2.0	5.0	−12.0	−28.0	−18.0	−13.0	−4.0	−13.0

Source: Quarterly Digest of Statistics (various issues), Central Statistical Office, Harare.

A CGE MODEL FOR ZIMBABWE

We use a computable general equilibrium model for Zimbabwe to illustrate the impact of minimum wage legislation under different trade regimes. Use of CGE analyses on Zimbabwe is fairly recent. Davies *et al.* (1994a, b) use a five-sector CGE model to analyse the macroeconomics of Zimbabwe in the 1980s. A similar model has been used by Mabugu (1996) to study a range of tax policy issues, while Chitiga (1996) has used it to assess the income distributional effects of government policies. In the model of Davies *et al.* there is a direct link between the factors used in production and the factor owners, while Chitiga develops a method of assessing the effects of changes in the functional distribution of income on the rest of the economy. These two approaches are the basis of the analyses undertaken in this chapter. Only the most important outlines of the model are provided below.

The model is real, distinguishing between policy instruments used by the government and their general equilibrium effects on production, employment, income generation, fiscal and foreign trade balances. The model further distinguishes between production sectors, households, two types of labour and the government. A constant elasticity of substitution formulation is used to model import and domestic demand in the consumption of goods from a sector. Private consumption demand is determined on the basis of the linear expenditure system. Aggregate investment is fixed in nominal terms, which means that the model uses an investment-driven closure. The rest of this section elaborates on features related to the labour market and foreign trade.

The demand for labour in the formal sector is fully endogenised. Each producer is assumed to minimise unit costs subject to given input prices and technology constraints. Each industry in the model uses both labour skill categories, i.e. skilled and unskilled, but in varying proportions. The demand for labour of skill category i by industry j, Ld_{ij}, can be written as a function of the industry's total demand for labour, Ld, relative prices of the different skill types of labour, w_i, and of technical change variables, A.

$$Ld_{ij} = Ld_{ij}(Ld, w_i, A) \tag{1}$$

where $i =$ skilled, unskilled; $j =$ sectors.

These labour demands can be aggregated across industries to obtain total labour demand for each skill category as follows:

$$Ld_i = \sum Ld_{ij} \tag{2}$$

Two labour market closures can be used, depending on the emphasis sought. For example, unskilled wages could be set exogenously with employment endogenised or the supply of skilled workers could be set *a priori* and skilled wages endogenised. Given a slack labour market, with institutionally determined wages, the first alternative closure seems appropriate.

It is assumed that each industry is operating on its demand curve for labour, that is, that employment and labour demand are equal. Unemployment is thus possible, since the model does not require that markets should clear. The economy can thus be thought of as operating inside as opposed to on its production possibility curve. An increase in the demand for labour, under these assumptions of slack labour markets, leads to an increase in the number of persons employed in some sectors. These new employees come from two sources: those who were previously employed (relocation to expanding sectors) and those previously unemployed.

In modelling foreign trade, we distinguish between tradables and non-tradables. In one version of the model, a foreign exchange rationing mechanism is introduced to capture the situation in the 1980s (for details see Mabugu 1996). In the second, the foreign exchange rationing mechanism is removed, to represent the more market-oriented conditions of the 1990s. The current account is now endogenous, with the nominal exchange rate fixed. All foreign currency needs for inputs, food and consumer goods are satisfied by drawing on the current account balance.

RESULTS FROM SIMULATIONS

To study impacts during the foreign exchange rationing period, minimum wages for all unskilled workers were raised by 5 per cent. Employment of unskilled workers falls across the board (see Table 7.3) as the costs of production increase owing to increased wage costs. On the demand side, higher wages raise demand, especially for food, and households engaged there receive higher income. In line with findings by Knight (1997) the minimum wage policy is effective in raising the real incomes of unskilled workers.

In our case, a 5 per cent increase in minimum wages raises total unskilled earnings by 3.7 per cent, that is, by less than the minimum wage increase, because other income sources increase less (for example, higher minimum wages may come at the cost of increased monitoring so that 'moonlighting' activities decline). However, skilled incomes rise by only 0.9 per cent. This partly implies that a reduction of unskilled employees relatively depresses skilled wages.

Under the regime of foreign exchange rationing a 5 per cent increase in the minimum wage leads to a slight fall in GDP. This is partly because minimum wage increases hurt the exportables sector directly through increased input costs and through a relative appreciation. Indeed, as Table 7.3 shows, it is exportables that suffer the largest decline in unskilled employment. Minimum wages under foreign exchange control regimes limit producer

Table 7.3 Effect of a 5% increase in minimum wages under two trade regimes (% change from base run)

Variable	Forex rationing	Liberalised regime
GDP	−0.1	−0.03
Fiscal deficit	−2.4	−2.5
Current account	8.0	10.0
Unskilled income	3.2	1.1
Skilled income	0.9	−0.3
Food income	0.4	−0.5
Employment (unskilled)		
Services	−1.6	−0.5
Construction	−1.7	−0.4
Importables	−2.0	−1.7
Exportables	−3.7	−0.3

flexibility. Thus, while their labour costs rise, they cannot substitute for capital inputs owing to the limits on imports. Instead, they substitute skilled for unskilled workers. One could argue that since unskilled workers now receive wages that are above 'market clearing levels', a longer unemployment queue results. It is also noteworthy that an increase in the minimum wage increases the fiscal deficit by about 2.5 per cent, since a number of unskilled workers are employed by the government.

In the second simulation, foreign exchange rationing is removed (Table 7.3). Even here unskilled labour employment falls, though by much less, compared with the earlier experiment. Producers can now substitute machines for the more expensive unskilled workers, and not necessarily for skilled workers as before. This time, unskilled workers in the importables sector are the worst hit, as higher production costs lead to loss of market share, given the more open import regime. There is presumably also some reallocation of labour towards exportables made more profitable by liberalisation of the foreign exchange market. It can be noted that the growth impact (negative) of a minimum-wage increase is also smaller in the liberalised regime than in the control one. However, the impact on the current account is positive, since the depreciation on its own discourages imports.

CONCLUSION

In assessing Zimbabwe's response to economic reforms in recent years, questions have been raised about the causes of the relatively poor growth of the 1990s, compared with the more robust performance during the control regime of the 1980s. In this chapter, we have focused on one aspect of government policy, minimum-wage legislation, and its impact during two diametrically opposed policy regimes: foreign exchange control and liberalisation.

The results showed that the output and sectoral effects of minimum wages were greater in the control regime than in the more liberal one. This is because, in the latter, producers have a broader choice of adjustment strategies, including becoming more capital-intensive, and can thus preserve strategies. However, capital-intensive production is not necessarily good for growth in a labour-rich country, since the implied unemployment depresses domestic demand. It also causes social distress.

REFERENCES

Chitiga, M.R. (1996) 'Computable General Equilibrium Analysis of Income Distribution in Zimbabwe', Ph.D. thesis, Göteborg University.

Davies, R., Rattso, J. and Torvik, R. (1994a) 'The macroeconomics of Zimbabwe in the 1980s: a CGE model analysis', *Journal of African Economies,* 3 (2): 153–98.

Davies, R., Rattso, J. and Torvik, R. (1994b) 'Short-run Consequences of Trade Liberalization in Zimbabwe: a CGE Model Analysis', mimeo, Department of Economics, University of Trondheim.

Fallon, P.E. and Lucas, E.B. (1991) 'The impact of changes in job security regulations in India and Zimbabwe', *World Bank Economic Review*, 5: 395–414.

Harris, J. and Todaro, M.P. (1970) 'Migration, Unemployment and Development: a Two-sector analysis', *American Economic Review*, 60: 126–42.

Knight, J. (1997) 'Labour Market Policies and Outcomes in Zimbabwe', working paper, Oxford University: Centre for the Study of African Economies.

Mabugu, R. (1996) 'Tax Policy in Zimbabwe: Applying General Equilibrium Models', Ph.D. thesis, Göteborg University.

Part II

INSTITUTIONS

8

FINANCIAL INSTITUTIONS AND THE MOBILISATION OF RESOURCES FOR DEVELOPMENT

Victor Murinde

Financial institutions and markets in Africa have not attracted as much attention as in other developing areas. For example, financial institutions and markets in the 'tiger' economies of South East Asia have underpinned the 'Asian miracle', an apparent reversal of Gunnar Myrdal's (1968) 'Asian drama'. However, the severity of the financial crises at the end of the 1990s has surprised many observers, and provoked questions on the resilience of financial institutions. In Latin America, where economies have gone through various crises in the past decades, financial sector reform is now part of the development agenda. In the Middle East, attention has been on the rapid growth of Islamic financial institutions and the use of unique instruments, often running counter to established financial precepts (see Murinde *et al.* 1995). Recent shifts in the global economy have increased the urgency of financial sector reform in Africa.

The role of financial institutions and markets, especially with respect to the mobilisation of resources for development, warrants serious scrutiny. Africa remains one of the most aid-dependent regions of the world and aid flows have continued to be the basis of interaction between African countries and the former colonial powers (Mosley *et al.* 1991). These flows have become unpredictable, however. Thus although projections for aid inflows for 1990–96 were already low by historical comparison they still were not realised (Murinde 1998). The continent also faces more competition with respect to funds for international development. Indeed, as Tovias (1990) has argued, the single European market is already diverting trade, aid and investment from Africa to Eastern Europe. The aid route can thus no longer be relied upon to provide sufficient funding for development.

In the 1960s and 1970s direct foreign investment, especially by multinationals, was substantial. It dried up with the crisis while the financing that

came with structural adjustment programmes was attached to tough conditionalities. Thus multilateral funding, while alleviating the tight resource
constraints, may not be the solution to the dwindling external inflows.
They have not been sufficient to cover the needs of African countries. It has
been argued, for example, that the IMF's net flows to Africa during most of
the 1980s were negative (see, in particular, Mistry 1991). Finally, financial
flows from the World Bank to developing countries (LDCs) have also been
declining over time. Summers (1991) has shown that over the period
1975–80 net transfers by the World Bank group to LDCs was US$9 (in
1991 terms) *per capita* per annum and projected to decline to about US$2
by the year 2000.

This chapter argues that since Africa has been poor at attracting foreign
savings, researchers and policy-makers should try to identify domestic sources
of development finance in the continent itself. If carefully exploited, domestic
sources are capable of yielding stable financial flows. The chapter reviews the
different sources of domestic finance: commercial banks, informal and other
non-bank institutions, appraising the potential of each. The fiscal policy
stance needed to promote government savings is also investigated. However,
lack of data has made it difficult to quantify all aspects of our discussion.

DOMESTIC FINANCIAL INSTITUTIONS

The contribution of the financial sector to economic growth in Africa can be
looked at from the macroeconomic point of view, as in Levine (1997), or in
terms of the specific role played by stock markets and banks in economic
growth, as in Levine and Zervos (1998). The 'supply-leading' hypothesis predicts that growth in the financial system induces further growth in the real
economy. It is implied that lack of a developed financial system impedes economic growth. The policy prescription is that pricing and other reforms are
necessary to raise efficiency and growth in the financial system.

The 'demand-following' hypothesis predicts that economic growth induces
financial development. That is, increased growth as well as the commercialisation of agriculture and other traditional subsistence sectors create demand
for financial services. St Hill (1992) finds moderate support for the 'supply-
leading' hypothesis for a sample of thirty-seven LDCs while the 'demand-
following' thesis is established for a sample of nineteen industrial countries.
However, bi-directional causality may occur between economic growth and
financial growth, implying some ambiguity. Notwithstanding, a seminal paper
by Patrick (1966: 176–7) suggests that in the early stages of economic development a 'supply-leading' pattern is the more likely, because a direct stimulus is
needed to garner savings for investment. During later stages, when the financial sector is fully developed, the 'demand-following' pattern takes over. This
earlier finding has been substantiated by many studies focusing on Africa, in

Table 8.1 Financial assets held with financial institutions in a sample of African economies, 1995 (local currencies)

| Country | Central bank currency outside | Commercial banks | | Non-bank financial institutions |
		Demand deposits	Time and savings	
Algeria*	249.77	210.78	278.17	58.56
Benin*	50.65	107.80	85.98	2.84
Botswana	223	607	1,809	–
Burundi	23,976	18,730	10,681	123
Cameroon*	102.29	213.97	329.30	0.08
Congo (Kinsh.)*	1,684	187	630	–
Congo (Brazz.)*	81.58	49.16	24.34	0.14
Côte d'Ivoire*	451.4	490.7	485.3	1.5
Ethiopia	5,718	3,562	5,325	234
Gabon	100.69	117.90	139.87	–
Gambia	247.97	223.50	443.45	–
Ghana	546.3	371.1	434.4	51.0
Guinea	167,144	104,060	64,950	–
Guinea-Bissau	278.1	187.2	285.7	–
Kenya	28,891	38,994	119,851	12,988
Lesotho	74.76	445.91	601.05	–
Malawi	987.52	1,218.14	1,936.43	184.06
Mali	107.54	90.49	56.36	–
Mauritania	7,383	10,674	7,817	–
Mozambique	1,130.2	3,774.8	805.5	–
Namibia	415.6	1,581.9	2,851.6	6.9
Niger	59.64	38.42	33.61	1.82
Nigeria	23,121	20,180	30,360	2,479
Rwanda	17,257	22,586	23,401	1,363
Sudan	249	156	257	–
Swaziland	307.81	282.57	811.70	–
Tanzania*	244.31	183.97	329.52	–
Uganda	204,519	204,182	148,148	–
Zambia	77.8	140.2	310.8	1
Zimbabwe	1,823.5	9,351.8	5,237.6	3,633.5

Source: IMF (1997a).

Note: Units are millions of local currency, except countries marked*, where data are in billions of local currency. Since we use different currencies, no inter-country comparisons are made; the emphasis is on intra-country comparisons.

particular Kwarteng (1982), Abebe (1990), Ikhide (1992) and Lyons and Murinde (1994).

In direct opposition to the above findings, the structuralist strand of the literature suggests that the financial system has only an obscure role to play in growth, especially given that financial bottlenecks are an intrinsic feature of the African economies (Taylor 1991, Murinde 1993). The financial sector is small relative to the size of the economy, and consists of a narrow range of institutions, predominantly deposit-taking ones, including commercial banks, savings banks, post office savings banks and housing finance companies. There are only a few well established insurance companies, pension funds or portfolio investment houses. Since most markets are inefficient, dominated by controls, the policy prescription emanating from the structuralist approach is that government should focus on alleviating the financial bottlenecks via control of the financial sector.

Table 8.1 shows the distribution of financial assets held at various financial institutions in a sample of African economies as at the end of 1995.[1] It is useful to recall that central banks in Africa inherited a colonial model of central banking, i.e. they were instituted to replace currency boards. The East African Currency Board was, for example, replaced by central banks in each of the three regional countries in 1966. In most African countries the central bank is an appendage of government, with top management of the bank, including the board of directors, often changing with the government. Thus, as in the case of the colonial currency boards, central banks are motivated by political expediency and their role in economic development is fairly limited. In Table 8.1 data on individual countries indicate that the largest share of financial assets is held by commercial banks and other financial institutions, not by central banks. It is unlikely that the central banks' position in Table 8.1 would improve if government bonds and securities, as well as deposits of banks held with central banks were reported. This is because in almost all African countries bond markets are poorly developed.

There is, however, considerable scope for innovations in the field of development banking and finance. Thus, on top of the conventional role of the monetary authorities, central banks could also encourage the growth, efficiency and geographical spread of development finance institutions. This might be achieved by providing some equity capital or via the creation of a conducive environment (moral suasion) for existing financial institutions to diversify their activities. Central banks could support institutions that introduce new initiatives such as mortgage finance. Real estate is often the biggest depository of domestic capital and its development has positive impacts on the whole economy. Similarly, central banks could spearhead the development of securities and money markets, by enhancing their own capacity to undertake regulatory and supervisory operations in the financial sector. The point to note is that if economic agents believe in the efficacy of the banking system they tend to hold less currency outside it. Part of the central banks' task in Africa is to ensure that such trust is broadened and sustained.

Table 8.1 also shows the size of financial assets held with commercial banks in selected African economies as at the end of 1995. In general, commercial banks in Africa have also followed the colonial model. They are mostly expatriate, though some are locally incorporated – for example, Barclays and Standard Chartered in East Africa. They specialise in the provision of short-term credit, especially trade credit, working capital and personal credit. The table shows that, for all the African countries in the sample, the major component of the overall financial assets is held in commercial, rather than central, banks and non-bank financial institutions. Thus commercial banks are well placed to play an active role in financial mobilisation, especially since alternative savings vehicles are relatively undeveloped.

Table 8.2 presents indicators for the strength, size and soundness of the top banks in a sample of Africa economies. The percentage change in the capital strength of the banks indicates that some banks have experienced zero or, in some cases, negative growth (as in Cameroon, Ethiopia, Niger and Sudan). In some countries the top banks have contracted in terms of assets (examples are Gabon, Niger, and Rwanda). In terms of soundness, shown by the percentage change in the capital assets ratio, some banks display weaker performance than previously (examples are banks in Burundi, Ethiopia, Madagascar and Nigeria). In general, however, bank performance is good. For example, sixteen out of a sample of twenty-five top banks indicate improvement for all the three indicators: capital strength, assets size and soundness. This notwith-standing that smaller banks have had very weak performance.

It is important for government to promote the development of other types of banks and financial institutions for resource mobilisation. For example, in the on-going restructuring of the commercial banking sector, banks may be transformed into universal banks as well as specialised financial institutions. A universal banking system is characterised by long-term lending, equity investment, and cradle-to-grave paternalistic involvement in the business activities of the client. Its development would thus be an important way of resolving the sectoral rigidity of African economies and helping to raise the rate of capital formation.[2] In countries where specialised development banks already exist, the main problem is that credit is subsidised and specialised institutions are often reduced to credit rationing agencies. I argue, therefore, that specialised banks should be pushed towards free competition. This will reduce credit rationing and thus remove the moral hazard and adverse selection problems that face these institutions today. This done, newly established as well as existing specialised development banks, subsidiaries or consortia of commercial banks, would be able to meet the financial needs of the key sectors. Under this setting, specialised development banks become useful tools for the diversification of risk. A third and novel approach would be the establishment of people's banks: these would comprise a network of rural banks, each being autonomous to the locality it serves, but with functional procedures determined at national headquarters. In contrast to the existing co-operative banking system, each bank unit would operate on a scale dictated by the local economy. An example of a people's bank is the Rural Development Bank in Nigeria.

Table 8.2 Top banks in a sample of African economies

Country	Strength: capital		Size: assets		Soundness: capital/assets (%)	
	$million	Change (%)	$million	Change (%)	Latest	Previous
Burundi						
Société Burundaise de Financement (12/89)	6	3.0	34	6.1	17.02	17.53
Cameroon						
BIC&I du Cameroun (6/90)	39	-0.1	1,009	2.4	3.88	3.98
Congo						
Banque Commerciale Congolaise (12/89)	35	9.6	347	0.8	10.07	9.26
Ethiopia						
Commercial Bank of Ethiopia (6/90)	51	-0.9	2,445	14.6	2.07	2.40
Gabon						
BIC&I du Gabon (12/90)	43	23.0	406	-3.4	10.55	9.96
Ghana						
Ghana Commercial Bank (12/90)	100	350.7	672	47.3	14.90	4.87
Guinée						
BIC&I de la Guinée (12/90)	10	25.7	95	17.7	10.53	9.86
Guinée-Bissau						
Banque International de Guinée-Bissau (10/90)	5	n/a	49	n/a	10.26	n/a
Ivory Coast						
SGB en Côte d'Ivoire (9/90)	82	2.1	1,759	1.1	4.67	4.62
Kenya						
Kenya Commercial Bank (12/90)	72	72.6	704	10.5	10.23	6.55
Lesotho						
Lesotho Bank (12/90)	20	16.2	184	11.9	10.84	10.44
Madagascar						
Banque Nationale pour le Commerce (12/90)	11	7.8	174	10.5	6.31	6.47

Malawi						
National Bank of Malawi (12/90)	18	28.4	251	27.2	7.32	7.25
Mauritania						
BABM Islamique (12/90)	14	107.6	77	4.7	17.67	8.91
Mauritius						
Mauritius Commercial Bank (6/90)	44	38.7	686	20.2	64.10	5.56
Niger						
BALNCED (9/89)	5	–0.0	35	–8.4	15.62	14.30
Nigeria						
Union Bank of Nigeria (9/90)	84	19.9	1,158	15.7	7.24	6.99
Rwanda						
Banque de Kigali (12/89)	7	5.1	105	–1.2	6.41	6.03
Senegal						
SGB au Sénégal (9/90)	22	16.0	468	0.3	4.63	4.00
Sudan						
Bank of Khartoum (12/90)	29	–6.3	1,178	29.3	2.43	3.35
Tanzania						
National Bank of Commerce (6/89)	67	85.9	1,646	50.0	4.10	3.30
Togo						
Ecobank Transnational (9/90)	34	7.3	212	79.5	16.04	26.83
Congo Democratic Republic						
Banque Commercial Zairoise (12/90)	48	344.9	181	175.6	26.32	16.31
Zambia						
Zambia National Commercial Bank (3/91)	23	71.0	343	96.3	6.81	7.82
Zimbabwe						
Zimbabwe Banking Corporation (9/90)	34	16.6	601	27.7	5.72	6.26

Source: The Banker, No. 63, December 1991: 61–3.

Notes: n/a Not available. The date in brackets is the sampling point and changes refer to the situation a year earlier.

The third category in Table 8.1 relates to non-bank financial institutions, holding a very small proportion of the total financial assets. Institutions in this category are few and rather passive, comprising the post office savings banks, insurance companies, housing finance companies, savings and loan banks, credit co-operatives and agricultural credit outlets. While post office savings banks are operational in much of Africa, and thus have high potential for the mobilisation of savings, they operate outside the regulatory and supervisory sphere of the central bank. However, non-bank financial institutions, as a whole, are often geographically better spread and could be used to mobilise funds in a more predictable way. It is, therefore, necessary to promote their growth.

FINANCIAL POLICY

This section explores the prospects for mobilising financial resources through the manipulation of financial policy instruments in Africa, particularly interest rates and credit policies, to influence savings and investment.

The financial repression literature suggests that, given cost-plus pricing rules in imperfect markets, high interest rates raise prices. Interest rates should not be left to market forces. Active intervention in financial markets thus forms the core of the financial repression thesis (see, for example, Dornbusch and Reynoso 1989). Generally the government imposes controls either by setting ceilings on the nominal interest rate and credit volumes or by exhorting financial institutions to observe interest rate ceilings. To direct investment to 'priority' sectors and to decrease the cost of financing the budget deficit financial repression policies are used.

The remedial policy for financial repression is financial liberalisation. Following the seminal work by McKinnon (1973) and Shaw (1973), it is argued that during high inflation controls on interest rates result in negative real interest rates. This retards the growth of financial activities, in particular savers will divert savings from financial institutions into real estate, gold and foreign currencies to hedge against inflation. Banks will be unable to lend funds to the private sector for investment and working capital. The policy prescription is to raise nominal interest rates above the rate of inflation. Positive interest rates channel savings into the banking system, increasing loanable funds and thereby investment and growth.

However, evidence from econometric studies is far from clear-cut (Fry 1995, Owen and Fallas 1989, Hermes 1994). It is shown, for example, that although most studies tend to confirm the financial liberalisation thesis, there is little evidence of a positive correlation between real interest rates and savings. This suggests that the key link between financial liberalisation and growth is not empirically strong.

IMF (1997a) data show, for example, that Botswana and Malawi experienced negative real interest rates during most of 1985–92 but had positive growth rates. This was also true of Uganda during 1985–92 (except 1991). The growth stimulus in Botswana was mineral resources rather than interest rate changes. On the other hand, some African countries have maintained positive real interest rates but have been unable to generate much growth. Kenya, for example, enjoyed positive real interest rates during 1986–89 but growth was falling throughout the period. It is thus important to identify the factors underlying the response of savings to interest rate changes. One would expect the success of financial liberalisation in most of these countries to depend much more on the establishment of a good network of financial institutions, as well as on the asset formation culture of the people. Even in rural areas well designed savings schemes seem to be successful in mobilising voluntary savings among rural households (Durojaiye 1991).

It is also helpful to assess financial policy decisions in terms of the rate of return on investment. Entrepreneurs and investors will normally operate on a given or assumed internal rate of return: that is, the interest rate will feature not only on the cost side but also as a return on investment. Most local businesses in Africa are small-scale, many of them newly established by young entrepreneurs, and business confidence and consumer optimism are eroded when new businesses go into receivership as loan repayments to financial institutions become difficult to meet. The nominal interest rate should thus be flexible enough to accommodate market expectations. This could be done by letting financial institutions adopt a benchmark nominal interest rate which can be continuously adjusted depending on signals from the central bank regarding expected inflation and return on investment in leading sectors.

CAPITAL MARKETS

Most African governments are now keen to develop capital markets as a direct way of mobilising risk capital for the corporate sector. There has also been considerable support for the aim from the International Finance Corporation (IFC). It is expected that capital markets will improve domestic resource mobilisation and promote the efficient use of capital. They should also play the important role of attracting foreign portfolio investment, thereby integrating domestic economies into international financial markets.

Table 8.3 shows a sample of existing capital markets in Africa, which embrace securities markets, including government bonds, company equity and loan stock, and money markets. It shows that the general level of activity has been low. Thus while the Zimbabwe stock exchange has been in existence for close to 100 years, it has had sporadic growth and was soon overtaken by the Nigerian Stock Exchange, at least in terms of the number of listed

Table 8.3 Stock exchanges in a sample of African economies

Country	Stock exchange	Date of establishment	Revitalised	No. of companies listed 1992	Market capitalisation 1992 (US$ million)	Trading value 1992 (US$ million)
Egypt	Alexandria Stock Exchange (Bourse des Valeurs du Cairo)	1883/96	1981	656	2,594	293
Côte d'Ivoire	Bourse des Valeurs d'Abidjan	1976		24	331	4
Kenya	Nairobi Stock Exchange	1954		57	607	12
Morocco	Bourse des Valeurs de Casablanca	–	1981	62	1,876	70
Nigeria	Nigerian Stock Exchange (trading at Lagos, Port Harcourt and Kaduna)	1961		153	1,243	23
Tunisia[a]	Bourse des Valeurs Mobilière de Tunis	1937	1969	48	n/a	41
Zimbabwe	Zimbabwe Stock Exchange	1896	1951	62	628	20

Sources: IFC, Emerging Stock Market Factbook, Washington DC: IFC (1993).

Note: Stock exchanges are expected to be operational in Botswana, Ghana and Uganda by the year 2000.
[a] Activities of the Tunis Stock Exchange not reported by IFC (1993); however, the exchange is listed for the purposes of providing information on its management and trading days.

companies, market capitalisation, and trading volume. However, in view of changes in the international economic system, and the programmes initiated by the IFC, almost all the existing stock exchanges have been revitalised while new ones are under consideration. In a number of developing countries, notably India and Korea, the early expansion of stock markets was characterised by an increase in the number of companies going public and by enhanced offerings of shares from listed companies. In many other countries the divestiture of parastatals also gave a boost to stock market activity. In a truly dynamic context, therefore, privatisation, divestiture and financial market development go hand in hand.

However, economists have yet to reach a consensus on the effectiveness of capital markets in mobilising development finance. Sceptics argue that there are serious costs associated with risk-sharing and efficiency gains in LDC capital markets (Hellwig 1989). The first problem is that of agency. Markets represent an institutional arrangement under which shareholders bear the risk while management controls the investment and financial decision-making process. The separation of management and ownership imposes an agency cost, since management is able to pursue goals that differ from those of the shareholders, profit and market value maximisation (see also Stiglitz and Weiss 1986). Second, the stock market is associated with a more specific and fundamental type of cost, which concerns the efficiency with which project risks are diversified and priced. It has been shown that capital markets are plagued by imperfections and distortions which generate volatility in stock returns contrary to the predictions of modern financial theory. This bears adverse implications for capital formation (see Merton 1987). Third, it has been argued that take-over activities on stock markets tend to weaken competition and company efficiency by inducing a bias towards short-term profits and financial returns. The problem here is that unlike development banks, which tend to have long-term objectives, capital markets are characterised by short-term ones.

Additionally, recent studies of Africa are pessimistic on the subject of whether capital markets are capable of solving the problems of inadequate savings mobilisation, poor investment and low growth, resulting from market segmentation, at low levels of development, and thin trade. A study of the Nigerian Stock Exchange (Ekechi 1990) showed that stocks deviate from a random walk because the exchange market is so thin that most shares are not traded daily. Casual evidence indicates that transactions per day on the Nigerian Stock Exchange have fallen over the years.

Still, we argue that emerging capital markets offer a great deal of promise for financial and economic development in Africa. However, if they are to become successful in raising large amounts of equity finance for companies, the existing capital markets have to be revitalised. This calls for the introduction of institutional procedures and mechanisms, including new legislation, to rationalise them, thereby creating confidence on the part of investors

(Fry 1997). This extends to the passing of a comprehensive company law specifying, for example, the conduct of public companies, disclosure requirements and shareholders' rights. In addition, a strong regulatory agency, in the form of a capital market authority, is required. Law enforcement is particularly important, given the separation of management and ownership, and the fact that most financial institutions and public companies in Africa are plagued by poor accountability.

Development of capital markets can also be seen as an integral component of overall financial restructuring. Since there is complementarity between capital markets and the banking sector and other financial institutions there should be simultaneous reform of all the segments. Finally, mechanisms must be instituted for linking the emerging capital markets with international ones, notably by reducing controls and strengthening institutions.

FISCAL POLICY

Government finances are derived mainly via taxation and borrowing. The IMF (1997b) data on the revenues and expenditures of African governments indicate that tax revenue accounted for 95 per cent of income, with grants and capital revenue comprising the rest. The data thus underscore the importance of taxation as a vehicle for mobilising public finances. Typically, a high percentage of the total tax revenue is derived from indirect taxation, mainly export and import duties. Still, in most African countries the tax effort is poor, constrained by low institutional capacities for tax collection and administration. Moreover, even when collected a sizeable proportion of the tax revenue is embezzled. In the bulk of economies, excepting Botswana, Ghana and Swaziland, the overall budget deficit is high, accommodated mainly by recourse to domestic borrowing, although for some countries foreign grants are important. Since taxes will continue to constitute a major source of public revenue, the efficiency of taxation needs to be improved. Thus, in addition to the tax effort and expenditure control, improving the financing of the overall deficit is important.

THE INFORMAL FINANCIAL SYSTEM

An informal sector financial system has usually no legal standing and is not subject to government regulation. In African economies, informal market institutions flourish, filling the gap left by the rudimentary official financial markets. They are based on traditional foundations: pooling of financial resources, credit arrangements within the extended family, savings and loan associations of peer groups, clans, etc. Since the informal sector is not subject to controls, interest rate ceilings or reserve requirements, they operate in a more efficient manner than formal markets. While the sector's growth signifies the dynamic nature of local private sector initiative, it also demonstrates the failure of the official sector to fully provide these services. However, there is considerable interaction between the operators in the formal and informal markets (Germidis 1991, Thomas 1993).[3]

Table 8.4 highlights the extent of the informal financial sector in a sample of African countries. It shows that the sector has a leading role in the mobilisation of domestic financial resources, including fixed funds, loans for specific purposes (e.g. education, dowries and housing), and working capital for some key sectors (e.g. agriculture and commerce). Indeed, in most African countries the activities take place in several different forms: occasional lending by individuals and institutions of their surpluses directly to deficit units, regular moneylenders specialising in lending their own funds or intermediating for others, activities involving group finance, including various co-operative schemes. An example of the latter are rotating savings and credit associations (ROSCAS), which collect funds from members at regular intervals for the benefit, in rotation, of a member.

However, if instruments and institutions used in the informal financial sector are to be integrated into the formal one, it is necessary to regularise the legal and institutional framework. One attempt at this has been to introduce some official rural credit schemes. However, these are often overwhelmed by the pent-up demand for finance in the rural areas. In a Nigerian study, Olomola (1991) noted that the amount of credit available to small-scale farmers was often insufficient, while rural credit schemes were plagued by high rates of default. Furthermore, Nkoju and Odii (1991) analysed the loan repayment performance of smallholders under the Special Emergency Loan Scheme in Nigeria. They also found a poor repayment rate (only 27 per cent). This was blamed on poor disbursements, relying on political considerations in assessing loan approvals, loan diversion, and poor enterprise returns.

CONCLUSION

In the global competition for development finance Africa's future access threatens to become even more sporadic than it is today. It is thus imperative for African governments to exploit all possible domestic sources for the mobilisation of development finance. However, while commercial banks are the most important financial intermediaries, they still have problems of capital inadequacy and inefficiency. Non-bank financial institutions that supply trade, insurance and related services are underdeveloped or plagued by performance problems. In this regard, there is a need to reform African central banks, and to make them better at bank regulation and supervision. In an increasingly complex global market, they will also be expected to undertake important research tasks, the results of which will guide policy-makers.

Table 8.4 The extent of the informal financial sector in a sample of African countries

Country	Savings	Credit	Urban informal sector	Type of lender	Non-monetise production (% of GDP)[a]	Population concerned
Ethiopia	Volume of savings mobilised by ekubs = 9–8% of GDP	–	Significant	Informal money lenders	45	Addis Ababa: 60% of urban population in an ekub. Everyone is member of at least one idir
Zimbabwe	–	87% of farmers used informal sources of credit	Significant	Informal money lenders	16	–
Zambia	–	43% of farmers' credit needs were met	Significant	Commercial money-lending on the rise	7	80–90% of the urban population participates
Nigeria	95% of farm loans	Informal sector	Significant	Informal credit agencies	–	80% of the urban population

Sources: Germidis (1991: 45), Thomas (1993).

Notes:

– denotes missing data.

a Figures from the late 1970s.

At the macro level governments need to improve their budgetary performance as well as the efficiency of their tax policies. Overall, financial policies need to be reformed to ensure positive real interest rates for savers and viable investments for the economy as a whole. African governments need to be increasingly imaginative in devising strategies for financial mobilisation as well as for raising the credibility and attractiveness of their markets. A regional monetary authority could, for example, enjoy greater independence and thus credibility than a national central bank. A common regional currency would also be an effective vehicle for facilitating cross-border commerce and for speeding up regional economic integration.

NOTES

1 The sample includes countries which had data in the IMF Financial Statistics for 1997 under the entries for financial assets. However, the data were not complete; for example, data on personal savings in bonds and shares were not available.
2 A parallel banking system that addresses equity participation in investment is the Islamic banking model, which, however, rejects the use of interest rates. In the Sudan the banking system is, for example, fully Islamised.
3 It can be argued that the existence of the informal sector reflects the failure of the formal system. The solution then lies in reform of the formal sector and not necessarily in the fusing of the formal and informal.

REFERENCES

Abebe, A. (1990) 'Financial Repression and its Impact on Financial Development and Economic Growth in the African Least Developed Countries', *Savings and Development*, 14 (1): 55–85.

Dornbusch, R. and Reynoso, A. (1989) 'Financial Factors in Economic Development', *American Economic Review Papers and Proceedings*, 79 (5): 204–9.

Durojaiye, B.O. (1991) 'Rural Household Consumption–Savings Behaviour in Low-income Nations', *African Review of Money, Finance and Banking*, 1: 85–95.

Ekechi, A.O. (1990) 'On Testing for Stock Market Rational Speculative Bubbles: the Case of LDC Markets', *Savings and Development*, 3 (14): 285–98.

Fry, M.J. (1995) *Money, Interest, and Banking in Economic Development*, Baltimore: Johns Hopkins University Press (second edition).

Fry, M. (1997) 'In Defence of Financial Liberalisation', *Economic Journal*, 107 (442): 754–70.

Germidis, D. (1991) *Financial Systems and Development: What Role for the Formal and Informal Sectors?* Paris: OECD Development Centre.

Hellwig, M. (1989) 'Asymmetric Information, Financial Markets, and Financial Institutions', *European Economic Review*, 33 (1): 277–85.

Hermes, N. (1994) 'Financial Development and Economic Growth: a Survey of the Literature', *International Journal of Development Banking*, 12 (1): 3–22.

Honohan, P. (1993) 'Financial Sector Failures in Western Africa', *Journal of Modern African Studies*, 31 (1): 49–65.

Ikhide, S.I. (1992) 'Making a Leading Sector of the Banking System', *International Journal of Development Banking*, 10 (1): 75–84.

IMF (1997a) *International Financial Statistics Yearbook*, Washington DC: IMF.

IMF (1997b) *Government Finance Statistics Yearbook*, Washington DC: IMF.

Kwarteng, K. (1982) 'Banking and Finance in Africa: a Review Article', *Savings and Development*, 6 (3): 247–63.

Levine, R. (1997) 'Financial Development and Economic Growth: Views and Agenda', *Journal of Economic Literature*, 35 (2): 688–726.

Levine, R. and Zervos, S. (1998) 'Stock Markets, Banks, and Economic Growth', *American Economic Review*, forthcoming.

Lyons, S.E. and Murinde, V. (1994) 'Cointegration and Granger-causal testing of hypotheses on Supply-leading and Demand-following Finance', *Economic Notes* 23 (2): 308–16.

Maizels, A. and Nissanke, M. (1984) 'Motivations for Aid to Developing Countries', *World Development*, 12 (9): 879–900.

McKinnon, R.I. (1973) *Money and Capital in Economic Development,* Washington DC: Brookings Institution.

Merton, R.C. (1987) 'On the Current State of the Stock Market Rationality Hypothesis', in R. Dornbusch, S. Fischer and J. Bossons (eds) *Macroeconomics and Finance*, Cambridge MA: MIT Press.

Mistry, P. (1991) *African Debt Revisited: Procrastination or Progress,* The Hague: FONDAD.

Mosley, P., Harrigan, J. and Toye, J. (1991) *Aid and Power: The World Bank and Policy-Based Lending,* London: Routledge.

Murinde, V. (1993) 'Budgetary and Financial Policy Potency amid Structural Bottlenecks', *World Development*, 21 (5): 841–59.

Murinde, V. (1998) *The Predictability of Official Flows to Africa: an Econometric Analysis*, Discussion Papers in Corporate Finance, 3 (98), University of Birmingham

Murinde, V., Naser, K. and Wallace, R.S.O. (1995) 'Is it Prudent for Islamic Banks to make Investment Decisions without the Interest Rate Instrument?', *Research in Accounting in Emerging Economies*, 3: 123–48.

Myrdal, G. (1968) *Asian Drama: An Enquiry into the Poverty of Nations,* Harmondsworth: Allen Lane.

Nkoju, J.E. and Odii, M.A.C.A. (1991) 'Determinants of Loan Repayment under the Special Emergency Loan Scheme (SEALS) in Nigeria: a Case Study of Imo State', *African Review of Money, Finance and Banking*, 1: 39–52.

Olomola, A.S. (1991) 'Credit Control Policies for Improved Agricultural Financing in Nigeria', *African Review of Money, Finance and Banking*, 1: 23–37.

Owen, D. and Fallas, O.S. (1989) 'The New Structuralist Critique of Financial Liberalisation: the Role of Unorganised Money Markets and Unproductive Assets', *Journal of Development Economics*, 31 (2): 341–55.

Patrick, H. (1966) 'Financial Development and Economic Growth in Underdeveloped Countries', *Economic Development and Cultural Change*, 14 (2): 174–89.

Shaw, E.S. (1973) *Financial Deepening in Economic Development*, Oxford: Oxford University Press.

St Hill, R.L. (1992) 'Stages of Banking and Economic Development', *Savings and Development*, 16 (1): 5–21.

Stiglitz, J.E. and Weiss, A. (1986) 'Credit Rationing and Collateral', in J. Edwards, J. Franks, C. Mayer and S. Schaefer (eds) *Recent Developments in Corporate Finance*, Cambridge: Cambridge University Press.

Summers, L. (1991) 'Research Challenges for Development Economists', *Finance and Development*, 38 (3): 2–5.

Taylor, L. (1991) *Income Distribution, Inflation, and Growth: Lectures in Structuralist Macroeconomic Theory*, Cambridge MA and London: MIT Press.

Thomas, J.J. (1993) *The Informal Sector in Developing Countries*, London: Macmillan.

Tovias, A. (1990) *The European Communities Single Market: the Challenge of 1992 for sub-Saharan Africa*, World Bank Discussion Papers 100, Washington DC: World Bank.

9

INSTITUTIONS AND RURAL DEVELOPMENT IN UGANDA

Issues arising

John Ddumba-Ssentamu

Since the 1960s rural development has been on the policy agenda of most African governments. This was a natural outcome of the pro-rural, pro-poor political policies pursued after independence. However, that it remains a priority some thirty years later partly reflects paucity of resources, which have made it impossible to extend modern infrastructure and services to the countryside, and partly the low level of political commitment. As in many other African economies, Uganda's rural dwellers are among the poorest and most disadvantaged groups in the country. They are not only poorly endowed in human and physical capital but also have, owing to their often disadvantageous location in the country, little influence on political decisions, even those affecting them directly. In the era of economic reform, considerable emphasis has been put on institution building, and on enhancing the role of markets in the economy. It can be argued that if the bulk of the population remains poor and unable to take part in economic activities, as is still the case with the majority of rural dwellers in Uganda today, it will be difficult to establish a viable market-based economy (Kiggundu 1997).

In the past, strategies for rural development were laid out in detail in the national development plans (see Republic of Uganda 1966). They included poverty eradication, mainly via the creation of employment in rural areas, in particular agriculture. For the country as whole, ensuring food self-sufficiency was a key goal, though equally important was the maintenance of adequate nutritional standards. Agriculture was also an important source of exports, and farmers were to be supplied with the requisite inputs, including fertiliser and equipment, at affordable prices. Similarly, domestic prices for export crops were to be kept attractive in order 'not to discourage the farmer' (Republic of Uganda 1965). However, concerns over foreign exchange generation, control of the urban cost of living, and raising rural purchasing power to spur budding import-substituting industry, were not necessarily mutually consistent. Part of the difficulty of meeting the goals of rural development thus lay in this friction between compassion for the rural poor and the need to preserve the support of the urban elite.

Discussion in this chapter centres on the issue of developing institutions that are responsive to the needs of the rural sector. Although it has been argued in recent debate that the role of government in the economy should be confined to regulation and policy guidance, and away from direct involvement, rural institutions will not grow in a vacuum. There is a need to create economic and political conditions under which viable rural institutions can evolve.

UGANDA'S RURAL SETTING

Uganda is predominantly rural, with agriculture as the main source of livelihood. The sector generates close to 90 per cent of export earnings, employs more than 80 per cent of the labour force and is a key source of raw materials for agro-processing industries. Farming is done, almost exclusively, by about 2.5 million smallholders on holdings which are less than 2 ha each. Most of the food produced is for own consumption, while cash requirements are met from the sale of coffee, cotton and tobacco or surplus food (Republic of Uganda 1994). Estate-based agriculture is mainly in the tea and sugar industries, although peasant out-growers are engaged in the south and west. In the north-west, tobacco farming is done by peasants who sell their output direct to the local branch of a tobacco multinational. It has been said that the predominance of smallholders in Ugandan agriculture implies that the benefits of liberalisation and growth in the sector have been more equitably distributed among rural dwellers than in countries with more concentrated land ownership structures (World Bank 1993).

The first post-independence decade saw a rapid decline in agriculture's relative contribution to the economy as manufacturing and service sectors began to expand under policies of import substitution and as government extended its services in a bid to cover as many parts of the country as possible. However, the chaotic economic policies of the 1970s and 1980s brought modern industry to a standstill, while public services contracted. Agriculture remained the only viable sector: farmers reverted to supplying urban dwellers or to subsistence production. However, after Uganda embarked on the Economic Recovery Programme of 1987, part of which was directed at the rehabilitation of manufacturing, the share of agriculture in GDP fell gradually. Still, by the mid-1990s agriculture remained the single most important sector in the economy, contributing close to 45 per cent of GDP. According to a recent *Integrated Household Survey* (Republic of Uganda 1994), agriculture is also the predominant source of household income in Uganda, accounting for 60 per cent of the total, although its share is much higher in rural areas and among the urban poor. For the latter households, the bulk of income derives from food crops, including *matooke*, sweet potatoes, cassava, maize and beans. This is in sharp contrast to earlier decades, when most income derived from traditional cash crops such as coffee, cotton, tobacco and tea (Republic of Uganda 1965).

Using a poverty line of Shs 6,000 in monthly expenditure (about US$10), in 1992/93 prices, 55 per cent of the population was defined as poor, 57 per cent in rural areas and 38 per cent in urban ones. With an estimated 96 per cent of the core poor living in rural areas, poverty is not only more widespread there, it is also deeper. Poor households tend to be larger, to have older and less educated heads, are likely to be headed by a woman, and have high dependence ratios. However, with urbanisation, and increasing push factors in rural areas, including civil strife, poverty in parts of the urban areas now sometimes exceeds anything comparable in the countryside (Maxwell and Zziwa 1990).

INSTITUTIONS OF RURAL DEVELOPMENT

As in other African countries, the rural development concept in Uganda has been largely amorphous. It was based on results from a number of poorly co-ordinated projects and institutions in areas such as agricultural extension services, primary health care, co-operatives and NGO intervention of various kinds. The years of political and economic chaos aggravated the situation in three ways: first, the government's ability to extend the infrastructure to the countryside was severely curtailed. Many regions of the country became isolated from the centre. Second, with the decline in the infrastructure, services became scarce, notably access to credit. This negatively affected attempts at modernisation and the introduction of new agricultural technologies (Nabuguzi 1993). But probably the most serious outcome of the period of decline was the lapse of political leadership at the local level. It became difficult to mobilise rural people for development-oriented projects (Brett 1994).

INSTITUTIONS OF RURAL CREDIT AND FINANCE

Uganda's financial sector is one of the least developed in sub-Saharan Africa. It is small in terms of the volume and value of transactions, while the range of services is limited (World Bank 1991). In rural areas, the provision of financial services is constrained by the high costs of intermediation, scarce knowledge of the socio-economic environment and the scattered micro nature of rural enterprises. The inability of banks to reach the rural population both for disbursement and recovery, and the rigid terms and conditions for agricultural lending, have minimised the impact of formal financial institutions on the rural sector. In recent years a number of private banks have been established, including a number run by Ugandans, but they have not eradicated the urban bias of banking services. Commercial banks are located almost exclusively in larger urban centres (Kampala, Jinja, Mbarara, Mbale and Masaka) even though over 80 per cent of the population live in rural areas. Prior to 1972 the country had 290 bank branches, that is, about one branch to 34,000 people. In the 1980s the ratio was one branch to 80,000 people, and, following the closure of several Uganda Commercial Bank (UCB) branches, the ratio became one branch to every 164,000 people in the mid-1990s.

Although an average of 45 per cent of total bank loans and advances went to agriculture in the 1980s, most of them were for crop financing, that is, for the purchase and marketing of export crops such as coffee. This assured quick returns while minimising risk. Very limited funds were available for direct agricultural investment or for other productivity-increasing measures, including input purchases, land improvement or even agricultural research.

In a bid to reduce the financial constraints on rural production, the government instituted a Rural Farmers' Credit Scheme in 1987, run by the UCB. The results were poor, with government failing to realise any of its objectives. What had been envisaged as the beginning of a revolving fund for rural farmers became a source of cheap loans for politicians and UCB employees. The scheme collapsed shortly after it had taken off. Still, in the mid-1990s government embarked on the *Entandikwa* Credit Scheme (Republic of Uganda 1995). Its long-term objective was to reduce poverty by increasing opportunities for income generation and by employment creation. Emphasis is on the rural and urban poor, rural artisans, women, youth and the disabled. In practical terms the scheme provides seed money for people to embark on sustainable development projects, including the development of managerial skills via training and technical assistance. The scheme is being implemented through local government institutions and the NGOs and is said to be better run than the UCB one. However, credit programmes targeting small farmers and other poor groups have generally failed in Uganda, partly owing to financial deficiencies and partly to failure to make a positive impact on rural productivity. Moreover, in government hands such programmes have tended to become mere extensions of political patronage, with the revolving fund character necessary for their sustenance often lacking.

A number of institutions have tried to bridge the resource gap in the countryside by providing rural households with direct financial assistance, advice or marketing infrastructure on a regular basis. They include co-operative societies, farmer groups and NGOs. As experiences from Bangladesh show, institutions with access to grass-roots structures have comparative advantages in rural finance operations, thanks to low overheads and transaction costs. Further, the informal nature of the organisational set-up, which can be adjusted to suit rural needs, and a rural bias in lending programmes enhance community participation in policy formulation (Jain 1996, Pal in the next chapter). Still, these institutions have serious human and financial resource constraints which limit the range of services offered.

Co-operative societies are relatively old institutions in Uganda. They grew out of the need to mobilise farmers for various schemes, including the regularisation of export-crop farming in a bid to ensure promptness, high quality, and to limit farmer exploitation. The primary society is the unit operating at the grass-roots level. Initially, primary societies functioned solely as rural agents in the marketing of cotton, coffee and other agricultural produce. Gradually some societies became involved in financial intermediation. In 1996 there was a total of 5,900 registered primary societies, of which close to 60 per cent were in crop marketing, 10 per cent in the mobilisation of savings and credit in rural areas. The latter was mostly under the Co-operative Credit Scheme, started as early as 1961, while the rest were engaged in trading and related activities.

In terms of rural mobilisation, co-operative societies have had a comparative advantage *vis-à-vis* formal firms. They often have superior local knowledge, while a broad membership enables them to engage in group lending, relying on peer pressure for loan recovery. As a result, they generally have lower intermediation costs than formal banks. In the past, however, primary societies were a source of much rural disillusionment. In the case of coffee, for example, primary societies were often unable to pay farmers promptly. In quite a number of cases, members were saddled with debts arising from mismanagement of the society. This, coupled with poor transport services and high indirect taxes, forced peasants to abandon coffee production in the 1970s and parts of the 1980s. Under the new Co-operative Statute, provision has been made for a co-operative society to go into liquidation when over 50 per cent of its capital has been used up. This, it is hoped, will instill more discipline in the co-operative movement while weeding out societies that are not viable. With economic reforms under way in the rest of the economy, primary societies are now seen by some banks and donors as a basis for the establishment of a rural financing structure in Uganda. However, part of the co-operative movement's failure to make a lasting impact on rural development in the past was due to interference from central government (Bunker 1991).

Farmers' groups are another form of rural mobilisation that has been growing rapidly in the past decade. They promote growth in rural areas by pooling resources and providing farmers with credit, on reasonable terms. The bulk are informally organised, however, while the number of registered ones is small. Many of the former are female-dominated and run, while some of the latter have both male and female members. The degree of variation is thus greater than that of primary-society activities. The success of farmers' groups is attributed to their focus on social issues and their greater independence. There is, for instance, no national umbrella body to oversee their activities. This also means, however, that they often lack legal registration and do not operate as legal business entities, making them prone to abuse and political pressure. Their ability to access funds from formal institutions is also weak.

The past decades have seen a sharp increase in the role of local and foreign NGOs in development activities in Uganda. The most innovative NGOs have been able to carry out micro-programmes outside the national budget and have thus been a useful complement to government-aided projects. A number are at present engaged in various rural development activities, including income generation and community development. A few are engaged in the provision of credit to the rural population. In the absence of banking facilities, they have served as an alternative means of linking rural households with formal financial institutions.

It should be noted, however, that dependence on NGOs is not without risk, especially since many of their activities are subject to the availability of donor funds. Very few local NGOs have developed the capacity to survive on their own funds, and there has been considerable fragmentation and duplication of effort. Perhaps most important is how to establish a partnership for development between NGOs and the government that transcends the current competition for peasant loyalty.

An example of a successful local NGO is the Uganda Women's Finance and Credit Trust, established in 1984. Membership is open to all Ugandan women either as individuals or in groups. By 1991 it had nine branches located in Mbale, Masaka, Kamuli, Mbarara, Iganga and Kampala. The main aim of the UWFCT is to facilitate women's access to credit for small-scale business undertakings. Although the initial funding came from various donors, UWFCT is now dependent solely on mobilising members' savings and on profits from its own business operations. UWFCT helps women prepare projects, which can then be co-financed with other financial institutions. It also provides loans, at reasonable terms, to women in the countryside. Besides, it has developed the ability, with respect to personnel training and branch networks, to undertake financial intermediation, including the development of a cost-effective capacity to reach target groups in both rural and urban areas (Agricultural Policy Secretariat 1996, Kasisira 1992).

Development of rural financial institutions will thus depend crucially on their capacity for innovation, with regard to organisation, resource mobilisation and functional flexibility. It will be necessary to abandon some traditional banking practices, based on the praxis of a bygone era, and adopt new methods that will direct rural efforts towards economically rewarding activities.

However, a number of issues have to be borne in mind: experience indicates that most successful forms of rural financing are demand-driven (Graham 1992). Saving instruments and procedures need to be tailored to the needs of rural people, in terms of convenience, flexibility and safety. The success of any rural financial programme is tied to its capacity to mobilise savings.

This helps increase the capital of the loan fund, discourages hazardous loan practices and improves loan amortisation. Saving thus establishes a basis for investment. In Uganda projects, government as well as donor-funded, which stressed rural lending but ignored saving invariably failed.

Since it has been difficult for commercial banks to open branches in rural areas, existing rural financial intermediaries, such as primary co-operative societies, self-help groups, micro-rural enterprises and NGOs should be encouraged. First, via the provision of adequate infrastructure in the country-side and, second, by providing them various incentives, including tax breaks. However, direct controls should be avoided. In the past too much government interference was injurious to the co-operative movement and care must be taken to prevent current efforts from meeting a similar fate.

POLITICAL AND SOCIAL INSTITUTIONS

Perhaps the most important constraint on rapid rural development has been at the level of political mobilisation. Rural dwellers have had few avenues for influencing policy at the national level, especially with regard to the distribution of resources. In Africa the rural–urban dichotomy became apparent much earlier on and attempts were made to eradicate the resource gaps in the 1960s. The most famous of these was Tanzania's Arusha Declaration, which was followed by similarly worded statements in neighbouring countries.

However, while a socialist approach to rural development, based on public control of the means of production, i.e. land in the countryside, excited much optimism in the development community in the post-independence decade, it ultimately proved unworkable. It has been argued that the efforts failed to generate rural development because they presumed that the government was better placed to define the needs of the farmers and other rural dwellers than the affected groups themselves. Collective ownership at the village level stifled local initiative and brought local production to a standstill in countries which applied this model of development (Keppler 1981).

On coming to power in 1986, the National Resistance Movement (NRM) of Yoweri Museveni tried to establish organisational forms at the local and grass-roots levels that would have sufficient authority to respond effectively to the needs of the rural households. A similar approach has been attempted in other African countries, including Ghana and Burkina Faso. Uganda's local council system comprises a hierarchical structure of councils and committees stretching from village to district level. The adult population in each village constitutes a village council (LC1) which selects nine of its members to an LC1 committee. The latter then selects two members to form the LC2 council, composed of nine members. The process is repeated at the sub-county (LC3) and county (LC4) levels. Each committee has a chairman, vice-chairman and secretary, as well as secretaries for youth, women (must be female), information, mass mobilisation and education, security and finance (Brett 1993, 1994, Republic of Uganda 1994).

In terms of maintaining law and order, settling disputes, managing services and regulating local economic activities, the local council system has had an appreciable impact in the countryside. Local councils can make by-laws, set and collect fees for various services and enforce environmental regulations. It is envisaged that the LC will become the political agent at the local level and the most important generator and executor of ideas for development in the decades ahead. It is feared, however, that LCs may be captured by the state, and that this will reduce their usefulness as agents of mobilisation and change in the countryside.

In many respects, rural development in Africa is about female empowerment. Tadria (1997) has argued that, in spite of their enormous economic contribution, women remain the most neglected group in Africa, especially in the countryside. In Uganda they constitute more than 50 per cent of the total population; over 90 per cent live in rural areas, where they account for the bulk of the labour input into food and cash crop cultivation. Nevertheless, women's access to productive resources, including land, capital and technology, is poor. They are also disadvantaged in terms of literacy, access to health facilities and safe water, and modern employment. Their level of schooling is poorer than average: 43 per cent of rural women in Uganda are functionally illiterate, compared with 28 per cent of men. Women are also overrepresented among the poorer groups (Republic of Uganda 1996). While much of this is a cultural and socio-economic legacy of the past, women have been disadvantaged by their poor access to policy-makers.

As a phenomenon in development, self-help is seeing something of a renaissance in Uganda. In rural Uganda the colossal task of providing social services has often overwhelmed the government, and households have had to devise their own means of service provision. In education, parent–teacher associations were credited with keeping primary education largely intact in the years of political and economic chaos. There have also been attempts to devise other means of providing services, such as health, on a collective basis. The onslaught of the AIDS epidemic has left many families in dire social need. Medical costs for the victims are exorbitant, as are the funeral costs, when victims succumb to the disease. Organisations at grass-roots levels have sprung up to address these new social needs. Activities involve the construction of minor bridges, access roads, the improvement of water supplies through the protection of wells and streams and the construction of community centres. Members also assist in home improvement campaigns as well as in comforting bereaved families. The more socially oriented groups are known as *Munno mu kabbi* associations, most common in southern Uganda, where membership is often compulsory for all adults in a village. Such groups are undoubtedly important social safety nets for rural dwellers.

JOHN DDUMBA-SSENTAMU

REFORM OF LAND TENURE

Land tenure systems differ across Uganda, with a mix of traditional praxis, colonial regulations and post-colonial legislation. Prior to the Land Reform Decree of 1975, which invested all land ownership in the government, there were four main types of land tenure: customary, freehold, mailo tenure and leaseholds.

The bulk of land is held under customary tenure, which varies according to traditional practices of ethnic groups. This system does not recognise individual ownership of land, but individuals have user rights and could let land out temporarily, pledge crops thereon, or dispose of land according to customary laws of inheritance. In turn, the 'family' has the right to settle disputes, approve all land transactions, prohibit the sale of land to undesirable persons, and has first refusal on land offered for sale in its jurisdiction. The wider community has the right to graze animals within its jurisdiction, as long as homesteads and crops are preserved. The community also reserves the right of access to water, salt licks and other key resources.

Freehold rights were first established in agreements between the colonial government and the kingdoms of Buganda, Ankole and Toro at the beginning of the century. Still, outside Buganda, few freehold titles were actually issued. Across much of Buganda today, a landlord/tenant system is still the basis of land ownership. This 'mailo' system has, however, been substantially modified since its introduction in 1900: tenant rights are protected and rents remain nominal. Moreover, tenancies are inheritable, while dispossession is difficult and must be adequately compensated. Mailo land titles are easily transferable, and have been used as collateral in credit transactions. This has been a key factor in the development of a land market. Registered title to land, by both individuals and co-operatives, is now common in central and western Uganda.

Leaseholds are provided by private owners, or by the government under the Public Lands Act of 1969. These have been used by influential farmers to obtain access to large tracts of land in underutilised areas. Thus while leasehold provides a flexible form of land tenure, abuses associated with it have increased disparities in land ownership. Under the system, politically powerful and rich individuals have been favoured, displacing peasants or turning them into squatters on land that was, under customary tenure, theirs.

Uganda's multiple system of land tenure has negatively affected rural development. First, it has increased the risks of tenure and thus lowered investment in land improvement. Second, it has introduced inefficiencies in the land market. Third, the role of land as collateral has become less certain. The system has also led to considerable fraud, leading to multiple claims, especially on urban plots. Proposals for reform are based on the adoption of freehold land tenure, with ultimate ownership vested in the government but with titleholders free to transact on the market. The reform seeks to protect the rights of customary tenants on public land and permit them to obtain freehold tenure.

However, as in the case of Tanzania (Tenga 1997), questions regarding land alienation in the reform process have arisen. What, under a market system, will 'protect' peasants from themselves, i.e. from selling land to rich individuals or groups under stress, turning them and their families into landless poor in the countryside? Forms of communal ownership may continue to be necessary, as a rural safety net, at least during a long process of transition. There has also been concern over the impact on the environment of freeing land markets. Recently the de-gazetting of Namaanve Forest near Kampala for development as an industrial estate led to much debate. Some saw it as a pointer to what can be expected when powerful economic groups vie for land on which to erect projects favoured by the government.

Effective land markets call for a high degree of transparency, and administrative competence is necessary to encourage investment in sound land management and utilisation. The Uganda land market has been characterised by considerable confusion in past decades, with unauthorised dealerships, poor information flow and generally inadequate legislation. Since land is the most important single asset in the country, reform of land transactions should go a long way in supporting parallel reforms in the rest of the economy. To unleash the dynamic forces that lead to rural development, it is also necessary to combine land reform with a supportive macroeconomic framework. Notably, with regard to price reforms, the supply of services and extension of the infrastructure to rural areas.

CONCLUSION

Since independence, rural development has been the focus of government policy. However, concrete results in terms of improvements in rural productivity and standards of living have been few and far between. An impediment has been the lack of institutions and resources. An even more serious constraint is lack of input by the groups concerned. To increase the level of consultation on development issues, the government has, in recent years, emphasised the importance of involving grass-roots levels in the political process. Will villages be able to translate their wishes into concrete action under these new forms? How will the resource-poor regions of the country fare in their attempts at improving their lives? Rural development will, no doubt, continue to be central to Uganda's development debate in coming years.

REFERENCES

Agricultural Policy Secretariat (1996) *Private Sector Development Project: National Strategy and Programme of Action for Private Sector Development in Rural Areas*, Kampala: Ministry of Agriculture.

Brett, E.A. (1993) *Providing for the Rural Poor: Institutional Decay and Transformation in Uganda*, Kampala: Fountain Publishers.

Brett, E.A. (1994) 'Rebuilding Organisation Capacity in Uganda under the National Resistance Movement', *Journal of Modern African Studies*, 32 (1): 53–80.

Bunker, G.S. (1991) *Peasants against the State: The Politics of Market Control in Bugisu, Uganda, 1900–83*, Chicago and London: University of Chicago Press.

Graham, C. (1992) 'The Politics of Protecting the Poor during Adjustment: Bolivia's Emergency Social Fund', *World Development*, 20 (9): 1233–51.

Jain, P.S. (1996) 'Managing Credit for the Rural Poor: Lessons from the Grameen Bank', *World Development*, 24 (1): 79–89.

Kasisira, G.L. (1992) 'Credit to Ugandan Women: The Experience of the Uganda Women's Finance and Credit Trust Ltd', MA dissertation, Kampala: Makerere University.

Keppler, R. (1981) 'Zambian Agricultural Structure and Performance', in B. Turok (ed.) *Development in Zambia*, London: Zed Press.

Kiggundu, R. (1997) 'Economic Reforms and Rural Households in Uganda', paper presented at the Partnership Africa conference, Stockholm, June.

Maxwell, D.G. and Zziwa, S. (1990) *Urban Agriculture: a Case Study of Kampala*, Kampala: Makerere Institute of Social Research.

Nabuguzi, E. (1993) 'Peasant Responses to Economic Crisis in Uganda: Rice Farms in Busoga', *Review of African Political Economy*, 56: 53.

Republic of Uganda (1965) *Uganda 1964*, Kampala: Ministry of Information and Broadcasting.

Republic of Uganda (1966) *Second National Development Plan*, Kampala: Ministry of Economic Planning.

Republic of Uganda (1994) *Integrated Household Survey 1992/93*, Kampala: Ministry of Finance and Economic Planning.

Republic of Uganda (1995) *Entandikwa Credit Scheme – Operational Guidelines*, Kampala: Ministry of Finance and Economic Planning.

Republic of Uganda (1996) *Demographic and Health Survey 1995*, Kampala: Ministry of Finance and Economic Planning.

Tadria, H.M. (1997) 'Poverty and Gender in Africa', in H. Kifle, A.O. Olukoshi and L. Wohlgemuth (eds) *A New Partnership for African Development: Issues and Parameters*, Uppsala: Nordiska Afrikainstitutet.

Tenga, R. (1997) 'Processing a Land Policy: the Case of Mainland Tanzania', paper presented at the Partnership Africa conference, Stockholm, June.

World Bank (1991) *Uganda Financial Sector Review*, Washington DC: World Bank.

World Bank (1993) *Uganda: Agriculture: A World Bank Country Study*, Washington DC: World Bank.

10

BUILDING AFRICAN
INSTITUTIONS
Learning from South Asia

Mariam S. Pal

In the face of persistent and even growing poverty, Africans have been search-
ing for new ways of building sustainable African institutions which are able
to address poverty reduction and human development. Whereas, in the past,
much credence was given to methodologies devised by experts from developed countries, there is now a surge of interest in the experience and success
of other developing countries, i.e. a south–south focus. The recent explosion
of poverty lending through micro-finance provides a particularly strong
example of this trend. Latin America and South Asia, specifically Bangladesh,
have shown that developing countries can build indigenous institutions
which address sustainable poverty reduction in ways which respond to their
people's needs more appropriately than imported concepts from industrialised
countries.

The Grameen Bank in Bangladesh, led by Mohammed Yunus, has galva-
nised support worldwide for its group-based approach to poverty lending
and social development. Growing from a small pilot project in 1976, it has
become a mass movement, which in 1997 had more than 2 million members.
It has also inspired the establishment of Grameen Bank replications in countries as diverse as Malaysia, Nigeria, the United States and Bolivia, all of
which have taken the key concepts of the Grameen Bank and used them to
develop their own institutions. A special fund, the Grameen Trust, provides
assistance to groups from the developing world seeking financial assistance to
establish Grameen Bank replications and create similar institutions in their
own countries. As Mohammed Yunus (1997) said, 'Just like food, credit is
a human right.'

This chapter will explain the Grameen Bank model and discuss how it
could be drawn upon in the context of African institution building. A general
overview will be given of how the model works and which features need to be
considered in replicating it. This is followed by a general discussion of actual

replication in Malawi and Burkina Faso. The chapter concludes with a review of the lessons learned from replicating the Grameen Bank in Africa and their implications for building African financial institutions.

THE GRAMEEN BANK APPROACH TO POVERTY LENDING

African countries have been showing considerable interest in the Grameen Bank model and its potential to assist in the development of indigenous poverty-focused institutions. The failure of institutions such as agricultural and rural development banks, and the limitations of commercial banking systems in most African countries, have meant that thousands, if not millions, of Africans living below the poverty line must rely on traditional sources of credit in order to fund both consumption and non-consumption expenditures. The increased monetisation of the African economy, especially in rural areas, has meant a growing demand for credit which remains largely unmet. In response to this situation, micro-finance funds patterned on the Grameen approach have been established in a growing number of African countries. They include Malawi, Guinea-Conakry, Tanzania, Ethiopia, Nigeria, Burkina Faso, Kenya, Lesotho, Mauritania, Uganda and Zimbabwe.

The Grameen Bank model is quite familiar, having received considerable attention both in development circles and in the media as a successful approach to poverty reduction. The fact that it was conceived in a poor developing country, Bangladesh, has only heightened international fascination with the institution's success. However, although the Grameen Bank concept is widely known, the details of how it works are often less clear. This section will provide a broad overview of the history and main characteristics of the Grameen Bank.[1]

The Bangladeshi economic and cultural context is unique. The population density is one of the highest in the world, agricultural land is scarce and the fragile economy is constantly threatened by natural disasters. These three factors contribute significantly to the endemic poverty that exists in the country. Women, who are the primary focus of the Grameen Bank's activities, are the worst-off, whether from an economic or a social perspective. They are exploited as cheap or free labour, have very few rights and suffer from poor health, malnutrition and illiteracy. As poverty and male out-migration escalate, more women become *de facto* household heads, responsible for large families but having very few means at their disposal to increase their income. A complex system of socio-cultural practices, known as *purdah*, restricts women from interacting with male officials or travelling very far from their home, e.g. to go to a bank. In this context the Grameen Bank approach, which favours women and which effectively brings the bank to them, has attracted nearly 2 million members, most of them women. The Grameen

Table 10.1 Grameen Bank activities

Number of members	2,131,107
Female	2,010,819
Male	120,288
Cumulative disbursement	US$1,993 million
Number of branches	1,084
Number of villages	36,935

Source: Grameen Bank (1997).

Bank is today an impressive institution, employing 10,000 people, of whom approximately 85 per cent work in the field (see Khandker *et al.* 1994).

The figures for 1997 illustrate the magnitude of the Grameen Bank's activities (Table 10.1). However, these figures fail to portray the very high growth rates enjoyed by the Grameen Bank. For example, in the period 1989–92 total membership more than doubled from 600,000 to 1.4 million, the number of villages grew from 15,073 to 30,619 and the value of loans tripled (Grameen Bank 1993).

The Grameen Bank lends money for productive, income-generating purposes to the poorest of the poor. In Bangladesh, as in the rest of the developing world, the poor are overwhelmingly women. The Grameen Bank requires that its members should be part of a group, save regularly, undergo special training prior to becoming members and contribute to collective funds such as the group fund and emergency fund. It grants loans for income-generating activities (consisting of general and seasonal, i.e. agricultural, loans) as well as for house construction or improvement, tube well construction and sanitary latrine construction.

One of the most interesting features of the bank is the combination of an agenda for social and economic development with banking for the poor. Members must agree to abide by a code of behaviour known as the Sixteen Decisions. These include promising to construct a sanitary latrine, drinking only boiled or tube well water, having a small family, sending the children to school, arranging dowryless marriages for them and eating a balanced diet. While not financial in nature, these pledges recognise that the positive benefit of increased income which may accrue to a woman can be undermined if her family's health is poor owing to dirty drinking water or if her savings are wiped out by having to pay a dowry upon her daughter's marriage.

The Grameen Bank approach to credit delivery to the poor is based on a decentralised system which targets the poor in rural Bangladesh. The main features of this credit system are:

1 an exclusive focus on the poorest of the poor in the community;
2 organisation of borrowers into small homogeneous groups;
3 special loan conditionalities which are particularly suitable to the poor;

4   the simultaneous undertaking of a social development agenda;
5   the creation of a loan portfolio with sufficient flexibility to meet diverse
    development needs of the target group.

Two units form the basis of Grameen Bank activities at the field level: the 'centre' and the 'branch'. The centre and the branch are the foundations of an elaborate organisation promoting self-reliance and social development.

Every group consists of five members. Six to eight groups form a centre (thirty to forty borrower members). Each group has a secretary and a chairperson, and all centres are headed by a centre chief and deputy chief. Group formation is either in response to a public information session held by the local branch manager or by groups of women who approach the branch manager to become members of the bank. Potential members undergo membership training which lasts for seven consecutive days. This training includes learning about the rules and regulations of the Grameen Bank, the Sixteen Decisions, issues in the social development programme and learning to sign one's name. When training has been completed, the branch manager tests the new members (demonstration of their signatures plus an oral examination) to determine their knowledge of the training course subjects. If all of them pass, the group is given provisional recognition. If members do not pass, a further period of training is required. Formal recognition of all group members is given to the group only after a visit by the bank worker to all the houses of the new members. The purpose of this is to verify whether all new members really qualify according to the Grameen Bank's rules and regulations, especially regarding their economic status.

Centre meetings are held weekly and always at a specific time and place. Centres are required to elect a centre chief and a deputy chief who will serve for one year. They must undergo special training over a seven-day period (two hours a day) prior to being recognised as a centre chief. Centre meetings are presided over by the bank worker/assistant and the women represented by their centre chief. The main activities that occur at these meetings are the remittance of group and individual savings, loan repayments and approvals of new loans. Applications for new loans are presented to the centre and approved by all members. The weekly meeting also provides the members with an opportunity to discuss any problems that they may be facing in their family lives or with their income-generating projects and to seek help from other group members to find solutions.

In the Grameen Bank system, the branch services the centre. It is the basis of all activities, since the growth and expansion of the Grameen Bank are horizontal rather than vertical. Branch offices are the first level of activity in an area. As the level of activity grows in a region, branches are expanded horizontally until they are of sufficient number to justify the establishment of a zonal office. The zonal office will then further break down the region's activities according to areas. The branch office is where the credit programme is planned and managed. All loan applications are processed for approval by the area staff. Detailed records of all transactions are kept at the branch.

Upon formal recognition, a group becomes eligible for loans. The group itself must decide the amounts of the loans (up to a maximum of approximately US$125) and which individuals will receive them. Usually the Grameen Bank encourages groups to approve their first loans to the two poorest members, then the next two poorest, followed by the remaining member. As a rule, the secretary or chairperson should not be the first to receive a loan. This is to discourage the notion that there is a reward associated with taking on the responsibility of being a group chairperson or secretary. If the first members to receive loans also repay them on time, then the next two will receive their loans within several weeks, followed by the final member. Such group pressure provides a powerful incentive to prompt repayment.

A loan is disbursed to the borrower one week after it has been approved and must be utilised for its stated purpose within one week of disbursement. This is verified by the bank worker/assistant.

The majority of Grameen Bank loans are repayable within a period of less than one year. Members who have demonstrated a good repayment record can apply for a housing loan which is repayable over a longer period of time not exceeding ten years. Once a loan has been completely repaid this is noted in the register of loan payments and verified by the branch manager.

Loans are provided to borrowers for a number of different purposes. The most common loan, and the one which is the first to be taken out by new members of the Grameen Bank, is the general loan. Other loans available include seasonal loans (usually taken out to grow a cash crop for quick sale), tube well loans and sanitary latrine loans. Borrowers pay an interest rate of 20 per cent per annum on general, seasonal and tube well loans which reflects the rates which are charged on the official money market in Bangladesh. Interest at the rate of 8.5 per cent per annum is paid to members on all deposits and funds.

Each group must purchase one share in the Grameen Bank. This serves two purposes: to ensure that the bank is actually 'owned' by the poor and to provide a capital base. Once savings in a group fund have reached the amount of US$15 the group is obliged to purchase shares amounting to US$12 (i.e. five shares).

Social development is the cornerstone upon which the Grameen Bank's success has been built. The Sixteen Decisions are the charter, and form the rallying point for social development amongst Grameen Bank members. From this platform spring the loans for housing, latrines and tube wells as well as special funds (the group fund, emergency fund and children's welfare fund). Training is also given to reinforce the social development agenda through a variety of workshops held for members.

REPLICATION: CAN AN ASIAN IDEA FIT INTO THE AFRICAN CONTEXT?

While it can be argued that many constraints are shared by the poor world-wide, e.g. many are women, all are powerless and large numbers are trapped in a vicious circle of low income, low savings and no collateral. It is also equally true that the poor cannot be helped in the same way in every context. Differences in the enabling environment, particularly those relating to society and culture, mean that the exact replication of any one approach to credit-based poverty reduction is impossible. In the case of replicating the Grameen Bank, an Asian model, in Africa, it is appropriate to question how this can be done. Furthermore, the fundamental features of the Grameeen Bank must be well understood to appreciate their relevance to another geographical, eco-nomic and cultural context.

The notion of replication is thus complex. The extent to which successful poverty reduction programmes can be replicated in or adapted to a different cultural and economic environment is difficult to predict with accuracy. In the past there has been a tendency to think that one approach can be applied to a variety of situations. Hulme (1991) refers to this as the 'blueprint method'. For example, the popularity in the recent past of schemes such as co-operatives and integrated rural development projects attest to it. Unfortunately, many of these initiatives have ended in failure (Chambers 1983).

The most common view of replication considers that the process should be based on a *learning approach*. Such institutional transfer relies on learning from other successful programmes by establishing a small pilot project that is adapted and modified until a model which is suitable to the local environment has been developed. In this way the main features of the original model accommodate the existing cultural and economic environment; at the same time the pitfalls and risks associated with uniform replication are avoided.

In this context two core issues will be examined: the definition of the essential Grameen model and identification of the issues relating to its replication.

The essential Grameen

The essential Grameen model consists of the basic elements of the 'core' Grameen model. The essential Grameen draws only on the principal activities and requirements of this model. For example, those culturally specific components of the Grameen Bank such as aspects of the Sixteen Decisions are not part of the essential Grameen and cannot be replicated. However, defining a different set of decisions or a charter which members should abide by could be carried out in another context.

Accordingly, the essential Grameen can be defined as an approach to building institutions which provide credit-based poverty alleviation based on the following concepts:

1 strict focus on low income groups and on women whose poverty is defined by land ownership;
2 the Sixteen Decisions;
3 bringing the bank to the poor through weekly meetings and frequent regular contact with the borrowers;
4 compulsory regular savings;
5 strong emphasis on training for members and bank staff;
6 participatory, highly decentralised management;
7 transparent administration and open transactions;
8 homogeneous group formation;
9 integration of a socio-economic development agenda with banking for the poor;
10 flexible approach to meeting the needs of the poor.

Clearly, not all elements of the Grameen Bank approach can be replicated in every context of the African environment. The African continent is far from homogeneous in terms of its institutions, cultures and economies. Furthermore, each country has its own policy environment and historical context within which development occurs. Likewise, it must also be recognised that significant internal variation (cultural, economic or otherwise) occurs within many African countries.

Can it be replicated?

Given the nature of such differences, the essential Grameen, as defined above, cannot be wholly replicated in Africa. Some of the concepts are difficult to replicate or would require major modifications. As well, other factors which are specific to Africa must be considered. Therefore, these elements should be considered when replicating the essential Grameen in an African setting:

1 definition of a poor target group by land ownership. Land based poverty is not as widespread in Africa as it is in Asia;
2 the nature and content of the Sixteen Decisions;
3 weekly meetings may not be possible, owing to problems relating to distance and transport (for members as well as for the bank workers). The concept was developed in the context of one of the most densely populated regions of the world;
4 the division of labour in Bangladesh is such that the poor produce a wide range of goods and services for their own rural economy. This has provided opportunities for several hundred different types of income-generating

activities. Such diversity may not be found in all African economies, especially rural ones;

5 participatory and highly decentralised management may not work where distance is a problem, as in much of rural Africa. This limitation also has an impact on how the bank is brought to the poor and on issues such as the regularity of savings and loan repayments. Obviously, this is not a consideration in urban areas;

6 group formation may need to be modified according to the local context, e.g. it may not be possible to insist that only one member of a family joins the group in sparsely populated rural areas. There is also the consideration of ethnic groups in Africa. Would groups be formed only from members of one ethnic group?

7 the social development agenda may not be possible in all environments;

8 the staff time needed to carry out the intensive supervision and monitoring required by the Grammen Bank model may be too expensive, and alternatives (such as computerised accounting systems) may need to be developed.

It should be noted that the requirement of compulsory regular savings has not been highlighted as requiring modification in the African context. Indeed, the saving habit is very strongly inculcated in Africa, especially among women. Savings groups are very active in most parts of Africa and operate under different forms and names. Rotating savings and credit associations, or ROSCAs, operate like miniature credit unions based on mutual trust. Members must make regular contributions and take turns withdrawing money. Such schemes operate all over the African continent and are known by various names – *igut* in Ethiopia, *tontines* and *osusus* in West Africa, *Chilemba* in Malawi, Zambia and Zimbabwe and *xitique* in Mozambique. Participation in such schemes is high – for example, it has been estimated that in Cameroon 70 per cent of the population participate in the informal financial sector and that savings in this sector are estimated to be more than 50 per cent of the country's total savings (African Development Bank 1994: 200–5).

Interestingly, when replication of the Grameen Bank was first raised as a possible approach to poverty in other Asian countries, some observers felt that the model was too closely linked with the specific context in Bangladesh which had given rise to it. However, this argument seems to have been refuted by the very successful introduction of Grameen Bank-type programmes in other countries such as the Amanah Ikhtiar Malaysia (AIM) in Malaysia and SAVECRED in Sri Lanka. In these cases, the Grameen Bank was not exactly *replicated* but rather the approach and philosophy have been adapted to the local environment. For example, the strong leadership of Muhammad Yunus is often cited as a focal point for rallying members' support and commitment. In the case of the AIM project, this commitment to the organisation was linked with Islamic principles rather than through an association with any one individual, thus refuting the 'charismatic leader' argument of those sceptical about the model's replication.

By contrast, it is worth noting that where exact or uniform replication of the Grameen Bank model has been attempted it was a failure. The Malawi Mudzi Fund was modelled directly on the Grameen Bank and encountered serious problems several months after disbursement started. Although the basic structure and systems of the bank were copied directly by the Malawi Mudzi Fund, there was a failure to recognise that successfully transferring the model to the Malawian context involved much more than simple replication (Hulme 1993). For example, since the Malawi Mudzi Fund was run by the government, borrowers perceived that the loans, like those from other government programmes, did not need to be paid back. This will be discussed further in the following section.

THE GRAMEEN BANK IN AFRICA

African attempts at replicating the Grameen Bank model have been undertaken in nearly a dozen African countries in all regions of the continent. The first replication was attempted in Malawi with the Malawi Mudzi Fund in 1988. Since that time, as awareness of and interest in the Grameen Bank have grown in Africa, NGOs, donors and community-based organisations have been increasingly active in supporting and mobilising lending to the poor through supporting the establishment of new institutions as well as through support for and reform of existing ones.

Conceptually, the African replications of the Grameen Bank model share several major characteristics that could be considered necessary for success. First and foremost, there is a focus on poverty. Second, credit has been identified as a barrier facing the poor when attempting to increase their income through agricultural or informal sector activities. Third, women constitute an important proportion of the poor and demonstrate their willingness to form small groups.

The Malawi Mudzi Fund

The Malawi Mudzi Fund (MMF) was the first attempt by an international donor to actually replicate the Grameen Bank model in another environment. In the mid-1980s, building upon its success as one of the early supporters of the original Grameen Bank in Bangladesh, the International Fund for Agricultural Development (IFAD) proposed that a similar scheme should be introduced in Malawi. The programme, known as the Malawi Mudzi Fund (*mudzi* means village) was originally designed as a component of a larger smallholders' credit scheme jointly funded by IFAD and the World Bank in Malawi (Smallholder Agricultural Credit Administration). The MMF was targeted at the poorest of the poor or the core poor, the majority of whom are women and who were largely excluded from the smallholders' credit scheme.

With its relatively high population density and widespread rural poverty, Malawi seemed a good location in which to attempt replication of the Grameen Bank model. Furthermore, experience with credit to farmers had been extremely positive, the government's SACA programme having achieved repayment rates of close to 100 per cent, an excellent record compared with the usual performance of such schemes in Africa. However, it is important to note that the high population density is fragmented into communities or villages that are far apart and punctuated by difficult roads, limited transport and very low purchasing power in terms of markets for the products of income-generating activities.

As in Bangladesh, it was assumed that if affordable credit were available, poverty would be reduced, owing to the increased income generated from the activities pursued by borrowers. Similarly, significant benefits were expected to accrue to the poor through increased savings.

The main features of the MMF are similar to the Grameen Bank and are based on the five-person group concept. Loans are made to individuals who own less than 1 ha of land or whose assets are worth less than the value of five bags of maize. Members must meet weekly and make contributions to their savings accounts on this basis. All members must also contribute to a group fund. The amount, as at the Grameen Bank, is 5 per cent of the total loan value. Loan repayments, initially over a period of fifty-two weeks, are now made over a twenty-six-week period. This is the only significant deviation from the Grameen Bank model.

Initially the MMF enjoyed great success. Lending activities began in June 1990. In the first four months, loan repayment rates were high, 100 per cent repayment being recorded for six out of seven branches and 91 per cent of scheduled repayments covered. However, by the end of the first year of operations, only 54 per cent of all loans were being repaid. As a result, all new loans were stopped in March 1991.

A month later, lending recommenced. Savings were required of all members for twelve weeks prior to loan disbursements as a measure to encourage financial discipline. First-year borrowers were separated from second-year borrowers so as to reduce any negative demonstration effects. By the end of 1991 repayment rates of 81 per cent had been achieved but monthly loan repayment rates were falling.

In the middle of 1992, when donors conducted a mid-term review of the MMF, the results were not encouraging. Loan disbursements and recoveries and savings were well below the anticipated levels and operational costs were excessive, with a ratio of four units spent to every unit lent. By 1994 repayment rates of up to 75 per cent were being reported for the MMF. Loan repayment eventually reached nearly 100 per cent but owing to its high operating costs (six times the volume of outstanding loans) the MMF was forced to suspend operations and merge with another rural finance institution.

Observers have suggested that a major problem was that requirements were not insisted upon, such as attendance at weekly meetings and regular contributions to savings accounts. This may have reinforced the existing perception, noted by some, that government loans need not be paid back. In addition, disbursement activity started before savings activities were properly established. This was in order to meet previously established targets. At the Grameen Bank in Bangladesh, lending is driven by client needs rather than by targets established by management. This is an important element in decentralised management based on a bottom-up approach. While the use of a scheduled approach to achieve objectives is necessary for any managerial task, the aspect of flexibility is essential to success.

Burkina Faso[2]

Credit with Education

The Credit with Education (CE) project commenced operations in 1993. It was designed jointly by the American NGO Freedom from Hunger and the Réseau de Caisses Populaires de Burkina Faso. Credit with Education is funded jointly by USAID, UNICEF and IFAD. In essence, the scheme builds upon an existing *caisses populaires* (or credit union) movement which has been operating in Burkina Faso since 1972, modelled on the Canadian Caisse Populaire Desjardins format.

Although the Burkinabé *caisses populaire* movement has been highly successful, the poorest people, especially women, were not being reached. Only 26 per cent of *caisse populaire* members in Burkina Faso were women. The *caisse villageois* or village bank concept was designed to address this situation.

The CE approach combines village banking with basic health education. In Burkina Faso Freedom from Hunger works with the Union Centrale des Caisses Populaires (UCCP). The *caisses villageoises* are located near *caisse populaires* in order to facilitate access to a bank to deposit savings and loan repayments. Each group comprises five members, all of whom must save and complete preliminary training to become *bona fide* group members.

Each *caisse villageoise* has, on average, about thirty women members and is made up of smaller groups of five or six women who already know each other well and who therefore trust one another. These smaller units are known as solidarity groups. Hence the loan approval process and the mutual guarantee system of loan repayment operate at two levels: first the solidarity group and then the whole *caisse villageoise* membership.

CE members are required to meet weekly during the first year of their participation (except during the rainy season, when such meetings are held bi-weekly) in order to ensure that they receive adequate exposure to the entire education curriculum (especially the priority health and nutrition topics) but also to diminish the risks which are associated with loan repayment. At the end of the first year, if the *caisse villageoise* has demonstrated that it is credit-worthy, it will then be able to meet only bi-weekly and eventually only monthly.

Women are attracted to join the village bank or credit association in order to gain access to credit and to have a safe place to deposit their savings. Most had already participated in ROSCAs but found access to funds limited. These women are required to attend regular meetings to conduct financial transactions such as loan disbursement and repayment and depositing savings. Regular meetings also provide the women with an opportunity to learn about health and nutrition issues. This education is organised in the form of short classes. The topics include birth spacing, breast feeding, infant and child nutrition, the management and prevention of diarrhoea and immunisation.

The programme also operates in conjunction with local health clinics operated by the government of Burkina Faso. UNICEF's local office was already working to strengthen the capacity of these rural health clinics. In addition to the existing clientele, women who are members of Credit with Education are trained to utilise the centres and can use their increased income to pay for the services which they may need.

By 1997 Credit with Education had 18,000 members, was operating in both the Central Region and the Central Plateau Region of Burkina Faso and was able to cover all its expenses with income from loan repayments and the interest on members' savings, thus becoming a sustainable institution. Total outstanding loans stood at US$791,138 and the average loan size was US$65. The loan cycle is four months, although borrowers who perform well are eligible to move to a longer, six-month loan cycle and be eligible to borrow a larger amount. A membership fee of CFA 250 (US$0.50) must be paid by all women who wish to join a *caisse villageois*, and savings (100 CFA or US$0.20 per week) are mandatory. Members must leave their savings in the bank until the end of the loan cycle as a form of guarantee. Each woman is given a passbook in which savings and loan repayments are noted. No interest is paid on the savings, kept in a current account at the *caisse populaire*. The members decide amongst themselves who will deposit the savings on their behalf.

Sahel Action

The Sahel Action project was initiated in 1988, funded by the French and Burkina Faso governments. It was jointly conceptualised and designed by European and Burkinabé researchers. It is based, in principle, on the Grameen model but with adaptations to the local context. Sahel Action began in 1988 in one village that had been severely hit by the Sahelian drought of the 1980s. Initially, an analysis was undertaken of the local agricultural production systems and what could be done to improve incomes. It was found that, while potentially profitable activities existed, the farmers lacked the means to finance them, e.g. to purchase the necessary inputs. In the past, before the · Burkinabé rural economy became monetised, cash was not necessary to obtain inputs. Thus the role of credit in breaking a vicious circle of poverty became crucial. Furthermore, the vital economic role of women was also identified, in terms of their contribution to the rural household economy and also the number of traditional income-generating activities usually undertaken by women.

The organisers of Sahel Action, guided by the Grameen Bank model's principles, sought to identify why existing credit schemes in Burkina Faso did not reach the poorest people and why loan recovery was not very successful. It was found that three factors contributed:

1 Loan recovery is insufficiently adapted to production systems, e.g. loan repayments are not scheduled to coincide with the periods when crops are sold and cash is available.
2 Credit is not granted to those who are most in need or to those undertaking the most profitable activities.
3 Loan recovery is based on a model copied from industrialised economies which is anonymous rather than linking repayment with group responsibility.

Sahel Action's programme was designed to overcome these factors. The core elements of the programme are:

1 an understanding of the economic strategies of poor farmers;
2 an appreciation of the reasons for the failure of conventional credit schemes;
3 an attempt to integrate new approaches to credit for the poor into the programme, particularly the Grameen Bank model.

Sahel Action's organisers first consulted the women farmers, many of whom, like CE members, were also involved in ROSCAs. As a result of this participatory process, they identified a number of elements that the potential beneficiaries themselves felt were important to ensuring project success. These include the Grameen Bank notion of a group guarantee (as opposed to the anonymous or impersonal relationship between the lender and the borrower) adapted to the African context, the choice by clients themselves of the nature of the activity to be financed (so long as it is profitable), the harmonisation of the loan repayment structure and production system, the identification of simple low cost management techniques and the formulation of credit rules which involve beneficiaries and are subject to review by the users themselves.

Following the practice developed by the Grameen Bank, loans are granted to members in succession, provided borrowers make timely loan repayments.

For example, in a group of five women, loans are granted on a monthly basis. If borrower A repays her loan as required after a period of one month then borrower B will be able to obtain her loan the following month, and so on, until all members have received their loans. Failure to complete repayment leads to a freeze on new loans until existing loans are paid back.

Actual loan repayment occurs over a period of fifty-six weeks or thirteen months. The first weekly instalment goes into an emergency fund which permits the recovery of unpaid debts, among other uses. The next fifty loan payments, i.e. weeks 2–51 constitute capital reimbursement. The last four weeks are for loan repayment at a rate of 2 per cent of the initial capital borrowed. This corresponds to an interest rate of 19 per cent per annum. The interest rate charged is subject to change, depending on the evolution of costs.

Sahel Action members also contribute to a group fund when they receive their loans, another practice similar to those of the Grameen Bank. The amount paid to the group fund is 5 per cent of the total loan value. This fund is kept in a local bank, is managed by the members and serves to familiarise them with credit management.

The reasoning behind this fund is that the group can lend money from it to members in difficult times or if they want to supplement their activities with a group loan. It could also help them to build up an asset base jointly at the local bank and to, over time, increase their influence and leverage at the bank as a result. However, experience has shown that most women leave their money in the group fund until they have repaid their loan, then want to withdraw it and use it for other purposes. The organisers have experienced difficulty in establishing the strong group solidarity which is needed for a group fund to grow.

Sahel Action works in four of Burkina Faso's thirty provinces and has a membership of more than 10,000 women. Membership is based on groups of five, who are then further organised in larger groups associated with a particular village. Loans range, on average, between US$50 to US$100 and are given for income generating activities.[3] While weekly savings are not required, members must contribute to a group fund when a loan is disbursed and pay into an emergency fund upon the first loan payment. Repayment rates are nearly 100 per cent.

Sahel Action does not have a social component to its activities. This project exists for the sole purpose of helping poor women gain access to credit. It is hoped that, through the provision of credit, members can empower themselves in order to improve various aspects of their lives and those of their children.

Sahel Action covers only a relatively small percentage (about 20 per cent) of its costs from interest income. Its main challenge is to increase the funds it raises internally in order to become less dependent on donor largesse and more sustainable as an African institution. Interest on savings, a potential source of income, is unavailable to Sahel Action, since individual savings are not required.

LESSONS LEARNED

Undoubtedly, African institutions concerned with sustainable poverty lending recognise that valuable lessons can be gleaned from successes in other developing countries. In the context of this 'south–south' transfer of knowledge, the Grameen Bank approach provides development practitioners with a successful model. While it would be unrealistic to attempt to replicate the system without modification in another environment, the evidence points to the fact that there are numerous essential elements which are generally relevant to the African situation. In particular, the group approach and inculcation of the savings habit stand out as two very important ingredients in reproducing the Grameen Bank model 'recipe' in Africa.

The discussion of the three Grameen Bank model replications in Africa provides three illustrations of how the model has been adapted to Africa, with varying degrees of success. In Malawi an exact duplication, though redesigned after initial failures, proved too expensive to sustain. Sahel Action adopted parts of the essential Grameen (group lending, group funds with no compulsory savings or social development agenda) but was unable to achieve financial sustainability. By contrast, CE introduced group lending, made savings compulsory and addressed social development through compulsory training and partnership with UNICEF. It is covering its costs with interest income and can thus be considered sustainable. Of the Grameen Bank model replications examined, only CE has succeeded in building an African institution.

Conceptually, several key characteristics are necessary for successful replication of the Grameen Bank model in the African context. First and foremost, a large proportion of the population in the area where such a project is being proposed should be poor. The measure of poverty will vary according to the local definition, i.e. in terms of income, in-kind wealth, land ownership, etc. Second, credit should be identified as a barrier facing the poor in attempting to increase their income through agricultural or informal sector activities. Third, women should constitute an important proportion of the beneficiaries and should be able to demonstrate their willingness to form themselves into the small groups which are at the heart of the Grameen Bank's organisational model. In addition, as the African examples illustrate, financial sustainability must be adopted as an objective in order to ensure the establishment and/or reinforcement of institutions involved in poverty lending.

Experience drawn from the two replications in Burkina Faso demonstrates that the nature of the adaptation can vary even within a country. For example, while Credit with Education offers its members health classes, Sahel Action's managers assume that the monetary gains realised by its beneficiaries will assist them to improve the quality of their lives. Similarly, Sahel Action members' savings are held in local banks, while Credit with Education has made a formal arrangement with the Union Centrale des Caisses Populaires, limiting the membership to those living within a reasonable distance of a *caisse populaire*. CE members are required to save in individual accounts, whereas Sahel Action members contribute to a group fund.

Lastly, it is also interesting to note the importance that informal savings schemes such as tontines play. In the case of the women participating in Credit with Education and Sahel Action, all were either current members or had been members of rotating savings and credit associations. The link between traditional and modern approaches to credit for the poor certainly merits further exploration as a foundation upon which financial institutions can build.

The Grameen Bank model offers Africans a vision of sustainable poverty lending which, though developed in Asia, can be replicated elsewhere. In the quest for new African institutions that respond to the needs of the poor, looking south rather than north can be not only inspirational but workable.

NOTES

The content of this chapter should not be ascribed to the Asian Development Bank or to the African Development Bank.

1 This section draws on Pal (1995).
2 The information in this section is based on field visits carried out by the author in Burkina Faso in October 1994 and was updated in October 1997.
3 The breakdown of these activities is as follows: trading 28 per cent, food processing 48 per cent, soap production 12 per cent, handicrafts 6 per cent, other 6 per cent.

REFERENCES

African Development Bank (1994) *African Development Report*, Abidjan: African Development Bank.

Chambers, R. (1983) *Rural Development: Putting the Last First*, London: Longman.

Hulme, D. (1991) 'International Transfer of Institutional Innovations: Replicating the Grameen in other Countries' in R. Prendergast and H. Singer (eds) *Development Perspectives for the 1990s*, London: Macmillan.

Hulme, D. (1993) 'Replicating Finance Programmes in Malawi and Malaysia', *Small Enterprise Development*, 4 (4): 4–15.

Grameen Bank (1992) *Annual Report 1992*, Dhaka: Grameen Bank.

Grameen Bank (1997) *Grameen Dialogue, July*, Dhaka: Grameen Bank.

Khandker, S., Khalily, B. and Khan, Z. (1994) *Is Grameen Bank Sustainable?* Human Resources and Operations Policy Working Paper 23, Washington DC: World Bank.

Pal, M.S. (1995) *An Examination of the Grameen Bank Model and its Replication in Burkina Faso*, Environment and Social Policy Series, Abidjan: African Development Bank.

Yunus, M. (1997) 'Opening Statement', Microcredit summit, Washington DC, 2–4 February.

11

MARKET POWER AND PRODUCTIVITY IN ZIMBABWEAN MANUFACTURING

Kupukile Mlambo and Thomas Sterner

By African standards the industrial performance of Zimbabwe is quite impressive. In spite of (or, according to some observers, on account of) the international embargo during the Unilateral Declaration of Independence (UDI) under Ian Smith, Zimbabwean industry grew rapidly and acquired a certain degree of diversity, although concentrating mainly on import substitution. By 1982 Zimbabwe could have been described as well on the route to industrialisation, with manufacturing accounting for 25 per cent of GDP, close to the levels of Korea and Brazil and higher than the average of the upper-middle income countries. During the 1980s, however, even Zimbabwe has seen its industry stagnate and this is sometimes attributed to the fact that the phase of 'easy' import substitution has now been passed (see Green and Kadhani 1986). Clearly capital equipment is outdated and industry has been facing serious shortages in imported materials. Recent reports have blamed the control regime set up under the import substitution regime (see Jansen 1982, World Bank 1987).

Earlier studies such as Jansen (1982) and Shaaeldin (1989) have shown that the growth in Zimbabwean manufacturing has not resulted from total factor productivity but mainly from the high rates of protection under the import substitution regime. Earlier work by Mlambo (1993) has also underlined the importance of various other factors in explaining the true development of productivity growth. These factors notably include capacity utilisation, public expenditure and finally the role of market power, which will be the focus of this chapter.

It is quite common in studies of productivity to assume perfectly competitive markets, that is, that economic agents are price takers and carry out their optimisation subject to given prices. However, most commentators have pointed out that Zimbabwean manufacturing is characterised by highly concentrated industrial activity in terms of both products and location, thus rendering the price-taking assumption hypothesis inappropriate. On product concentration, Riddell (1990: 389) has observed that 'The dominant forms of manufacturing production in Zimbabwe are monopolistic and oligopolistic and not those of perfect, or even imperfect, competition; over 80 per cent of all manufactured products are made by only a few producers and just over half by single manufacturers.'

In terms of spatial concentration, Zimbabwean manufacturing activity is concentrated in three centres, namely Harare, Bulawayo and the Kwekwe–Redcliff industrial complex, which account for over 80 per cent of all manufacturing output and employment. Throughout most of the period observed (at least from 1965 to 1980) the economy was practically closed, owing to sanctions, and there was for all practical purposes no effective competition from imported goods, which of course heavily adds to the effects of monopolistic or oligopolistic collusion.

Bennell (1990), using unpublished firm-level data for 1970 and 1986, also found high levels of product concentration. Bennell calculated one-firm and four-firm concentration ratios (CR1, CR4) for the manufacturing sector and found the following pattern: out of fifty-four four-digit ISIC industries, (1) forty-two could be classified as highly concentrated oligopolies (CR4 0.75–1.0), (2) six as moderately concentrated oligopolies (CR4 0.5–0.749), (3) five as slightly concentrated oligopolies (CR4 0.25–0.499), and only one industry, namely wearing apparel, had a CR4 value below 0.25.

Under the conditions of the Census and Statistics Act, Bennell (1990: 5) could not publish CR1 values, but he was nevertheless able to conclude on the basis of his results that 'single enterprises accounted for half of total turnover in twenty-five of the fifty-four (46 per cent) manufacturing industries, and in only ten industries was the CR1 value below 0.25'. His results also show that over time there has been a tendency for industries to move to more concentrated levels. For example, between 1970 and 1986 six industries, namely cement, textiles, other foods, tobacco, spinning and knitting, moved from moderately concentrated to highly concentrated oligopolies.

Bennell also calculated prime cost mark-ups and found that the majority of industries have mark-ups that lie between 25 per cent and 75 per cent. The study by Bennell, although an important contribution to the market structure debate in Zimbabwe, is, however, not based within a framework of production theory. Instead Bennell adopts traditional applied industrial organisation methods of estimating the influence of market structure and of the industry characteristics on price–cost margins. Second, the study does not relate price–cost mark-ups to important issues of capacity utilisation and cyclical variations.

The purpose of this chapter is twofold. First, we estimate the gap between market price and marginal cost at the aggregated industry level. Second, we relate the results to observed procyclical movements in total factor productivity growth. The study applies a production theory-based model similar to that of Appelbaum (1982) and Bernstein and Mohnen (1992). We employ the translog short-run or restricted cost function to measure firms' market power. Three inputs are used, namely labour, energy and capital. Capital is treated as a quasi-fixed factor, while labour and energy are variable inputs.

The chapter is divided into six main sections. The next section sets out the theoretical framework for estimating price–cost margins. The following one lays out the econometric model to be estimated. A translog function is chosen as the functional form for the cost function, and for the inverse demand function we choose a log-linear function. The econometric estimation methods and sources of data are presented in the third section, while the fourth contains the estimation results for the production function. In the fifth section we come to our main objective, namely a discussion of the effects of cost–price margins on observed total factor productivity.

THEORETICAL FRAMEWORK

Consider a representative firm j operating in a non-competitive industry with N firms that produces homogeneous output Y. Assume that the technology facing this industry can be described by a transformation function $F(Y, V, K, t) = 0$, where $V = (V_1, \ldots V_n)$ refers to the vector of variable inputs, K to a vector of fixed inputs, and t captures shifts in technology. The restricted or variable cost function for firm j, obtained from minimising total variable costs subject to $F(.)$, is given by

$$C_v = C_v(Y_j, \ P, \ K, \ t) \tag{1}$$

where P is a price vector of variable inputs and K is a vector of quasi-fixed inputs. The variable cost function is assumed to be increasing in the variable factors and output, and decreasing in quasi-fixed factors. It is also concave and homogeneous of degree 1 in the variable factor prices, and convex in the quasi-fixed factors. And, finally, its derivative with respect to P yields the demand for the ith factor input V_i:

$$V_i = \frac{\partial C_v}{\partial P_i}(Y_j, \ P, \ K, \ t) \quad i = L, E \tag{2}$$

The market demand function facing the industry is assumed to be given by:

$$Y = D(P_Q, \ Z) \tag{3}$$

where P_Q is the market price of output Y, and Z is a vector of exogenous variables that affect the demand for firm j's output. Alternatively we can define the inverse demand function:

$$P_Q = D^{-1}(Y, Z) \tag{4}$$

The inverse product demand equation is assumed to be twice differentiable, non-negative and non-increasing in output quantity.

Firm j's monopolistic profit maximisation problem may thus be written as:

$$\max_{Y_j}[D^{-1}(Y, Z).Y_j - C_v(Y_j, P, K, t) : Y = D(P_Q, Z)] \tag{5}$$

The optimality condition corresponding to this profit maximisation problem is given by (Appelbaum 1982):

$$P_Q(1 - \theta_j\varepsilon) = \frac{\partial cv(Y_j, P, K, t)}{\partial Y} \tag{6}$$

where $\varepsilon = -[(\partial P_Q/\partial Y).Y/P_Q]$ is the inverse demand elasticity, and $\theta_j = (\partial Y/\partial Y_j).Y_j/Y)$ is the firm's conjectural variation elasticity. If the industry is perfectly competitive in the market for Y_j then $\theta_j = 0$ and we have the usual equalisation between price and marginal cost. If the industry is a pure monopoly, then $\theta_j = 1$. In the latter case monopoly power is given by ε, the inverse of the price elasticity of demand. The term given by $\theta_j\varepsilon = [P_Q - \partial C_v/\partial Y_j]/P_Q$ is a kind of 'cost mark-up' and defines the degree of oligopoly power of firm j. Following Cowling and Waterson (1976) and Appelbaum (1982), for a single product case, the industry's degree of oligopoly power can be stated as:

$$M = \sum_j S_j \theta_j \varepsilon \tag{7}$$

where $S_j = Y_j/Y$. The value of M will span from zero to unity. If the industry is perfectly competitive, then $M = 0$, and if it is a pure monopoly, then $M = \varepsilon$.

MODEL SPECIFICATION

To apply the framework discussed in this section requires firm-level data, which unfortunately are not available to us. However, if we assume that the distribution of firm-specific variables is constant and ignore other aggregation problems, the framework can be applied to industry-level time series data (see Bernstein and Mohnen 1992). Assuming that the variable cost function depends only on industry variables, then at equilibrium firms in this industry face the same marginal costs, which implies that the conjectural elasticities must be the same as well (see Appelbaum 1982). This implies that, as long as equilibrium exists, $\theta_j = \theta (j = 1, \ldots N)$ is the equilibrium value of the conjectural elasticities.

We will assume the industry employs two competitively priced inputs, labour (L) and energy (E), and one quasi-fixed input, capital (K). The industry variable cost function is assumed to be a translog function, and is written as:

$$
\begin{aligned}
\ln C_v = {} & \beta_0 + \beta_Y \ln Y + \beta_L \ln P_L + \beta_E \ln P_E + \beta_K \ln K + \beta_t t \\
& + \tfrac{1}{2}[\beta_{YY}(\ln Y)^2 + \beta_{LL}(\ln P_L)^2 + \beta_{EE}(\ln P_{EE})^2 + \beta_{KK}(\ln K)^2 + \beta_{tt}t^2] \\
& + \beta_{EL} \ln P_E \ln P_L + \beta_{YL} \ln Y \ln P_L + \beta_{YE} \ln Y \ln P_E \\
& + \beta_{YK} \ln Y \ln K + \beta_{LK} \ln P_L \ln K + \beta_{EK} \ln P_E \ln K \\
& + \beta_{Yt}t \ln Y + \beta_{tK}t \ln K + \beta_{tL}t \ln P_L + \beta_{tE}t \ln P_E
\end{aligned}
\tag{8}
$$

where, by Young's theorem, $\beta_{ih} = \beta_{hi}$. For the variable cost function to be well behaved, it must be homogeneous of degree 1 in prices, given Y, K and t. This implies the restrictions:

$$
\beta_L + \beta_E = 1 \text{ and } \sum_j \beta_{ij} = 0 \quad j = L, E \text{ and } i = L, E, K, Y, t
\tag{9}
$$

Cost-minimising input demands are obtained via Shephard's lemma as:

$$
S_i = \frac{\partial \ln C_v}{\partial \ln P_i} = \beta_i + \beta_{ii} \ln P_i + \sum_{h \neq i} \beta_{ih} \ln P_h + \beta_{Yi} \ln P_i + \beta_{Ki} \ln K \ln P_i + \beta_{ti} t
$$

$$
i, h = L, E
\tag{10}
$$

The long-run equilibrium condition for capital, the quasi-fixed input, is defined as:

$$
S_K = -\left(\frac{\partial \ln C_v}{\partial \ln K}\right) = -[\beta_K + \beta_{KK} \ln K + \sum_{Ki} \beta_{Ki} \ln P_i + \beta_{YK} \ln Y + \beta_{Kt}t]
$$

$$
i, h = L, E
\tag{11}
$$

According to equation (11) the aggregate capital stock to variable cost ratio (S_K) depends on variable input prices P_L and P_E, cyclical product market conditions as reflected in Y, and the bias in technical change β_{tK}. Using the estimated parameters, the rate of technical change can be defined as:

$$\varepsilon_{Ct} = -\frac{\partial \ln C_v}{\partial t} = -(\beta_t + \beta_{tt}t + \sum_i \beta_{ti} \ln P_i + \beta_{Yt} \ln Y + \beta_{tK} \ln K) \quad (12)$$

Following Morrison (1986) the cost side (or dual) measure of productivity growth in the presence of scale economies and temporary equilibrium is:

$$\dot{TFP} = \varepsilon_{Ct} - \varepsilon_{CK}\frac{\dot{K}}{K} - (\varepsilon_{CY} - 1)\frac{\dot{Y}}{Y} \quad (13)$$

where $\varepsilon_{CK} = \partial \ln C_v / \partial \ln K$ and $\varepsilon_{CY} = \partial \ln C_v / \partial \ln Y$.

The inverse output demand function is given by:

$$\ln P_Q = b_0 + b_1 \ln Y + \zeta^T \ln Z \quad (14)$$

where ζ^T is a vector of the parameters related to Z variables, and b_1 is the inverse demand elasticity defined as:

$$\varepsilon = \frac{\partial P_Q}{\partial Y} \cdot \frac{Y}{P_Q} = \frac{\partial \ln P_Q}{\partial \ln Y} = b_1 = \frac{1}{\eta} \quad (15)$$

where η is the price elasticity of demand.

Given that the firm equates perceived marginal revenues to marginal cost (see equation 5) equation (6) can be written as:

$$S_Y(1 - \theta\varepsilon) = \beta_Y + \beta_{YY} \ln Y + \sum \beta_{Yi} \ln P_i + \beta_{YK} \ln K + \beta_{Yt}t \quad (16)$$

where $S_Y = \partial \ln C_v / \partial \ln Y = P_Q Y / C_v$ and θ is the industry conjectural variation, which at equilibrium does not vary across firms but varies across products. This parameter is estimated within the model.

This completes our discussion of the model to be estimated, which includes equations (8), (10), (14) and (16). In the next section we discuss the estimation and the results obtained.

DATA AND ESTIMATION

To formulate an econometric model, as shown above, we have appended an additive random disturbance term u_i in each of the share equations (10), the cost function (8) for the translog and the inverse demand equation (14). It is assumed that the error terms are jointly normally distributed with zero mean.

The model is estimated subject to the parameter restrictions stated in (9). Christensen and Greene (1976) have shown that in estimating the translog model statistical degrees of freedom can be increased by estimating jointly the cost function and the cost shares as a multivariate regression system, given that the cost share parameters are a subset of the cost function parameters. Such a procedure is very attractive in cases such as ours, where data are limited.

The system can be estimated either by the maximum likelihood method or by the Zellner iterative estimation procedure. Kmenta and Gilbert (1968) have demonstrated that the parameter estimates obtained by these two methods are numerically equivalent. Owing to the singularity of the variance–covariance matrix, we followed the most common approach of arbitrarily dropping one of the share equations, the energy input share equation in our case. The model was then estimated using Zellner's iterative procedure. The results will be invariant to the equation deleted (see Barten 1969).

The empirical data consist of industry-level annual time series data for the period 1964 to 1987. Domestic expenditure has been included as the exogenous variable that enters the inverse demand equation. The sectoral price deflator, obtained from Statistics Zimbabwe is used as proxy for the industrial product price index. Quantity and price data on labour, capital and energy also come from Statistics Zimbabwe, and the two publications *The Census of Production* and *Quarterly Digest of Statistics*. The branches of industry included in this chapter correspond to the ISIC codes 3000, 3100, 3200, 3300+3400, 3600, 3700+3800. Real output is gross manufacturing output deflated by the manufacturing GDP deflator. Expenditure on labour includes both wages and salaries, while the physical index of labour input is number of employees (since hours of work are not available).

Statistics Zimbabwe does not publish data on capital stock and so these data had to be prepared using the perpetual inventory method ($K_t = (1 - d) K_{t-1} + I_t.$). The capital user cost was calculated as $U_K = P_I(r + d)$, where P_I is the price index of investment goods and $(r + d)$ is the sum of real interest rate and depreciation. The necessary data on investments, depreciation rates and the book value of capital assets in 1970 were taken from Statistics Zimbabwe and from UNIDO (1984). Quantities and costs of energy were obtained from the same sources. The data on energy consumption were divided into electricity, coal and other fuels. These were aggregated into a composite energy measure and the price of energy was calculated as a Divisia index. For more details the reader is referred to Mlambo (1993).

Cost function estimates

The model was estimated for total manufacturing; food, drink and tobacco; textiles and clothing; wood, paper and pulp; non-metals; metals and metal

Table 11.1 Goodness of fit and log-likelihood values

	Total	Food	Textiles/clothing	Wood/paper	Non-metal	Metals
$R^2(\ln C_v)$	0.993	0.998	0.983	0.95	0.992	0.96
DW	1.11	1.76	1.628	1.17	1.48	1.47
$R^2(SL)$	0.65	0.794	0.712	0.99	0.395	0.20
DW	1.51	1.51	1.79	1.85	0.89	1.28
$R^2(PQ)$	0.974	0.967	0.923	0.988	0.962	0.972
DW	0.54	0.77	0.35	0.65	0.36	0.50
$R^2(SY)$	0.938	0.942	0.644	0.66	0.873	0.934
DW	1.98	1.39	0.54	1.31	1.41	0.69
L ratio	300.9	313.8	285.8	304.6	293.9	269.0

products. In addition the impact of price–cost margins on productivity measurement was also calculated. In Table 11.1 we report the relevant statistics for the model. The results show that the fit of the model is quite good. The R^2s for the variable cost function and the inverse demand equation are generally above 0.92 for all industries. The R^2 for the labour share equation is, however, rather low. The Durbin–Watson statistics indicate that some autocorrelation may be present, especially in the case of the inverse demand equation. Bernstein and Mohnen (1992) also report the presence of first-order autocorrelation in the inverse product demand equations. In our case, except for textiles, and non-metals for the inverse demand equation, at the 0.01 level of significance, the test statistic for each equation and in all industries falls in the inconclusive region.

Given that our primary interest lies with measuring the degree of market power, we shall confine our comments on the parameters to a few general observations. Most of the parameters in Table 11.2 are significant at the 5 per cent and 10 per cent levels. According to Alderman (1984), the β_{ib} parameters contain the same information as the more widely used Allen–Uzawa elasticities.

A few observations can be made about these parameters regarding substitution. The parameter β_{KL} has a positive sign in most industries except in food and in wood and paper. A positive sign shows that labour and capital are substitutes: an increase in the price of labour will increase the share of capital and vice versa. Labour and energy were, however, found to be complements.

The β_{ti} parameters contain information about the bias in technical change. In general, our findings suggest that we should expect technical change to be both labour and capital-saving. Technical change is labour-using in wood and paper, and capital-using in aggregate manufacturing and in textiles and clothing. The parameter β_{tt} is positive in all cases except in non-metals. This suggests a decreasing rate of technical change in the majority of Zimbabwean manufacturing industries.

Table 11.2 Estimation results (asymptotic standard errors in parentheses)

Parameter	Total Manu-facturing	Food	Textiles and clothing	Wood and paper	Non-metal	Metals
β_0	0.0583	0.7549	0.0899	1.7472	0.6330	0.9009
	(0.176)	(0.145)	(0.553)	(0.218)	(0.153)	(0.359)
β_K	0.1270	0.4924	−1.0718	0.7828	1.0870	1.3774
	(0.177)	(0.233)	(0.377)	(0.364)	(0.734)	(0.288)
β_L	0.7726	0.5132	0.6497	0.3818	0.5939	0.7090
	(0.094)	(0.056)	(0.105)	(0.064)	(0.050)	(0.175)
β_Y	0.5309	0.8540	0.9773	0.7591	1.0791	0.2840
	(0.164)	(0.240)	(0.048)	(0.249)	(0.343)	(0.212)
β_{KK}	−0.4131	−1.2487	−0.9329	0.1719	−1.4755	−0.6300
	(0.325)	(0.536)	(0.462)	(0.670)	(0.742)	(0.366)
β_{LL}	0.2443	0.0112	0.0523	−0.2603	0.0811	0.1697
	(0.070)	(0.042)	(0.001)	(0.031)	(0.030)	(0.162)
β_{YY}	0.0679	0.0349	0.4727	0.3324	0.1667	−0.0092
	(0.057)	(0.114)	(0.204)	(0.102)	(0.075)	(0.016)
β_{KL}	0.0106	−0.0311	0.0277	−0.0486	0.0522	0.0306
	(0.004)	(0.004)	(0.009)	(0.032)	(0.015)	(0.042)
β_{LE}	−0.1397	−0.0368	−0.0212	−0.0851	−0.0047	−0.1009
	(0.023)	(0.016)	(0.009)	(0.023)	(0.025)	(0.059)
β_{YL}	0.1055	0.0518	0.0186	0.0867	0.0267	0.1210
	(0.033)	(0.040)	(0.025)	(0.033)	(0.022)	(0.088)
β_{YE}	−0.0771	−0.0850	0.0148	0.0003	0.1208	−0.0285
	(0.029)	(0.037)	(0.020)	(0.047)	(0.081)	(0.022)
β_{YK}	−0.0593	−0.0226	−0.0189	−0.0607	0.0039	−0.0029
	(0.045)	(0.062)	(0.022)	(0.066)	(0.035)	(0.008)
β_t	0.0169	−0.0171	0.0406	−0.1090	0.0278	−0.1173
	(0.002)	(0.016)	(0.062)	(0.029)	(0.030)	(0.048)
β_{tt}	0.0020	0.0017	0.0009	0.0022	−0.0029	0.0100
	(0.001)	(0.001)	(0.004)	(0.002)	(0.003)	(0.003)
β_{Yt}	−0.0162	−0.0195	−0.0372	−0.0039	−0.0361	−0.0125
	(0.004)	(0.006)	(0.018)	(0.007)	(0.013)	(0.009)
β_{tK}	0.0118	−0.0457	0.0662	−0.0599	−0.0939	−0.0650
	(0.010)	(0.018)	(0.023)	(0.032)	(0.053)	(0.019)
β_{tL}	−0.0141	−0.0013	−0.0109	0.0072	−0.0051	−0.0073
	(0.006)	(0.003)	(0.006)	(0.004)	(0.003)	(0.010)
b_0	0.0518	−0.0015	0.0545	−0.0009	0.1224	0.0567
	(0.027)	(0.037)	(0.041)	(0.020)	(0.031)	(0.027)
ζ_2	1.0913	1.1035	1.0532	1.0228	0.9917	1.0753
	(0.044)	(0.051)	(0.096)	(0.024)	(0.042)	(0.042)

Price-cost mark-ups

Parameters that interest us are the equilibrium value of the conjectural variation elasticity (θ) and the inverse demand elasticity (ε). Therefore, although they are estimated together with the parameters reported in Table 11.2, we have chosen to report them separately in Table 11.3. The degree of oligopoly power for aggregate manufacturing can be calculated from equation (7). However, given that we have assumed that firms in the industry produce a single homogeneous output, and that θ is an equilibrium value, the degree of oligopoly power M is just a product of the conjectural elasticity and the inverse demand elasticity (i.e. $M = -\theta\varepsilon$). For total manufacturing the conjectural elasticity is 0.52, and is significantly different from zero. The inverse output demand elasticity, which is also statistically significant, is -1.0223. The degree of oligopoly power is therefore found to be 0.513. This result suggests that, at the aggregate level, Zimbabwean manufacturing firms exert a sizeable degree of monopoly power.

The price–cost mark-up found here for aggregate manufacturing suggests rather a high degree of oligopoly power compared with the values found by other researchers in other countries. Tybout (1990) applied a methodology suggested by Hall (1986) to the manufacturing sectors of four developing countries, Chile, Colombia, Turkey and Côte d'Ivoire. With the exception of Chile, he found substantial mark-up estimates of 0.31 for Colombia, 0.67 for Turkey and 0.24 for Côte d'Ivoire. Our results for total manufacturing give mark-ups above Colombia and Côte d'Ivoire, but below Turkey. Morrison (1992b), using a production theory-based approach, found mark-ups of between 0.11 and 0.23 for US manufacturing, and between 0.07 and 0.48 for Japanese manufacturing.

Table 11.3 Estimated inverse demand and conjectural elasticities and mark-ups (asymptotic t ratios in parentheses)

Industry	ε	θ	M
Total manufacturing	−1.0223	0.5190	0.513
	(−4.98)	(2.33)	
Food, drink and tobacco	−1.0795	0.0442	0.048
	(−4.40)	(0.15)	
Textiles / clothing	−0.4366	0.7057	0.308
	(−2.74)	(2.74)	
Wood and paper	−0.8969	0.4035	0.362
	(−9.98)	(0.68)	
Non-metals	−0.4501	0.1468	0.066
	(−4.03)	(2.93)	
Metals	−0.9110	0.9629	0.877
	(−5.66)	(4.46)	

Turning next to the sub-sectors, in two sub-sectors, namely food, and wood and paper, the industry level conjectural elasticity is not statistically significant from zero. The remaining three sub-sectors, namely textiles and clothing, non-metals, and metals, give θ parameters that are statistically significant. We can thus conclude that the degree of non-competitiveness is not significant in foodstuffs and wood and paper, but is significant in the remaining industries. The values of the conjectural elasticities vary across industries, ranging from 0.04 for foodstuffs, drink and tobacco to 0.96 for metals.

In all industries, the t values given in parentheses in Table 3 indicate that the inverse elasticity of demand (ε) is significant and that it always has the expected negative sign. Foodstuffs, drink and tobacco has the highest inverse elasticity of demand (-1.08), while textile and clothing has the lowest (-0.44).

Price–cost differentials are also listed in Table 11.3. The results show that price–cost differentials or degree of oligopoly power are highest for metals and lowest for foodstuffs. From equation (7) it is clear that the value of M, the degree of oligopoly power, is directly related to θ. As a result, although wood and paper has a lower conjectural elasticity value compared, for example, with textile and clothing, it nevertheless has a higher value of oligopoly power. Metals, which have the second lowest demand elasticity (or second largest inverse demand elasticity) but the highest conjectural elasticity also has the highest oligopoly power measure. Overall, price–cost margins appear higher in durables industries than in non-durables. This can be attributed to the nature of price controls, which have been an important feature of the economic policy environment in Zimbabwe. In some industries, like capital goods manufacturing, price controls were virtually non-existent, while in foodstuffs they were rigorously applied, by the government either setting the price of the goods, or approving the pricing formula.

The general result here is that, for Zimbabwean manufacturing, prices exceed costs by a margin between 4 per cent and 90 per cent across industries. By way of comparison we may refer to the detailed empirical work of Bennell (1990), carried out at a more disaggregated level. Bennell classifies individual industries by their percentage mark-ups, which range between 0 per cent and 75 per cent, with the majority of industries concentrated in the range 25–50 per cent. These include some industries in foodstuffs, textiles, wood and furniture and paper, iron and steel and metal products. Industries with higher price–cost margins, according to Bennell, include soft drinks and tobacco, footwear, chemicals, and glass and cement. Those with low price–cost margins include dairy, beer, wines, motor vehicles and transport equipment. Comparing with our results in Table 11.3, we find that like Bennell's our results include textiles and clothing, and wood and paper, within the range 25–50 per cent. Our results, however, exclude metals and metal products, and non-metals, from this range, placing the former in a higher range, the latter in a lower range together with food, drink and tobacco. The 0.51 mark-up we found for total manufacturing accords rather well with the results found by Bennell.

Market power and profitability

The existence of market power in Zimbabwean manufacturing raises a number of interesting questions. According to the structure–conduct–performance paradigm in industrial economics, there is a positive causal relationship between market power and profitability. Given that our study indicates evidence of market power in Zimbabwean manufacturing, we should expect firms to be highly profitable. Second, we should expect new firms to enter manufacturing and by competition erode the profits. However, Bennell regressed mark-ups on CR4, advertising expenditure (to capture barriers to entry), and the percentage increase in a particular industry 1985–86 (to capture the state of the market in each industry), and found no relationship between market power and profitability. He attributed this result to the impact of government price controls. Price controls were one of the main pillars of industrial policy in Zimbabwe, but they do not offer a full explanation, since they were not equally effective for, nor fully applied to, all type of goods, and moreover the base used to calculate the profit margin was often vague.[1]

Hall (1986, 1987, 1988, and 1990) has pointed out that excess capacity and returns to scale will counteract profitability from market power, implying that profits will approximate zero even with mark-ups. The argument of Hall is basically that, in industries with market power, fixed costs, especially if related to capital, are sufficient to keep equilibrium pure profits close to zero for potential entrants while the incumbents retain market power. In earlier work (Mlambo, 1993: chapter 3) we reported capacity utilisation measures that suggest the existence of excess capacity in total manufacturing, and a majority of the sub-sectors. The measure of capacity utilisation we used assumed quasi-fixity of capital, implying that fixed costs are largely traceable to capital in Zimbabwe manufacturing. The fact that we found excess capacity suggests that, for the incumbents, output can be increased without a large accompanying increase in marginal cost. We can thus conclude that excess capacity partly explains the joint occurrence of market power and low profitability found by Bennell, and serves as a threat to potential entrants. It is, however just part of the explanation, given that some industries, like textiles and clothing, and wood and paper, show capacity utilisation measures that for some observations exceed unity. For these we turn to the explanation of returns to scale.

Hall (1988) and Morrison (1992b) have argued that the profitability implied by mark-ups arises from potential returns to scale. The issue we are interested in here is whether there is any evidence of increasing returns to scale in Zimbabwean manufacturing. We shall utilise the returns to scale (RTS) measure suggested by Caves et al. (1981). They define RTS for a variable cost function as:

$$RTS = \frac{1 - \partial \ln C_v / \partial \ln K}{\partial \ln C_v / \partial \ln Y} \qquad (17)$$

Table 11.4 Scale economies in Zimbabwean manufacturing: sample averages (standard errors in parentheses)

Industry	ECY	ECK	RTS
Total manufacturing	0.4326	0.2896	1.667
	(0.042)	(0.058)	(0.287)
Food, drink and tobacco	0.6324	0.0517	1.743
	(0.171)	(0.401)	(0.977)
Textiles and clothing	0.3763	0.4379	1.5923
	(0.064)	(0.298)	(0.917)
Wood and paper	0.6264	0.0428	1.5011
	(0.058)	(0.373)	(0.507)
Non-metals	0.5608	0.2989	1.4279
	(0.133)	(0.597)	(1.165)
Metals	0.0989	0.7547	2.504
	(0.034)	(0.508)	(1.458)

Note: $ECY = \partial \ln C_v / \partial \ln Y$; $ECK = \partial \ln C_v / \partial \ln K$.

In Table 11.4 we report sample average returns to scale for aggregate manufacturing and the sub-sectors. Although the standard errors of some of these returns to scale indices are large, they nevertheless give an indication of the magnitude of returns to scale. For total manufacturing and the sub-sectors under consideration the returns to scale index is above unity, indicating increasing returns to scale. In metals we found substantial mark-ups, which as can be seen in Table 11.4 suggest substantial returns to scale. Thus for Zimbabwean manufacturing a case can be made for the conclusion by Hall (1988) and Morrison (1992b) that returns to scale attenuate profitability.

To conclude this section, we have, within a short-run equilibrium framework estimated market power in Zimbabwean manufacturing. Our results suggest that Zimbabwean manufacturing firms exert substantial oligopoly power. Using earlier results about capacity utilisation and new ones generated in this chapter, we have concluded that there are grounds for accepting Hall's (1988) hypothesis that mark-ups and excess capacity and returns to scale offset each other in generating profits. In the next sub-section we will consider the effect of market structure on productivity growth measurement.

Market structure and productivity growth

In industrial organisation literature, market structure is often considered, through its effect on the income and cost structure of the firm, to have a significant effect on investment in technology. The impact of market power on technological progress was first discussed by Schumpeter (1960), who argued that monopolistic firms were better suited to promote technological progress. According to Schumpeter, firms innovate in order to earn higher profits, but innovation is risky and costly. Firms will have no incentive to undertake costly and risky innovation unless there is a prospect of at least some market power. On the other hand monopolistic firms have at their disposal a pool of funds for this kind of investment.

In opposition to the Schumpetarian proposition, is the argument that the pressure on profits in competitive markets induces firms to innovate faster. The monopolistic firm is insulated from such pressures because it already earns supernormal profits in the pre-innovation period. However, when the argument is applied to oligopolistic markets, the arguments are less clear-cut. Firms operating in oligopolistic markets face a threat from potential entrants, and thus may have a greater incentive to innovate in order to maintain their market share.

The issue is, however, really an empirical one, and of late the role of price–cost mark-ups in explaining observed slowdown in total factor productivity growth has received much attention from researchers in the field. Denny *et al.* (1981) used a long-run equilibrium framework for Canadian telecommunication carriers, and found that about one-fifth of growth in productivity could be explained by the presence of market power. Hall (1988), after revaluing output at marginal cost, concluded that some of the observed decline in productivity growth in US manufacturing can be attributed to the existence of price–cost margins. His results were corroborated by Domovitz *et al.* (1986 and 1988), who extended and refined the Hall methodology. For developing countries, Tybout applied the refined Hall methodology and found that total factor productivity growth improves slightly with the incorporation of price–cost margins. Morrison and Diewert (1990) and Morrison (1992a), working within a short-run equilibrium framework, also conclude that for the United States, Canada and Japan traditional productivity methods which ignore market power underestimate productivity growth (see also Westbrook and Tybout 1993).

We have adjusted the traditional productivity growth measurement for price–cost mark-ups within the framework suggested by Hall. Under perfect competition and instantaneous adjustment productivity growth is defined as:

$$\varepsilon_{Yt} = \frac{\dot{Y}}{Y} - \sum_i S_i \left(\frac{\dot{v}_i}{v_i}\right) = \frac{\dot{c}}{c} - \sum_i S_i \left(\frac{\dot{P}_i}{P_i}\right) = -\varepsilon_{Ct} \qquad (18)$$

where $S_i = w_i V_i / P_Q Y$ and $s_i = w_i V_i / C$. Hence the equality of the primal and the dual rate of productivity growth is given by the assumption that $P_Q Y = C$ (or $P_Q = MC$). In previous work (Mlambo 1993) we considered a case where the quasi-fixity of some inputs violates the output price marginal cost equality. Another reason for $P_Q \neq MC$ is the existence of market power. To correct for market power, Morrison (1992a) suggests, all we need to do is adjust the demand side as follows. Suppose the firm operating in a non-competitive industry faces a downward-sloping demand curve represented by the inverse demand function $P_Q = D^{-1}(Y)$. The first-order conditions for profit maximisation will be given by $P_i = P_Q(1 + \varepsilon)\partial F/\partial V_i$, where as before ε is the inverse price elasticity of demand. Given that price–cost margins are positive, TFP growth should be calculated as:

$$\varepsilon_{YT}^M = \frac{\dot{Y}}{Y} - (1 + \varepsilon)\sum_i S_i \frac{\dot{V}_i}{V_i} \qquad (19)$$

In the light of our definitions of S_i and s_i and that $1 + \varepsilon = C/P_Q Y$, implying that $S_i = s_i(1 + \varepsilon)$, we can rewrite (19) as:

$$\varepsilon_{Yt}^M = -\varepsilon_{Ct} = \varepsilon_{Yt} - \varepsilon\sum_i S_i \frac{\dot{V}_i}{V_i} \qquad (20)$$

From equation (18), once a reliable measure of market power is known, TFP growth adjusted for mark-ups can be measured, with the error bias represented by $\varepsilon\sum_i S_i(V_i/V_i)$ (see Morrison 1992a). In the next sub-section we discuss for Zimbabwean manufacturing the effect of incorporating market power on measured productivity growth.

Mark-ups and productivity estimates for Zimbabwean manufacturing

To facilitate discussion of the role of price–cost margins in productivity measurement we have used equations (13) and (20) to decompose TFP growth into three components, technical change, returns to scale effect, and price–cost margins.

The pattern of productivity growth and its decomposition for total manufacturing are given in Table 11.5. The table shows that in the 1980s there was a tendency for productivity growth to decline slightly. TFP growth between 1980 and 1987 was 2.3 per cent, compared with 2.7 per cent for the period 1965–79. Most TFP growth in the earlier period occurred between 1965 and 1973, before the energy crisis and the intensification of the war of liberation. The decline in productivity growth therefore began in the mid-1970s.

Looking at column 4 of Table 11.5 we see that despite our feeling that Zimbabwean manufacturing is very concentrated, price–cost margins do not actually explain more than quite a minor share of what is registered as total factor productivity. Presumably this can be taken to imply that the degree of oligopolistic power over the price–cost margin has been fairly stable. It is increasing degrees of monopolisation that would give high figures for this factor. We also note that the returns to scale effect has played a fairly subordinate role and that most of what is registered as productivity growth is

Table 11.5 Decomposing TFP growth: total manufacturing (%)

Period	Technical change effect	Returns to scale effect	Price–cost margins	TFP growth
1965–87	2.406	0.0478	0.0636	2.52
1965–73	3.258	0.2068	0.2302	3.69
1974–79	1.410	−0.214	−0.162	1.03
1980–87	2.194	0.0656	0.0458	2.31
1965–79	2.519	0.0383	0.0730	2.70

thus actual technical change – or productivity increase in the pure sense of the word. This conclusion appears to hold firm for each of the sub-periods. Note that during the period 1974–79, which was the last period of UDI, when the regime was squeezed by the oil embargo and by domestic and international pressure, the price–cost margin effect was actually negative. Presumably this can be attributed to the effect of rather harsh price controls during the period. During this period of slow growth the returns to scale effect was also negative and technical progress slow, giving low overall figures for TPF.

In Table 11.6 we report the results for various industries and note that as concerns the observed TPF growth the differences are fairly minor. The relative contributions of technical change, returns to scale and price–cost margins, however, vary between branches. Price–cost margins play a really important role only in the metal industry, which is hardly surprising, given that we have identified it as the industry in which the degree of market concentration or oligopoly power was highest, see Table 11.3. On the other hand, we find that in foodstuffs and in non-metals, which according to Table 11.3 had the lowest degree of oligopoly, the price–cost margin factor is practically negligible in explaining the observed total factor productivity. For an industry such as wood and paper the situation is intermediate, with some influence from cost–price margins and also a rather strong returns to scale effect, leaving rather little to be explained by pure technical progress.

Table 11.6 Decomposing TFP growth, various industries, 1965–87 (%)

Industrial sector	Technical change effect	Returns to scale effect	Price–cost margin effect	TFP growth
Food, drink and tobacco	1.56	0.13	−0.05	1.7
Textiles and clothing	2.70	0.49	−0.70	2.5
Wood and paper	0.64	0.74	0.66	2.0
Non-metal	1.60	−0.052	0.08	1.6
Metals	0.14	0.0154	2.40	2.5

The results for the various sub-periods for each sub-sector are not reported but are available on request. In general they confirm the procyclical pattern found for total manufacturing, with very reduced total factor productivity growth for the period 1974–79 in all sectors and rather low productivity growth in all sectors except foodstuffs for the 1980s.

CONCLUSION

In this chapter we have calculated price–cost mark-ups for Zimbabwean manufacturing using a short-run equilibrium model. The results showed that mark-ups exist and are significant for total manufacturing, metals, wood and paper, and textiles and clothing. Mark-ups are low for foodstuffs and non-metals. Returns to scale were also calculated for each industry, and the results indicated increasing returns to scale in all industries under consideration.

For each industry, we decomposed TFP growth into the technical change effect, the returns to scale effect and the price–cost margin effect. We found that for foodstuffs and non-metals the effect of price–cost margins is weak but important in metals, showing that productivity increases in this sector are highly illusory, since they are largely the effect of increasing market concentration. In wood and paper we found returns to scale to be more important. For total manufacturing, price–cost margins are cyclical, having a positive effect in the good years and a negative effect in the bad years when the cutting edge of competition sharpens. TFP growth shows a slight decline for total manufacturing, textiles and clothing, wood and paper, and metals. For foodstuffs, and non-metals, TFP shows a tendency to increase slightly over time.

NOTES

The views expressed here should not be ascribed to the African Development Bank. The authors would like to thank participants at the Asia-Pacific Economic Modelling Conference, Sydney, 24 August 1994, especially the Symposia on Productivity Growth, for comments, as well as Lennart Hjalmarsson and Arne Bigsten for comments on an earlier version of the chapter.

1 A World Bank (1987) mission relates this anecdote about a manager who, asked what his margin was, replied, 'My margin is twenty per cent.' When asked, 'Twenty per cent of what?' he answered, 'Twenty per cent of everything that I can put in.'

REFERENCES

Alderman, H. (1984) 'Attributing Technological Bias to Public Goods', *Journal of Development Economics*, 14 (3): 375–93.

Appelbaum, E. (1982) 'The Estimation of the Degree of Oligopoly Power', *Journal of Econometrics*, 19: 287–99.

Barten, A.P. (1969) 'Maximum Likelihood Estimation of a Complete System of Demand Equations', *European Economic Review*, 1: 7–73.

Bennell, P. (1990) 'Market Power and Markups: Manufacturing Industry in Zimbabwe, 1970–86', Working Papers in Economics, Department of Economics, University of Zimbabwe.

Bernstein, J.I. and Mohnen, P. (1992) 'Price–Cost Margins, Exports and Productivity Growth: with an Application to Canadian Industries', *Canadian Journal of Economics*, XIV (3): 638–59.

Caves, D.W., Christensen, L.R and Swanson, J. (1981) 'Productivity Growth, Scale Economies, and Capacity Utilisation in US Railroads 1955–74', *American Economic Review*, 71 (5): 994–1002.

Christensen, L.R. and Greene, W.H. (1976) 'Economies of Scale in US Electric Power Generation', *Journal of Political Economy*, 84: 655–76.

Cowling, K. and Waterson, M. (1976) 'Price–Cost Margins and Market Structure', *Economica*, 43: 267–74.

Denny, M., Fuss, M. and Waverman, L. (1981) 'The Measurement and Interpretation of Total Factor Productivity in Regulated Industries, with an Application to Canadian Telecommunications', in T.G. Cowing and R.E. Stevenson (eds), *Productivity Measurement in Regulated Industries*, New York: Academic Press.

Domowitz, I., Hubbard, R.G. and Petersen, B.C. (1986) 'Business Cycles and the Relationship between Concentration and Price–Cost Margins', *Rand Journal of Economics*, 17 (1): 1–17.

Domowitz, I., Hubbard, R.G. and Petersen, B.C. (1988) 'Market Structure and Cyclical Fluctuations in US Manufacturing', *Review of Economics and Statistics*, LXX: 55–66.

Green, R.H. and Kadhani, X. (1986) 'Zimbabwe: Transition to Economic Crises 1981–83: Retrospect and Prospects', *World Development*, 14 (8): 1059–83.

Hall, R.E (1986) 'Market Structure and Macroeconomic Fluctuations', *National Bureau of Economic Research Reprint*, 845: 285–322.

Hall, R.E. (1987) 'Productivity and the Business Cycle', *Carnegie-Rochester Conference on Public Policy*, 27: 421–44.

Hall, R.E. (1988) 'The Relation between Price and Marginal Cost in US Industry', *Journal of Political Economy*, 96 (5): 921–47.

Hall, R.E. (1990) 'Invariance Properties of Solow's Productivity Residual', in P. Diamond (ed.) *Growth/Productivity/Employment*, Cambridge MA: MIT Press.

Jansen, D.J. (1982) 'Zimbabwe: Government Policy and the Manufacturing Sector', Larkspur CA.

Kmenta, J. and Gilbert. R. (1968) 'Small Sample Properties of Alternative Estimators of Seemingly Unrelated Regressions', *Journal of the American Statistical Association*, 63: 1180–200.

Mlambo, K. (1993) 'Total Factor Productivity Growth: an Empirical Analysis of Zimbabwe's Manufacturing Sector based on Factor Demand Modelling', Ph.D. thesis, Göteborg University.

Morrison, C.J. (1986) 'Productivity Measurements with Non-static Expectations and Varying Capacity Utilization: an Integrated Approach', *Journal of Econometrics*, 3 (1–2): 51–74.

Morrison, C.J. (1992a) 'Unravelling the Productivity Growth Slowdown in the United States, Canada, and Japan: the Effects of Subequilibrium, Scale Economies and Markups', *Review of Economics and Statistics*, LXXIV (3): 381–93.

Morrison, C.J. (1992b) 'Markups in US and Japanese Manufacturing: a Short-run Econometrics Analysis', *Journal of Business and Economic Statistics*, 10 (1): 51–63.

Morrison, C.J. and Diewert, W.E. (1988) 'Productivity Growth and Changes in the Terms of Trade in Japan and the US', Department of Economics Discussion Paper 88–09, University of British Columbia.

Morrison, C.J. and Diewert, W.E. (1990) 'New Techniques in the Measurement of Multifactor Productivity', *Journal of Productivity Analysis*, 1: 267–85.

Riddell, R.C. (1990) 'Zimbabwe' in R.C. Riddell (ed.) *Manufacturing Africa: Performance and Prospects for sub-Saharan Africa*, London: ODI.

Schumpeter, J.A. (1960) *Capitalism, Socialism, and Democracy*, New York: Harper & Row.

Shaaeldin, E. (1989) 'Sources of Industrial Growth in Kenya, Tanzania, Zambia and Zimbabwe: some Estimates', *African Development Review*, 1 (1): 21–39.

Tybout, J.R. (1990) 'Researching the Trade/Productivity Link: New Directions', paper prepared for the World Bank research project on Industrial Competition, Productive Efficiency, and their Relation to Trade Regimes, RPO 647–46, 3 August.

UNIDO (1984) *Study of the Manufacturing Sector of Zimbabwe*, Vienna: United Nations Industrial Development Organisation.

Westbrook, M.D. and Tybout, J.R. (1993) 'Estimating Returns to Scale with Large, Imperfect Panels: an Application to Chilean Manufacturing Industries', *World Bank Economic Review*, 7 (1): 85–112.

World Bank (1987) 'Zimbabwe: an Industrial Sector Memorandum', Washington DC: World Bank.

12

REGIONALISM IN AFRICAN DEVELOPMENT

Peter Kimuyu

The world economy seems to be evolving towards increased globalisation at the same time as regionalism is being emphasised. The two trends have not necessarily been self-reinforcing. For example, expansion of the European Union to encompass countries from Eastern Europe has caused apprehension not only in Africa, where the loss of concessions is feared, but also in the richer American and Asian regions. The advent of the North American Free Trade Area sent many countries in North, Central and South America, traditionally dependent on the American market, scrambling for preferential trade status with the United States in a bid to prevent loss of market shares and investments. It is generally acknowledged that the decision of the ASEAN countries to deepen their collaboration with North America was a direct response to the increasing economic power of China, and the possible loss of markets to emerging economies in other parts of the world. In the light of the goals of the newly created World Trade Organisation, empowered to ensure the removal of impediments to free trade, the current proliferation of trade blocs is puzzling. There is concern that the potential gains from open trade and multilateralism, as envisaged in the Uruguay Round, could be lost (Bhagwati 1997, Nagaoka 1994, Gibb and Machalak 1994).

The fear of African countries is that, while they are too weak to resist external pressure for concessions, they are equally unable to exert much influence on the emerging configurations (Collier and Gunning 1995). These weaknesses are reflected in the poor record of many of Africa's regional co-operation projects during the past decades. The political aspects of regional co-operation played a far more important role than the purely economic ones, with integration seen as a condition of the total liberation of the continent. However, in recent gatherings, countries have emphasised economic co-operation as the basis of their individual and collective prosperity. It is now argued that only economic strength can lend credence to political integration. This change of attitude, coupled with rapidly changing domestic economic structures, may provide the continent a better bargaining position in its efforts to derive more benefit from the expanding global economy. In 1994 the Abuja Treaty setting up the African Economic Community was formally ratified, and the Community itself was declared ahead of schedule in 1997.

The purpose of this chapter is to put African efforts at regional co-operation in the perspective of the rapidly changing global economy. The chapter revisits the case for integration, reviews the integration experience in Africa, and suggests a number of ways in which efforts could be made more productive under African conditions.

THE CASE FOR INTEGRATION

Regional integration has been debated extensively in the economic literature. It is above all, said to create scale economies that enable countries to embark on large infrastructural and industrial projects, and to undertake profit-able product differentiation. Co-operation also reduces the costs of economic restructuring and increases investment opportunities by allowing inter-ndustry specialisation and trade (Asante 1995, Krugman and Venables 1996, Robinson 1988). Furthermore, integration enables the transfer of technology through the exchange of goods, services and factors of production. This, in turn, creates opportunities for the acquisition and mastery of production skills, the diversification of economic activities driven by pursuit of rents resulting from specialisation, and the expansion and strengthening of the regional industrial base. All these factors lead to more efficient use of resources, thereby increasing regional welfare. In terms of policy, regional arrangements are sometimes seen as agencies of restraint on domestic govern-ments. They force them to undertake sometimes unpopular, but necessary, decisions, thereby enhancing credibility. This in turn attracts both domestic and foreign investors.

Among the goals of regional integration is trade creation. However, on its own, regional co-operation is not a guarantee of it, especially since customs unions are sometimes used to protect inefficient industries. As indicated by theory, customs unions lead to trade creation when imports from high-cost sources are substitutable for low-cost partner sources and to trade diversion when imports from low-cost world sources are substituted for high-cost union sources. While trade creation has welfare-increasing production and consumption effects, trade diversion reduces welfare. In this 'static model', benefits result when trade creation exceeds trade diversion. However, since by definition trade is restricted in a customs union, the most favourable outcome would still be only 'second best' (Robinson 1988).

It should be noted, however, that the neoclassical argument assumes perfect competition, full employment, constant returns to scale, perfect internal mobility of factors of production and equality of social and private costs among member states. For many African countries these assumptions are unrealistic. Benefits have tended to accrue to the well-off countries, which then become regional centres and thus more attractive to investors *vis-à-vis* regional partners (Mullei 1987). Moreover, since trade taxes are the most popular form of taxation in Africa, the revenue impact of tariff reductions can be large.

Some attention has recently been paid to the 'contemporary school' which sees integration as an alternative development strategy, providing a basis for industrialisation (see Hussein 1997). Here regional co-operation is seen as the best way of reducing structural obstacles to development, since it enables nations to acquire improved technologies and to reach superior technology niches. Emphasis is put on manufacturing, where goods demanded by an expanding world market are made. The demand for raw commodities, which dominate African production, is on the other hand inelastic and dependence on it implies a 'secular' decline in growth and welfare. Industrialisation is thus seen as critical for economic growth and development and countries benefit most when it is undertaken regionally.

Regional co-operation also helps developing countries withstand external exposure, and to break away from their traditional dependence on the former colonial powers. This, it is argued, is bound to increase regional self-reliance, as well as bargaining power in the global market (Anyang' Nyong' 1993, Asante 1995). Since regional co-operation is best guaranteed by politically strong regional institutions, with sufficient powers to discipline errant members, it is suggested that the surrender of national autonomy and political power to the regional organisations is a viable proposition.

Recent contributions to the growth literature have also underscored the benefits of regional integration. Elbadawi and Ndulu (1996) have argued, for instance, that deepening regional integration makes it possible to shift national economies to levels where they can begin to strategically complement each other in world trade. Regions are able to suck in enough investment and to bring about an adequate level of technological transfer, thereby creating the dynamics necessary for the development of manufacturing (Motta and Norman 1996). Furthermore, by permitting policy co-ordination and harmonisation, especially in the areas of transport, energy and fiscal arrangements, integration is bound to fuel growth, the so-called dynamic effect of integration. Additionally, regional investments generate externalities that have positive effects on human and physical capital development, increasing the potential for further growth. By mitigating marginalisation, integration is critical in sustaining long-term growth and development (Laporte 1995). It has also been argued that regional co-operation encourages competition between countries, especially in the area of liberalisation, leading to general policy improvement.

In a continent which has experienced serious cross-border conflicts and civil war, regional co-operation can be an important stabilisation mechanism. The role of integration in the process of constructing foundations for peace is itself important in creating the environment necessary for institution building and for attracting foreign and domestic investment. Rwanda's application to join the East African Community could be seen in this light.

CONSTRAINTS ON AFRICAN REGIONAL CO-OPERATION

In spite of many attempts at integration, there have been few instances of outright success in Africa. Lack of resources and institutions to maintain member discipline have led to a general lack of commitment (Oyejide 1997). The homogeneity of the sub-Saharan African economies has also been identified as a serious constraint on intra-regional trade (Elbadawi and Ndulu 1996). Many of the economies depend on primary products for exports, while levels of industrialisation are low throughout the region. This has restricted the dynamics of comparative advantage, making competition and learning by doing difficult to realise. Parallels are often drawn with Asian countries, where proximity to Japan has enabled vast opportunities for learning and copying while at the same time benefiting from Japanese investment and technology. With the end of apartheid South Africa may provide the 'leadership', investment, and competition necessary for rapid growth in the region. Still, the recent trade disagreements between Zimbabwe and South Africa suggest that the road ahead may not be smooth (Masaya and Mamhare 1993).

For quite a long time, protectionist policies were strong features of African economic policies, with regionally based reciprocal discrimination leading to the redistribution of benefits between co-operating countries. But since some benefited more than others this also led to friction. Thus, even as countries sought regional co-operation, many others preserved strong economic and political ties with the former colonial powers. As a consequence, transport and communication networks are still oriented towards trade with the metropolitan countries, while inter-country trade remains poor. For example, intra-regional trade in ECOWAS was only 6 per cent of total trade at the beginning of the 1990s (Rwegasira 1997).

With regard to commitment, African countries have been unable to articulate minimum conditions for co-operation. Three important issues for success are often left unresolved: how much power to cede to the regional body, how to meet the human and financial resource commitments, and how to incorporate regionally adopted policies into national programmes. However, independent governments have been very reluctant to cede power to regional bodies over which they have little direct control. Thus policy-making institutions in the regional groupings have little power and hence little leverage on governments. They cannot impose sanctions for non-compliance or even enforce treaties and agreed policies. Furthermore, many regional bodies are seriously short of money and are thus slow to honour financial commitments, while the wish to give the staff of the secretariat a regional profile leads to overstaffing. Regional bodies thus tend to be top-heavy, with managers and chief executives appointed on political grounds rather than on those of demonstrated competence.

THE INTEGRATION RECORD

There has, over the years, been a proliferation of integration schemes in the different sub-regions. As early as 1958 a joint committee was established in Ghana to co-ordinate economic planning in Africa. In Ethiopia two years later the creation of a council for economic co-operation, which led to the formation of the United Nations Economic Commission for Africa (UNECA), was proposed. Thereafter, efforts were made to establish conventions on international transport, transit trade in landlocked countries, and a framework for commodity export pricing.

New opportunities for inter-state interactions accompanied the formation of the Organisation of Africa Unity (OAU) in 1963. Soon afterwards the ECA and OAU set up a committee on trade and development, drawing participation from fourteen independent member states, to deal with problems of customs and common markets, and to study and resolve constraints on intra-African trade. During an OAU heads of state meeting in Ethiopia in 1973 a declaration on economic independence, development and co-operation was adopted. It compelled member countries to establish procedures and mechanisms for co-ordinating trade policies in order to move the continent towards economic growth, via joint trade and development institutions, and the adoption of modern marketing techniques. Further, a 'Lagos Plan of Action' was drawn up in 1980 under which African governments committed themselves to pursuing collective self-reliance and the strengthening of existing groupings, as well as initiating new ones. The ultimate goal was the creation of an African Economic Community by the year 2000.

However, while there has been considerable official interest in regional co-operation the integration record has varied from region to region. In West Africa integration attempts antedate independence. The West African Customs Union was, for example, established as far back as 1956 by countries then comprising part of French West Africa, including Benin, Burkina Faso, Guinea, Côte d' Ivoire, Mauritania, Niger, Senegal and Mali. This union underwent major changes during the following decades, finally becoming the West African Economic Community in 1973.

Countries belonging to the Communauté Financière Africaine (CFA) franc zone have managed to pursue a more decidedly economic agenda. Unlike other schemes, CFA monetary co-operation was guaranteed by the French government, which backed the currency and preserved its parity with the French franc. This also implied the surrender of monetary policy independence by all zone countries, and an unprecedented degree of interference in money and other economic matters by France. The devaluation of the

CFA franc in early 1994 was, for instance, mainly due to French unwilling-ness to underwrite the balance of payments deficits that members countries were accumulating as a result of the overvaluation of the CFA franc in the 1970s and 1980s. Still, the monetary arrangement gave the region a broader basis for economic co-operation than in other parts of Africa. Economic pol-icy, including the financing of common transport and telecommunications projects, is better co-ordinated, while trade within the region is higher than in other parts of the continent. A regional *bourse* is being planned, with its operations located in Abidjan (African Development Bank 1997). Still, the prospective adoption of the euro as a common currency in the European Union and the resistance of Germany to continued support of the CFA franc by France when the new currency is finally adopted have created con-siderable anxiety among zone countries. This, however, also provides zone countries with the opportunity of going it alone under their own pre-mises.

The sixteen-member Economic Community of West African States (ECO-WAS) is an important grouping which includes French and English-speaking countries. Its goal is to promote greater commercial interaction, by eliminat-ing trade barriers, encouraging the adoption of a common industrial policy, and ensuring a fair distribution of benefits from economic integration. However, political uncertainties in West Africa, including civil war in Liberia and Sierra Leone, have tended to lower the effectiveness of the regional body. Paralysed for many years by political differences, ECOWAS has recently become more active, thanks to the end of autocratic regimes in the region, the economic turn-round in the 1990s and the successful co-ordination of Liberia's return to peace. Other changes in West Africa, such as reduced French influence, have also been favourable to regional integration efforts.

Integration attempts in Central Africa have been least cohesive. There are currently three main groupings: the first (the Central African Customs and Economic Union) consists of Cameroon, the Congo, Gabon, the Central Afri-can Republic and Chad, all of them former French colonies. The second group (the Economic Community of Countries in the Great Lakes) draws its mem-bers from countries formerly under Belgium: the Democratic Republic of the Congo, Burundi and Rwanda. The third group (the Economic Community of Central African States) incorporates Angola, Burundi, Cameroon, the Central African Republic, the Congo, Equatorial Guinea, Rwanda, São Tomé e Príncipe and the Democratic Republic of Congo.

In the more culturally homogeneous North African region co-operation has been mainly bilateral, with the Maghreb sub-region, consisting of Algeria, Libya, Morocco and Tunisia, being the main grouping. Attempts at setting up a preferential trade area for the region, with Algeria, Egypt, Libya, Morocco, Tunisia and Sudan, failed owing to political differences, and perhaps the wish on the part of individual countries, not to jeopardise the on-going efforts to establish favourable links with the European Union (Sekkat 1996).

With regard to the Horn of Africa, Hettne (1996) has argued that the weakening of previously powerful nation states has opened new avenues to greater regional co-operation. Notable among these are efforts to avert the environmental degradation caused by years of strife and adverse weather conditions (see Hansson in Chapter 16). An Intergovernmental Authority on Drought and Development (IGADD) with members including Djibouti, Ethiopia, Eritrea, Ethiopia, Somalia, Sudan, Kenya and Uganda was established in 1986. Though initially preoccupied with security issues, the body has been able to play an increasingly important role in regional economic affairs, with the emphasis on development, trade and conflict resolution.

The East African Community, PTA/COMESA and SADC

Regional co-operation in East Africa has a long tradition going back to the formation of a customs union in 1917. The region had a common currency board, common railways, harbours and air services. The education system was based on common curricula, and universities had a common admission policy. The East African Community (EAC) established in 1967 was once lauded as the best example of regional co-operation in Africa. It sought to promote balanced industrial development, through the harmonisation of incentives and tax systems. However, with regard to technical and financial services there was substantial concentration in Nairobi and Mombasa. This was said to give the two towns and Kenya as a whole an undue advantage in infrastructural development, industrialisation and job creation at the expense of Tanzania and Uganda (Hazlewood 1975). Political differences between governments made further co-operation impossible and the EAC was disbanded in 1977. However, the attraction of an East African market comprising close to 75 million people continued to be a strong argument for closer ties. Thus, a few years ago, regional leaders decided to resume co-operation, even though initially on a smaller scale. Below we dwell at some length on the East African experience, using it to illustrate the challenges of regional co-operation in Africa.

Though pressure for the re-establishment of the East African Community was already building up in the late 1980s, the Community did not resume work in earnest until 1996, when Kenya appointed a new Secretary General to the secretariat in Arusha, Tanzania. This marked the start of a whole range of activities. In the area of transport and communications the three countries plan to introduce a common policy on road utilisation, railways, inland water, maritime and air transport, posts and telecommunications and meteorology. Other innovations include the introduction of a standard East African identity card, making passports unnecessary within the region.

Currencies are convertible and there have been attempts to co-ordinate economic policy. In the area of combating crime, the countries now share information, helping to reduce car hi-jackings, arms smuggling and drug trafficking. The Attorneys General of the three countries have met to prepare the relevant legislation. Besides, bodies that survived the break-up of the first attempt, including the East African Development Bank, the Inter-university Council of East Africa and the East African School of Librarianship, have been strengthened. In the wake of its ferry disaster Tanzania has called for the mapping of Lake Victoria to ensure safe passage and funds are being solicited jointly for the purpose. Furthermore, all three countries have joined efforts to fight the rapidly spreading water hyacinth plants that are threatening marine life on the lake.

It can be argued that while co-operation was mainly driven by governments earlier, today's developments are pushed to a large extent by the private sector. To encourage regional investment, a free flow of capital is essential. It is thus suggested that citizens of the East African countries should buy shares from each other's stock exchanges. With this in mind, the latter are already co-operating with a view to creating a more formal method of collaboration. The more experienced Nairobi Stock Exchange has assisted in the setting up of the Kampala Stock Exchange, while similar contacts have been made with the Dar-es-Salaam Stock Exchange. In 1997 a memorandum of understanding was signed on the development of stock exchanges in East Africa.

Thus the renewal of East African co-operation is seen as capable of attracting investment, expanding tourism, and spurring trade and industrial development. Much has happened in East Africa to ensure convergence, including Uganda's return to more normal conditions, and the pursuit of similar economic policies in the region. However, it is close on twenty years since the end of the earlier co-operation, and there are many areas of concern still. Kenya remains much more industrialised than either Tanzania or Uganda. The two countries fear being overwhelmed by Kenyan firms. For example, though production in Uganda picked up in the 1990s, its taxes, especially on fuel, are much higher than in Kenya. Smuggling has resulted. On the other hand, the availability of food in Uganda has enabled reverse smuggling to Kenya. Closer co-operation in East Africa will have to be redefined to meets the demands of much changed regional dynamics.

The treaty setting up the Preferential Trade Area (PTA) for Eastern and Southern Africa was signed at the end of 1981 and came into force in September 1982. Two factors made its establishment especially important. First, the collapse of the East African Community, comprising Uganda, Kenya and Tanzania, with origins from the pre-independence years. Second, political and economic destabilisation by the Republic of South Africa demanded a united response. Third, it was hoped that closer co-operation would shield member countries from external shocks. By 1994 the PTA had been transformed into a Common Market of Eastern and Southern Africa (COMESA).

Its membership comprised a total of twenty-two states: Angola, Burundi, the Comoros, Djibouti, Eritrea, Ethiopia, Kenya, Lesotho, Madagascar, Malawi, Mauritius, Mozambique, Namibia, Rwanda, the Seychelles, Somali, Sudan, Swaziland, Tanzania, Uganda, Zambia and Zimbabwe. Support institutions included a secretariat in Lusaka, a PTA clearing house and a reinsurance company (ZEP-RE) in Harare, and a PTA development bank in Bujumbura.

The PTA members set themselves an ambitious agenda: to promote co-operation and integration in all fields of economic activity, notably in trade, customs, industry, transport, communications, agriculture, natural resources and monetary policy. They would pool resources, remove trade barriers, and encourage competition and competitiveness in the region.

The PTA countries, and later those of COMESA, were similar in terms of economic structure, level of development and the level of state participation in the economy. All countries are primary commodity producers, with those in southern Africa depending a great deal on mining while those farther north are mainly producers of agricultural goods. In terms of transport and communications infrastructure, the countries were not linked adequately. The similarities became a hindrance to trade and regional co-operation, as they provided little basis for complementarity (Manundu et al. 1995).

Another constraining factor was the severe shortage of foreign exchange due to external shocks and a poor export base. Strict foreign exchange controls meant that individual currencies were overvalued while related controls made trade difficult. In manufactures, for example, PTA members sought to prevent multinationals in the region from capturing markets from 'indigenous' firms. Tariff structures and other rules relating to share ownership were thus introduced. However, countries such as Kenya and Zimbabwe, which had relatively large manufacturing sectors, including multinationals, felt unduly punished for their earlier success at attracting foreign investment and opposed the arrangements.

To create a dynamic climate for trade, the countries needed to co-ordinate their economic policies, in the areas of fiscal, monetary and industrial policy. In a bid to increase monetary policy harmonisation in the region, the use of market-determined exchange rates was advocated, while members were encouraged to reduce their fiscal deficits and to exercise restraint in their credit policies. Furthermore, there was emphasis on the need to co-ordinate policies in the areas of industry, energy and the environment as well as in efforts to ensure food security. During its first decade PTA/COMESA adopted a harmonised commodity description and coding system that would provide a basis for the development and eventual establishment of a common external tariff. Tariffs were also reduced by up to 70 per cent in the region during this period. With a view to matching buyers and sellers, and to promote trade, the PTA headquarters undertook surveys of the supply and demand for products from the region. In the early 1980s PTA trade was dominated by Kenya and Zimbabwe, with 43.3 and 18.7 per cent, respectively. All in all, five countries accounted for 85 per cent of total intra-regional exports. In the first decade PTA trade grew by 1.2 per cent per year, that is, less than average regional GDP growth. However, the traditional trade patterns were not changed much. Thus almost half of Kenya's intra-PTA trade went to Uganda while most of Zimbabwe's went to Zambia.

However, regional co-operation in the COMESA region was complicated by the role of post-apartheid South Africa. The Southern Africa Development Co-ordination Committee (SADCC), founded in 1980 to galvanise the 'front-line states' in their struggle against apartheid South Africa, was broadened to include the former enemy itself. Neighbouring countries preferred co-operation within a framework that included South Africa, the regional economic power, to taking part in one without it. Treaties to upgrade inter-action between member countries were signed, an overriding concern being to ensure that socio-economic differences among countries did not lead to political instability. Co-operation was established in a vast number of areas (see Harvey and Hudson 1993, Weeks 1996) and the grouping was renamed the Southern Africa Development Community (SADC). As discussed by Baldwin (1993) in his domino theory of regionalism, a configuration such as that of SADC, with natural congruence and an economic motor, is bound to generate considerable interest from within the region as a growing number of countries seek to become members. Mauritius applied to join SADC and was accepted in 1995, while more recently the Democratic Republic of the Congo and Seychelles have been admitted as new members. With the entry of the Democratic Republic of the Congo, SADC has one of the world's highest concentrations of non-oil mineral producers, and thus some serious global leverage. Countries which continue to belong to both organisations such as Tanzania are seriously burdened by the membership fees (see Mndeme-Musonda et al. 1997).

With the expansion of economic co-operation centring on SADC in southern Africa, the COMESA institutions, such as the secretariat in Lusaka and clearing house in Harare, seem to have been overtaken by events. To the north, the rejuvenated East African Community is going to demand much attention from the participating countries. COMESA may remain largely an article of faith.

CONCLUSION

In Africa's search for integration the political rationale has been stronger than the economic. Many regional groupings were created in the first instance more as an expression of African solidarity than of economic integration and market development. This meant that some groups became too big and unwieldy. But even in seemingly better integrated regions, trade between partners has grown very little, while the former colonial rulers are still the main trading partners, and raw materials the main exports. Failure to expand economic co-operation was partly due to the economic crisis that confronted most African economies from the early 1970s. Countries were engulfed in economic reform, and the sense of siege prevented them from looking at economic reforms from a regional perspective. Thus, in spite of the proliferation of regional organisations, Africa's economic policies remain poorly co-ordinated.

In retrospect, while much was expected of the regional groupings, the secretariats supposed to run them were short of resources. Even more important, they lacked the power to enforce commonly agreed policies. Trade policy is a good example. In many countries an inadequate structure for income taxation made trade taxes the most important source of government revenue. Thus agreements to reduce tariffs at the regional level have been difficult to implement in individual countries. Similarly, while a number of joint projects have been suggested, notably in the area of transport, domestic bureaucracies seem able to delay implementation indefinitely.

The past few years have seen a resurgence of interest in regional co-operation in Africa, with the emphasis on trade issues. This has helped to remove earlier barriers, mostly of a political nature, that had split co-operation along received geographical and linguistic lines (for example, Francophone or Anglophone Africa). In West Africa, Guinea-Bissau has joined the CFA franc zone, while Mozambique is building close relations with its anglophone neighbours and the Democratic Republic of the Congo is doing likewise. The East African Community seems set for a more serious integration effort, with collaboration in most areas, including economic policy co-ordination and measures to ensure joint security. Following a decade of adjustment, countries are pursuing relatively similar policies. This may make them more willing to co-ordinate policies regionally. An important task will be to develop strategies that will help incorporate African countries profitably into the global economy.

REFERENCES

African Development Bank (1997) *African Development Report*, Oxford: Oxford University Press.

Anyang' Nyong', P. (1993) 'Regional Integration, Security and Development in Africa' in O. Obasanjo and F.G.N. Mosha (eds) *Africa Rise to Challenge,* Lagos: Alf.

Asante, B.S.K. (1995) 'The Need for Regional Integration: a Challenge for Africa', *Review of African Political Economy*, 22 (66): 573–7.

Baldwin, R. (1993) *A Domino Theory of Regionalism*, Discussion Paper 857, London: Centre for Economic Policy Research.

Bhagwati, J. (1997) 'The Watering of Trade', *Journal of International Economics*, 42: 239–41.

Collier, P. and Gunning, J.W. (1995) 'Trade Policy and Regional Integration: Implications for the Relations between Europe and Africa', *World Economy*, 18 (3): 387–410.

Elbadawi, I.A. and Ndulu, B.J. (1996) 'Long-term Development and Sustainable Growth in sub-Saharan Africa', in M. Lundahl and B. Ndulu (eds) *New Directions in Development Economics: Growth, Environmental Concerns in the 1990s*, London and New York: Routledge.

Gibb, R. and Michalak, W. (eds) (1994) *Continental Blocs: The Growth of Regionalism in the World Economy*, Chichester, New York and Toronto: Wiley.

Harvey, C. and Hudson, D. (1993) 'Post-apartheid Regional Financial and Monetary Co-operation', in B. Odèn (ed.) *Southern Africa after Apartheid: Regional Integration and External Resources*, Uppsala: Scandinavian Institute of African Studies.

Hazlewood, A. (1975) *Economic Integration: The East African Experience*, Nairobi and Oxford: Oxford University Press.

Hettne, B. (1996) 'Developmental Regionalism', in M. Lundahl and B. Ndulu (eds) *New Directions in Development Economics: Growth, Environmental Concerns in the 1990s*, London and New York: Routledge.

Hussein, N.M. (1997) 'Africa's External Sector and Economic Growth – Possible Areas for Development Co-operation', in H. Kifle, A.O. Olukoshi and L. Wohlgemuth (eds) *A New Partnership for African Development*, Uppsala: Nordiska Afrikainstitutet.

Krugman, P. and Venables, A.J. (1996) 'Integration, Specialization, and Adjustment', *European Economic Review*, 40 (3–5): 959–68.

Laporte, G. (1995) 'Regional Co-operation and Integration in Africa: Agenda for Action at the National Level', paper presented at the first Open Forum on Regional Co-operation and Integration Today, Maastricht.

Manundu, M., Mwaura, Z.N., Nganda, B.M., Ogai, J.S. and Kimote, J.M. (1995) *Kenya's Trade with COMESA Countries: Strategies and Policy Options*, Nairobi: Office of the Vice-President and Ministry of Planning and National Development.

Masaya, T.R. and Mamhare, G.M. (1993) 'Zimbabwe – Experience with Regional Integration', *International Review of Administrative Sciences*, 59 (4): 663–70.

Mndeme-Musonda, F., Mjema, G. and Danielson, A. (1997) 'Tanzania 1997. The Urge to Merge: the Revival of East African Cooperation', Macroeconomic Report 7, Stockholm: Swedish International Development Co-operation Agency (Sida).

Motta, M. and Norman, G. (1996) 'Does Economic Integration cause Foreign Direct Investment?', *International Economic Review*, 37 (4): 757–83.

Mullei, A.K. (1987) 'Determinants of the Effects of Economic Integration among African Countries', *Eastern Africa Economic Review*, 3 (1): 21–5.

Nagaoka, S. (1994) 'Does Regional Integration promote Global Liberalization? A Case of Endogenous Protection', *Journal of the Japanese and International Economies*, 8 (4): 551–64.

Oyejide, T.A. (1997) 'Trade Policy and Regional Integration in the Development Context: Emerging Patterns, Issues and Lessons for sub-Saharan Africa', paper prepared for the plenary session of the May workshop of the African Economic Research Consortium, Nairobi.

Robinson, P. (1988) 'The Conceptual Framework of Regional Integration Analysis and Appropriate Technology', proceedings of the Workshop on Regional Integration and Co-operation in sub-Saharan Africa, Abidjan.

Rwegasira, D. (1997) 'Economic Co-operation and Integration in Africa – Experiences, Challenges, and Opportunities', in H. Kifle, A.O. Olukoshi and L. Wohlgemuth (eds) *A New Partnership for African Development*, Uppsala: Nordiska Afrikainstitutet.

Sekkat, K. (1996) 'Regional Integration among the Maghreb Countries and Free Trade with the European Union: a Challenge for both Sides of the Mediterranean', *Journal of Economic Integration*, 11 (4): 421–52.

Weeks, J. (1996) 'Regional Co-operation and Southern African Development', *Journal of Southern African Studies*, 22 (1): 99–117.

13

TRANSFORMING ECONOMIC AND POLITICAL STRUCTURES FOR GROWTH

The Zambian experience

Manenga Ndulo

Zambia's recent economic and political experience has tended to epitomise those of sub-Saharan Africa: external shocks, the reintroduction of multi-party politics, debt escalation, etc. Combined, these factors have made it immensely difficult for the country to establish credibility. It is landlocked, with a relatively small but rapidly expanding population. Though it has grown nationally by 3.2 per cent per annum since 1965, urban population growth has been faster. Today the majority of Zambians live in urban areas, making it one of the most urbanised countries in Africa. Income distribution is perversely and highly skewed and poverty levels have been rising in the past decades. It has been estimated that close to 70 per cent of the population live below the poverty line (Sheshamani 1997).

The economic disruptions of the past decades have limited employment opportunities. Between 1965 and 1995, a period of over three decades, formal sector employment grew by only 12.8 per cent. However, formal sector employment in the mid-1990s was 15 per cent less than in 1975, when it peaked. Unemployment and underemployment are widespread and it is estimated that more than 75 per cent of the working population are affected. The recent restructuring of the civil service, and the liquidation or privatisation of parastatals, have not improved the situation much.

Economic policy and performance in Zambia have been heavily influenced by the performance of the copper industry: its revenue generation, employment, exports and related politics. Mining activity and the associated infrastructure also turned the Copperbelt into one of the most prosperous regions of the country. In the 1960s copper generated a substantial part of GDP, followed by a sharp decline during the following twenty years. However, the copper sector still generates substantial foreign exchange

earnings as well as public revenue. Although dominated by a few crops, notably maize, the country's agriculture has considerable potential. Still, rain-fed
agriculture has also implied weather shocks, low levels of productivity and
poor income generation. Droughts are common, and have been exceptionally
serious during the period of economic reform.

At independence in 1964 Zambia pursued liberal economic policies that
included encouragement of the private sector. However, by the end of the
1960s this stance had started to change, especially following Kaunda's
pronouncement of the philosophy of Humanism, an ideology based on a
mixture of Christian, socialist and traditional African values. It entailed
inward-looking and nationalistic economic policies.

With hindsight, it can be said that following major external and internal
shocks the economy reached a turning point in 1975. Policy-makers realised
that changes in economic policy were required if the economy was to remain
on course (see ILO 1977). Policy statements and budgets emphasised the need
for public expenditure austerity, including reductions in subsidies to the
parastatals. In 1976 the kwacha was devalued for the first time. However,
the measures failed to reverse the economic crisis, which seemed to have
broader and much deeper causes. Delay of broad economic reform meant
the loss of an early opportunity to correct the direction of the economy.

This chapter examines how Zambia adjusted to its external and internal
crises during the period 1975–97. We analyse how the state transformed its
economic and political institutions in response to exogenous factors. It is
important to note that the major reforms in Zambia, after 1989, were undertaken against the backdrop of a changed attitude to globalisation and openness. As part of structural adjustment, there was substantial realignment of
fiscal, monetary and exchange rate policies. Political systems have also been
liberalised.

Our discussion covers two periods: 1975–88 was characterised not only by
shocks but also by attempts at economic reform, marked by policy reversals
and centralisation of power. This period is contrasted with 1989–97, which
began with attempts at defining policies that would lead to 'growth from
own resources' (Republic of Zambia 1989) and ended with concerted efforts
at economic reform and privatisation, supported by the IMF, the World
Bank and other donors. The latter period also marks the reintroduction of
multi-party democracy.

A CONSTRAINED RESPONSE, 1975–88

The economy has performed relatively poorly since 1975, exhibiting mixed
results between 1989 and 1997. For the entire period, real output grew at
an average rate of only 0.26 per cent. Thus, given a population growth rate
of 3.2 per cent per annum, the standard of living has fallen sharply in the

past two decades. By the mid-1990s *per capita* GDP had fallen below a third of that of 1975. From being a lower middle income country, as per the World Bank's definition, Zambia had become one of the world's poorest. The period also saw a serious drop in capital formation. While the ratio of domestic investment to GDP was above 30 per cent in 1975, it had fallen to 9.9 per cent by 1995. The burden of this scaling down was borne by the infrastructure, including roads, other communications and social utilities. The spillover effects of the retrenchment included increased isolation of the countryside and deterioration in service quality in many urban areas.

External shocks and internal rigidities led to rising inflation, which reached an unprecedented 20 per cent in 1984, while sharper increases were to follow. By the end of the decade inflation had reached three-digit levels. In the 1990s inflation continued to be of serious concern, with average rates of close to 150 per cent during 1990–93. It then fell markedly as macroeconomic policies became more effective. Average inflation was down to about 40 per cent by the mid-1990s.

The difficult macroeconomic situation was also reflected in the weak balance of payments. In the 1960s favourable copper prices had ensured strong export revenue inflows. However, the oil shocks of the early 1970s, the copper price shock of 1975 and the servicing of a rising external debt led to a weak current account. Total external debt in 1995 was estimated at US$6,366 million, that is, three times GDP and five times total export earnings. This makes Zambia one of the most indebted countries in sub-Saharan Africa. As in other countries in the region, the debt problem arose mainly from the government's treatment of the external shocks of the 1970s as temporary. The necessary adjustment was postponed, with resource gaps closed by external borrowing. Subsequently the country accumulated payment arrears and has had to request debt rescheduling from creditors at regular intervals (Adam *et al.* 1994, Andersson and Ndulo 1994).

The period 1975–88 was dominated by three major events. First, a sharp economic decline induced by worsening terms of trade, much more severe between 1974 and 1980, but recurring until the end of the 1980s. Though it was mainly to blame for the collapse of copper prices and sharp increases in import prices, notably oil and manufactures, South African threats were of great concern. Zambia's trade routes, traditionally through South Africa, were disrupted and other, less efficient, routes to the sea, notably via Tanzania, had to be found. All this led to political tension and rising military expenditure.

The first major reform-related programme was reached in the period 1976–77 and a stand-by facility of SDR 19 million was made available by the IMF. Too confined to arrest the economic decline, this programme was followed by a bigger stand-by facility of SDR 250 million, in 1978–80, called the Action Programme, which sought to introduce 'economic prices'. It was soon felt, however, that a fully fledged programme was necessary to begin addressing

Zambia's serious structural dislocation. An extended fund facility worth SDR 800 million was negotiated in 1982 with the aim of supporting a medium-term structural adjustment programme. Reductions in aggregate demand were emphasised, including a freeze on wages as well as on government employment. Most prices were decontrolled and interest rates were allowed to increase in a bid to encourage savings. Still the country failed to meet the optimistic targets set by the IMF. The policy-makers failed to go far enough in the areas of price liberalisation or subsidy reduction to enable a continuation of the extended fund facility. A smaller loan worth SDR 211.5 million was negotiated for the period 1983–84 and yet another for 1984–86.

During 1985 the economy was faced with severe pressure on its fiscal and external balances. Rising inflation in the face of stagnant wages made labour markets restive. Public sector workers, notably junior doctors, took to 'work to rule' tactics while miners threatened even more serious union action. Towards the end of October 1995 the government disbanded the foreign exchange allocation committee, and a foreign exchange auction programme began. There were a number of exemptions, including party and government expenditures, debt servicing, use by ZCCM and medical and education supplies. The pressure on the system led to a rapid depreciation of the kwacha from K2.35 to K7 to the dollar in a matter of weeks (Ndulo and Sakala 1987). The 'austere' budget of 1986 nevertheless had a deficit of K1,789 million. In spite of efforts to fine-tune the performance of the auction, including advance payments on the bids and an increase in interest rates to a minimum of 30 per cent, the speculative mood in the economy persisted. Following a year of economic disruption and much fluctuation in the auction-determined exchange rate, the government decided to fix the kwacha–dollar rate between K9 and K12.5. Subsequently the auction was suspended for two months, and it was ultimately replaced by a two-tier system with a priority rate and an auction rate. At the auction, and reflecting the smaller amounts of foreign exchange available to the private sector, the kwacha rate slid towards K20 to the dollar.

With mounting social unrest and political disaffection, Zambia abandoned the IMF–World Bank supported programme in May 1987, replacing it with a New Economic Recovery Programme. As Kayizzi-Mugerwa (1990) has noted, the programme was presented at a particularly critical period in Zambia. Mining had ceased to be the engine of the economy, with no replacement in sight. The size of the public and parastatal sectors could no longer be sustained on current revenues, with expenditure on social services coming under considerable pressure. Further, the debt burden had grown beyond the country's ability to service it without threatening core services. Last, failure to reach a workable agreement with the IMF and World Bank had put supplementary finances from other donors on hold. In many respects the New Recovery Programme was an attempt to return to the traditional policies pursued in the more affluent 1960s, and which had lent the country the aura of a welfare state. With a view to 'mobilising the masses', policies became increasingly expansionary. Still, there seemed to be some economic improvement in 1988, with increases in capital formation, the current account and agricultural output. In retrospect, however, these were the result of 'external factors' such as adequate rainfall and good copper prices than of policy reform.

Thus in terms of policy the period 1975–88 depicts an interesting evolution. On the one hand, the government was quite conscious of the need to undertake reforms in order to halt the rapid erosion of the economy, while on the other it operated under severe constraints imposed by the party, the parastatal sector and trade union interests. Pulling in different directions, the two factors meant that efforts at reform would be weak, with uncertain results. Any hint of political opposition would result in policy reversal. Uncertainties were thus created among economic actors and even among the donor community. With the accumulation of 'programme packages' it became impossible to tell whether the government was serious in pursuing reforms or simply trying to muddle through the crisis.

Several factors inhibited the evolution of a serious economic policy framework during this period. Mainstream political views and the general ideological inclination of the country opposed market forces as a means of resource allocation and as a tool of economic management. In a speech about this time President Kaunda had referred to 'two decades of fruitless co-operation with the IMF' during which there were 'mounting social and political tensions and a drastic decline in the living standards of the people'. It is interesting to note that even the business class, which benefited greatly from the controls, did not initially support liberalisation. For example, when the foreign exchange auction system was introduced in 1985 the chairman of the Zambia Association of Chambers of Commerce and Industry denounced it as unworkable (see *Times of Zambia*, 13 October 1985). It has also been noted by Andersson and Kayizzi-Mugerwa (1989: 26) that wars of liberation in the region introduced something of a siege mentality, which influenced economic thinking. There was undue emphasis on self-sufficiency and economic nationalism.

It can be argued, further, that what now seems in retrospect to have been overt donor influence on economic policy, ultimately unacceptable to Zambia, was simply a reflection of the country's failure to devise credible policies. A brave attempt to do so in the New Economic Recovery Programme soon failed owing to serious problems of financing. As in other African countries political power was centralised, while the bulk of the economy was in the hands of government-owned companies. The country thus needed to undertake microeconomic reforms alongside the far-reaching ones it was attempting to put in place at the macro level. As no such reforms were attempted for much of the 1980s, severe distortions remained in the economy.

The crisis and the attempts at reform had important impacts on political structures in Zambia. The underlying strength of the economy in the

1960s and early 1970s had given the ruling party, UNIP, a strong basis for expanding patronage and influence. The President of the country was able to pursue his philosophy of Humanism without encountering opposition, as the system seemed to have sufficient resources to cater for the needs of the elite (Bates and Collier 1995, Gulhati 1989). In the 1980s the intricacies of structural adjustment meant that the main responsibility for economic policy shifted from the political leadership to technocrats in the Ministries and the central bank, supported by the IMF and the World Bank. However, politicians were blamed for the poor economic results. This dichotomy was ultimately the cause of Kaunda's declining popularity. Consistent economic policies could be pursued only when the technocrats and the politicians were pulling in the same direction. This was not to happen until the tumultuous changes that saw UNIP removed from power by the opposition's Movement for Multi-party Democracy (MMD).

MANAGING REFORM, 1989–97

Zambia's experiment with 'growth from own resources' failed precisely because the country had few resources of its own to finance the ambitious recovery programme. Adverse weather patterns, and another decline in copper prices, greatly constrained the options open to the government. In 1989 Zambia was forced to 'return to the fold'. An Economic Recovery Programme was introduced, underpinned by a shadow agreement with the IMF and bilateral donors. Since the country was in serious arrears with the multilateral institutions, it would not normally have qualified for assistance. To remedy the situation, a rights accumulation programme was introduced by the IMF which would ensure access to adjustment funds when an acceptable level of performance, including a reduction in arrears, was reached. The programme consisted of a series of quarterly targets and conditionalities. The bilateral donors used the conditionalities to ensure that the government remained on track and aware of the consequences of faltering. Policy-makers accepted these stiff conditions, which may also have cost the government the election. There was fear that, owing to pressures related to the pending presidential and parliamentary elections, the reforms would collapse (Adam 1994: 5, Andersson and Ndulo 1994). However, following the MMD's landslide victory, reforms were pursued even more vigorously.

Since then reform has concentrated on five main areas (World Bank 1996): first, economic stabilisation, including monetary and fiscal reforms, the liberalisation of foreign trade, promotion of exports and reform of the financial sector. Second, the government has committed itself to private sector expansion via privatisation and market development. Third, recognising the potential of agriculture in the economy, policy-makers have emphasised the need for reforms to raise agricultural productivity and income generation.

Fourth, it is necessary to remove the constraints that excessive external debt has imposed on the economy by restructuring the public sector. Five, all the above changes also imply fundamental alterations in governance.

Since the early 1990s there have been major achievements in all the above areas. As something of a nominal anchor, the government has committed itself to a balanced budget, which has in turn implied a tight monetary policy. By 1995 the budget deficit, as a percentage of GDP, was down to 0.1 per cent, compared with an average of over 15 per cent in second half of the 1980s. The capital account has been fully liberalised, with foreign exchange transactions now freely conducted in foreign exchange bureaux. The tariff system has been harmonised, with nominal tariff now ranging between 0 per cent and 25 per cent. In the financial sector, government has removed controls over interest rates, while the licensing of more banks and investment houses has increased competition in the sector. Still, a rapidly expanding financial sector has generated problems of regulation and credibility. Initially low capital requirements meant that a number of financially unsound institutions entered the financial sector. In recent years the government has had to close many such institutions, while the central bank has undertaken 'fire brigade' operations.

If the 'new' government is to claim a distinguishing feature from the Kaunda regime, it must be the enthusiasm with which it embarked on privatisation. At the beginning of the 1990s Zambia was still referred to as a difficult case for liberalisation. The prospects of privatisation, other than of small and marginal companies and units, were considered small. All this was before Zambia embarked on one of the most rapid privatisation programmes in Africa. In its status report of July 1996 the Zambia Privatisation Agency could report unprecedented progress. In less than two years the agency had managed to divest a total of 140 firms out of a 'working portfolio' of 235 companies. Further, another thirty firms were under advanced negotiations for privatisation while twenty were in liquidation or receivership. The privatised companies vary from small transport firms to large holdings in the hotel industry, in agriculture and manufacturing. The privatisation methods included public flotation, as in the case of the Chilanga Cement Company, company splits and the exercise of pre-emptive rights, as in the case of Zambia Breweries, the return of the companies to the original owners, or a management buy-out. Government also relinquished its shares in many companies, such as Rothman's Zambia, to the Privatisation Trust Fund for flotation to the public. However, in many cases the companies, already redundant, were simply dissolved. The number of foreign purchases was also substantial. The firm of Tate & Lyle acquired 40 per cent of Zambia Sugar for about US$20.8 million, while the Commonwealth Development Corporation acquired the rest for US$50 million. Tata, the Indian multinational and long-term manager of the Pamodzi Hotel in Lusaka, bought 70 per cent of the hotel's shares, with the rest to be floated on the fledgling stock exchange. There was considerable participation by Zambians, especially in the agricultural sector and in the purchase of small manufacturing companies, hotels and shops.

However, the privatisation of the heaviest portions of the parastatal sector is still incomplete. These include the huge Zambia Consolidated Copper Mines (ZCCM), valued at US$2.2 billion, with its many subsidiary companies, the railway system, power generation, telecommunications, the insurance parastatal as well as the state-owned commercial banks. However, much ground has been covered already and studies have been undertaken of the most important companies in preparation for privatisation. By the end of 1997 four mines, including Chibuluma and Luanshya, had been sold while negotiations for the purchase of the large operations at Nchanga and Nkana mines, comprising 70 per cent of ZCCM's mining activities, were going on with the American company Phelps-Dodge.

An interesting aspect of Zambia's privatisation effort has been the decision to commercialise some government departments. With support from the World Bank and the European Union, the government hired consultants to assist in the privatisation of various training and management institutions in human and natural resource development, including tourism, the administration of law, printing and information services, etc. Among the most interesting targets for commercialisation are the Government Printer, the Registrar of Patents and the management of ports and harbours.

On completion, Zambia will have undertaken one of the fastest privatisation programmes on record in Africa. By mid-1997 the government had sold off close to 70 per cent of the 326 state-run companies accumulated since the privatisation of the early 1970s. Still, the privatisation process has not been entirely free of friction. There have been resignations of government officials over anomalies in the privatisation of the copper industry, while the charge that the government is selling the family silver is still voiced frequently.

The government has been able to undertake such radical reform because it felt that it had the political mandate to transform the country's political and economic structures in order to arrest economic decline and begin a process of growth. The much freer economic debate has also led to a gradual convergence of views on economic policy, namely the recognition that it was not necessary for government to intervene at all levels of the economy. That pursuit of prudent fiscal and monetary policies was crucial to the development and well-being of the private sector. It has thus been argued that the policy problem of the 1980s was not so much lack of economic diversification as failure to manage external shocks by adopting less rigid policies (Maipose 1994: 71). It can be said that with MMD's assumption of power the debate over market reforms effectively came to an end. Henceforth concern would be over the level of emphasis rather than the policy thrust.

In spite of the broad reform effort, the impact on real output growth remained diffuse. Rapid policy shifts lowered credibility, which in turn weakened the investment response (Adam and Bevan 1995). Real GDP fell on average by 1.3 per cent for much of the first half of the 1990s, while investment averaged 10.5 per cent of GDP during the period. The slow growth was also due to lingering rigidities in the main sectors. Copper continued its downward slide, while agriculture responded poorly to the changes in relative prices. The agriculturally most productive parts of the country still suffered from poor infrastructure provision, notably the lack of a reliable marketing chain. The liberalisation of agricultural marketing implied for many farmers an increased level of uncertainty. Maize marketing was, for example, adversely affected by the financial squeeze in the economy. Merchants had little working capital, and areas far from the capital were unable to sell their produce or received prices that were much below those obtaining in urban centres. Non-price factors have thus tended to limit the response of farmers and other economic actors.

With regard to expenditure control, the government seems to have made rapid progress in the 1990s. As a percentage of GDP the fiscal deficit averaged 13.7 during 1975–88, falling to 4.5 per cent of GDP in the reform period. Since the current account deficit also narrowed in the latter period, economic reform seems to have helped remove internal and external imbalances.

However, improved fiscal discipline did not translate into lower inflation at once. Indeed, while the rate of inflation averaged 24.58 per cent from 1975 to 1988, it accelerated rapidly between 1989 and 1995, reaching an average of 115.01 per cent. This was mainly because inflation had been repressed via price and wage controls during the period of market intervention and control, with associated costs due to queues, parallel markets and loss of allocative efficiency. Much of the increased inflation, being a direct result of the opening-up process, is likely to be of a one-off character.

Subsequently, tight monetary policy, the introduction of a cash budget and a policy stance bent on running budgetary surpluses have finally reined inflation in, with the rate falling to 38.7 per cent in 1995. However, in spite of this recent progress, Zambia is still a high inflation country, even by African standards, many countries having had single-digit inflation during the period. An average seignorage rate of 7.8 per cent during 1989–95, compared with the usual norm of 2 per cent, indicates persistence of macroeconomic imbalances.

GOVERNANCE AND INSTITUTIONAL REFORM

Institutional and political reforms that enhance good governance are necessary for good economic management and sustainable growth. Indeed, fostering good governance, including accountability, participation, transparency and openness is now thought to be as important in the promotion of local initiative, policy innovation and resource mobilisation as good macroeconomic policy (Ndulu 1993: 53–68). As already noted, the poor performance of the economy during 1975–88 was due to policy inconsistency, emanating from the dynamics of the one-party political system under UNIP. By its very nature the system generated centrally controlled institutions, enhancing the power of the party leadership (Gulhati 1989). With the onset of social and economic decline the system failed to evolve meaningful policy options for crisis management. There were few avenues for venting popular discontent arising from the declining standard of living.

The sustainability of the economic reforms and the prevention of reversal are ultimately determined by the degree of domestic consensus over the changes. To achieve consensus demands broad debate. The period 1989–95 was a time of immense political and institutional change in Zambia, partly enabled by broad public discussion of the reform programme. It can be said that from the point of scepticism, and even hostility, the debate was able to garner a majority in favour of change by the beginning of the 1990s. However, in spite of an expanding private sector and a growing civil society, the *coup* attempt at the end of 1997 showed that the process is far from complete.

Uniquely for Zambia, the election of 1991 was fought on the basis of the need for real reform. Thus the new MMD government felt that it had received an overwhelming mandate to proceed with reforms, including a complete restructuring of the economy. It would seem, however, that the push for governance and political reforms petered out after the MMD's first mandate. The liberalisation of the economy has since been accompanied by noticeable reticence in the political arena. The political inertia led to an increased threat of policy reversal, dampening in turn the investment and growth prospects of the economy. Thus while economic reforms have been implemented rapidly there has been little public service reform, and the civil service remains politicised. Reminiscent of the Kaunda days, the President continues to wield immense power (Chanda 1996).

In recent years the real power of decision-making in government seems to have shifted from the Cabinet to an influential group of ruling party members. Already the debate over institutional and political issues is relatively circumscribed, resulting in failure to prepare the legal reforms required to strengthen the reform programme. Ultimately this leads to disrespect for the rule of law and to constraints on civil liberties, notably freedom of the press. Given that the latter persist, there soon follows serious erosion of judicial independence, lack of accountability and transparency, and generally a lack of acceptance of internationally accepted norms of governance (Chanda 1996).

CONCLUSION

This chapter has discussed the evolution of economic policy in Zambia in two distinct periods: one a time of economic and political controls and the other characterised by a move towards liberal economics and politics. During 1975–88 the economy failed to evolve the capacity necessary to respond to internal and external shocks. Economic policy was broadly inconsistent, and prone to reversal. Social and political institutions were likewise constrained by the centralising tendencies of the ruling party. The economy was locked in internal and external disequilibria, characterised by declining growth rates and *per capita* incomes.

Since 1989 the country has undergone a dual reform: at the political level, a multi-party system was introduced, while in the economic area policy-makers have attempted to implement one of the most ambitious privatisation and market development programmes in sub-Saharan Africa. On both counts the results have been mixed. The resumption of high and sustainable growth is still difficult. In the past decade real economic growth has been negligible and *per capita* incomes continue to decline. Sustained growth will demand increases in domestic and foreign investment which can be ensured only by a strong commitment to sound macroeconomic policy. The latter is inevitably a product of the political process, making it imperative to strengthen all aspects of good governance. This will be the best way to enhance policy credibility and ensure policy irreversibility. Both are necessary to prevent the reform process from faltering.

REFERENCES

Adam, C. (1994) 'The Fiscal Costs of Premature Financial Liberalization: Some Evidence from Zambia', mimeo, Oxford University: Centre for the Study of African Economies.

Adam, C., Andersson, P., Bigsten, A., Collier, P. and O'Connell, S. (1994) *Evaluation of Swedish Development Co-operation with Zambia*, Stockholm: Ministry of Foreign Affairs.

Adam, C. and Bevan, D. (1995) 'Investment, Uncertainty, and the Option to Wait: Implications for Government and Donor Policies in Zambia', mimeo, Oxford University: Centre for the Study of African Economies.

Andersson, P. and Kayizzi-Mugerwa, S. (1989) *Mineral Dependence, Goal Attainment and Equity: Zambia's Experience with Structural Adjustment in the 1980s*, Macroeconomic Studies 4, Stockholm: Swedish International Development Co-operation Agency (Sida).

Andersson, P. and Ndulo, M. (1994) *Hyperinflation, Stabilization and the New Recovery Program in Zambia*, Macroeconomic Studies 51, Stockholm: International Development Co-operation Agency (Sida).

Bates, R. and Collier, P. (1995) 'The Politics and Economics of Policy Reform in Zambia', *Journal of African Economies*, 4 (1): 115–43.

Chanda, A.W. (1996) 'Zambia's Fledgling Democracy: Prospects for the Future', *Zambia Law Journal*, 25–8: 125–54.

Gulhati, R. (1989) *Impasse in Zambia: The Economics and Politics of Reform*, Washington DC: World Bank.

International Labour Organisation (1977) *Narrowing the Gaps: Planning for Basic Needs and Productive Employment in Zambia*, Addis Ababa: ILO.

Kayizzi-Mugerwa, S. (1990) 'Growth from own Resources: Zambia's Fourth National Development Plan in Perspective', *Development Policy Review*, 8 (1): 59–76.

Maipose, G. (1994) 'Government and Administration in a Liberalised Economy: Problems and Prospects' in M. Banda, C. Fundanga and C. Ng'andwe (eds) *Economic Development and Democracy: Critical Issues in the Third Republic*, Lusaka: Economic Association of Zambia.

Ndulo, M. and Sakala, M. (1987) *Stabilization Policies in Zambia 1975–85*, World Food Programme Research Working Papers 13, Geneva: International Labour Organisation.

Ndulu, B.J. (1993) 'The Role of the State and the Market in Reformed Economic Management in sub-Saharan Africa' in Swedish International Development Co-operation Agency (Sida), *Redefining the Role of the State and the Market in the Development Process*, Stockholm: Västergötlands Tryckeri.

Republic of Zambia (1989) *Fourth National Development Plan 1989–93*, Lusaka: Government Printer.

Sheshamani, V. (1997) *Economic Policy Reforms, Economic Growth and Sustainable Human Development: A Comparative Study of India and Zambia*, Tokyo: Institute of Developing Economies.

World Bank (1996) *Zambia: Prospects for Sustainable Growth 1995–2005*, Washington DC: World Bank.

Zambia Privatisation Agency (1996) *Progress Report*, Lusaka.

14

THE OTHER AFRICA

Economic development in Lusophone countries

Renato Aguilar

The terms Anglophone and Francophone Africa commonly refer to the regions where the dominant languages of the former colonial powers are used, even if only by an elite minority. However, the designations in no way exhaust the pastiche of language groups and affiliations that characterise modern Africa, with a large majority who do not speak any European language at all. Among countries falling outside the two dominant colonial spheres are those of Lusophone Africa, the former Portuguese colonies, including Angola, Mozambique, Guinea-Bissau, Cape Verde and São Tomé e Príncipe. It should be remembered that Portugal was not only the first European power into sub-Saharan Africa but also the last out.

However, although these countries are also known as PALOPS *(Países Africanos de Lingua Oficial Portuguesa)*, that is, African countries with Portuguese as the official language, the use of Portuguese varies a lot among them. In the smaller ones of West Africa *crioulo*, a pidgin Portuguese, is dominant. Guinea-Bissau is surrounded by French-speaking countries, and the language is used widely in that country. In Mozambique, Portuguese is important in the urban areas, although English is also common. Portuguese has its strongest position in Angola, where it is clearly the preferred language in urban areas, and extensively understood in rural ones. Still, French is spoken widely in the northern parts near the border with the Democratic Republic of the Congo. Former Portuguese colonies are also unique in not sharing a common colonial history with any of their neighbours.

This chapter looks at recent economic development in Lusophone African countries. Their independence was invariably a result of armed struggle, attained after the Portuguese revolution of 1974. All five tried, with varying degrees of success, to implement a socialist system at home. However, in spite of this shared colonial experience, their development as independent countries has been quite varied. Tensions and social cleavages caused by the wars of independence led to civil war in Angola and Mozambique while the smaller countries in West Africa have maintained peace. The differences in the post-independence experience were partly the result of disparities in natural resource endowments, and of the role the colonies played within the Portuguese colonial administration, and how they, as independent states, responded to the challenges of international politics and global markets.

COLONIALISM AND THE STRUGGLE FOR INDEPENDENCE

The Portuguese were among the first explorers of the African coastline and by the end of the fifteenth century traders and explorers were visiting regularly. This was partly thanks to royal interest and backing, although individual expeditions were mainly organised privately. With time, Portugal's colonial empire became an unparalleled example of overextended resources: one of the smallest and poorest countries in Europe was trying to manage one of the most extensive colonial empires in history. It was thus inevitable that in much of Africa effective Portuguese control was initially confined to a few trading posts on the coast and, in the hinterland, to some essential centres of communication (Murteira 1988).

This did not prevent Portuguese traders and explorers from penetrating practically every corner of sub-Saharan Africa. Their main activity in West Africa was trade in gold, ivory and slaves. The latter was a pervasive feature of Portuguese history in Africa, with disguised forms of slavery persisting well into the twentieth century.

The Berlin Conference held at the end of the nineteenth century was to change Portugal's reluctance to acquire territory. The country embarked on a series of expeditions and wars in areas where it had established influence, the goal being to put as much territory under its effective control as possible. The result was a much expanded Portuguese Africa, inordinately large in relation to the size and resources of the colonial power. A direct consequence of this change in policy was an increased flow of European settlers. Thus at the eve of independence the largest colonies, Mozambique and, especially, Angola, had a sizeable white population. However, most of the latter were unskilled and largely uneducated, so that there were white workers even for the most menial of jobs. This became a serious obstacle to the advancement of the African population, limiting the role of the labour market in social mobility.

By the end of the 1960s Portugal found itself fighting colonial wars in Angola, Mozambique and, an especially harsh one, in Guinea-Bissau. Cape Verde was saved from war because the leaders of the independence movement, PAIGC (African Party for the Independence of Guinea-Bissau and Cape Verde), made the tactical choice of fighting in the jungles of Guinea-Bissau rather than in the barren and overpopulated islands. These African independence movements were closely allied with the democratic movements then fighting dictatorship in Portugal.

Cape Verde played a central role among Portuguese colonies in Africa. Uninhabited when the Portuguese arrived, the islands soon became a strategic outpost in Atlantic maritime trade. A permanent base for Portuguese exploration and colonial adventures was established there, along with complementary agricultural activities, mostly sugar cane production. For the latter purpose, slave populations were brought in from Guinea, which then occupied most of Senegambia, but also from as far away as Angola. Thus Cape Verde became quite a mixture of ethnic groups, who developed their own *crioulo* culture (Lobban 1995).

Following the Portuguese revolution of 1974, all of Portuguese Africa became independent. In Guinea-Bissau the PAIGC declared independence unilaterally, taking effective control of the country. Though there was a half-hearted attempt by the new Portuguese authorities to keep control of Cape Verde, massive demonstrations and the return of Cape Verdean leaders from the war in Guinea-Bissau showed that it would be futile. Cape Verde and Guinea-Bissau remained under the same government until the military *coup* of 1982, which deposed Luis Cabral. The countries then went their separate ways.

In the former southern African territories, independence marked the start of civil war. In Angola the Popular Movement for the Liberation of Angola (MPLA) quickly defeated the National Front for the Liberation of Angola (FNLA). The National Union for the Total Independence of Angola (UNITA) was then a small and weak group which, with support from South Africa and the United States, eventually became the most persistent opposition to the MPLA government. In Mozambique the Front for the Liberation of Mozambique (FRELIMO) took power and was soon opposed by the similarly named Mozambique Liberation Front (RENAMO), a splinter movement, with support from South Africa.

Socialism and central planning were common characteristics of policies pursued by Portuguese-speaking Africa after independence. A possible explanation of this was lack of Western support to the rebel movements for fear of offending Portugal. The movements were thus pushed towards the socialist bloc, the main source of weapons and financial and diplomatic support.

Throughout Portuguese-speaking Africa, these experiments in socialism failed to generate sustained growth or to resolve the serious social problems generated by the civil war. Attempts to produce workable national plans proved futile. By the mid-1980s the countries had conceded failure and concerted efforts were made to shift towards market-oriented economic policies. However, the pace and depth of the reforms necessary before their economies returned to growth were seriously underestimated.

ADJUSTMENT AND GROWTH

In this section we present a synopsis of recent economic developments in each of the Portuguese-speaking countries.

Angola

Angola became independent in 1975 and the first government would include members of the three recognised political parties: the MPLA, UNITA and the FNLA. However, earlier friction between the three groups developed into open military confrontation, with the country divided into three zones, with Luanda, the capital, under the control of the MPLA. The civil war rapidly acquired an international dimension, with the intervention of former Zaire and white mercenaries on the side of the FNLA in northern Angola, a South African invasion of southern Angola in support of UNITA, and Cuban military advisers and troops supporting the MPLA (Bhagavan 1986, Carneiro and Abreu 1989, Marcum 1987).

After consolidating power over much of the country, the MPLA succeeded in forming a government under Agostinho Neto. Soon after installation the government adopted a Marxist-Leninist orientation and declared its strategic aim as the establishment of a socialist economy, based on central planning. However, the short and medium-term aims were the recovery of economic activity. Thus, in the first years of independence, there was little collectivisation and nationalisation, save the take-over of banks and other properties abandoned by Portuguese settlers. International trade was run by a state monopoly and prices were set administratively.

At independence, Angola had one of the largest industrial sectors in sub-Saharan Africa. It was, however, highly dependent on imported capital and raw materials, and was directed mainly at the domestic market. Oil production had already become Angola's largest export item, helping to raise *per capita* GDP to US$200 in 1973, at the time among the highest in Africa. However, incomes were very unequally distributed, with the native population having incomes that were only about 10 per cent of those of the white population (UNDP/World Bank 1989).

On the labour market, independence was preceded by a wave of strikes. This led to considerable disruption of commerce in urban and rural areas. There followed a massive emigration of Portuguese settlers, including many educated Angolans who had worked for the colonial administration. Thus, unlike other African countries, independence meant an enormous external shock for Angola, that almost paralysed the whole economy. In effect, Angola has never quite recovered from this shock, since the economic policies pursued and the war made it difficult to alleviate the effects (Gunn 1987). The Angolan economy and politics have thus been formed by a combination of external shocks, military conflict and the dynamics of resource exploitation.

The Portuguese had built their control strategy on a system of alliances and military confrontations with local kingdoms. Among other things this enabled them to exploit the slave and other hinterland trades in the earlier colonial period. The enormous natural resource endowments made the country relatively rich, while at the same time exposing it to external shocks. The ultimate shock, at least to the Portuguese settlers, was the speed at which independence was achieved. There followed a mass departure of skilled labour. Failure to adjust to these shocks explains the poor state of the economy today.

The first oil crisis of the early 1970s made oil the country's main export, signalling the beginning of its battle with the Dutch Disease effects of resource dependence. Coupled with the effects of the war on industry and agriculture, oil became the only viable industry in the country. A protected and booming oil sector drained most of the human resources, leading to serious decline in the rest of the economy. However, though the shocks drastically affected the economy, the government refused to adjust to them or to the new economic structure that had resulted.

Recurrence of external shocks and the reluctance of policy-makers to adjust to them have created a peculiar style of economic policy in Angola. The institutions responsible for economic policy, already weak at independence, have been weakened considerably. Civil war, related corruption, and the peculiar role of the oil sector in the economy, especially as generator of funds for the war effort, and general lack of fiscal discipline have prevented the central bank and the Ministry of Finance from pursuing effective policies. The former is largely an extension of the government and SONAGOL, the oil parastatal. Though central planning has since been abandoned, the Ministry of Planning has not been able to replace it with an effective alternative. The half-hearted measures currently pursued have only weakened the clout of policy-making institutions (Aguilar and Zejan 1990).

In the wake of economic reforms, a number of weakly co-ordinated centres of decision-making on economic matters have emerged. The lines of authority are unclear, with Ministries often overridden by the presidency. Thus, although programmes may be duly approved by the Ministries, their execution can be delayed by interference from some other policy-making centre. Sudden and drastic changes in policy orientation are often made without explanation. Policy pronouncements, though made often, are rarely implemented, or are continuously postponed. This has created a serious credibility problem for the government.

By the mid-1980s Angola's policy-makers had come to the conclusion that not much headway would be made without external financial support, notably from the international financial institutions. In 1987 co-operation was initiated with the World Bank and discussions were undertaken aimed at a formal structural adjustment programme. While waiting for the latter, the World Bank started some programmes in support of capacity building. The International Monetary Fund, on the other hand, has sent regular missions to Luanda, and some reforms and policy measures have been agreed with the government, including a modest set of targets. IMF missions have often left Luanda with an optimistic *aide-mémoire* in the expectation of a full agreement in the near future. Subsequent missions invariably discover that little was done in Luanda, leading to the breakdown of negotiations.

In the 1990s there was some partial price liberalisation, although a significant degree of relative price distortion remains in the system. Notably, the exchange rate is still overvalued, while fuel prices remain low. There has been little attempt to liberalise markets; they continue to be heavily regulated, dominated by monopolies created earlier by the government. Market inflexibility remains the single most important hindrance to economic activity.

Thus, after ten years of negotiations, Angola has yet to come to a definitive agreement with the international financial institutions. Most analysts argue, however, that such an agreement would help reverse the difficult economic situation the country finds itself in today.

Guinea-Bissau

Following independence in 1974, Guinea-Bissau tried to implement a centrally planned economic system tailored on the Soviet model. It became virtually closed, with weak international links. With donor support, the government made some efforts at industrialisation, but with disastrous results. Large state monopolies and extensive rationing dominated domestic markets, while poor marketing structures and low productivity characterised agriculture. The rural sector suffered considerable destruction during the independence war, and there was massive displacement of populations.

Beginning in the early 1980s, a switch of orientation from controls towards a market-oriented economy was frequently voiced. This change was parallel to political developments that culminated in the overthrow of Luis Cabral.

In 1983 an Economic Recovery Programme was introduced and weekly currency devaluations were embarked on by the end of the year. Negotiations with the International Monetary Fund and the World Bank led eventually to the first structural adjustment programme, followed in 1984 by a new stabilisation plan. The reforms were limited to the devaluation of the peso, price deregulation and the introduction of some private commercial activity.

In the transition from a centrally planned economy to a market-oriented one 1986 was a critical year, with the government issuing a number of decrees aimed at liberalising the economy. The first decree liberalised trade, ending state monopolies in domestic and international trade. The second one freed most prices, the only exceptions being basic goods, including rice and petrol. Thus, for the first time since independence, the minimum conditions necessary for the development of the private sector had been set. It was now possible for the country to embark on its first formal structural adjustment programme with support from the IMF, the World Bank and other donors.

The agreement reached in 1987 related to a three-year structural adjustment facility amounting to SDR 5.25 million. The World Bank also signed its first structural adjustment credit, which was instrumental in mobilising complementary donor funds in support of the reform programme.

In the first phase of adjustment, important structural changes were introduced. Furthermore, price liberalisation helped remove the most serious distortions in the economy. The local currency was also devalued, reducing the black market premium. Quantitative restrictions were removed on 75 per cent of imports, and the state monopoly of the cereal trade was abolished. In the public sector, some effort was made to put public investment in order, including steps towards privatisation. This led to the creation in 1989 of a special unit for the management of the reform of public enterprises (UGREP), which became the lead agency for privatisation.

In spite of the successful introduction of adjustment measures, the government's weak managerial capacity became a serious impediment. There was a general lack of reliable information and a paucity of technical staff, while the legal framework was inadequate. Fragmentation of government into small semi-autonomous entities, with poor co-ordination between them, made it difficult to pursue a consistent policy. The government was not able to control credit expansion or to reduce the budget deficit. Inflation resulted, reaching 100 per cent in 1987, and it was still above 80 per cent in 1988. Failure to limit new debt creation, or to implement a medium-term debt strategy, meant that the debt burden would continue to worsen.

During the course of the second structural adjustment agreement with the World Bank, covering the period 1989–91, the government was able to show improved performance. Thus 1990 ended with a falling rate of inflation, some exchange rate appreciation, and a reduced budget deficit. However, performance deteriorated in 1991, with increasing signs of monetary and fiscal policy slippage.

In spite of the price liberalisation, the change in relative prices between tradables and non-tradables in the urban sector had little immediate effect on rural activity. This was because the rural sector was cut off from the formal market during the civil war and economic crisis and it would take time to reincorporate it (Aguilar and Zejan 1992).

Having accomplished economic stabilisation, the government sought to embark on important structural changes, including the restructuring of the public sector via privatisation. However, although administrative capacity had improved, notably data collection and analysis, the Ministry of Finance's ability to formulate budgetary priorities, execution and control had remained weak. Since government was failing to meet targets, relations with the IMF and World Bank remained worrisome.

In February 1992 the government embarked on an IMF shadow programme, that is, without actually getting money from the Fund, but for the purposes of establishing policy targets for December 1993. It had the following ingredients: a real GDP growth rate of 3 per cent, a reduction in annual inflation from 70 per cent to 47 per cent, and a reduction in the current account deficit from 49 per cent of GDP to 29 per cent. The shadow programme managed to halt economic deterioration and the country was able to agree a new Enhanced Structural Adjustment Facility (ESAF) with the International Monetary Fund in 1994, and new sector adjustment loans and a third structural credit with the World Bank. In the wake of the new programme, round-table discussions were held in Geneva with the international community in support of Guinea-Bissau. Up to US$357 million in financial aid was requested. In February 1995 Guinea-Bissau met the Paris Club with a view to rescheduling its external debt. The bilateral donors decided to grant Guinea-Bissau 'Naples terms', that is, the most generous terms for rescheduling available at the time (Aguilar and Stenman 1993, 1994, 1996).

After more than ten years of structural adjustment, at least in terms of programmes supported by the international financial institutions and donors, Guinea-Bissau is now quite a different country from the one that decided to change orientation in 1983 or the one that finally embarked on the programmes in 1987. The following are some of the features that emerged in the course of the decade.

Since 1987 *per capita* GDP has increased by 25 per cent. This is clearly above the average in Africa during the period. However, the target should have been doubling GDP during the course of each decade. Although the country halved its current account deficit during the same period, its balance of payments remains unsustainable, and foreign aid will remain crucial for years to come. Relative prices are now wholly market-determined, and the impact of this has finally reached the countryside, inducing a vigorous agricultural export response.

The vigorously implemented privatisation and enterprise reform programme has seen most of the state monopolies divested or liquidated and there has also been some retrenchment in public sector employment. By some estimates the number of registered private businesses has more than doubled. There is also a large and dynamic informal sector. However, the financial sector is still small, and its service provision poor. Still, it can be said that ten years ago there was for all practical purposes no financial sector at all.

However, though it is one of the more successful examples of adjustment in Africa, there have been a number of failures. First, a paramount goal of structural adjustment is to make the economy responsive to market signals. The structures emerging in Guinea-Bissau will not be efficient, nor will they be competitive. In a small and poor country, it is difficult to see how the present levels of monopolistic concentration could be reduced. The absence of strong regulatory agencies to curtail monopolies implies that market signals are poorly transmitted. The privatisation programme remains incomplete. Again, in a small country privatisation has meant the unravelling of a complex system of vested interests and a number of difficult political problems to transcend. On the other hand, the original privatisation programme overestimated the value of the assets to be privatised, as well as the technical capacity of the government to carry out the necessary procedures.

There have also been problems in the design and implementation of adjustment policies. Expectations of rapid output responses to changes in relative prices were exaggerated. In reality the initial response was poor, and it took several years before progress was made. Finally, education has been inadequately addressed. Education services are still very shallow and the country lacks institutions for training the technical staff required by the public and the private sector.

Mozambique

With its area of over 800,000 km^2 and close to 16 million people, Mozambique is one of the largest countries in Africa. It is also a classic example of Portuguese colonisation: the focus was on control of port installations and of diverse strongholds in the hinterland. This has meant that the country has adequate structures to provide transit facilities and communications for its landlocked neighbours while its own hinterland remains very remote. A long border with South Africa has also provided proximity to a dynamic neighbour, where Mozambique also expects to find a market for its excess energy output.

Earlier, proximity to South Africa was important because during apartheid RENAMO had the overt support of South Africa in its war against the government. There was extensive damage to the economy and the most important railways and road links were closed. As in other parts of the former Portuguese colonies, the civil wars caused massive displacement of rural populations, causing extensive disruption.

As one of the 'front-line states' opposing South Africa's apartheid policies, Mozambique received considerable financial and moral support from the international community. This enabled it to survive under extremely difficult economic conditions.

It is not surprising, then, that peace, finally achieved in 1992, created huge expectations of economic and social development. Some positive results, especially improvements in service delivery, can already be seen. On the other hand, with the return of peace the standards used by the international community to judge Mozambique's performance have hardened. Still, in light of the extensive damage caused by the war, the limited infrastructure and lack of human capital, Mozambique is still considered a 'special case' in donor circles.

Table 14.1 Mozambique: macroeconomic indicators, 1981–87 (% change)

Indicator	1981	1982	1983	1984	1985	1986	1987
Real growth							
GDP	0.5	−3.4	−12.9	0.9	−8.8	0.9	4.4
Imports	1.8	11.5	−20.3	−13.4	−13.1	28.0	7.6
Exports	−10.9	7.8	−37.1	−37.2	−2.0	−8.3	8.3
Current account deficit (% GDP)							
Including official transfers	−9.7	−14.4	−18.2	−15.4	−1.5	−5.2	−4.4
Excluding official transfers	−12.0	−16.9	−21.4	−18.1	−3.6	−7.5	−13.6

Source: World Bank (1995).

Lack of reliable data makes it difficult to analyse, with accuracy, Mozambique's economic performance. The World Bank has estimated that GDP could be 50 per cent higher than current estimates. It has also been noted that up to 30 per cent of the investment expenditures are actually public consumption (Stenbeck 1996). Still, most indicators suggest that the economy had started deteriorating rapidly by the mid-1980s (Table 14.1). Table 14.1 illustrates the extent of the crisis faced by Mozambique in the 1980s, the decade when government decided to change policy orientation. GDP was falling for most of the first half of the 1980s. The drastic reduction in imports from 1983 to 1985, while improving the current account, also meant fewer consumer goods and inputs to industry. The negative performance, coupled with the effects of the war, led to a sharp decline in standards of living, increasing levels of poverty.

In 1987 the government introduced an Economic and Social Rehabilitation Programme with support from the IMF, the World Bank and other donors. The programme marked the start of concerted efforts at structural adjustment in the country. Appreciable progress enabled the country to embark, in 1990, on a three-year Enhanced Structural Adjustment Facility, which expired in December 1993 (IMF 1994, World Bank 1995). Table 14.2 presents results for the period 1988–95. The period began with good performance, with an average growth rate of 4 per cent per annum. Imports expanded steadily as well as exports. However, at beginning of the 1990s the situation deteriorated again, though after the peace agreement of 1992 growth resumed.

More worrying, however, were the current account outcomes. Data suggest a continuous deterioration due to net deficits on the service account. Thus the imbalances of Mozambique's economy were still in place by the mid-1990s, indicating that the structural adjustment programme had failed to bring about fundamental change in the economy. Sectors have responded rather weakly to the changes in relative prices. It is possible that the weak infrastructure and the lingering effects of the long civil war are still obstructing a rapid

Table 14.2 Mozambique: results of adjustment, 1988–95 (% change)

Indicator	1988	1989	1990	1991	1992	1993	1994	1995
Real growth								
GDP	5.4	5.4	1.0	4.9	−0.8	19.3	5.4	4.3
Imports	−2.0	2.8	3.8	3.1	−4.7	13.7	−2.6	−15.0
Exports	4.4	8.4	13.1	23.6	−7.0	−1.9	10.8	6.6
Current account deficit (% GDP)								
Including official transfers	−35.9	−35.5	−22.0	−16.5	−18.6	−21.9	−20.8	−20.8
Excluding official transfers	−49.9	−52.1	−49.8	−48.2	−51.9	−52.5	−55.5	−43.0

Source: World Bank (1995).

response from producers in urban and rural areas. It is also possible that the huge inflows of foreign funds in recent years led to currency appreciation, thereby inhibiting production.

Are the reforms politically sustainable? There seems to be considerable political will and commitment to the broader aspects of economic reform and structural adjustment. Reforms are still openly debated and given wide coverage. However, it should not be forgotten that the government still faces considerable political problems in proceeding with the programme. The main opposition party, RENAMO, opposes the main thrust of the reforms. On the other hand the party in power, FRELIMO, retains a heavy ideological inheritance from the past, with a partiality for central planning and control. Thus commitment to the reform programme is by no means universally supported within government (Soares 1994).

It is, however, important to note that the international perspective has changed radically for Mozambique. First, collapse of the Soviet Union meant the loss of an important political and commercial ally. Second, the return to democracy in South Africa had an important demonstration effect, forcing the country to move into multi-party democracy. But, as noted above, the country lost its leverage with the donor community and is now seen pretty much as another African country that should reform under similar conditions to those of its neighbours. Mozambique's ability to pursue independent policies has thus narrowed considerably.

Finally, let us look at performance in three areas that have received considerable attention in the ten years of structural adjustment. These are inflation, the public sector investment programme and external debt. Persistent inflation has been a feature of Mozambique's economy during the last few years. As in many other transition economies, it has been partly a result of repressed inflation, inherited from the system of central planning. However, the poor sequencing of economic reforms, imperfect liberalisation of the markets, and general weakness of monetary policy, plus weak financial institutions, have also contributed to the problem.

Second, there has been concern among donors regarding the future of public investment. Mozambique's current public investment programme is assumed to contain a large share of hidden current expenditure. Further, the programme is said to reflect donor interests and priorities, rather than those of Mozambique. The consequence has been low efficiency of the public investment, partly reflected in a too high incremental capital output ratio. To improve public investment, it is necessary to evolve well designed country as well as sector strategies, specifying priorities and defining options. Second, it is important to develop local capability in identifying, preparing and appraising projects

Third, the external debt problem is a central issue in Mozambique. To achieve a viable balance of payments situation, the country needs a radical restructuring of its external debt. However, as a result of adjustment programmes, multilateral debt is still on the increase. This is a debt pattern frequently found in countries undertaking structural adjustment programmes. However, since no arrears may be accumulated on this type of debt, it has become more demanding of the country's resources. The other problem is that of debt to Russia. There is considerable uncertainty about the volume and terms under which the debt was contracted. Most of the loans were for the purchase of military hardware, making it even more difficult to establish a rationale for repayment.

The island states

Let us make some brief mention of developments in Cape Verde and São Tomé and Príncipe. Cape Verde comprises a number of islands in the Atlantic Ocean. Its population is only slightly more than 400,000. There has been a high level of migration, and Cape Verdeans can be found in all Lusophone countries, the United States, France and other parts of Europe. Cape Verde played a special role in the Portuguese colonial set-up, and became more a province of the metropolitan country than a colony. It became a communications and trade hub in the Atlantic for Portugal's African empire. Many Cape Verdeans were educated for direct integration into the colonial administration on the continent. The struggle for independence, as already noted, was waged together with Guinea-Bissau, the two subsequently forming 'one country with two governments'. They became separate countries in 1982. Following a spell of socialism, Cape Verde had turned to multi-party democracy by the 1990s.

São Tomé e Príncipe are even smaller, with an estimated population of about 135,000 inhabitants. The islands were uninhabited on the arrival of the first Portuguese explorers and the Portuguese used them as a slave depot. What the islands states have in common is a degree of insularity from the continental concerns. Life has gone on pretty much as before. And structural adjustment concerns have not been at the forefront.

CONCLUSION

Portugal's colonial adventure in Africa was largely a case of improvisation. A small, impoverished country at the European periphery, it had to find its own way. The purely mercantile model used during most of the period of Portuguese colonialism in Africa ended during the second half of the twentieth century with attempts at European settlement, in Angola especially but also in Mozambique. The Portuguese language is no doubt an important legacy. Although, as noted above, there are challenges from French and English, Portuguese will remain important, even if mainly in the *crioulo* form now used widely in the former colonies of West Africa. As a small country Portugal has not been able to provide the training opportunities desired by its former colonies. Many students from Lusophone Africa have found their way into Britain and France.

Civil wars have been another common feature, while poor management aggravated the already difficult social conditions. Serious reforms were not embarked on until the mid-1980s. The delay was partly a result of the legacy of central planning and control, from which it has been difficult to make a complete break. This problem was especially serious in Angola, which is today the only country that has been unable to embark on structural adjustment.

Finally, although a common colonial background would seem to be a uniting factor, the Portuguese-speaking African countries have little real co-operation. Partly owing to distance, trade between the countries is practically non-existent, with perhaps the exception of some trade between Guinea-Bissau and Cape Verde. However, Portugal itself retains a central position as trading and financial partner for all the countries. It is difficult to foresee a situation where trade among these countries would increase significantly. Partly in a bid to free themselves from the trade patterns, countries are taking own initiatives. Guinea-Bissau has recently joined the CFA zone countries, retaining the CFA franc as its currency. Mozambique, on the other hand, has become the first non-English-speaking country to become a member of the Commonwealth. Both Angola and Mozambique are members of the Southern African Development Community (SADC). Lusophone countries seem to be shedding their colonial legacy and charting new paths to development on the basis of a broader and much older collaboration with their African neighbours.

REFERENCES

Aguilar, R. and Zejan, M. (1990) *Angola: A Macroeconomic Analysis*, Macroeconomic Studies, Stockholm: Swedish International Development Co-operation Agency (Sida).

Aguilar, R. and Zejan, M. (1992) *Guinea-Bissau 1992: Getting off the Track*, Macroeconomic Studies, Stockholm: Swedish International Development Co-operation Agency (Sida).

Aguilar, R. and Stenman, Å. (1993) *Guinea-Bissau 1993, Facing New Temptations and Challenges*, Macroeconomic Studies 43, Stockholm: Swedish International Development Co-operation Agency (Sida).

Aguilar, R. and Stenman, Å. (1994) *Guinea-Bissau 1994: On the Eve of Tomorrow*, Macroeconomic Studies 56, Stockholm: Swedish International Development Co-operation Agency (Sida).

Aguilar, R. and Stenman, Å. (1996) *Guinea-Bissau 1995: Missing the Beat*, Macroeconomic Reports 5, Stockholm: Swedish International Development Co-operation Agency (Sida).

Bhagavan, M.R. (1986) *Angola's Political Economy 1975–1985*, Uppsala: Scandinavian Institute of African Studies.

Carneiro, D.D. and Abreu, M.D. (1989) *Angola: Growth and Adjustment in Scenarios of Peace*, Stockholm: Sida.

Gunn, G. (1987) 'The Angolan Economy: a History of Contradictions', in E.J. Keller and D. Rothchild (eds) *Afro-Marxist Regimes: Ideology and Public Policy*, London: Lynne Rienner.

International Monetary Fund (1994) *Republic of Mozambique: Enhanced Structural Adjustment Facility: Policy Framework Paper for 1994–96*, Washington DC: IMF.

Lobban, R.A. (1995) *Cape Verde: Crioulo Colony to Independent Nation*, Boulder CO: Westview Press.

Marcum, J.A. (1987) 'The People's Republic of Angola: a Radical Vision Frustrated', in E.J. Keller and D. Rothchild (eds) *Afro-Marxist Regimes: Ideology and Public Policy*, London: Lynne Rienner.

Murteira, M. (1988) *Os estados de língua portuguesa na economia mundial: Ideologias e práticas do desenvolvimento*, Lisbon: Presença.

Soares, P.F. (1994) *Moçambique. Evolução económica 1992–93*, Lisbon: Banco de Portugal.

Stenbeck, C. (1996) *National Accounts for Mozambique: Preliminary GDP Estimates for 1994*, Stockholm: Statistics Sweden.

UNDP/World Bank (1989) *Angola: An Introductory Economic Review*, New York: UNDP.

World Bank (1995) *Country Assistance Strategy of the World Bank Group for the Republic of Mozambique*, Washington DC: World Bank.

Part III

THE FUTURE

15

THE NEW SOUTH AFRICA

Growth or stagnation?

Mats Lundahl

South Africa's second post-apartheid elections are scheduled for 1999. By then, the African National Congress (ANC) will have been in power for five years, nominally at the head of a Government of National Unity, together with the National Party (until April 1996) and Inkatha, but in fact carrying out a purely ANC policy agenda. Coming to power on the crest of rising expectations among the black majority, the ANC failed only by a narrow margin to obtain the two-thirds majority that would have made it possible for it to rule alone.

The apartheid era, from the triumph of the National Party in the 1948 elections to the release of Nelson Mandela and other political prisoners in early 1990, saw the creation of the most elaborate system of economic and social discrimination in world history. Discrimination was not new in South Africa, however, having been a feature of that part of the African continent since the arrival of the first European settlers in 1652. What was new in 1948 was the systematic thoroughness with which discriminatory legislation was pursued. The results were evident at each and every level of society, permeating all facets of everyday life. In the end, the economic costs of the system were huge: low efficiency, low growth, isolation from the international economy, and low incomes, malnutrition, ill health, bad housing and inferior education for the black majority.

Thus for more than forty years the rights and economic opportunities of the majority of the South African population were constrained by the National Party government. All available indicators tell an identical story: there was an enormous gap between whites and blacks, with Asians and coloureds somewhere in between. Then, in 1990, the tide began to turn. National Party president, Frederik Willem de Klerk, finally realised that the apartheid system had no role to play in the new dispensation and had to be relegated to history. The road to democratisation lay open and could not be closed again. Once opened, the initiative quickly went into the hands of the ANC. After forty years in power, the National Party was seriously burdened by its tumultuous past. It was incapable of projecting a credible view of what the new South Africa should look like. The task of wooing voters to its side on the basis of well argued political and economic programmes proved formidable. There was thus little it could do but fall in line, hoping to salvage something by participating in a government of transition.

This chapter will examine some of the most important economic issues confronting the new leaders in South Africa. The ANC made a number of promises during the 1994 elections, most fundamentally dealing with redistribution, to be implemented up to 1999. They were spelled out in the ANC's economic strategy called the Reconstruction and Development Programme (RDP), subsequently adopted by the Government of National Unity. The RDP is essentially a strategy for narrowing the gap between the rich and the poor, with its goals formulated in terms of extending access to education, housing, electricity, water, sanitation, health services and land (ANC 1994).

BACKGROUND

In the years between de Klerk's decision to open up the democratic process to all South Africans, irrespective of race, and the 1994 elections, the scope for and the economic limitations on redistribution were thoroughly examined by South African economists. The verdict was fairly unanimous: unless drastic measures were resorted to, the scope for a static redistribution of income was small. If the visions contained in the RDP were to be realised, the economy needed to grow and at a much higher rate than before (Lundahl and Moritz 1996: chapters 9–10).

The inter-racial distribution problem has been better analysed than virtually any other economic problem that South Africa faces (see Lundahl and Moritz 1994). I will, therefore, not dwell on it in any detail here. Instead, I will focus on the necessary (but not sufficient) condition for greater equality: growth. How can the ANC-led government inject new life into an economy that was in decline from the 1970s to 1993 and which, thereafter, has only had a rate of growth that barely matched that of the population (South African Reserve Bank 1997a: 5)? An economy that seeks increased income equality via redistribution needs to generate growth. There is simply no way round it.

The year 1999 will be a historic one for South Africa in the sense that it will mark the end of the transition to democratic majority rule. The winner of the parliamentary elections will then form a government without having to pay any political dues to the minority. The winner – the ANC – will take everything. Whatever happens on the road to 1999, the ANC will win a comfortable victory, simply because no alternatives have emerged since 1994 to threaten its dominance. The National Party will be relieved to get half the number of seats it obtained in 1994. With de Klerk gone and its name smeared, the party will gradually fade out of the picture. No serious liberal alternative exists, and no such alternative is likely to emerge in the near future. But even if one should exist by 1999, it would not be able to make much of a dent in the ANC ranks. Inkatha remains an ethnically based party, one which stands and falls with its leader Buthelezi. No populist splinter group has broken away from the ANC. This situation is unlikely to last but requires a trigger in the form of a cataclysmic event. So far, no such occasion has presented itself, and it is unlikely to come before the elections.

The ANC thus rules supreme. It does not have to discuss its policies with other parties unless it wants to. But, as we will demonstrate below, the probability that the present economic strategy will fail to deliver the promised results is very high. Then, possibly, another policy package will have to be tried. However, in the absence of credible political threats to the ANC hegemony, the changes will be marginal, perhaps even cosmetic. Some strategy for the twenty-first century must be put in place before the elections, because the voters will demand it. It will not mean that the preferences of the voters will have changed, however. They will still demand satisfaction of their basic needs, the cornerstone of the Reconstruction and Development Programme. It is hardly realistic to expect any abrupt about-turn with regard to how the needs will be met.

Thus growth will be the overriding economic consideration up to the 1999 elections, and quite probably after that as well. In 1999 Nelson Mandela will resign as President and Thabo Mbeki will take over. *Ceteris paribus*, that is not likely to lead to any other changes in economic policy than would have resulted otherwise. Being ultimately responsible for the recent development policy, Mbeki represents continuity, not change.

GETTING GROWTH GOING

Arguments about to how to get growth going in South Africa have not been lacking. The country has a long and not very successful experience of import substitution in manufacturing, from the 1920s until the change of policy in recent years (see Horwitz 1967, Botha 1973, Lipton 1985, McCarthy 1988, Fine and Rustomjee 1996). In spite of this, when the ANC's economic policy began to take shape after 1990, one of the most favoured ideas was that growth could spring out of industrialisation based on the domestic market (van der Berg and Siegbrits 1991, Moll 1991, Standish 1992). The demand in this market, if suitably stimulated, would be directed mainly towards low-price necessities that could be produced with the aid of labour-intensive techniques that furthermore would demand few imported inputs.[1] This would create a

215

virtuous spiral, with increasing incomes leading to increasing demand and output. For that to materialise, however, demand would first have to be stimulated. Arguments were thus advanced for a redistribution-driven 'kick-start' of the economy. Construction of dwellings for low-income earners on a large scale being a good example. The sector does not require a huge volume of imported inputs, while it is at the same time labour-intensive.

Although the kick-start idea was partly based on the existence of unutilised capacity in labour-intensive sectors, such as construction, it is obvious that when these sectors expand their output they may have to rely on intermediates and other inputs from sectors where there is little such capacity, thus inhibiting growth. Also, nothing guarantees that the demand generated by increased incomes will be directed exclusively towards goods produced in sectors with excess capacity. Thus to what extent it is possible to kick-start the economy remains an empirical question.

In 1989 the average capacity utilisation in manufacturing was 84.5 per cent, not much lower than the 86.3 per cent reached in 1981 – a year with high gold prices and insignificant balance of payments restrictions (Moll 1991: 318). In 1995 the figure was 83 per cent (Standing *et al.* 1996: 25). However, restrictions on the growth rate could also come from imports. At the beginning of the 1990s a 1 per cent increase in domestic expenditure, on average, increased imports by almost 2.2 per cent (Moll 1991: 317). Thus, in the worst case scenario, the kick-start process would be held back by balance of payments difficulties as well.

An alternative way of generating growth that has been suggested is a change in demand patterns, triggered by a redistribution of income and wealth in favour of black South Africans. The latter are believed to spend relatively more on labour-intensive domestically produced goods, and less on imports, than whites. The Development Bank of Southern Africa has suggested that incomes spent by Africans tend to yield a contribution to GDP that is almost 21 per cent higher than that from incomes spent by whites. Further, black consumption is 21 per cent more labour-intensive and 4 per cent less import-intensive than that of whites (Krietzinger-Van Niekerk *et al.* 1992: 14).

Whether a redistribution-driven demand increase generates growth is to a very large extent determined by what happens on the production side. For example, will the output pattern adjust easily when the demand side of the economy emits signals that differ from those of the past? If not, growth will not easily be generated. Unfortunately, there seem to be good reasons for suspecting that adjustment may be sluggish. Here the extent of excess capacity is of fundamental importance, but obstacles may arise in other ways as well. For example, it may not be easy to shift from capital-intensive to labour-intensive methods of production. Elasticities of substitution may be low, at least in the short run, which is the relevant time spectrum if the aim is to kick-start the economy.

The assumptions with respect to demand made by the kick-start and domestic market advocates have also been questioned. Poor people do not necessarily demand mainly labour-intensive goods. Branches of industry like non-electrical appliances, furniture, clothing, leather and metal products, shoes and food would be suitable for small-scale, labour-intensive production, but since the income elasticities of demand for most of these do not exceed 1, embarking on them may slow down the kick-start process (Standish 1992: 121).

Critics have also pointed out that the idea of growth from redistribution has much in common with the 'macroeconomic populism' of the type practised in some Latin American countries in the recent past, on the basis of deficit financing via the government budget (see Dornbusch and Edwards 1990). The expansion process works only during the initial phase when, in addition, real wages and employment both increase, inflation is kept low through price controls and imports are resorted to in order to ease the bottle-necks created by the increasing demand. In the second phase the country runs out of foreign exchange, and the bottlenecks become visible. The price level increases, the currency appreciates in real terms, and the investment level falls, while real wages remain high. The government budget deficit increases but the rate of growth declines. Finally, the country enters a balance of payments crisis, the currency reserves are almost wiped out, shortages of goods ensue and the budget deficit and the rate of inflation both increase rapidly, while the tax base is simultaneously eroded. Increased foreign support becomes necessary to maintain growth. Since this is often not forthcoming, the economy heads for macroeconomic chaos, and drastic medicine is required to stabilise it. Stagnation sets in.

For whatever reason, the kick-start advocates failed to convince the Government of National Unity that their case was a good one. During the last few years – with a couple of exceptions (notably NIEP n.d.) – the idea of growth from redistribution has faded into the background. This, however, does not mean that the growth theme has been abandoned – on the contrary, it has been given added emphasis – only that now most of the participants in the South African economic debate appear to be convinced that causality runs, or must run, in the opposite direction: from growth to redistribution. According to this view, the task of economic policy is to stimulate growth directly. Only then will South Africa see a rise in employment and incomes as well as increased scope for redistribution in favour of the poor population segments.

The 'growth first' strategy has been accepted by the ANC. The Reconstruction and Development Programme (ANC 1994) also has as one of its main objectives the increase of the growth rate to around 5 per cent by the turn of the century. Though the RDP is fundamentally a basic needs programme, it was realised that without growth the scope for redistribution and poverty reduction would be extremely limited. The programme can also be seen as 'a version of a home-grown structural adjustment programme' (Kahn 1997: 2). The strategy builds on a revision of the trade and industry policy, in the direction of increased openness, increased human capital formation through education and a consistent and growth-fomenting macroeconomic policy. Measures should be devised to stimulate manufacturing exports, increase competitive pressure by lowering tariffs and instituting anti-trust legislation. Small and medium-size enterprises were to be targeted for support: capacity building, training, technological development, infrastructure, marketing, etc. Fiscal and monetary restraint was also seen as contributing to a stable policy environment, conducive to an inflow of foreign capital.

The RDP never got off the ground, however (Lundahl 1997). Lack of capacity at the local level, where the projects were to be implemented, made it fall behind schedule from the very outset. By mid-1995 the Office responsible for the implementation of the RPD had discovered that virtually all basic needs projects were behind target. Lacking a clear and co-ordinated implementation programme, the initiative had been left to the individual government Ministries, and had thus taken place only in a very *ad hoc* fashion. But the RDP was also overtaken by events. Alternative or complementary strategies were formulated at the same time, reducing the RDP's focus and thrust. Plans were announced, for example, for a national growth and development strategy that would ensure that the resources necessary for delivery would be forthcoming.

At the same time, the South African Foundation, representing big business, had produced its own growth document, *Growth for All*, where a major economic reform programme was sketched (South African Foundation 1996). The point of departure was clearly in line with the RDP: the need for an annual growth rate of around 5 per cent if employment was to increase by 3.5–4 per cent, so as to avoid an open unemployment rate of 40 per cent or more in 2004. The *Growth for All* strategy rested on five pillars: (1) law and order, (2) macroeconomic stability and financial liberalisation (notably the scrapping of exchange controls), (3) a reduction of the budget deficit by at least 1.5 percentage points per year, tax cuts and reforms, (4) increasingly competitive markets, with deregulation and privatisation, as well as increased wage flexibility in the labour market and, finally, (5) measures to liberalise foreign trade and encourage an inflow of foreign capital. All the pillars were not of equal importance. Two elements stood out as central: wage flexibility to ensure that employment increased and contraction of the budget deficit through a reduction of government expenditure in order to signal to investors (especially foreign ones) that macroeconomic stability would prevail in the future.

As could be expected, the *Growth for All* strategy did not appeal to the trade union movement, notably the Congress of South African Trade Unions (COSATU). The unions were not late in producing a counter-strategy: *Social*

Equity and Job Creation (1996). This strategy proceeded very much along Keynesian lines, putting emphasis on the ability of the state to create jobs without having to woo the private sector by stimulating demand and employment via fiscal expansion. Hence the unions argue that there is no need for a rapid tightening of fiscal policy, especially not via the expenditure side. Instead, the taxation of high-income earners and corporations should increase, with proceeds used for transfers and other welfare-increasing measures in favour of the poor. The unions did not see any need for wage flexibility either. On the contrary, high wages would keep demand up, and worker training could be used to increase labour productivity so as to keep cost-push inflationary pressure at bay.

Two opposing growth strategy proposals had thus been produced. In the meantime it had also become clear that with the prevailing growth rate the RDP stood little chance of being implemented according to the envisaged timetable. For that, investment in the infrastructure would have to grow by 21 per cent per annum and the local authorities (municipalities, etc.) would have to increase their infrastructure funding by no less than 30 per cent per year. With a growth rate of GDP of 3 per cent, constant government spending and a reduction of the budget deficit of 0.5 percentage points per year, that level of expenditure was completely out of the question. If the RDP was to be saved, the growth rate had to be increased. The question was: how?

The ANC-led government by and large opted for the solution suggested by the South African Foundation. In June 1996 a new macroeconomic strategy was ready: *Growth, Employment and Redistribution (GEAR)* (Department of Finance 1996a, b). The growth target is roughly the same: around 6 per cent per annum at the turn of the century. Central in the new strategy is the signalling aspect: by demonstrating that a consistent, stabilising macroeconomic policy is firmly implemented, investor confidence in South Africa is bound to increase. The slashing of the budget deficit is to be accelerated and monetary policy is to remain tight. Investment will be stimulated by tax incentives, and a gradual relaxation of exchange rate controls to enable free movement of capital. To ensure competitiveness in the world market, tariffs will continue to be lowered. Further, a number of public corporations will be privatised and the state will instead concentrate on the provision of infrastructure. By and large, the idea that greater flexibility, notably with respect to wages, is needed in the labour market has also been accepted, but this flexibility is to be traded for price restraint and job-creating investment on the part of employers.

GROWTH: THE ACTUAL RECORD

The 1970s and 1980s were bad years for the South African economy. Between 1970 and 1985 the real growth rate of GDP was a mere 2.6 per cent per annum on average, barely enough to match the rate of population growth (Nattrass 1988: 25). By the mid-1980s growth rates were negative. The figures for the latter half of the 1980s were positive, but below 2 per cent on average (Republic of South Africa 1994: 21), while in 1990–92 economic decline set in, continuing until 1993 (South African Reserve Bank 1995a). The ensuing recovery has, however, proved to be highly uneven. Thus while the growth rate jumped to an (annualised) 6 per cent during the latter half of 1993 (ibid. 1995c: 7), it was only 1.5 per cent on an annual basis for the year. In 1994 it grew by 2.5 per cent, rising to 3.5 per cent in 1995, but then fell to 3 per cent in 1996 (ibid. 1997a: 5).

This relative improvement also conceals substantial fluctuation, with a decline of 1 per cent during the first half of 1994, followed by a 5.5 per cent expansion over the rest of the year (ibid. 1997a: 7). There was then a somewhat steadier expansion of 3.5 per cent, 2.5 per cent, 3.5 per cent, 3 per cent and 3.5 per cent over the ensuing six-month periods to the end of 1996, and another dip to a mere 1 per cent during the first half of 1997 (ibid. 1997a: 6). With a population growth rate of around 2.2 per cent per annum (Standing et al. 1996: 25) these growth rates are not impressive. In per capita terms, the one for 1994 is virtually naught and the next two years yielded a mere 0.8–1.3 per cent per capita growth. Using the higher figure, it would take over fifty years to double per capita income in South Africa, while with the lower one it would take over eighty years. Should the slowdown that began in 1997 continue, the time horizon will have to be stretched even more.

The recovery initiated in 1993 began on a broad basis, with strong growth in the secondary and tertiary sectors. Agricultural output has gone through a number of swings caused by variable weather conditions. In 1993 production increased by no less than 29 per cent, followed by a 12 per cent increase in 1994 (South African Reserve Bank 1995b: 7, 1996: 3). Severe drought, leading to food imports in 1994, led to a 15 per cent fall in agricultural output, followed in 1996 by a 26 per cent increase, due to exceptionally good weather. In the first half of 1997 an annualised decline of 21 per cent was projected (ibid. 1997a: 6). Thus what happens in agriculture is ultimately conditioned by the weather.

Gold mining has been a consistently weak performer, with a negative contribution to overall growth throughout 1994–96. In the latter year gold output reached its lowest level in forty years. The gold content of the ore is falling and mining itself is done at deeper and deeper ground levels, increasing the risks and costs of operation (ibid. 1995c: 8, 1996: 3–4, 1997a: 5–6). Under the circumstances, this is hardly the sector that will help generate strong job-creating growth in the future. Generally speaking, non-gold mining has fared better, but mining output as a whole is sensitive to international price movements, as witnessed during the second half of 1996 (ibid. 1997a: 5).

Outside the primary sector, output performance has been better from the second quarter of 1993 to the second quarter of 1995, with manufacturing displaying the highest growth rate. Thereafter, output slackened, as household demand weakened and inventory accumulation was reduced. The year 1996 was an almost stagnant one. The depreciation of the rand during most of 1996, however, prepared the ground for renewed expansion in 1997 (ibid. 1995b: 7–8). Construction, in turn, has contributed only modestly, with growth rates of 1.5–2 per cent, among other things because of a late start during the upturn, but also due to slower than expected expansion of demand from the RDP programme. The utilities sub-sector of electricity, gas and water, on the other hand, has expanded rapidly, with growth rates reaching 3.5 per cent in 1994–95 and 5 per cent thereafter. This has mainly been the result of the extension of the national grid to formerly disadvantaged areas (ibid. 1995c: 8, 1996: 4, 1997a: 6–7).

The growth rate in the tertiary sector, finally, has also increased, from about 2.5 per cent up to 1995 and 3–3.5 per cent, thereafter, before falling during the first half of 1997. Transport and communications and commerce have displayed the highest growth rates, with financial services slightly behind. However, as demand has weakened and production elsewhere in the economy has experienced weaker growth, these sectors have also slowed down considerably (ibid. 1996: 4).

It is readily seen from this cursory overview that the recent growth performance has been both weak and uneven. Recorded growth rates have improved *per capita* incomes only marginally. In a situation where there are strong and repeated demands for substantial redistribution, such growth levels are far from sufficient. Virtually all observers and political actors agree that it is not an acceptable state of affairs. The sectoral composition of growth also gives cause for concern. What happens in agriculture cannot be controlled too much. Gold mining, once the engine of the economy, has shrunk to the point where it now accounts for a mere 2.5 per cent of GDP (ibid. 1997a: 5), a share likely to fall further. The output of other minerals is crucially dependent on what happens in the world market. Tertiary sector production is intimately connected with the overall level of economic activity. This leaves manufacturing, and it is around it that the growth debate has centred. Already in 1950 manufacturing had become the largest sector of the economy in terms of output (Nattrass 1988: 25), partly as a result of the import substitution process referred to above. However, long before 1994 this process had run its course. Besides, in April that same year South Africa had signed the Marrakesh Agreement establishing the World Trade Organisation. As a result, the import substitution road had for all practical purposes been closed. New ways of expanding the manufacturing sector had to be found. It is in this light that the GEAR strategy is of significance.

GEAR makes clear predictions with respect to growth up to the year 2000 (Department of Finance 1996b: 11). A base scenario (ibid.: 10–11) assumes a

9.6 per cent depreciation of the real exchange rate for 1996, with only very small changes after that, and a gradual reduction of the budget deficit up to a level of 3 per cent of GDP in fiscal 2000/01. Further, a reduction of government consumption is assumed, along with a reduction of tariffs from 10 per cent of import value to 8 per cent. Real wage increases in the public sector of 1 per cent per annum are coupled with increased public capital formation (with 2–3 per cent per year), positive, but falling real interest rates and modest (1.4 per cent per annum) private wage increases. These assumptions would generate overall growth rates of 3.3 per cent in 1996, 2 per cent in 1997, 2.5 per cent in 1998, 2.9 per cent in 1999 and 3.3 per cent in 2000, i.e. rates that would not be able to ensure positive *per capita* income growth for three of the five years in the projection. This is clearly insufficient. At these rates the Reconstruction and Development Programme would be in jeopardy.

The GEAR strategy attempts to speed up the growth rate by introducing the following changes as compared with the base scenario. (1) Faster reduction of the budget deficit, to 4 per cent (instead of 4.5) in 1997, 3.5 per cent in 1998 and 3 per cent in 2000. (2) Accelerated tariff reform, substantial increases in public investment, up to a growth rate of almost 17 per cent in 2000 for public authorities (against 2.4 in the base run) and 10 per cent in public corporations (against 3 per cent). (3) Also included are reduced wage increases in the private sector, confining increases to 0.7 per cent per annum, and increased non-gold exports (a growth rate of 10 per cent by 2000, against 5.3 in the base scenario). (4) Finally, substantial increases in private investment are assumed (growth rate of 17 per cent, against 7.1 in the base scenario) as well as increased foreign capital inflows, in the form of direct investment, rising from US$155 million in 1996 to US$804 million in 2000. Supposedly this medicine would increase GDP growth to 3.5 per cent in 1996, 2.9 per cent in 1997, 3.8 per cent in 1998, 4.9 per cent in 1999 and 6.1 per cent in 2000 (ibid.: 12–13).

But will it? As we have seen, the actual growth rate for 1996 was 3 per cent, not 3.5 per cent, and the annualised rate for the first half of 1997 falls far short of the GEAR target for the year as a whole. Will the same pattern prevail in the future – that is, with actual growth rates falling persistently below those predicted in the accelerated GEAR scenario? Unfortunately there are good reasons to fear that such may be the case.

Why GEAR won't work (1) The investment problem

The main snag regarding GEAR is that it builds on a number of variables which, from the point of view of the government, are by and large exogenous. The most important is investment. The government attempts to get growth going through an expansion of private investment, but, to the extent that private investors want to witness growth before they invest, we are back to square one. This is obviously a chicken-and-egg problem, certainly a vicious circle, and there is no obvious way of breaking it. The problem manifests itself in several ways. We shall deal with each one in turn, beginning with the determinants of investment.

What determines investment is a tricky question in any economy, while the South African case presents more complications than most. Basically, investment is a matter of expectations with respect to the future. If investors are not confident that the future will be favourable, they will not invest. The question is then how confidence is built. What do investors look at when they form their expectations? The GEAR strategy makes very definite assumptions about what governs this process: government policy. By emitting the right kind of signals the government can convince both domestic and foreign investors (notably the latter) that a policy environment which is likely to be conducive to stability will prevail. These signals induce investment.

An alternative interpretation runs in terms of 'crowding out' (Weeks 1996). Increased fiscal discipline will reduce the need for public sector borrowing and this will in turn exert a downward pressure on interest rates that will allow companies in the private sector to finance their expansion. This, however, presupposes that the demand for investment funds is sensitive to changes in interest rates. In a situation where it is highly uncertain what the future will bring, this elasticity may be low and little new investment results. Thus the mechanism that is supposed to trigger investment may be lacking. Furthermore, the GEAR scenario predicts that falling interest rates will go hand in hand with an increased deficit on the current account of the balance of payments, covered by a capital inflow from abroad. Given the recent history of monetary policy in South Africa, this is hardly a likely sequence of events. Still, deterioration of the current account is likely to lead to a tightening of monetary policy, with higher, not lower, interest rates.

Fiscal austerity and low interest rates are two possible ways of getting investment going. Neither will work in isolation. As noted above, investors may also want to see signs of growth, because growth implies market opportunities (Gibson and van Seventer 1995). Nobody is likely to invest in an economy heading for a stagnant future. This is a balanced growth *cum* free rider problem. If all investors are waiting for all other investors to get their act together, nothing will happen. To what extent then does government policy have an influence on growth independently of that which results from government-induced private investment? The GEAR answer is: 'Through exports.' GEAR is a strategy for the open economy, and the government envisages a stimulus to exports that works through three different routes: exchange rate policy, labour market flexibility and tax incentives and other supply-side measures.

The first measure is already in place. From January to November 1996 the rand underwent a depreciation (from an initial overvaluation) *vis-à-vis* the dollar from R3.64 to R4.70 (Kahn 1997: 2). This windfall gain for exporters was complemented with compensating tariff decreases to ensure that resources did not flow into import-competing industries instead of into exports and to maintain competitive pressure in the economy.

The other two measures are much more problematic. In May 1996 a presidential commission on labour market policy presented a report entitled *Restructuring the South African Labour Market.* It is an 'accord' on employment and growth that would bring about the necessary labour market flexibility. The idea is to arrive at a negotiated tripartite solution − a tit-for-tat − between labour, employers and government. Each of the three parties is supposed to bring something to the negotiating table: moderate wage demands (and other demands related to working conditions) in the case of the unions, price restraint and increased investment in that of employers' organisations and social service and infrastructure provision in the case of the state. This construction does not solve the problem, because it *assumes* that investment will be forthcoming in a situation where exports are, on their own, a crucial element in generating the growth needed for higher investment. We end up in a chicken-and-egg situation again. The reasoning becomes circular.

This is not the only problem with a social accord. It may never come into being, because the negotiators may fail to deliver what it stipulates or simply because they doubt each other's ability to honour it. The fragile link in the accord chain is the employers. Business in South Africa hardly speaks with a single voice. The large corporations to a large extent speak for themselves, while on the more organised collaborative level there are the South African Chamber of Business, the South African Foundation and others. Who then speaks for 'business'? Even if a 'player' with some kind of mandate can be located or constructed there is no guarantee that what is decided at the negotiating table will be honoured by the individual companies. In a market economy decisions with respect to investment and pricing are made at the firm level, not centrally. Unless firms believe in the future they will not invest or refrain from raising prices if they cannot cover their costs. This, of course, the labour movement realises. Business will not be able to come up with a credible commitment. Hence there would be no point in attempting to negotiate a social pact. Once more, the mechanism that is supposed to put investment in motion is missing.

This leaves us with the supply-side measures. Such measures have already been attempted. Between 1990 and mid-1997 a General Export Incentive Scheme (GEIS) was in existence. To what extent this scheme, which targeted exports directly and encouraged the use of local inputs, actually managed to stimulate exports is still debatable. Critics claim that its effects were marginal at best − no less than 75 per cent of the payments went to the iron and steel industry (Nomvete *et al.* 1997: 45) − and that the support went to the wrong kind of firms, sometimes fraudulently. At any rate, GEIS had to be phased out, since the direct targeting of exports violates the WTO statutes. New measures had to be devised, including accelerated depreciation on new investments, tax holidays, support to small and medium-size firms, marketing support, credit schemes, technological development, etc. Whether these new efforts will be more fruitful than the GEIS scheme remains to be seen. However, since the net appears to have been cast too widely across branches and firms, and with the aid of too many (sometimes possibly conflicting) criteria, this is hardly likely to be the case. Successful targeting requires a good crystal ball. Sectors, sub-sectors and individual product lines where South Africa has a comparative advantage must be found. This is not an easy exercise, hardly one likely to be conducive to short-run growth. If it works at all, it would do so in the medium to long run.

It is also possible that the wrong industries are being targeted. Recent research indicates that South Africa's comparative advantage is to be found in resource-intensive, low technology and medium-wage industries, like those of non-ferrous metals, iron and steel, paper and printing and shipbuilding. All these are also relatively capital-intensive, which means that an expansion of output may be dependent on investment – both in terms of physical capital and in the form of the human capital required to handle the equipment (Nordås 1996). If so, the conclusions are clear. (1) The best supply-side measure would be education. (2) Once more we are facing the problem of how to get investment going. The present supply-side measures do not seem able to do the trick.

The role of the foreign trade sector appears peculiar once imports are taken into account. GEAR envisages an increase in the deficit on the current account of the balance of payments up to the year 2000 (Department of Finance 1996a: 7). In a simple national income identity setting, the impact of this on the growth rate is *negative*, not positive (Weeks 1996: 10–13). How exports work in the GEAR framework is impossible to say, since the underlying model, for some strange reason, has never been made public.

A final question mark has to do with the targeting of foreign investment. At present, foreign capital is flowing into the economy (ibid. 1997b: 1), but it is the 'wrong' kind of capital: either portfolio investment or replacements of the capital stock that was run down during the years of sanction. There is little net expansion of direct investment. It might have made more sense to primarily target domestic firms instead. That South Africa should be able to attract foreign direct investment without the growth of domestic capital formation does not sound a likely proposition. Foreign investors are likely to watch the behaviour of domestic investors very closely. Thus to the extent that investment picks up one would expect domestic companies to take the lead and foreign companies to follow suit once they are convinced that the economic environment is safe, sound and conducive to future growth.

Why GEAR won't work (2) Built-in policy brakes

Investment is not the only problem with the GEAR strategy. It is simply the first hurdle. Assuming that investors react the way GEAR predicts they will, and that growth somehow gets going, a second line of obstacles awaits to be overcome: the austere fiscal policy needed to reduce the budget deficit, and the tight monetary policy 'that has characterised the South African economy for close to a decade. There is a considerable risk that short-run stabilisation considerations will conflict with the growth target.

Already the basic scenario of GEAR calls for a continuous reduction of the government budget deficit, with 0.5 percentage points (of GDP) per annum, to 4.5 per cent in 1997 and a final 3.0 per cent in 2000. The GEAR strategy for accelerated growth envisages an even faster convergence path, with a reduction in 1997 that is twice as large as in the base run. This would be followed by 0.5 percentage point reductions thereafter, in order to arrive at the 3.0 per cent target already by 1999 (Department of Finance 1996b: 11, 13). The higher-growth scenario would thus call for a much more contractionary fiscal stance than the one prevailing in the low-growth one.

Seen in an international perspective, South Africa is not a low-tax economy. The share of taxes in GDP is on the same level as that prevailing, on average, in countries with similar *per capita* income (Lachman and Bercuson 1992: 29). Whether the tax base can be broadened and existing taxes raised can always be debated. What matters in the present context is that the central element of GEAR is increased private investment and that the way to higher investment is via the emission of the right signals. This effectively precludes tax increases and puts the entire burden of adjustment on the expenditure side.

Relying on expenditure cuts creates problems. First, they should in principle be made in such a way as to minimise the harmful effects on growth, i.e. the cuts should be selective and target some expenditures and budget votes more than others. In practice, however, such targeting tends to be difficult. Government departments tend to watch each other and defend their own territories. In this situation the likelihood that the cuts will be effected in an 'egalitarian' way, that is, without due regard to efficiency and growth considerations, is high.

Should the economy grow more slowly than expected, the problems will be compounded. The computations for government revenue build on some assumed growth path of GDP. Thus if the actual rate falls short of that targeted, revenues will fall short of target as well. This implies, in turn, that, if the targeted budget reduction is to materialise, expenditures must be reduced at a faster rate than planned. Thus the policy becomes more contractionary than originally intended, public investment suffers and the burden of 'getting growth going' through investment will increasingly be placed on the shoulders of the private sector. The use of tax holidays to stimulate growth has similar effects. They reduce potential revenue and shift the burden of adjustment to the expenditure side. On the other hand, situations could arise where companies create new firms or subsidiaries just to be able to continue to enjoy tax holidays.

Unless education is exempted, the expenditure cuts will also hamper human capital formation, in a situation where skilled labour is badly needed. The apartheid legacy has implied an acute shortage of skilled people. From the mid-1970s onwards, this has contributed to the poor growth (Lundahl *et al.* 1992: 312–17). This shortage, which, as we have seen, may have serious consequences for export growth, still persists and to the extent that expenditure cuts take place across the board will be exacerbated.

The skills issue takes us from fiscal to monetary policy. For a number of years, monetary management has been tight. In 1989 the South African Reserve Bank tightened the monetary screw in a bid to defend the rand. This tight policy still prevails. The autonomy of the bank is guaranteed in the new constitution, which means that since the main task of monetary policy is that of combating inflation the bank could easily pull in a direction that is likely to hamper growth. Contractive action can be set off in different ways, and one of them is via the skill constraint. Growth increases the demand for skilled labour. Unless the supply can be expanded, upward pressure on skilled wage rates will result and, to the extent that wage contracts for unskilled labourers are indexed to the development of skilled wages, 'contamination' will result. The overall wage level will thus tend to rise and with it the general price level. In such a situation the Reserve Bank will react by tightening monetary policy. Interest rates, already high, will rise even further, and there will be pressure on the Department of Finance to fall in line so as not to compromise the stabilisation effort. The result is that growth, if only temporarily, will be held back. Firms cannot invest and consumer demand falls.

Possibly the growth rate at which the skill constraint may spark off a monetary contraction has been reduced during the last couple of years. South Africa is to an increasing extent experiencing a brain drain of educated whites, who have seen their labour market shrink as affirmative action measures take hold. At the same time, with rising labour costs, there will be a tendency for techniques in manufacturing to become more capital, and hence also skill, intensive.

The trade-off between stabilisation and growth that runs via monetary policy could also come into play as a result of balance of payments trouble. When GDP increases so do imports, and marginal import propensities appear to be high in South Africa. During the recovery from late 1993 to late 1996 the average import penetration ratio (the value of imports in relation to GDP at constant prices) increased from 19 per cent to 27 per cent. In part this was due to the repeal of trade sanctions and the lowering of tariffs, but there is no doubt that GDP increases tend to result in increased demand for imports as well, via increased real domestic expenditure (South African Reserve Bank 1997a: 23). To the extent that the increases consist of inputs for the export sectors the pressure on the balance of payments will presumably be tolerable, at least in the somewhat longer run, but non-traded goods require imported inputs as well, and in addition there is a demand for imported consumer goods. Thus growth easily leads to a deficit on the current account of the balance of payments and to a tendency for the rand to depreciate, which makes the Reserve Bank tighten the monetary screw to reduce the threat of imported inflation.[2] Again growth is choked in the process.

In sum, GEAR stands out not so much as a growth strategy but as one for macroeconomic discipline. Unfortunately, the way it is formulated appears to introduce a conflict or trade-off between growth and stability in the sense that stabilisation efforts will get in the way of growth. The government is committed to reducing the budget deficit at a brisk pace and fiscal policy hence has to be contractionary. However, in the best-case scenario, tight monetary policy can be avoided. GEAR envisages a reduction of tariffs that may put competitive pressure on firms and make them refrain from price inflation. However, inflationary pressure may mount from other quarters, not least the labour market. If such be the case, monetary policy will be tightened and the growth rate will be reduced. That puts us back where we started: with investment. Unless domestic and foreign companies react positively in the face of austere policies and turn a blind eye to the lack of growth, the GEAR package will fail to lift the economy.

THE POLITICAL ECONOMY OF LOW GROWTH

The conclusions from the foregoing should be clear. There is a very real risk that GEAR will fail to deliver the growth necessary for meeting the objectives of the Reconstruction and Development Programme. The crucial elements of the strategy are outside the control of the government and there are strong built-in policy checks on growth. Together these factors will choke the growth process. The South African economy will continue to muddle through, the way it has done since 1993, with some years slightly better than others. Factors like the weather will continue to be decisive for the growth rate, which is likely to remain around 3 per cent, until the turn of the century. This is far from enough to enable the delivery of the contents of the RDP. The growth constraint on redistribution and social spending will become stronger, while emphasis on growth will presumably be even more pronounced in the debate, with new (or old) suggestions about how to proceed continuing to enliven it. At the same time, the expansion of formal employment will be sluggish and the disadvantaged among the population will be required to wait or to adjust their expectations downwards.

This message will be delivered in a situation where the gap between the haves and the have-nots among blacks increases rapidly. Between 1975 and 1991 the richest 20 per cent of the blacks increased their real income by almost 40 per cent. All other black groups saw their position deteriorate, the poorest 40 per cent by no less than 41.4 per cent (McGrath and Whiteford 1994: 11). This pattern is likely to have been reinforced since 1991. In the post-apartheid economy, the better-educated blacks are the ones with the brightest future prospects. Political change and correctness make it imperative to hire blacks at all levels of the formal labour market. The problem of the poor is that they are not part of this market and the backlog of unemployed is already enormous. Since, on present trends, perhaps only some 5–6 per cent of the annual addition to the labour force is absorbed by the formal segment (van der Berg 1991: 22, Standing *et al.* 1996: 109), one can only imagine what sentiments may be building up outside it and the social consequences, including crime, of exclusion.

Pressure is mounting from another quarter as well. After the presentation of the GEAR document, the trade union movement, notably COSATU, has gradually distanced itself from the economic policies of the ANC government. The issues of labour market flexibility and wage restraint have driven a wedge between the traditional allies. COSATU, to an increasing extent, is expressing grass-roots sentiments against ANC policy, with the aid of the strike weapon. Not only has it become increasingly vocal with respect to GEAR, but the labour movement as a whole has also reacted against the proposed Basic Conditions of Employment Act, arguing that it provides far fewer employee benefits (in terms of working hours, maternity leave, overtime payment, etc.) than demanded. It is now too late in the day to forge a social accord on the labour market; it should have been done back in 1994, immediately after the elections, in the general mood of conciliation that prevailed at the time. Today, with slow growth and little employment creation, the historic moment seems to have passed.

Sooner or later these sentiments will be vented in a different way. Economic and political solutions other than those advocated by the present ANC coalition will be sought. Even though the outcome of the process may not be as dramatic as predicted by Lester Venter (1997), where a new 'African National Labour Party' arises, to the left of the ANC, takes over the government in 2004, and begins to implement a generally populist policy, including the redistribution of a non-growing cake, political pressure may still force the ANC to do something similar. Ultimately, politicians cannot remain isolated from popular sentiment. Economic policy easily moves in cycles (Krueger 1993) and if populism is allowed to carry the day, the consequences sketched in the discussion of distribution-fuelled growth will quickly be felt by all South Africans.

NOTES

Thanks are due to Brian Kahn, Murray Leibbrandt, Lieb Loots, Nicoli Nattrass, Ben Smit and Servaas van der Berg for liberally sharing their views of the problems facing the South African economy with me. An earlier version of the chapter was presented at a seminar at the School of Oriental and African Studies, University of London, on 1 December 1997. I am grateful to the participants in that seminar, especially Ben Fine, for helpful suggestions.

1 For criticism of the argument that import substitution behind tariff walls was the main engine of industrial growth in South Africa, see Fine and Rustomjee (1996).
2 During 1996 the Bank rate was increased from 15 to 17 per cent, and the prime overdraft rate of the banks exceeded 20 per cent part of the year (Department of Finance 1997: 27). Since then, the Bank rate has come down one percentage point.

REFERENCES

ANC (African National Congress) (1994) *The Reconstruction and Development Programme*, Johannesburg: Umanyano Publications.

Botha, D.S.S. (1973) 'On Tariff Policy: the Formative Years', *South African Journal of Economics*, 41 (4): 321–55.

COSATU (and others) (1996) *Social Equity and Job Creation: The Key to a Stable Future. Proposals by the South African Labour Movement* (issued by the Labour Caucus at Nedlac incorporating Cosatu, Nactu and Fedsal).

Department of Finance (1996a) *Growth, Employment and Redistribution: A Macro-Economic Strategy* (Appendices), Pretoria.

Department of Finance (1996b) *Growth, Employment and Redistribution: A Macro-Economic Strategy* (Appendices), Pretoria.

Department of Finance (1997) *Budget Review 1997*, Pretoria.

Dornbusch, R. and Edwards, S. (1990) 'Macroeconomic Populism', *Journal of Development Economics*, 32 (2): 247–77.

Fine, B. and Rustomjee, Z. (1996) *The Political Economy of South Africa: From Minerals-Energy Complex to Industrialism*, London: Hurst.

Gibson, B. and van Seventer, D.E. (1995) *Restructuring Public Sector Expenditure in the South African Economy*, Pretoria: Development Bank of Southern Africa.

Horwitz, R. (1967) *The Political Economy of South Africa*, London: Weidenfeld & Nicolson.

Kahn, Brian (1997) *Capital Flows and Balance of Payment Crises in South Africa*, London: Weidenfeld & Nicolson.

Krietzinger-Van Niekerk, L., Eckert, J.B. and Vink, N. (1992) *Toward a Democratic Economy in South Africa: An Approach to Economic Restructuring*, Pretoria: Development Bank of Southern Africa.

Krueger, A.O. (1993) *Political Economy of Policy Reform in Developing Countries*. Cambridge MA and London: MIT Press.

Lachman, D. and Bercuson, K. with Ballalli, D., Corker. R., Christofides, C. and Wein, J. (1992) Economic Policies for a New South Africa, IMF Occasional Paper 91, Washington DC: IMF.

Lipton, M. (1985) *Capitalism and Apartheid. South Africa 1910–84*, Aldershot: Gower.

Lundahl, M. (1997) *The South African Economy in 1996: From Reconstruction and Development to Growth, Employment and Redistribution*, Stockholm: Sida.

Lundahl, M., Fredriksson, P. and Moritz, L. (1992) 'South Africa 1990: Pressure for Change', in M. Lundahl, *Apartheid in Theory and Practice: An Economic Analysis*, Boulder CO: Westview Press, pp. 293–358.

Lundahl, M. and Moritz, L. (1994) 'The Quest for Equity in South Africa – Redistribution and Growth', in B. Odén, T. Ohlson, A. Davidson, P. Strand, M. Lundahl and L. Moritz, *The South African Tripod: Studies on Economics, Politics and Conflict*, Uppsala: Scandinavian Institute of African Studies, pp. 141–212.

Lundahl, M. and Moritz, L. (1996) *Det nya Sydafrika: ekonomi and politik efter apartheid*, Stockholm: SNS Förlag.

McCarthy, C.L. (1988) 'Structural Development of South African Manufacturing Industry', *South African Journal of Economics*, 56 (1): 1–23.

McGrath, M. and Whiteford, A. (1994) *Inequality in the Size Distribution of Income in South Africa*, Occasional Papers 10, Stellenbosch: Stellenbosch Economic Project, Centre for Contextual Hermeneutics, University of Stellenbosch.

Moll, T. (1991) 'Growth through Redistribution: a Dangerous Fantasy?', *South African Journal of Economics*, 59 (3): 313–30.

National Institute for Economic Policy (NIEP) (n.d.) *From the RPP to GEAR: The Gradual Embrace of Neo-liberalism in Economic Policy*, Johannesburg: NIEP.

Nattrass, J. (1988) *The South African Economy: Its Growth and Change*, second edition, Cape Town: Oxford University Press.

Nomvete, B.D., Maasdorp, G.G. and Thomas, D. (eds) (1997) *Growth with Equity*, Cape Town: Africa Institute for Policy Analysis and Economic Integration.

Nordås, H.K. (1996) 'South African Manufacturing Industries – Catching up or Falling behind?', *Journal of Development Studies*, 32 (5): 715–33.

Presidential Commission to Investigate the Development of a Comprehensive Labour Market Policy (1996) *Restructuring the South African Labour Market*, Cape Town: CTP Book Printers.

Republic of South Africa (1994) *South African Statistics*, Pretoria: Central Statistics Service.

South African Foundation (1996) *Growth for All: An Economic Strategy for South Africa*, Johannesburg.

South African Reserve Bank (1995a) *Quarterly Bulletin* 195, March.

South African Reserve Bank (1995b) *Quarterly Bulletin* 197, September.

South African Reserve Bank (1995c) *Annual Economic Report 1995*, Pretoria.

South African Reserve Bank (1996) *Quarterly Bulletin* 199, March.

South African Reserve Bank (1997a) *Annual Economic Report 1997*, Pretoria.

South African Reserve Bank (1997b) *Quarterly Bulletin* 205, September.

Standing, G., Sender, J. and Weeks, J. (1996) *Restructuring the Labour Market: The South African Challenge*, Geneva: International Labour Office.

Standish, B. (1992) 'Resource Endowments, Constraints and Growth Policies', in I. Abedian and B. Standish (eds) *Economic Growth in South Africa: Selected Policy Issues*, Cape Town: Oxford University Press, pp. 99–127.

van der Berg, S. (1991) 'Prospects for Redistribution of Primary and Secondary Incomes in the Transition to Democracy', unpublished paper for the Conference of the Economic Society in South Africa, Stellenbosch, 2–3 October.

van der Berg, S. and Siegbrits, K. (1991) 'Redistribution and Growth', paper presented to a workshop of the Economic Trends Group, Cape Town, 22–4 November.

Venter, L. (1997) *When Mandela Goes: The Coming of South Africa's Second Revolution*, London: Doubleday.

Weeks, J. (1996) *Macroeconomic Strategy: Implications for the North West Province*, London: School of Oriental and African Studies, University of London.

16

THE POLITICAL ECONOMY OF THE HORN

Göte Hansson

The Horn of Africa, comprising Djibouti, Ethiopia, Eritrea, Somalia and the Sudan, has had a recent history characterised by wars, civil unrest, droughts and famine, and widespread poverty. The poor natural resource endowment, in particular lack of land suitable for agricultural production, implies that the arid soils do not lend themselves easily to cultivation without huge investment in irrigation. Households have tried to offset this by migrating from place to place in search of water and food for themselves and their animals. This has turned the Horn of Africa into the world's highest concentration of traditional pastoralists. Markakis (1994: 218) has noted that scarcity remains a harsh fact of life in the region.

Apart from the harsh living conditions, its conflict-prone politics have also contributed to the perennial conflicts. In the past, dictatorship and centralism featured in most of the countries in the Horn. As a consequence of the conflicts and inadequate policy design, with ideology rather than economic reality as the main thrust, social standards in the region have become quite low, even by sub-Saharan African comparison (UNDP various years). However, during the 1990s the political and economic situation in the region has changed quite dramatically.

In Ethiopia, following more than thirty years of civil war, relative peace was attained when the socialist military government, led by Mengistu Haile Mariam, was replaced by a transitional government in 1991. Following elections in 1995, a new government was formed, dominated by the EPRDF (Ethiopian People's Revolutionary Democratic Front), which had won the earlier war. In 1991 the transitional government gave Eritrea the option to secede. Following a referendum in May 1993, the latter became a sovereign state.

Another geopolitical change that dates back to May 1991 was the breakaway of the northern part of Somalia to create the Republic of Somaliland. In February 1997 the 'new' state introduced its own constitution. Thus in Somalia, as in Ethiopia, the changes of the early 1990s led to national disintegration.

In addition, Sudan has seen far-reaching political changes during the past decade. Since 1989 the unstable political situation, arising from conflicts between the north and south, worsened. Towards the end of the 1990s the civil war shows no sign of coming to a peaceful end. A number of observers have argued that the secession of the south may be the long-term solution to the crisis in Sudan (see Gurdon 1994: 109 f.). If the latter happens, it would mean that all countries in the Horn of Africa, save Djibouti, would have been divided into two separate nations. This outcome is particularly intriguing in the light of the Organisation of African Unity's insistence that Africa's post-colonial (geopolitical) borders should be kept intact.

Djibouti is the only country in the Horn of Africa that, so far, has escaped severe internal conflicts and movements for secession, even though in the north of the country tension has risen between government forces and the Afar community. It is, however, still too early to evaluate the effects on Djibouti's internal stability of the government reshuffle of June 1995, following a peace accord with the Front for the Restoration of Unity and Democracy (FRUD), making two FRUD members Ministers. Djibouti is the only country in the region that is classified as a lower middle-income country by the World Bank (1996, 1997); the rest are low-income countries, ranked at the very bottom of the group.

The political dynamics of the Horn have been closely linked with global politics. With the end of the Cold War, and the demise of the Soviet bloc, the countries of the Horn lost an important source of moral, ideological, military and economic support. In a sense, the countries of the Horn were left pretty much to themselves, and to some extent to the international donor organisations that extended emergency relief.

Countries in the Horn are among the most indebted in Africa and the debt burden will remain an important restriction on their governments' ability to meet economic and social demands. In order to mobilise foreign assistance, in the form of direct development assistance and via debt reduction, various economic reform programmes have been introduced: in Ethiopia since 1990, in Eritrea since 1992/93, and in Sudan since the late 1970s (see Hansson 1995a, b, c, 1996b, 1997a, b). In Djibouti intensive talks about economic reforms between the government, France, an external backer, and the IMF in May 1997 led to an agreement on reforms that is, however, still to be implemented (EIU 1997: 3, 39).

The aim of this chapter is to analyse the prospects for economic development in the Horn of Africa. It looks at a set of crucial questions related to the potential as well as the existing problems of the region. Although the focus is on the economic prospects, with a number of development scenarios outlined, our discussion also outlines political developments. The approach used can best be described as political economy, where, in addition to domestic aspects, due attention will be paid to international political economy as well. Further, the chapter looks at regional integration, issues of ethnicity, self-determination and relations with the global powers.

REGIONAL INTEGRATION IN THE HORN

In discussing economic growth in the Horn, we must of necessity make a number of assumptions. For example, peace and stability have to be assumed to prevail. Likewise, broadened international development co-operation is necessary to enable aid to flow to the region. Regional attempts at closer co-operation also need to be successful. With regard to the latter, de la Torre and Kelly (1992: 25 ff.) have argued that though the issue of regional integration has attracted much political attention in sub-Saharan Africa, resulting in the largest number of regional groupings in the world, concrete outcomes have been few. Aside from structural factors which impair the benefits of increased regional integration, the generally poor implementation of regional projects has also affected results (de la Torre and Kelly 1992: 32, Kimuyu in Chapter 12).

Turning to the potential for economic integration in the Horn, we note that with regard to economic factors that are crucial to successful integration, including the liberalisation of trade and foreign investment, the process is only now beginning to take shape in the region. Although a number of reform programmes have been announced, progress is still behind that in other regions of Africa. Ethiopia has come furthest with its reforms, but even there a considerable amount of work still needs to be done. The discretionary element in the allocation of resources is still prevalent. The Mengistu government did not fully appreciate the potential of international trade and the system was put under considerable restrictions. Quotas were relied upon, implying more distortion and welfare loss than if other forms of trade policy had been adopted. The Mengistu government also favoured a fixed and overvalued exchange rate, a policy that was counterproductive from the point of view of trade (see Hansson 1995a: chapter 3). Since 1991 far-reaching trade liberalisation has been introduced, first by the transitional government and then by the EPRDF government that replaced it (see Hansson 1995a: chapter 7, 1995c, 1997a). This move towards greater flexibility in economic policy has been positive, not least for investors in Ethiopia. Notably, trade must be given a chance to work as an 'engine of growth' through bilateral, regional and multilateral collaboration. Djibouti has also undertaken a number of liberalisation measures, while Eritrea has announced an economic reform programme that is close to that of Ethiopia, especially with respect to trade policy (see Hansson 1996a, b).

With regard to macroeconomic policy implementation and performance, Ethiopia is even here the leading performer in the region (Hansson 1995a, b, c, 1997a). Again a similar process seems to be under way in Eritrea

(Hansson 1996b, World Bank 1994). The two countries seem to co-ordinate economic policy to some degree; most recently new national currencies were introduced to replace the Birr, which has been used since the 1970s. Elsewhere in the Horn, countries have yet to embark on formal stabilisation programmes.

Thus, from the point of view of purely economic factors, regional integration involving all Horn countries seems unlikely over the next decade. A free-trade area comprising Eritrea, Ethiopia and Djibouti seems a more feasible alternative. In fact, following Eritrean independence, a free-trade area was formed with Ethiopia in January 1992 (UNDP 1993: 3). It is not too unrealistic to assume that the ultimate long-run objective of this Ethiopian–Eritrean co-operation is the creation of an economic union between the two countries. Beyond the rather poor prospects of regional economic integration in the Horn, one may look for prospects of unilateral and multilateral trade liberalisation. Also in this case Ethiopia and Eritrea seem to have come furthest among the Horn countries, even though only Djibouti has joined the World Trade Organisation.

From the political point of view, the prospect of successful regional integration in the Horn of Africa is even remoter. As noted above, the region's recent history and development have been characterised by military conflict at various levels of intensity, both internally in the individual countries and along the common borders. Even today, at the end of the 1990s, there are frequent reports of military conflict and war preparation in the region, e.g. between Eritrea and the Sudan and along the border between Somalia and Ethiopia. Thus, even in the case of Ethiopia, where the economic factors in favour of successful international or regional economic integration are promising, there are potential problems of border conflict.

Even more important for the prospects of economic integration are the issues of secession and internal conflicts in Ethiopia itself. Reaching a workable domestic consensus on the issue of secession is, at the moment, rather remote, especially in light of the emotion with which the question is attached. Thus even though the new constitution of the Federal Republic of Ethiopia, adopted in December 1994, seems to be unequivocal regarding the matter, the issue of secession will, if unresolved, remain a big question mark for economic development. The question has potential for generating internal conflict and, in the event of one region choosing secession, a host of international implications. It would be even harder to bring about conditions for future economic integration in the Horn of Africa.

In terms of broader regional co-operation, the Intergovernmental Authority on Drought and Development (IGAD) established in 1986, with a membership that includes Djibouti, Ethiopia, Eritrea, Somalia, Sudan, Kenya and Uganda, has been quite effective. Its initial mandate was limited, however, confined to combating drought and the threat of desertification through joint action and co-operation. In the 1990s IGAD's goals have been widened to include mechanisms of conflict resolution in the region as well as the promotion of closer economic co-operation. To mark this shift of emphasis IGAD adopted a new charter. Its vision of the future is as follows (IGAD 1996: 3):

> The sub-region has the required natural and human resources that could be developed to propel the sub-region to collective self-reliance where peace and security prevail. The vision is based on the determination of the governments of the sub-region to pool resources and co-ordinate development activities in order to face the present and future challenges, enabling the sub-region to interact and compete in the global economy on behalf of its inhabitants, eventually leading to regional integration.

In order to realise this vision, regional co-operation and integration are emphasised. Three priority areas have been identified: food security and environmental protection, conflict prevention, management and resolution, as well as humanitarian affairs and infrastructure development. As often in regional co-operation, the ambition is often greater than the ability to put it into operation. Still, even if member countries are able to realise only a few of their goals, they will have taken useful steps towards a prosperous Horn of Africa. In October 1997 peace talks were held under IGAD's auspices between the Sudanese government and the Sudanese People's Liberation Army. Talks between Uganda and Sudan have also been held under similar auspices.

However, the history of integration and co-operation in the region has, as already noted, been poor and the prospects for harmonious regional economic integration would seem bleak at the moment. The picture looks more optimistic when the perspective is confined to integration among the countries of Djibouti, Eritrea and Ethiopia. However, considering the central role of Ethiopia in any eventual integration process, it is crucial that the issue of secession does not break down into military confrontation and further disintegration. Much will be determined by the ability of the Ethiopian government to accommodate ethnic heterogeneity.

ETHNONATIONALISM AND ECONOMIC DEVELOPMENT

Countries in the Horn have been characterised as nations that have not completed their state formation, at least in the sense of possessing well defined and respected borders. The ethnic diversity of the region, and within individual Horn countries, is the explanation given for the porous borders and the lack of national cohesion. In Ethiopia the issue of ethnicity was, for instance, an important factor behind the long-running civil war, which

Table 16.1 Ethnic divisions in the Horn of Africa (%)

Djibouti:	
Somali	60
Afar	35
French, Arab, Ethiopian, and Italian	5
Eritrea:	
Ethnic Tigrays	50
Tire and Kunama	40
Afar	4
Saho	3
Ethiopia:	
Oromo, Amhara, Tigrean	72
Sidamo	9
Shankella	6
Somali	6
Afar	4
Gurage	2
Other	1
Somalia:	
Somali	85
Other	15
Sudan:	
African	52
Arab	39
Other	9

Source: CIA (1994, 1995).

hampered economic development for some thirty years. It has also been at the centre of debates during the process of formulating the new Ethiopian constitution, which formalised the right of secession (Hansson 1995b).

From the perspective of global geopolitics there is no clear-cut correspondence between ethnic and political borders. According to Connor (1994: 29) of 'a total of 132 contemporary states, only twelve (9.1 per cent) can be described as essentially homogeneous from an ethnic viewpoint'. In Table 16.1 ethnic divisions in the Horn of Africa are presented. For all countries except Ethiopia and Sudan, there is an ethnic group accounting for 50 per cent or more of the population.

The factors crucial to efficient state integration and thus successful nation building have been analysed by political scientists for decades. Among them, the role of ethnicity in the context of nation building has been under debate for some time, but the results are generally inconclusive. Some analysts have found the role of ethnicity to be marginal and thus to be ignored, while others have argued that its divisive nature makes ethnicity one of the major impediments to state integration (Connor 1994: chapter 2).

Populations are subject to at least two types of loyalty: that to the ethnic group and that to the state. By their nature, the two types of loyalty are not naturally harmonious. The implied conflicts have been demonstrated all too well in Bosnia, Rwanda and Afghanistan. By inhibiting the pace of urbanisation, industrialisation and the spread of education, conflicting ethnic loyalties can be a serious detriment to the process of social mobilisation.

To assimilate competing ethnic groups into the process of nation building, they must be able to identity with the state. In the literature there has been a long debate on what impact economic factors have on ethnically based separatist movements, in other words to what extent economic factors contribute to ethnic alienation. In this context, a major issue has been the extent to which economic factors are decisive for the amalgamation of ethnonationalism (the theory of economic deprivation). Looking at research outcomes, Connor (1994: 39) concludes that ethnic consciousness has been increasing, and not, as one would have expected, given rapid social change, decreasing. The form of government, the geography of the country or even the level of economic development have not been important determinants of ethnic disaffection. However, rapid economic development, accompanied by increased social mobility and communication, appears to increase ethnic tension and thus lead to increasing separatist demands. These are key issues that need to be incorporated when theorising nation building.

However, Connor (1994: 72) has noted that there is no consensus on how to achieve ethnic heterogeneity or even whether it can be accommodated without coercion. Still, the experience of developed countries provides some indicators: the degree of ethnic heterogeneity, the dynamics of secession, group attitudes to violence, and the extent of ethnic support. These points are amplified below (Connor 1994: 81 f.):

Ethnic heterogeneity obviously varies, but is high when members of ethnonational minorities manifest substantially less affection towards the state than do members of the dominant group. Minorities within the same state could, however, differ significantly in this regard. For most persons, however, the matter is not perceived in either/or terms. Affective ties to the state could coexist with heightened ethnonational consciousness.

With regard to secession, in most cases where a separatist movement is actively behind the demands, large numbers, usually a majority, of the ethnic group involved may not favour secession. In some cases, the percentage represented by pro-secessionists could remain relatively constant over long periods. Regardless of their attitude towards secession, however, there is usually an ethnic majority in favour of major alterations in the political system that would result in greater autonomy. However, where separatist parties are allowed to contest elections, their vote is often an inadequate indicator of separatist sentiment.

Third, group attitude to violence is important. In all cases for which there are attitudinal data, members of ethnic groups overwhelmingly reject the use of violence carried out in the name of the ethnic group. At the same time, a large percentage of the respondents, including many who do not favour separation, tend to empathise with those engaged in violence with an 'ethnic tag' and place the blame for it on others. There is thus a considerable degree of ambiguity in ethnic alliances.

Finally, separatist movements cannot thrive without support. Research shows that separatists draw their support from all social strata and age groups. However, support is drawn mainly from those under thirty-five years of age, with above-average education and income. Professional people are also disproportionately represented among supporters. There is, however, much less support among those aged fifty-five and above.

Without attempting to generalise too much, some of the above outcomes could help shed light on the situation in the Horn of Africa. In cases where there are a large number of competing ethnic groups, the chances of efficient accommodation of ethnic heterogeneity at the national level are smaller than when there is a dominant ethnic group that holds power. In the Horn of Africa an example of a dominant ethnic group holding power is that of Arabs in the Sudan. While black Africans form a bigger portion of the total population, they are ethnically diverse, with the largest minority group having less than 15 per cent of the total population. Arabs, who are also numerically superior in the northern and central parts, thus dominate. Still, it would appear that Sudan is a long way from containing the effects of the SPLA's opposition. In Djibouti there are just two major groups, the Somali-speaking Issa, who are in power and represent around 50 per cent of the population, and the opposition group, the Afar, who claim up to 40 per cent of the population. In Somalia six large clans dominate the political scene. In Eritrea there are five major ethnic groups and a number of smaller ones. In Ethiopia, finally, ethnic groups number more than 100. The two dominant ones are the Oromo and the Amhara, who could be said to be outside the groups providing support for the ruling EPRDF, which is dominated by the Tigreans. Thus it is extremely difficult to accommodate ethnic heterogeneity in the Horn, given such extensive differentiation. It is ironic, however, that the most ethnically homogeneous country, Somalia, is the one which collapsed.

With regard to changes made in the political system to enable ethnic autonomy, only Ethiopia has adopted a formal, if controversial, policy on the matter (Republic of Ethiopia 1994). In Somalia the secession of Somaliland was a result of military struggle and cannot be equated with steps taken within the political process to enhance regional autonomy. In early 1997 twenty-six Somali factions concluded a peace agreement in Sodere, Ethiopia, forming the National Salvation Council. It was followed by another meeting in Cairo in May 1997. However, challenging tasks remain to be resolved before a sustainable peace can be established. Thus, even with two governments in Mogadishu, Somalia cannot be classified as a country where the various clans or ethnic groups live in formal autonomy. Notably, the Somaliland Republic did not participate in the process that led to the Sodere agreement. The leaders of the Somaliland Republic emphasise that their independence is irreversible and have classified an invitation from the NCS to take part in the Sodere peace process as a 'flagrant interference in the internal affairs of Somaliland' (EIU 1997 1: 45).

In Eritrea, as opposed to Ethiopia, political parties based on ethnicity are not allowed, while in Sudan there has been a decades-long struggle between the dominant ethnic and religious groups. The subsequent divide between the northern and the southern parts of the country can by no means be described as a situation of autonomy for ethnic groups. The same could be said of the situation in Djibouti. Thus, with the exception of Ethiopia, ethnic group demands have not been responded to by increasing ethnic autonomy. It could thus be said that the accommodation of ethnic heterogeneity via autonomy has been subordinated to the greater need for centralised power in most of the Horn.

The Ethiopian experience has been unique in modern statehood. Already at the outset of the transitional government, the intentions of decentralising political power and giving the regions greater autonomy were outlined. Since regional divisions in Ethiopia are based on ethnicity, this move has given the various ethnic groups greater formal autonomy. This has not resolved the ethnicity question in Ethiopia, however. In fact autonomy and the possibility of secession have been some of the most debated issues since the removal of Mengistu in 1991. Thus, while there are groups that are ready to demand self-determination and independence, such as the Oromo and the people of the Ogaden, and would even resort to military struggle to meet their demands, there are others that are totally opposed to the dismemberment of Ethiopia. The Amhara are such a group. They have always supported Ethiopian unity and were even opposed to the liberation of Eritrea and the recent introduction of clauses in the new Ethiopian constitution making it possible for regions to secede. Historically, they have held a central position in government, and the bulk of the civil servants are from this group. With the demise of the Derg, Amhara opposition groups claim that they are discriminated against in the public sector job market.

Thus in Ethiopia there have been important changes towards increased regional and ethnic autonomy. However, it is still impossible to judge the extent to which opposition groups that demand independence have support among the population. The elections of 1995 failed to provide a useful indicator because most opposition groups boycotted them. Still, considering the large number of ethnic groups, and the absence of a numerically dominant group in power, as well as differences of attitude towards self-determination and independence, the accommodation of ethnic heterogeneity poses enormous challenges. The creation of a stable ethnic situation will demand great skill from any government in power. Ironically, it may well be that freedom to secede will become the glue that continues to hold the Ethiopian people together, since national unity will no longer be a diktat from the centre but a choice based on ethnic self-interest (see Bardhan 1997).

To conclude, the prospects of accommodating ethnic heterogeneity in the Horn of Africa are bleak. There is even a risk that ethnic conflict will continue both within and between the various countries. Its impact will be internationalised as migrants are uprooted and exposed to the elements. Such catastrophic outcomes were demonstrated by the effects of the flooding in Somalia in November 1997. Thus a considerable amount of resources will be directed to emergency relief of refugees and the internally displaced. Furthermore, the uncertainties that accompany civil wars and ethnic tension jeopardise the environment, since investment in agricultural land, forestry and water resource development becomes exceedingly risky under such circumstances and are abandoned. Last, since ethnic struggles and the related migration imply great costs in human and material terms, they should be lowered in order to create an environment that sustains economic development.

FROM COLD WAR TO NEW GEOPOLITICAL TENSIONS

As indicated above, a considerable amount of regional tension in the Horn was due to superpower rivalry. The demise of the Soviet bloc reduced the strategic importance of the region, at least in the eyes of the United States. There was a sharp reduction in the flow of resources to the region. This downgrading of the Horn in strategic terms has partly contributed to the national disintegration of the countries. In this section we briefly analyse the changes in the strategic importance of the Horn from the Cold War to the present. We ask whether new strategic interests are bound to arise and speculate on their nature and their possible impacts.

Soviet and American competition for the strategic upper hand in the Horn of Africa goes as far back as the end of World War II. The Soviet Union supported Somalia and Ethiopia because their regimes were among the most steadfast followers of the Soviet brand of socialism, with the emphasis on central planning and control and the expansion of a military-industrial complex. The United States, on the other hand, wished to stop the spread of communism, which stood against all the principles – capitalism, individual liberties and democracy – on which its style of government is said to be based.

However, Ethiopia and Somalia were not passive victims of superpower manipulation, but often turned the competition between the Soviet Union and the United States to their advantage (Ottaway 1982: 2). Proximity to the Suez Canal, the Red Sea, the Indian Ocean and the oil deposits of the Middle East, not to mention closeness to Israel, gave the countries of the Horn much more importance in strategic terms than their economic strength would have commanded. However, relations with the superpowers often meant sudden shifts in alliances. Such changes were easy to take, since Ethiopia and Somalia were ruled by autocratic regimes, and debate on national issues was quite circumscribed. The impressively high levels of foreign assistance obtained by these countries from the competing powers can be said to have been the material benefits of the Cold War (Ottaway 1982: 31).

The end of the Cold War at the close of the 1980s thus had consequences for the whole of the Horn. The Soviet Union and Eastern bloc allies now had another list of priorities, including attempts to address their own economic woes and the discontent of their populations. They were also turning away from support for autocratic regimes in Africa, especially when they were grappling with their own domestic demands for greater economic and political liberalisation.

Loss of Soviet support was marked in various ways across the African continent. However, Mengistu of Ethiopia bore the brunt of this shift in policy. Resource flows had begun to decline by the second half of the 1980s, and pressure for a change of policy began to mount (see Hansson 1995a: chapters 6–8). It is now clear, in retrospect, that changes in relations between the Soviet bloc and Ethiopia had a major impact on the moral and military capacity of the Ethiopian government. While the rapidly advancing ERPDF was the immediate reason for the collapse of the Mengistu government in May 1991, the decline had set in with the collapse of the Soviet Union earlier.

Need we fear a repeat of a Cold War situation? What implications would such an eventuality have for the Horn? In an analysis of the impact of the Cold War, Wohlforth (1994: 96) argues that it was partly due to fear of the rise of Soviet power. However, what sustained it was that the Soviet Union had the resources to wage war. The economic collapse of the Soviet Union implies that the challenger lost the ability to sustain competition at the Cold War level. Since the United States was left relatively unscathed, there is bound to be a long period of international stability among the major powers, essentially dictated by the unrivalled superiority of the United States. However, Russia remains a country of immense physical and human resources and it would not be prudent to count it out.

Still, from the perspective of the countries of the Horn, there seems to be less room for superpower manipulation. Their strategic geographical situation seems less important today, even though not entirely uninteresting. They have little to offer in return for support. Since earlier resource flows were tied to strategic considerations, the loss of strategic importance is bound to lead to a permanent decline in resource flows.

Though a new round of superpower rivalry involving the Horn may be considered a remote possibility, other threats have emerged in the region which have drawn the attention of the United States and its allies. The risk of wars in the Horn partly based on religious differences seems to have grown in recent years (Baker 1997: 67 f.). The most recent internal flare-ups in the region, together with the cross-border skirmishes, could be said to have a strong religious element. The recent tensions between Sudan and its neighbours Eritrea, Ethiopia and Uganda are often given as examples of the broadening implications of such conflict. Still, the picture emerging may be more complex than would first appear. For example, the mainly Christian and Animist SPLA in southern Sudan is allied with Muslim groups in the north of the country in their bid to remove the government in Khartoum. At the same time, the Sudanese government is accused by Uganda of providing sanctuary and arms to the Lord's Resistance Army, a Christian fundamentalist group waging war on the largely Christian government in Kampala. It may very well be that the switches in allegiance at the local level are indicative of a desire to fill the power gaps created by the departure of the superpowers at the regional level.

Another important source of regional tension may be the distribution of water rights. The Nile is the longest river in the world and many African countries depend on it for their livelihood. Its sources are controlled by Ethiopia, where the Blue Nile emanates, and Uganda, the source of the White Nile. The two arms join in the Sudan and flow as a single river down to Egypt and the Mediterranean. Aside from the conflicts, countries are considering ambitious electricity and irrigation projects. While the Nile waters seem adequate for the moment, they are far from inexhaustible. Co-ordination in the use of water resources will be necessary if the countries do not wish to jeopardise the source of their power generation, irrigation and water for human and animal consumption. The risk that the countries of the Nile valley could run into severe conflict is thus real enough. It could even have implications beyond the Horn.

CONCLUSION

The Horn of Africa is currently in political and economic distress, while the prospects of a rapid reversal of the poor performance of the past decade are poor. For a long time, civil wars and ethnic tensions have plagued the population. The latter has had little influence over the political and economic systems, and even less on the future. An important reason for this pessimistic prediction is that political uncertainty and instability pervade all the countries, preventing long-term investment in productive capacity or in measures for environmental protection. Thus it will be difficult to bridge the gap between the rapidly growing population and the declining economic base.

Ironically, the end of the Cold War was not positive for the countries of the Horn. Superpower rivalry and the attention it bestowed on the region is no more. Though much of the resource flow was in the form of ammunition, it was related to useful complementary flows. When the Cold War came to an end the position of the Horn of Africa in the 'market' for foreign assistance changed radically. Now assistance is mainly from Western countries and the multilateral aid organisations, including the IMF and the World Bank, with attached conditionalities. It is ironical that the Horn now competes for international aid with countries from the former Soviet bloc which, in the heyday of superpower rivalry, were the main backers of the regimes in the Horn.

We have also argued that in the medium term no country will be able to challenge the United States effectively, at least anywhere near the extent of the Soviet Union during the Cold War. Thus renewed foreign competition as a source of prosperity for the Horn is not to be expected. However, two sources of tension can be identified. The first relates to the possibility of increased religious conflict in the Horn and neighbouring countries, while the other relates to potential struggles over water rights. We have argued that these two scenarios are far from unrealistic. They are already cause for considerable unease, and could easily lead to armed conflict.

Regarding the implications for international assistance, it can be argued that nothing can be done for the region as a whole while insecurity and war persist. However, when peace is re-established, the most important type of assistance will be that which enables countries in the Horn to strengthen their political and economic institutions, and the development of human capacities. In order to stem rising poverty and environmental degradation, economic policy has to improve via the adoption of effective policies. To raise social standards, currently among the lowest in Africa, substantial resources need to be invested in education and health care. For a long time, resources were invested in wars, which killed people and destroyed the environment. A real change for the Horn may well be when human capacity development is given priority. In this regard donors still have an important role to play.

REFERENCES

Baker J. (1997) 'The Horn of Africa, with particular Reference to Ethiopia, by the year 2015: a Vision of Hope or Despair?', in Project 2015, East and West Africa – Regional Studies, Stockholm: Swedish International Development Co-operation Agency (Sida).

Bardhan, P. (1997) 'Method in the Madness? A Political Economy Analysis of the Ethnic Conflicts in Less Developed Countries', *World Development*, 25 (9): 1381–98.

CIA (1994, 1995) Country facts available on the Internet (for Eritrea: http://www.ic.-gov/94fact/country/74.html; for Ethiopia:(http://www.ic.gov/94fact/country/76.html; for Sudan: (http://www.ic.gov/94fact/country/224.html; for Somalia: (http://www.ic.gov/94fact/country/218.html; for Djibouti: (http://www.odci.gov/cia/publications/95fact/dj.html).

Connor, W. (1994) *Ethnonationalism – The Quest for Understanding*, Princeton NJ: Princeton University Press.

de la Torre, A. and Kelly, M.R. (1992) *Regional Trade Arrangements*, Occasional Paper 93, Washington DC: International Monetary Fund.

EIU (1997) *Country Report: Ethiopia, Eritrea, Somalia and Djibouti*, London: Economist Intelligence Unit.

Gurdon, C. (ed.) (1994) *The Horn of Africa*, London: UCL Press.

Hansson, G. (1995a) *The Ethiopian Economy 1974–94: Ethiopia Tikdem and After*, London and New York: Routledge.

——(1995b) *Ethiopia 1994 – Economic Achievements and Reform Problems*, Macroeconomic Studies 61, Stockholm: Swedish International Development Co-operation Agency (Sida).

——(1995c) *Ethiopia 1995 – Consolidation of Reforms: Implications for Foreign Aid*, Macroeconomic Studies 64, Stockholm: Swedish International Development Co-operation Agency (Sida).

——(1996a) 'From GATT to WTO: a Potential for or a Threat to LDC Development?', in M. Lundahl and B.J. Ndulu (eds) *New Directions in Development Economics*, London and New York: Routledge.

——(1996b) *Eritrea 1996 – a Peaceful Struggle for Sustained Independence*, Macroeconomic Report 12, Stockholm: Swedish International Development Co-operation Agency (Sida).

——(1997a) *Ethiopia 1996 – Government Legitimacy, Aid and Sustainable Development*, Macroeconomic Report 5, Stockholm: Swedish International Development Co-operation Agency (Sida).

——(1997b) 'The Horn of Africa beyond the Year 2015: Poverty or Prosperity?' in Project 2015, East and West Africa – Regional Studies, Stockholm: Swedish International Development Co-operation Agency (Sida).

IGAD (1996) *IGAD Strategy Framework*, Djibouti: InterGovernmental Authority on Development.

Markakis, J. (1994) 'Ethnic Conflict and the State in the Horn of Africa', in K. Fukui and J. Markakis (eds) *Ethnicity and Conflict in the Horn of Africa*, London: James Curry and Athens OH: Ohio University Press.

Ottaway, M. (1982) *Soviet and American Influence in the Horn of Africa*, New York: Praeger.

Republic of Ethiopia (1994) *The Constitution of the Federal Democratic Republic of Ethiopia* (unofficial English translation from the Amharic original), Addis Ababa.

Shambaugh, D. (1995) 'The United States and China: a New Cold War?', *Current History*, 94 (593): 241–51.

UNDP (1993) *Project of the State of Eritrea*, New York: United Nations.

UNDP (various years) *Human Development Report*, New York and Oxford: Oxford University Press.

Wohlforth, W.C. (1994) 'Realism and the End of the Cold War', *International Security*, 19 (3): 91–129.

World Bank (1994) *Eritrea Options and Strategies for Growth*, Report 12930–ER, Washington DC: World Bank.

World Bank (1996) *Eritrea Poverty Assessment*, Report 15595–ER, Washington DC: World Bank.

World Bank (1997) *World Development Report*, New York: World Bank and Oxford University Press.

17

AGRICULTURE, POLICY IMPACTS AND THE ROAD AHEAD

Wilfred Aboum-Ongaro

Discussion of Africa's economic prospects inevitably leads to inquiry as to the state of its agriculture. It is realistic to argue that even in the event of rapid economic diversification, agriculture will for a long time continue to play a leading role in generating incomes for the majority, providing food and industrial inputs, and producing the bulk of exports. Still, past policies and recent performance provide a rather poor projection for the future of agriculture on the continent.

Three issues are raised frequently in policy-related discussions of African agriculture. First, the continent's rather poor capacity to grow food seems to be worsening. Chronic food shortages have led to serious undernourishment among broad sections of the population and to stunting among children. Though far from the most populous continent, these problems have been more severe in Africa than in other developing regions (see Table 17.1). In the first half of the 1990s agricultural output grew, on average, by 1.5 per cent per annum, a significant decline from 3.5 per cent growth in the late 1980s (FAO/UN 1995, African Development Bank 1997). Countries partly adjusted to this shortfall by requesting food aid. Sub-Saharan Africa now accounts for 36 per cent of global food aid deliveries, compared with 11 per cent for Latin America and the Caribbean. There have also been rapid increases in cereal imports. Thus, although African conditions are ideal for cereal production, imports of cereals increased by 50 per cent in the decade following the mid-1980s, reaching 34 million tons in 1993/94 (World Food Programme 1995).

Second, inadequate macroeconomic incentives and poor technologies have lowered agricultural productivity, while a combination of political and fiscal constraints has led to a severe reduction in the resource flows to agriculture (Cleaver and Donovan 1995, Staatz 1996). Budgetary constraints have reduced governments' ability to extend services to the countryside, or to

Table 17.1 Estimates and projections of the incidence of the chronically undernourished in developing countries

Region	Period[a]	Total population (million)	% Undernourished
Sub-Saharan Africa	1969–71	268	36
	1979–81	357	39
	1990–92	500	41
	2010	874	35
Near East/North Africa	1969–71	178	25
	1979–81	233	10
	1990–92	317	10
	2010	513	7
East Asia	1969–71	1,147	41
	1979–81	1,393	17
	1990–92	1,674	16
	2010	2,070	5
South Asia	1969–71	711	33
	1979–81	892	33
	1990–92	1,146	22
	2010	1,617	15
Latin America and Caribbean	1969–71	279	18
	1979–81	354	13
	1990–92	443	14
	2010	593	8
Total	1969–71	2,583	35
	1979–81	3,228	27
	1990–92	4,064	20
	2010	5,668	13

Source: Alexandratos (1995).

Note: a Three-year average.

provide farmers with information on a regular basis. While tax administration has improved in some countries, the incidence of taxes on farmers, especially via taxes on energy and transport, both of which are used intensively in the production and marketing chain in agriculture, is high. Poor infrastructure continues to be a serious constraint. Farmers find it difficult to reach the market and thus often revert to subsistence. With regard to new technologies, the promising high yielding varieties, introduced in the 1960s, failed to transform agriculture to anywhere near the same extent as in Asia. Eicher (1995) has blamed this on economic policies that discriminated against agriculture, affecting the pace at which peasants adopted new technologies.

Third, poor resource husbandry, coupled with bad weather, and population pressure, led to land overutilisation. There has been rapid depletion of soils, forests and bush cover. Increasingly, marginal soils, and areas reserved for grazing, are coming under intensive cultivation, with severe consequences for the environment and the welfare of the rural populations. Environmental stress and rapid population growth are closely related, and the competition for natural resources has left whole societies worse off. While sub-Saharan Africa's population was estimated at 600 million in 1996, its total population is expected to double in less than thirty-five years (UN/ECA 1996b: 24). With rampant migration and urbanisation, over 700 million persons will then be living in cities. Yet, the rural sectors will be expected to supply the food needs of the urban dwellers.

In recent decades the AIDS epidemic has added to an already difficult economic and social situation (Way and Stanecki 1991). Many rural regions have been hit severely by the disease, affecting their engagement in economic activities. Risk, often high in agriculture, has thus risen further. Under the threat of the disease, farmers are unwilling to innovate or gather superior information. Many have resorted to traditional means of production, which demand a minimum of modern inputs.

This chapter provides an overview of current knowledge of the state of African agriculture. It draws on studies undertaken since the early 1980s, but with the emphasis on those from more recent years. While the causes of agriculture's poor performance are analysed at length, we also look at some of the solutions suggested for the reinvigoration of the sector. Also important in our discussion are issues of natural resource exploitation and environmental preservation.

AGRICULTURE, POPULATION AND THE ENVIRONMENT

Studies of sustainable agricultural development are increasingly focusing on the multiple and synergetic relationships between population growth, agricultural activities and the environment. In the face of limited resources, rapid population growth has led to environmental degradation which has, in turn, led to poor agricultural performance (UN/ECA 1996a, World Resource Institute 1992).

First, in the absence of sufficiently rapid and widespread technological change, a high population growth rate has led to land scarcity and brought about competition between crop and animal production. Second, the decrease of arable land *per capita* has gradually pushed farmers towards ecologically fragile land and range areas where soil and climatic conditions are unsuited to the cultivation of annual crops. As a result, yields have fallen substantially. Further, a reduction of grazing areas for animals has pushed pastoralists towards semi-arid areas, circumscribing their livelihoods (Tenga 1997). Third, traditional techniques of crop and livestock production based on customary land tenure and land use systems have, under population pressure, proved inadequate in addressing the problems of resource allocation. In fact the traditional methods of obtaining wood fuels and building materials, practised in most of Africa, have contributed to severe natural resource degradation and to agricultural stagnation (Stern *et al*. 1996). Thus in laying strategies for rural development land, population and environmental issues should be handled in tandem (see, for example, McIntire *et al*. 1992, Mink 1993, Cleaver and Schreiber 1994, Reardon and Vosti 1995, Marter and Gordon 1996).

The implication is that policies that fail to take a 'cross-cutting' approach to development will not be able to make a lasting impact (Ongaro 1994, Lufumpa in the next chapter). For example, food production is linked with population dynamics, the environment and gender issues. In the latter case because women are the main producers of food in the countryside, with their decisions affected by a variety of factors, including those impacting on their individual households. There is little doubt that agricultural success will, to a large degree, depend on what is achieved in efforts to include women more centrally in rural income generation and resource conservation (Thapa *et al*. 1996, UN/ECA 1996a).

Other factors with a strong bearing on agricultural production include civil strife, poor macroeconomic environments, inadequate physical and institutional infrastructure. The latter especially refers to poor roads, inefficient markets, underdeveloped rural credit markets, inadequate human resource development and insufficient research (FAO/UN 1994, Byerlee and Heisey 1996: 266). In what follows we briefly discuss how these factors have impacted on agricultural productivity. In a later section we look at a number of possible policy responses.

CONSTRAINTS ON AGRICULTURAL PRODUCTIVITY

Low productivity is the main cause of Africa's poor agricultural performance. Traditional systems, characterised by low-input, and in some areas shifting cultivation, have not generated the quantities of crop and livestock necessary to meet the needs of a rapidly expanding population. Thus while food grain yields in Asia and Latin America have risen since the mid-1960s, following the introduction of high-yielding varieties, those in Africa have remained stagnant (Alexandratos 1995: 439–62). In 1993–95 average cereal yields in Africa were over 40 per cent lower than in Asia and Latin America. Key to success in the latter regions was the adoption of new technologies, including improved seeds and fertiliser. However, the use of modern inputs such as fertiliser is still very low in Africa, where, on average, African farmers use 9–11 kg of fertiliser per hectare (ha), compared with an average of 83 kg/ha in the developing countries (Heisey and Mwangi 1996). Moreover, in spite of relatively abundant water supplies only 4–6 per cent of land under crops is under irrigation.

This inadequate use of new techniques is due not to farmer resistance but to poor rural access to information, and inadequate support services and credit. Reardon and Vosti (1995) have noted, in the case of Rwanda, that lack of capital has forced farmers to adopt labour-intensive techniques. Upper limits to yields are thus reached fairly quickly and a vicious circle of poverty has been created, with labour intensification leading to soil degradation, low productivity and poor earnings.

In spite of isolated success stories such as the introduction of upland rice in parts of West Africa, hybrid maize in Ghana, Kenya, Malawi, Nigeria, Zambia and Zimbabwe, and more recently high-yielding varieties of cassava in West Africa, the impact of agricultural research in sub-Saharan Africa has been poor (Ongaro 1994). In theory, the decision to adopt fertiliser by farmers is dictated by the interaction between soil characteristics, climatic factors and the nutrient–crop price ratio. When the first two factors are given, the nutrient–price ratio becomes the main determinant of adoption. In practice, many other factors come into play as well: the cost of operating capital for the crop season, information flows, and the extent of risk aversion. Some studies have contended that risk aversion is so high in African agriculture that the return on capital invested in fertiliser must be at least 100 per cent before significant adoption takes place (Heisey and Mwangi 1996, Reardon et al. 1997).

Thus the development of suitable technological packages requires location-specific research. However, the resources needed to support related services and projects often exceed the research funds of most countries. Countries with common ecological features could, for instance, co-operate in many agricultural research fields, thereby spreading risk and research costs. A first step could be to increase collaboration between national agricultural research systems. It is also necessary to involve universities, non-governmental organisations and the private sector in mainstream research efforts.

In the rest of this section we shall examine more closely six important impediments to agricultural production: incomplete technology transfer due to poor support systems, inadequate land tenure legislation, insufficient human resource development, poor socio-economic infrastructure and environmental degradation. We look at each of these in turn.

Improvements in agricultural production ultimately depend on the extent to which information is disseminated to farmers, enabling them to adopt new ideas, including new production techniques, better application of agricultural inputs, profitable marketing decisions, and improved methods of water and soil conservation. There is, however, little agreement on how best to transfer technologies to farmers. In Africa a wide range of extension systems have been used, with support from the international development community. They include traditional hierarchical approaches that employ large numbers of field staff, with relatively low levels of education, who work directly with farmers, with support from subject-matter specialists. Another form has been based on the co-operative movement, with its organs rendering services to farmers who are members, occasionally supplying inputs and other services. Profit-oriented agencies, often with support from multilateral donors, have also provided integrated specialist services to producers of certain high-value crops (livestock) at a fee. In a number of countries, farm research and extension services, adopting a multidisciplinary approach, are well developed and have been used to assist farmers.

Experience shows, however, that most extension information in Africa is transferred via a hierarchical system, in some countries modified by 'teaching and visits' (T&V) approach, funded entirely by the government. In Kenya the T&V system, since inception in 1980s, has proved effective in the transmission of modern farming techniques in rural areas (Blindish and Evenson 1993). Still, the system has been criticised for being too expensive and, for lack of flexibility, with little feedback. There is also the charge that T&Vs are a 'top-down' approach and thus fail to fully integrate farmers' needs and concerns. Research conducted into experimental stations has shown that there are serious deficiencies in transferring research recommendations to the farming community. Further, owing to limited financial resources, there is very little emphasis on verifying and testing improved technologies under realistic conditions. Research recommendations are thus often drawn from experimental research station trials, with few field applications. The outcomes may not be useful to farmers from other locations. Thus, while wheat farmers in the Narok and Kajiado districts of Kenya, near agricultural research stations, managed to increase their average yield three times by using recommended practices, this proved difficult to replicate in other areas. There was also sharp deviation from recommended methods, which may explain the yield gap (Hassan et al. 1993).

It has also been argued that in spite of the disproportionately large number of women engaged in agriculture, men tend to get more extension service advice, especially in relation to cash crops, where they dominate (Collier 1988, Staatz 1996). Providing for the needs of women farmers, who are responsible for the bulk of food production and whose decisions have a direct bearing on soil fertility and erosion, would help spread best practice in the countryside. Thus, as Cleaver and Schreiber (1994: 155) have noted, 'if extension services are to offer farmers the best techniques to suit their specific circumstances, they must provide "menus" of options for farmers to choose from – rather than deliver prescriptive composite "technology packages"'. Farmers should thus be allowed to converge, via experiment, on solutions that meet their needs.

Experience suggests that extension programmes have generally been successful when focused on high-value commodity producers. It is thus possible to differentiate the nature of extension services by the degree of commercialisation of the farmer group. The expansion of Kenya's dairy, tea and pig production in the past decades is a good example of a successful extension effort, which could now be handed over to the private sector. Already a number of firms are able to steer their extension programmes. The Kenya Tea Development Authority, for instance, carries out its own tea extension services with staff seconded from the Ministry of Agriculture. Other companies have undertaken extension services for crops relevant to their operation, as in the case of Kenya Breweries in barley farming. In Zambia the multinational Lonrho provides an integrated extension package to cotton farmers, including seed, chemicals and market advice. Extension workers are partly remunerated by bonuses directly related to output targets. Part of this system's success is due to the small number of farmers allocated to each extension agent, a small radius from which to operate and reliable means of transport (Francis *et al.* 1997). Another programme that emphasises this more flexible approach to rural mobilisation is Japanese-funded Sasakawa-Global 2000. It seeks to create a strong link between production enhancing centres: research, extension services, input distributors, credit lending systems and smallholders (Putterman 1995).

Land tenure systems have been studied widely, and it was generally believed that they had important impacts on agricultural performance and rural development. The modernisation approach stressed the need for proper land surveying, registration (entitlement) and a streamlined legal structure for dispute adjudication. Entitlement is assumed to increase tenure security, and to promote investment in more permanent structures. It is also said to boost the production of high-value crops. Land title is also used as collateral, thereby increasing access to institutional credit. Modernisation measures thus provide security of tenure and encourage the development of modern land management practices. This, in turn, increases investment in land improvement and possibly reduces pressure on the natural resource base. The dynamics of all these factors should lead to higher productivity and incomes, raising the standard of living.

However, recent work has questioned this overt emphasis on entitlement and related strategies as important for rural development. Pinkney and Kimuyu (1994) have argued, for instance, that entitlement is no more important for rural development than other measures which enable market access, such as a well functioning transport network. Access to markets enables farmers to generate cash income, which is necessary for engagement in rurally-based non-agricultural activities. The latter are important in reducing the risk inherent in over-dependence on agriculture. It has also been noted that although entitlement is considered important for access to credit, there is no guarantee that the money would remain in agriculture. Agricultural loans are fungible and funds can be diverted (Pischke and Adams 1980). There are many examples of wealthy farmers who have used their title to land to borrow money with which to embark on business in the urban areas.

However, rejecting the efficacy of entitlement as a development tool is by no means to advocate a return to traditional tenure systems, which have come under considerable pressure in recent years. In the past, communal land holding was effective because traditional institutions were strong, and pressure on land was low. However, these systems are now blamed for impeding agricultural innovation and causing environmental degradation. With the dissipation of traditional kinship ties and authority, individuals lack incentives to engage in long-term investment, production or conservation measures. Still, attempts at turning land into a marketable commodity have led to extreme results in some countries, with cases of 'land grabbing' by influential politicians and businessmen. Poor peasants have been exposed to the risk of landlessness (Cleaver and Schreiber 1994).

Lack of credit markets in rural Africa has been identified as one of the most serious impediments to agricultural productivity. Credit institutions are urban-based, making the gathering of information on rural dwellers for the purpose of assessing creditworthiness costly. Private institutions thus prefer not to lend to rural dwellers at all. Government institutions, often with non-market motives, have embarked on a number of rural lending schemes. Many have not been sustained, while in some cases the main beneficiaries were politicians and other urban-based individuals. The recent liberalisation of commodity marketing has reduced farmer dependence on government institutions for input supply and produce marketing. However, private sector initiatives are unevenly distributed, with a proliferation of private marketing outlets near urban centres and poorer market access in the remoter regions.

In the Sahel, the private sector has not been fully able to reduce the risks associated with farming, through geographical pooling or the interlinking of input and output markets, or by the timely provision of credit as the government did in previous years. The private merchants who are taking over agricultural marketing and distribution lack technical knowledge of fertiliser and other inputs. Moreover, they tend to operate from retail outlets that ensure high turnover, neglecting the marginal areas (Reardon et al. 1997). Similar observations have been made regarding cotton production in Mali, cocoa in Ghana, and maize in Malawi (FAO/UN 1994, Lele 1990). A major challenge is thus to identify an appropriate role for the public sector which ensures that services reach most parts of the countryside, but without regression into controls (Valdes and Muir-Leresche 1993). Experience from Cameroon illustrates that once the market is fully developed, the private sector can meet all farmers' needs, and at lower social cost. However, the public sector still needs to provide information and other support (Truong and Walker 1990).

Credit availability is closely related to market access. In both cases, an adequate infrastructure is important. Asian experience suggests that priority should be given to improving general communications, that is, transport and market infrastructure, and letting the private sector take care of commodity-specific processing, storage and market facilities (Bautista 1992). However, owing to low population densities, the per capita costs of communication/transport development in Africa are high. The resulting costs of transport have affected the structure and degree of tradability of Africa's produce. For example, cost mark-ups of 100–200 per cent on landed grain are common in many of Africa's landlocked countries. Mali's example is illustrative: following a bumper millet harvest, the average retail price in urban areas fell to 55 CFA/kg (then about twenty US$0.20). However, the import parity price at the retail level (for sorghum from coastal countries) was 99 CFA/kg, while the export parity price for millet and sorghum sold in Abidjan was only 12 CFA/kg (Delgado 1992). Deficient transport has thus hindered trade in agricultural products, reduced information flows and eventually the size of marketed surplus.

The last aspect looked at is rural human resource development. Basic education has been found to be important in farmer absorption of information regarding all aspects of agricultural production. Crucially, education also improves farmer strategies for dealing with risk. It is thus a key feature in enhancing efficiency in agriculture, by facilitating entrepreneurship and speeding up responses to changing market conditions and technological developments (Moock 1981, Bigsten 1984, Schultz 1988). Thus the fact that, in spite of recent progress, only 30 per cent of rural men and 20 per cent of rural women can read and write in Africa indicates that rapid agricultural development may be difficult to achieve in the short to medium term. Studies done at the World Bank have indicated further that the gains from education in agricultural productivity are larger for female than male farmers (World Bank 1989). Increasing female access to education should receive high priority. However, in a study of Masaka District, Uganda, Bigsten and Kayizzi-Mugerwa (1995) found that owing to the long period of crisis, education had ceased to be an asset in the countryside, with many farmers reverting to traditional methods where traditional knowledge was enough to meet their subsistence needs. Still, with the return of peace and a more dynamic environment, education would once again become important, since superior information is necessary for survival in a market environment.

THE FUTURE

Africa's major challenge is to reverse the long period of economic decline and stagnation. As already noted, much of the hope of improvement is based on the ability to generate and sustain agricultural growth. Srivastava and Alderman (1993) have defined sustainable agriculture as that which, in the long term, enhances environmental quality, preserves land and provides food, fodder and fibre. It should be economically viable in order to enhance the quality of life of farmers, as well as of society. Within the limits of this definition, it is clear that past and current practices have not been consistent with a sustainable African agriculture. However, agricultural policy reform is, as experience from more advanced regions shows, a particularly complex process. Historically agriculture has been subject to extensive intervention. Prices for agricultural products have, until recently, been controlled in most African countries, while factor markets have responded poorly to incentives, owing to the poor macroeconomic environment. Since costs and returns in agriculture depend relatively more on performance in other sectors of the economy, including transport and communications, manufacturing and the public sector, it is bound to be vulnerable to price and weather shocks as well as policy swings (Valdes and Muir-Leresche 1993). An unstable policy environment is thus bound to increase risk, reducing agricultural investment.

In this section we take a look at the future, especially at policies that should be pursued with a view to creating an environment conducive to the expansion of agricultural activities. The first issue looked at is research and how to disseminate the results to the farming community. In this regard, it is important to let target groups have some influence on research. It has been argued, for example, that the former settler economies such as Zimbabwe and Kenya developed sophisticated agricultural sectors because white commercial farmers were able to influence research and to demand results (Eicher 1995). On the other hand, maize farming was poorly promoted in Malawi because influential groups, such as those engaged in tobacco farming, were not interested in championing the interests of peasants (Smale 1995). Thus, when farmers have little influence on decisions bound to affect their welfare, as in efforts to enhance productivity, not much progress can be expected.

Owing to human and financial resource constraints, research institutions in Africa depend to a large extent on support from the donor community. The latter in turn, directly or indirectly, sets the agenda for national research, sometimes far removed from the realities of African agriculture. A serious setback is that university faculties of agriculture and related fields have not been fully integrated into national agricultural research efforts. Since the most capable individuals are found in those institutions, their exclusion or lack of participation is a serious impediment to the creation of national capacities. There are, however, a number of ways in which university faculties can be incorporated into national research. One approach is to let the national agriculture research system contract universities for specific research tasks. Another is to bring university researchers into mainstream programmes at the national level by establishing university-based agricultural research stations. In both cases, the goal is to overcome the gap between university and national research efforts. Still, resources at the country level are limited. Thus, bearing in mind that identical research projects are often pursued in neighbouring countries, regional collaboration and pooling of research funds may be the prudent way of the future.

Another issue relates to the transformation of traditional systems of agriculture in order to ensure that social and communal structures are preserved, while at the same time allowing flexibility. Though traditional farming systems are still used by the majority of the population, there has been little research on how to improve them. Emphasis has been on more modern methods which, however, have been poorly supported by the agricultural Ministries or have failed owing to incomplete adoption

It can be argued, however, that African agriculture has performed badly not solely for lack of appropriate research or because of the presence of too many traditional farmers in the countryside, rather it has performed inadequately because policies have impeded the flow and dissemination of useful information. While there is a proliferation of institutions at various levels of the public sector meant to ensure it, the ability to communicate has been seriously constrained by financial and human resource constraints. Thus extension workers have failed to link farmers with best practice, while markets have failed to send signals to farmers on output and quality. Research itself must be 'client-driven', with users in a position to influence the major research efforts. Whenever possible, governments should also encourage and support the emergence of private extension services. As indicated above, a good portion of African farming is profitable and, therefore, does not need subsidies.

Let us now turn to human resource development and the socio-economic infrastructure. Paucity of human capital resources is probably one of the most serious constraints on Africa's economic development. We noted above that basic levels of education are crucial to sustainable food production, and to agriculture more generally. However, a good level of education is even more important when a country chooses to expand its export base. In the global economy, skills are becoming increasingly the basis of international competition. While there is considerable scope for private initiative in the supply of heath and education services in urban areas, it is limited in the countryside. Given resource constraints, promoting adult and functional literacy programmes may be an appropriate starting point. Similarly, special attention needs to be accorded to rural women. The latter form the largest group in the countryside and their services in planting, cultivation, weeding, harvesting and the processing of food are indispensable. Thus widespread illiteracy among women is a drag on rural development as a whole, as well as on the well-being of their individual households. More important, women as mothers, and de facto social insurance in the rural areas, have considerable influence on succeeding generations and should be directly incorporated in all development strategies.

If well planned, carefully targeted, and efficiently operated, the socio-economic infrastructure is important for agricultural diversification (Bautista 1992), poverty reduction, and for opening up the countryside to new ideas and opportunities. Research across a number of African countries has shown that farmers with access to roads and transport infrastructure are quicker to adopt efficient techniques, use land more intensively, produce more surplus for the market, and employ more labour (Valdes and Muir-Leresche 1993, Putterman 1995). Rurally based infrastructure, including water supply, electricity and telecommunications, not only improves the standard of living in the countryside but also plays a crucial role in fostering reliable market structures, particularly the linking of agriculture and industrial sectors. Further, efficient infrastructure boosts national competitiveness within the world economy. At the regional level, an interconnected network of roads, rails and telecommunications is vital for trade, and improves access to ports for landlocked countries (see Ongaro 1995).

The development of the infrastructure to anywhere near meeting the demands of rapidly changing economies is not a task that can be left wholly to the public sector. Resource and other constraints suggest that the role of the private sector in infrastructure provision will have to increase in the future. Studies in Africa have shown a relatively high willingness to pay to ensure good-quality communications. Still a study of road user charges in Kenya (Laferrière and Nalo 1992) found that existing systems favoured passenger and heavy goods vehicles. One could thus argue that, by helping to improve communications, user charges would be beneficial to agriculture, since the bulk of road haulage is of agricultural exports. The construction and maintenance of the rural infrastructure could be done at the local level by the users themselves or by incorporating road construction in 'food for work' schemes. Various forms of aid relief, common in most of sub-Saharan Africa, could be partly diverted to the provision of complementary infrastructure.

Most governments in Africa are contemplating some form of land reform, for reasons already advanced above. It is believed that successful reform would lead to significant improvements in agricultural productivity and environmental quality. However, on its own land reform might simply disenfranchise the poor. Though customary tenure systems seem to be in crisis, research in Africa suggests that they adapt quickly to changes in resource availability. They thus provide a social threshold for many rural households. On the other hand, some land redistribution may be necessary to reduce the large asset and income disparities in the rural areas. It has been argued that the best way for governments to support rural development is by providing an appropriate legal and institutional environment, to enable more efficient transactions (Migot-Adholla et al. 1991).

Population growth and environmental degradation are closely linked, with causality running from population to environment. In both respects, the development of human capital, especially education and health care for women, has a positive impact on the environment. For example, some female education reduces family size; child survival improves with better nutrition and care. This ultimately slows down the growth of population. There are thus dynamic effects on population and the environment of education and health care provision.

Let us finally look at the dynamic linkages between agriculture and non-agriculture that will form the basis of Africa's industrialisation. Close to half of value added in African manufacturing is due to agricultural raw materials (Jaffee 1992). However, of even more interest is how agriculture interacts with non-agriculture in the countryside. Promotion of small non-farm enterprises (the manufacture of farm inputs, food processing, product distribution and sale) is important for several reasons. First, by providing alternative sources of livelihood, non-farm income reduces pressure on land. Second, non-farm income is also an important source of cash for investment in the farm and for the introduction of new technologies (Hazell and Haggblade 1993, Evans 1992). Third, a fast-growing agricultural sector requires fertiliser, pesticides and farm implements, thus creating demand for domestic industry, while at the same time supplying most of the inputs and raw materials needed in agri-based industries. Fourth, as rural households become richer their demand for consumer goods, including clothing, footwear, sugar, edible oils, etc., is bound to increase rapidly. Thus the agriculture–industry link has considerable development implications for Africa.

CONCLUSION

The performance of African agriculture will continue to be influenced by a variety of factors, many of them touched on here. A question remaining is whether the introduction of more liberal economic policies will be able to raise productivity and increase incomes in agriculture to levels close to those which have brought rapid growth and affluence to other parts of the world.

Though many structural and policy impediments remain, it is possible to argue that the recent policies of African governments towards agriculture and the rural sector have mostly been supportive. Rural mobilisation is now largely based on improved price and marketing policies, decentralisation and extension of the infrastructure and the provision of social services. Though it is still too early in the process to predict how successful they will be, the fact that the majority of countries have abandoned export taxes on crops and liberalised commodity markets will have a positive impact on rural initiative and development. Parallel developments in other areas of the economy, notably ensuring macroeconomic stability, suggest that many of the reforms will be long-term.

NOTE

The views expressed here are the author's responsibility and not those of the United Nations.

REFERENCES

African Development Bank (1997) *African Development Report 1997,* Oxford: Oxford University Press.

Alexandratos, N. (ed.) (1995) *World Agriculture: Towards 2010: An FAO Study,* New York: Wiley.

Bautista, R. (1992) 'Rural Diversification in the Philippines: Effects of Agricultural Growth on the Macro-economic Environment', *South-East Asian Journal of Agricultural Economics,* 1 (1): 25–44.

Bigsten, A. (1984) *Education and Income Determination in Kenya,* Aldershot: Gower.

Bigsten, A. and Kayizzi-Mugerwa, S. (1995) 'Rural Sector Responses to Economic Crisis in Uganda', *Journal of International Development,* 7 (1): 181–209.

Bindlish, V. and Evenson, R. (1993) 'Evaluation of the Performance of T&V Extension in Kenya', Technical Paper 208, Washington, DC: World Bank.

Byerlee, D. and Heisey, P.W. (1996) 'Past and Potential Impacts of Maize Research in sub-Saharan Africa: a Critical Assessment', *Food Policy,* 21 (3): 225–77.

Cleaver, K.M. and Donovan, W.G. (1995) 'Agriculture, Poverty, and Policy Reform in sub-Saharan Africa', World Bank Discussion Paper 280, Washington DC: World Bank.

Cleaver, K.M. and Schreiber, G.A. (1994) *Reversing the Spiral: The Population, Agriculture, and Environment Nexus in sub-Saharan Africa,* Washington, DC: World Bank.

Collier, P. (1988) 'Women in Development - Defining the Issues', Policy, Planning and Research Paper 129, Washington, DC: World Bank.

Delgado, C. (1992) 'Why Domestic Food Prices matter to Growth Strategy in Semi-open West African Agriculture', *Journal of African Economies,* 1 (3): 446–71.

Eicher, C.K. (1995) 'Zimbabwe's Maize-based Green Revolution: Precondition for Replication', *World Development,* 25 (5): 805–18.

Evans, E.H. (1992) 'A Virtuous Circle Model of Rural–Urban Development: Evidence from a Kenyan Small Town and its Hinterland', *Journal of Development Studies,* 28(4): 640–67.

FAO/UN (1994) *Structural Adjustment and the Provision of Agricultural Services in sub-Saharan Africa,* Rome: Food and Agriculture Organisation.

FAO/UN (1995) *Production Yearbook,* Rome: Food and Agriculture Organisation.

Francis A.P., Milimo, J.T., Njobvu, C.A. and Tembo, S.P.M. (1997) 'Listening to Farmers: Participatory Assessment of Policy Reform in Zambia's Agricultural Sector', World Bank Technical Paper 375, Washington DC: World Bank.

Hassan, R.M., Mwangi, W. and Karanja, D. (1993) 'Wheat Supply in Kenya: Production Technologies, Sources of Inefficiency, and Potential for Productivity Growth', CIMMYT Economics Working Paper 93-02, Mexico, DF: CIMMYT.

Hazell, P. and Haggblade, S. (1993) 'Farm and Non-farm Linkages and the Welfare of the Poor', in M. Lipton and J. Van de Gaag (eds) *Including the Poor,* Oxford: Oxford University Press.

Heisey, P.W. and Mwangi, W. (1996) 'Fertilizer Use and Maize Production in sub-Saharan Africa', CIMMYT Economics Working Paper 1, Mexico, DF: CIMMYT.

Jaffee, S. (1992) 'Enhancing Agricultural Growth through Diversification in sub-Saharan Africa', in S. Barghouti, S. Garbus and D. Umali (eds) *Trends in Agricultural Diversification: Regional Perspectives,* Washington, DC: World Bank.

Laferrière, R. and Nalo, D.S.O. (1992) 'Optimal Road User Charges and Income Distribution in Kenya', *International Journal of Transport Economics*, XIX (1): 61–83.

Lele, U. (1990) 'Structural Adjustment, Agricultural Development and the Poor: Some Lessons from the Malawian Experience', *World Development*, 18 (9): 1207–19.

Marter, A. and Gordon, A. (1996) 'Emerging Issues confronting the Renewable Natural Resources Sector in sub-Saharan Africa', *Food Policy*, 21 (2): 229–41.

McIntire, J., Bourzat, D. and Pingali, P. (1992) *Crop–Livestock Interaction in sub-Saharan Africa*, Washington DC: World Bank.

Migot-Adholla, S., Hazell, P., Blarel, B. and Place, F. (1991) 'Indigenous Land Rights Systems in sub-Saharan Africa: Constraint on Productivity?' *World Bank Economic Review*, 5 (1): 155–75.

Mink, S.D. (1993) 'Poverty, Population and the Environment', World Bank Discussion Paper 189, Washington DC: World Bank.

Moock, P.R. (1981) 'Education and Technical Efficiency in Small-farm Production', *American Journal of Agricultural Economics*, 58: 831–5.

Ongaro, W.A. (1994) 'Africa's and South East Asia's Agricultural Export and Import Markets: a Comparative Analysis of Africa's Opportunities in the 1990s and Beyond', Research Monograph 7, Addis Ababa: Joint ECA/FAO Agriculture Division.

Ongaro, W.A. (1995) 'Food Production and Consumption in the Context of Border Trading: an Application to Eastern and Southern Africa', Research Monograph 12, Addis Ababa: Joint ECA/FAO Agriculture Division.

Pinkney, T.C. and Kimuyu, P.K. (1994) 'Land Tenure Reform in East Africa: Good, Bad or Unimportant?', *Journal of African Economies*, 3 (1): 1–28.

Pischke, J.D. von and Adams, D.W. (1980) 'Fungibility and the Design and Evaluation of Agricultural Credit Projects', *American Journal of Agricultural Economics*, 62: 719–26.

Putterman, L. (1995) 'Economic Reform and Smallholder Agriculture in Tanzania: Discussion of Recent Market Liberalization, Road Rehabilitation, and Technology Dissemination Efforts', *World Development,* 23 (2): 311–26.

Reardon, T. and Vosti, S.A. (1995) 'Links between Rural Poverty and the Environment in Developing Countries: Asset Categories and Investment Poverty', *World Development*, 23 (9): 1495–506.

Reardon, T., Kelly, V., Crawford, E., Diagana, B., Dione, J., Savadago, K. and Boughton, D. (1997) 'Promoting Sustainable Intensification and Productivity Growth in Sahel Agriculture after Macro-economic Policy Reform', *Food Policy*, 22 (4): 317–27.

Schultz, T.W. (1988) 'Education Investments and Returns' in H. Chenery and T.N. Srinivasan (eds) *Handbook of Development Economics*, Amsterdam: Elsevier.

Smale, M. (1995), '"Maize is Life": Malawi's Delayed Green Revolution', *World Development*, 23 (5): 819–31.

Srivastava, J.P. and Alderman, H. (eds) (1993) *Agriculture and Environmental Challenges: Proceedings of the Thirteenth Agricultural Sector Symposium*, Washington DC: World Bank.

Staatz, John M. (1996) *Fostering Agricultural and Food System Transformation in Africa*, MSU Policy Synthesis 13, East Lansing: Michigan State University.

Stern, D.I., Common, M.S. and Barbier, E.B. (1996) 'Economic Growth and Environmental Degradation: the Environmental Kuznets Curve and Sustainable Development', *World Development*, 24 (7): 1151–60.

Tenga, R. (1997) 'Processing a Land Policy: the Case of Mainland Tanzania', paper presented at the Partnership Africa conference, Stockholm, June.

Thapa, K.K., Bilsborrow, R.E. and Murphy, L. (1996) 'Deforestation, Land Use and Women's Agricultural Activities in the Ecuadorian Amazon', *World Development*, 24 (8): 1317–32.

Truong, T.V. and Walker, S.T. (1990) 'Policy Reforms as Institutional Change: Privatizing Fertilizer Sub-sector in Cameroon' in D. Brinkerhoff and A. Goldsmith (eds) *Institutional Sustainability in Agriculture and Rural Development: A Global Perspective*, New York: Praeger.

UN/ECA (1996a) *African Population Newsletter* 69, Addis Ababa: ECA.

UN/ECA (1996b) *Report on the Economic and Social Situation in Africa 1996*, Addis Ababa: ECA.

Valdes, V. and Muir-Leresche, K. (eds) (1993) *Agricultural Policy Reforms and Regional Integration in Malawi, Zambia, and Zimbabwe*, Washington DC: International Food Policy Research Institute.

Way, P.O. and Stanecki, K. (1991) *The Demographic Impact of an AIDS Epidemic on an African Country: Application of the Iwgaids Mode*, Washington DC: International Research, US Bureau of the Census.

World Bank (1989) *Sub-Saharan Africa: From Crisis to Sustainable Growth: A Long-Term Perspective Study*, Washington DC: World Bank.

World Food Programme (1995) *The Food Aid Monitor: 1994 Food Aid Flows*, Rome: International Food Aid Information System.

World Resource Institute (1992) *World Resources 1992–93 – Toward Sustainable Development*, Oxford and New York: Oxford University Press.

18

TOWARDS SUSTAINABLE DEVELOPMENT

The poverty-environment nexus

Charles Leyeka Lufumpa

In the hierarchy of challenges confronting Africa, poverty eradication is one of the most important. However, it has also become increasingly clear in recent years that, for a poverty-reducing growth strategy to be sustainable, it must also address environmental concerns. In the Bruntland report of the World Commission on the Environment and Development (1987: 43) sustainable development was defined as 'development that meets the needs of the present without compromising the ability of future generations to meet their own'. It is thus important to look at Africa's poverty and environmental demands as part and parcel of the broader development challenge.

There are three reasons why poverty and the environment should be addressed as a twin problem. First, Africa's population is one of the fastest growing in the world. This is putting a lot of pressure on land and other natural resources. Second, the majority of the population depend on low-productivity, rain-fed agriculture for their livelihood and cash income. The first two points imply that, in the absence of a technological shift, the only way of increasing agricultural output is by extending farming activities on fragile land or by converting forest into farm land. Third, inadequate economic policies have increased the risks related to farming, thereby inhibiting the use of enhanced agricultural technologies.

While Africa's economic performance has seen a turn-around in the 1990s, large pockets of poverty remain in most countries (African Development Bank 1997a). Paucity of resources has forced communities to adopt survival mechanisms that have been harmful to the environment and thus to the long-term well-being of the population. The fact that the pressures for survival are immediate while the impact on the environment takes time to manifest itself gives rise to a time inconsistency problem that makes it difficult to enforce good behaviour. To develop a sufficient level of environmental consciousness demands, therefore, a considerable amount of social learning.

Policy-makers should be able to demonstrate that rapid population growth, inadequate food production, poor access to social services and increasing degradation of natural resources can create a vicious circle of poverty, especially in rural areas, that will be difficult to address solely on the basis of existing resources.

This chapter examines the factors jointly affecting poverty and environmental degradation in Africa. It is argued that while economic growth is a prerequisite in all attempts at addressing poverty and environmental issues, policy-makers need to ensure that it is not skewed in favour of a privileged few. It is important to provide the services and information necessary to enable the less privileged also to engage in mainstream economic activity.

POVERTY AND THE ENVIRONMENT

While Africa is in absolute terms not the world's poorest region, it is the only one where poverty is increasing strongly. In the mid-1990s close to 50 per cent of Africa's population of 700 million lived in absolute poverty. It has been estimated that while the number of the poor in developing countries should have declined by 400 million by the turn of the decade, sub-Saharan Africa itself will have seen a more than 25 per cent increase in the number of its poor. The region will then account for 30 per cent of the poor in developing countries, compared with 16 per cent in the mid-1980s.

Poverty indicators for Africa show that the majority of the poor live in rural areas, with agriculture, fishing and hunting as the main sources of livelihood. In both urban and rural areas, women as a group comprise a disproportionately large number of people living in absolute poverty (see also Kayizzi-Mugerwa and Lufumpa 1995).

With regard to the main social indicators, sub-Saharan Africa lags behind other developing areas. The crude death rate is about 15.6 per 1,000 people, compared with 8 or less in South America and Asia. Though infant mortality in the region has fallen by more than 30 per cent since the 1970s to 97 children per 1,000 live births, it still compares unfavourably with the average of 64 for low-income countries. Further, though most African countries can sustain several harvests a year, malnutrition is still widespread. It is estimated that 32 per cent of all the under-fives suffer from severe malnutrition or stunting, while only 53 per cent of the population have access to health services, compared with 80 per cent for developing countries as a whole.

Using its human development index (HDI), a measure incorporating aspects such as life expectancy, education and income levels in estimating the quality of life, the United Nations Development Programme (1997) classified all African countries, except Algeria, Libya and Tunisia, in the bottom half of the 175 countries covered. More than 75 per cent of the countries with scores in the bottom third of the index are African. These poor rankings highlight the region's widespread poverty and low human resource development. In a number of respects this pervasive poverty is closely related to a rapidly deteriorating environment. There are high levels of deforestation and soil degradation, falling water supplies, degradation of coastal areas and urban pollution. These have not only affected sources of livelihood but also the quality of life.

It is estimated that close to 5 million ha of natural forest were lost annually over the period 1981–90. This high rate of deforestation contributed significantly to soil degradation, making the latter one of the most serious problems facing Africa today. The Food and Agriculture Organisation (1986, 1993) has estimated that during the 1970s the annual deforestation rate in Africa was 0.5 per cent. This increased to 0.7 per cent, that is, about 4 million ha of forest per year, during the 1980s. Then only about 36 per cent of Africa's original closed tropical moist forests was left. The highest rate of deforestation has taken place in West Africa, where about 1.2 million ha of forest were felled annually over the 1980s. In that region, only about 15 per cent of original tropical moist forest remains. As a result of this high forest depletion, Nigeria, once a net exporter of wood products, is now a net importer.

Côte d'Ivoire provides another illustration of the impact of rapid forest resource depletion. Initially one of the most densely forested countries in West Africa, it saw, in the absence of controls, forest harvesting reaching 290,000 ha per year in the first half of the 1980s. This was equal to 10 per cent of total closed forest area in the country (US Congress 1984). High population density in Côte d'Ivoire's forest area gave rise to increased migration into neighbouring areas, which then also came under similar pressure. The vicious circle led to more forest clearance, the planting of coffee, cocoa and food crops, and exposure of vulnerable soils to erosion (African Development Bank 1997b).

Deforestation has been most serious in areas adjacent to urban concentrations. Here trees often are cut down without replacement and before maturity in order to meet the insatiable demand for fuel wood by urban dwellers, especially the poor in slums and other areas with poor access to the power grid, for cooking, heating and lighting. Taking into account the fact that about 90 per cent of the population in Africa uses fuel wood to meet energy needs (Lufumpa 1995), felling for this purpose is by far the most significant factor contributing to local deforestation.

A total of close on 500 million ha have been lost to land degradation. Besides deforestation, noted above, which accounts for 13 per cent of this, it is estimated that overgrazing, which leads to accelerated removal of vegetation cover and compaction of the soil, is responsible for another 49 per cent of land loss. Two other factors are important to note. First, among richer farmers, and on government farms, poor agricultural practices, including the excessive use of fertiliser and other chemicals, and the use of inappropriate equipment on fragile land, are responsible for the loss of a considerable amount of farm land. Second, bush clearing during land preparation for agricultural use or for other development activities and logging also has deleterious effects.

The high rate of environmental degradation in Africa also poses a serious threat to bio-diversity. The shrinking forest and vegetation cover, and the related degeneration of mangrove swamps, have contributed to the degradation of eco-systems and destruction of natural habitats, threatening the survival of many animal and plant species. Poor management of the eco-system, complicated by widespread poaching, has led to the near extinction of some species, notably the white rhinos of southern Africa. Similarly, elephant populations have been decimated in much of Africa, though the recent ban on the ivory trade has had some positive impact on the recovery of elephant populations, especially in southern Africa.

Water is also becoming an issue of serious concern (see Chapter 16). There is a fear that future regional conflicts may result from competition over water use. Partly owing to long spells of drought, Africa has less water today than in the 1970s (UNEP/OAU 1991). For example, the Congo basin, which incorporates one of the largest river systems in the world, has seen a significant reduction in water resources. Associated with falling water supplies is the issue of water pollution. In rural areas the population draw water from unprotected sources, such as wells and rivers. Many of these sources have been exposed to serious pollutants from industry, the infiltration of agricultural chemicals and fertiliser, and raw sewage. It has been estimated that in most of Africa sewage is discharged untreated into surface waters. These are often sources of drinking water for downstream communities, making populations vulnerable to 'environmental' diseases like cholera, typhoid, diarrhoea and dysentery.

Let us now look more closely at the nature of the poverty–environment nexus. Africa's poor are based in rural areas, depending on agriculture for their livelihood. Lack of sufficient land means that farmers increasingly resort to marginally productive land that is prone to degradation. The high population growth rates exert further pressure on the limited land, leading to serious encroachment on forests and other natural resources. As noted above, that in turn leads to soil degradation, deforestation and subsequent loss of productivity.

Civil wars, which have been common in Africa, also tend to aggravate pressures on the countryside. Since their immediate needs are shelter and food, displaced populations pay little attention to environmental concerns. Large concentrations of displaced people on confined areas often lead to localised deforestation and poor sanitary conditions, as recently demonstrated in the Democratic Republic of the Congo.

Small-scale farmers producing for their own consumption rather than for the market comprise the majority in many parts of Africa. Little if any modern inputs or equipment are used, implying that agricultural production, in particular food production, has remained quite below potential. In past decades Africa has been unable to feed its expanding population adequately, let alone generate a surplus to improve stocks and ensure a degree of food security. While population has been growing at 3 per cent per year, food production has increased by an average of only 1 per cent (El-Ashry 1992). Three other factors have impinged on African agriculture: poor price incentives for farmers, inadequate systems for the dissemination of information on productivity-enhancing technologies, and irregular land tenure legislation and practices.

Poor incentives have been a key impediment to agricultural production. In many post-independence plans, agriculture was accorded a prominent place (e.g. Republic of Zambia 1974), if mainly as an important source of cheap resources for the budding industrial sector. Thus from independence up to structural adjustment the tendency in many countries was to maintain low food and input prices for the politically vocal urban consumers and producers, respectively, but at the expense of rural producers. This was made possible by the maintenance of extensive market controls and parastatal companies for commodity marketing. Foreign exchange controls and export taxes also meant that, in spite of subsidies, the tax incidence on agriculture was high. There was thus a fundamental imbalance in the economy tilted against the rural sector. In not a few cases, peasants responded by withdrawing from the formal market altogether (Bunker 1991).

A number of studies (Borlaug and Dowswell 1995, Ongaro 1990) have tried to respond to the question of why farmers in sub-Saharan Africa have been slow to adopt production-increasing technologies. Among the explanations offered are that farmers have inadequate access to markets, and thus to cash income, and have few means of spreading the risks related to earning a living from agriculture. In a study of the social articulation of risk in West Africa, Carter (1997) has noted that risk blunts the adoption of technologies as well as strategies for specialisation. Groups unable to deal with risk are exposed to deepening poverty and food insecurity, even as their better-endowed neighbours prosper. In this regard, off-farm employment was found to be a crucial and stabilising feature of rural households, as it limits the risk involved in over-reliance on agricultural production. Thus policies that promote industrial growth as well as non-farm employment are important also to the well-being of agriculture (Keller 1996, Oehmke and Crawford 1996).

In a study of Kenya Evans (1992) found that the most innovative farm households were those that had managed to combine farm incomes with off-farm ones. There is greater interaction with the urban areas, a more efficient flow of information, and a greater willingness to try new techniques. These factors create a 'virtuous circle' of improved resource use, leading to sustainable exploitation of natural resources. It is important to add that farmer education is a key factor. Lockheed *et al.* (1980) argued that a dynamic agricultural environment can be taken advantage of only by farmers with some education, while in environments not supportive of agricultural innovations traditional knowledge is often sufficient.

The low agricultural productivity has also been blamed on the poor nature of rural institutions, especially with respect to land ownership: security of tenure and land entitlement (see Feder and Feeny 1991). It has been argued that rural responses are very dependent on access to and hence the distribution of land. When access is insufficient, rural responses tend to become perverse. In particular, subsistence farmers who still use shifting cultivation have shortened their fallow periods as available land becomes scarcer. This has meant that more forest and woodland is cleared to create additional agricultural land. The result is deforestation with the attendant problems of soil degradation and continued loss of soil fertility.

LOOKING AHEAD

The issues raised above suggest two important conclusions, namely that poverty is a serious cause of environmental degradation and, if not arrested, environmental degradation affects economic growth, further worsening the situation of the poor. Thus to achieve sustainable development requires growth not only to be pro-poor but also to take account of environmental concerns. Strategies for poverty reduction and the efficient management of natural resources are threefold:

1 Policy-makers need to have a good knowledge of the exogenous factors influencing farming, forestry, grazing or fishing and how to manage them. The goal should be to achieve a broad-based and equitable economic growth.
2 Policy-makers should be able to compare how various economic strategies impact on poverty and the environment.
3 It is necessary to put in place an institutional framework which ensures that the long-term goal of sustainable development is achieved: that is, a framework that incorporates environmental factors in growth strategies. This implies among other things the development of legal and land tenure systems, as well as the adoption of best practices for urban and rural development (Castle *et al.* 1996).

In promoting broad-based and equitable growth, one needs to focus on the revival of the rural economy, where agriculture is the predominant activity. This will also be beneficial to the rest of the economy, since in many countries agriculture accounts for as much as 60 per cent of foreign exchange earnings and up to 40 per cent of GDP.

With regard to reforming agriculture, many countries have started the slow but steady process of privatising their economies, leading in some to more competitive agricultural commodity markets, prompt payment of farmers, and to some signs of recovery in the countryside. On the whole, however, agriculture continues to have extremely low levels of productivity and few countries have established a viable level of food security. It would seem, therefore, that there are ingredients still lacking in the macroeconomic environment to ensure sufficient increases in agricultural investment, output and productivity, all of which are necessary in raising capacity for technological innovation and in the creation of a virtuous circle of development.

A substantial number of rural impediments to agriculture are non-market in nature, however. Poor infrastructure has implied that remote areas continue to have poor access to the market, while a combination of low levels of education and poor access to credit have hindered many peasants from adopting even the simplest of technologies. Thus while macroeconomic reforms are necessary to create incentives for technology adoption, governments need to complement them with non-market reforms in land, property rights and the infrastructure, in order to make farmer efforts worthwhile. Probably a case can be developed for making subsidies available to traders in remote regions of the country with a view to improving market access.

The best way to empower poor people is to let them benefit from their factors of production: land and labour. However, poor people are likely to be illiterate, unskilled, in poor health and with little or no access to capital. It is necessary therefore to improve access to social services and to credit. Education and health investments have, for example, well known benefits to society as a whole. They raise the individual welfare of the users while improving the human capital of the country as a whole. Education, for instance, raises labour productivity, with farmers with some years of schooling improving their ability to absorb information on new farming methods and markets. On the other hand, educated mothers are more likely to have fewer and better-nourished children, since they are better able to follow family planning advice.

However, the situation of women needs special emphasis. In a study of rural India, Agarwal (1996) found strong gender linkages between rural production, poverty and the environment, especially with respect to time use, income generation, health, social support networks and concern for the environment. Women are by far the biggest contributors to production in the countryside and also the main gatherers of food, fuel and water. Still, having no assets of their own, women have few means of taking the initiative. Two of the most serious constraints are access to land and agricultural credit. In principle, women have access to communal or family land, although few own it, via direct purchase or inheritance. Where land is available, access to agricultural credit is poor. It has thus become difficult for women to plant high-yielding varieties, which demand high volumes of modern inputs, such as fertiliser. To increase efficiency in the countryside thus requires the improvement of women's access to land and capital. A higher income-generating capacity has implications for the welfare of many rural households, since women are the *de facto* social insurance in the countryside. It has been argued that women are more apt to spend their extra income on their children and the aged than are their male counterparts (Tadria 1997).

An adequate rural infrastructure is important for enhancing rural productivity, facilitating access to markets and thus providing incentives for increasing output. This facilitates the integration of rural markets, while an improved marketing and food storage infrastructure enhances food security and reduces post-harvest losses. The latter often account for up to 30 per cent of total yield. Curtailing such losses would thus increase available supplies and reduce food insecurity. In the absence of proper storage facilities, many poor farmers are compelled to sell their surplus production at harvest and at distress prices. Improved storage facilities would enhance the opportunities of the poor to participate in the market. Farmers would also be able to increase their own food security by storing food for drought periods.

Much of the environmental degradation in Africa is caused by activities related to overgrazing and agricultural production. Pastures are considered common property with free access for everyone. Under such circumstances, the distribution of private benefits is to a large extent dependent on the size of the herd one is able to put out to pasture. The carrying capacity of the land is soon exceeded as more animals are allowed to graze than can be supported by the available pasture. Forage becomes scarcer and soil becomes more and more compacted, leading to further deterioration of the pasture. The adoption of better grazing and farming practices, and of improved animal husbandry techniques, is necessary in a bid to reduce environmental damage, raise productivity and incomes and so reduce poverty.

One of the key issues in addressing environmental problems relates to land tenure. Africa's unusually complex land tenure systems have made it difficult to create incentives to improve resource management, especially on the part of farmers and herdsmen. It has not been possible to pursue environmentally conscious production systems that encourage long-term improvements in pasture and farm land. In the absence of well specified rights to land use, farmers may not find it worth while to undertake them. They need to be assured that their investment will not be appropriated (Lufumpa 1991).

Rapid population growth has accelerated encroachment on ecologically fragile land, leading to serious degradation, diminished productivity and lower incomes. Reducing the rate of population growth should, therefore, form an integral part of strategies aimed at improving the welfare of the people and ensuring that natural resources are managed in a sustainable manner. Population policies aimed at lowering fertility should be integrated in overall development strategies (Tiffen 1995)

Expansion of electrification programmes in rural areas, via simple environmentally friendly technologies, could also reduce the rate of exploitation of the natural resource base. Further, promotion of energy efficient stoves on a large scale would help reduce fuelwood waste and thus impact positively on efforts to reduce deforestation.

With regard to water, it is necessary to highlight its importance in sustaining income generation, maintaining acceptable health standards, and even in power generation. While threats to water supplies are not all man-made, there is little doubt that deforestation, poor agricultural practices, as well as the dumping of industrial and household waste, have ruined many rivers and lakes in Africa. Marshland has been put under agriculture in many countries, initially with favourable results in terms of output. However, its productivity declines rapidly, while the eco-system is perhaps ruined for ever.

Finally, it should be emphasised that economic policies which increase overall efficiency are also beneficial to the environment. The removal of distortions and improvement of people's access to productive resources and social services not only enhance the prospects of growth and poverty reduction but also reduce the wasteful use of natural resources, so abating environmental degradation. However, the review in this chapter, as well as experience in Latin American (Pichón, 1997), suggests that the interaction between growth and the environment can be complex and problematic, with no simple solution. Besides being innovative, policy-makers must also attempt to reconcile the demand for higher resource productivity with demand for increased resource protection. The goal should be not to restrict use but more broadly to avoid the irreversible use or destruction of natural resources.

NOTE

The views expressed here should not be ascribed to the African Development Bank.

REFERENCES

African Development Bank (1997a) 'Côte d'Ivoire: Proposal for a Loan for the Financing of the Agricultural Sector Adjustment Loan', working document, Abidjan: ADB.

African Development Bank (1997b) *African Development Report 1997*, Oxford: Oxford University Press.

Agarwal, B. (1996) 'Gender, Environment and Poverty Interlinks: Regional Variations and Temporal Shifts in Rural India 1971–91', *World Development*, 25 (1): 23–52.

Borlaug, N.E. and Dowswell, C.R. (1995) 'Mobilising Science and Technology to get Agriculture moving in Africa', *Development Policy Review*, 13 (2): 115–34.

Bunker, G.S. (1991) *Peasants against the State: the Politics of Market Control in Bugisu, Uganda, 1900–83*, Chicago: University of Chicago Press.

Carter, M.R. (1997) 'Environment, Technology, and Social Articulation of Risk in West African Agriculture', *Economic Development and Cultural Change*, 45 (3): 557–90.

Castle, N.E., Berrens, R.P. and Polasky, S. (1996) 'The Economics of Sustainability', *Natural Resources Journal*, 36 (4).

Congress of the United States (1984) *Technologies to Sustain Tropical Forest Resources*, Washington DC: Office of Technology Assessment.

El-Ashry, M. (1992) *Natural Resource Management and Agricultural Productivity in sub-Saharan Africa*, IFAD Staff Working Paper Series, Rome: IFAD.

Evans, E.H. (1992) 'A Virtuous Circle of Rural–Urban Development: Evidence from a Kenyan Small Town and its Hinterland', *Journal of Development Studies*, 28 (4): 640–67.

Ezumah, N.N. and Di-Domenico, C.M. (1995) 'Enhancing the Role of Women in Crop Production: a Case Study of Igbo Women in Nigeria', *World Development*, 23 (10).

Feder, G. and Feeny, D. (1991) 'Land Tenure and Property Rights: Theory and Implications for Development Policy', *World Bank Economic Review*, 5: 135–53.

Food and Agriculture Organisation (1986) *African Agriculture: The Next 25 Years*, Rome: FAO.

Food and Agriculture Organisation (1993) *Report on Forest Resources Assessment 1990*, eleventh session of the Committee on Forestry, Rome: FAO.

Kayizzi-Mugerwa, S. and Lufumpa, C.L. (1995) *Poverty Alleviation in Africa: Putting the Challenge in Perspective*, Environment and Social Policy Working Paper Series 11, Abidjan: African Development Bank.

Keller, W. (1996) 'Absorptive Capacity: on the Creation and Acquisition of Technology in Development', *Journal of Development Economics*, 49 (1): 199–227.

Lockheed, M., Jameson, D. and Lau, L. (1980) 'Farmer Education and Farm Efficiency: a Survey', *Economic Development and Cultural Change*, 29 (1): 37–76.

Lufumpa, C.L. (1991) *'An Economic Analysis of Agroforestry Systems in Zambia: Application of Risk Programming and Risk-Free Modeling Techniques,'* Ph.D. dissertation, Ames IA: Iowa State University.

Lufumpa, C.L. (1995) *Agricultural Sector Adjustment Programs and the Environment*, Environment and Social Policy Working Paper Series, Abidjan: African Development Bank.

Oehmke, J.F. and Crawford, E.W. (1996) 'The Impact of Agricultural Technology in sub-Saharan Africa', *Journal of African Economies*, 5 (2): 271–92.

Ongaro, W.A. (1990) 'Modern Maize Technology, Yield Variations and Efficiency Differentials: a Case of Small Farms in Western Kenya', *East African Economic Review*, 6 (1): 11–30.

Pichón, F.J. (1997) 'Colonist Land Allocation Decisions, Land Use, and Deforestation in the Ecuadorian Amazon Frontier', *Economic Development and Cultural Change*, 45 (4): 707–44.

Republic of Zambia (1974) *Second National Development Plan* (1974–78), Lusaka: Government Printer.

Seabright, P. (1993) 'Managing Local Commons', *Journal of Economic Perspectives*, 7: 113–34.

Tadria, H. (1997) 'Poverty and Gender in Africa', paper presented to the Partnership Africa Conference Abidjan, January.

Tiffen, M. (1995) 'Population Density, Economic Growth and Societies in Transition: Boserup Reconsidered in a Kenyan Case Study', *Development and Change*, 26 (1): 31–65.

United Nations Development Programme (UNDP) (1997) *Human Development Indicators*, New York: Oxford University Press.

United Nations Environment Programme (UNEP) (1992), *The State of the Environment (1972–1992) Saving our Planet: Challenges and Hopes*, Nairobi: UNEP.

UNEP and Organisation of African Unity (1991) *Regaining the Lost Decade*, Nairobi: UNEP.

World Commission on Environment and Development (1987) *Our Common Future* (the Bruntland report), Oxford University Press.

19

PRIVATISATION AND MARKET DEVELOPMENT

Steve Kayizzi-Mugerwa

Privatisation is unquestionably one of the most important policy changes in Africa since the achievement of independence in the 1960s. The policy focus of the post-independence years was state control of the 'commanding heights': to ensure balanced growth and income equality. Indeed, similar arguments were flourishing in Labourite Britain and on the European continent at the time. Thus when structural adjustment policies were embarked on in the early 1980s, it was generally assumed that privatisation would be an extremely sensitive subject, to be dealt with carefully, and even then implemented over a long period of time (Berg 1992). In its assessment of structural adjustment in Africa, the World Bank (1994) also felt that privatisation, especially of the bigger firms, was unpopular, and had to be relegated to subjects on which there was still disagreement on how to proceed.

It is thus surprising that while aspects of monetary and fiscal reform as well as institutional rehabilitation remain difficult to implement, privatisation has proved easier to push through than the assessments of the 1980s and early 1990s had predicted (Kanbur 1995). In Zambia, for example, the sale of the giant mining parastatal ZCCM was unthinkable only a decade ago – considered the equivalent of selling the family silver. Yet the government was not only in the process of selling it at the end of the 1990s but had already divested itself of the bulk of the parastatal sector as well, in what has been one of the fastest rates of privatisation in Africa to date (African Development Bank 1997).

Across Africa, and irrespective of earlier political ideology, countries have undertaken far-reaching privatisation measures. In many cases, foreign companies and individuals have been allowed to purchase companies with 'no strings attached'. In others, governments have preserved a percentage of the shares with a view to selling them to the 'general' public when the fledgling stock exchanges are strong enough to undertake the exercise.

But even more interesting is the change in the internal debate on privatisation. In Ghana and Uganda, for example, the ruling 'movements' had initially professed a dislike for 'liberal' economics, including privatisation. However, they went on to pursue some of the most far-reaching liberalisation programmes in Africa. Likewise, though the local media were loudly anti-structural adjustment, with privatisation equalled to 'foreignisation', they have shown considerable enthusiasm for private sector ownership in recent years, in some cases even deriding governments for dragging their feet. Part of the explanation may of course be that the bulk of the media is now in private hands.

This chapter surveys the privatisation debate in Africa. Three issues are emphasised: first, we look at the rationale of state control and why it failed; second, we examine the dynamics of privatisation, including the impact on firms, markets and corporate governance; third, we outline the regulatory and support structures needed for successful private sector development. The chapter ends with a look at selected privatisation experiences in Africa.

THE INDIGENOUS QUESTION

At independence many African countries felt a strong need to create employment and to extend the physical and social infrastructure to the countryside. However, the modern African economies were dominated by foreign companies and businesses belonging to minorities; the former were feared, seen as too close to the former colonial rulers, while non-African minorities were resented for dominating domestic commerce. Indigenous entrepreneurs were very few, with fairly limited technical skills, and often incapable of raising much capital (Killick and Commander 1988). Thus many post-independence governments saw state ownership as the only means of overcoming the legacy of underdevelopment.[1] Public enterprises, it was argued, would provide the scale economies and finances needed to realise the goals of the national development plans. Wangwe (1992) argues, for example, that it was only thanks to public firms that Tanzania was able to achieve some industrialisation from what, at least by comparison with its neighbour Kenya, was a position of considerable disadvantage. Public companies were also expected to contribute to state revenue, in terms of taxes and dividends. Moreover, parastatals were expected to set an example in corporate behaviour, not only in the treatment of their workers, say with regard to the implementation of minimum wage legislation, but also in the uplifting of the technological base of the country via on-the-job training and learning-by-doing effects. The conscious establishment of parastatals in all regions of the country would lead to more balanced growth, while pricing and subsidy policies would help governments achieve a number of their distributional objectives (Chang and Singh 1993). As became increasingly evident in the 1970s, parastatals also provided the government with the means to exercise political patronage.

Initially, the nationalising governments focused on the 'strategic' sectors of the economy, such as mining, banking and textiles. However, the sense of what was 'strategic' changed with the political demands. Details of today's privatisation programmes indicate that governments had gone well beyond the original intention of state ownership, i.e. to promote rapid growth and ensure income equality. These goals were superseded by the need for control and political patronage. Thus firms recently privatised in Benin include those in textiles, tobacco, cement, transport, refrigeration at ports, abattoirs, cinemas, hotels, sugar production, fruit juice manufacture, food oils, water and electricity, tourist promotion and many more (Forum Afrique Expansion 1996). Since a similar proliferation of state ownership was evident in Egypt, Nigeria, many parts of East Africa and in the other countries belonging to the CFA franc zone, 'strategic' was merely a euphemism for total economic control.

However, by the end of the 1970s, the achievements had been modest. Parastatals and nationalised companies failed to become business entities in the conventional meaning. Audits were rare and 'ghost' workers were maintained on the payrolls. In many cases, governments were forced to provide direct and indirect subsidies, the latter via tax reductions or tax write-offs. These 'soft budget' constraints encouraged waste, tying up social capital and obstructing the flow of services, such as water, electricity, roads, railways and harbours. Instead of contributing to the budget, as intended, public firms became a major cause of fiscal imbalance (Gersovitz and Paxson 1996, Eriksson 1991). Internally, parastatals were confronted by extremes. Thanks to controls, subsidy levels were sometimes too high, so that even inefficient firms could show a profit. Most often, price policies were too restrictive so that productivity fell at otherwise efficient firms. Apart from the distortions of the incentive structures and the negative impact on resource distribution, the parastatal sector's financial deficits had a serious impact on fiscal and monetary policy – with upward pressure on interest rates and prices. Exchange rates, then often controlled, became seriously overvalued. In a number of cases, parastatals incurred foreign debts, with government guarantees, contributing directly to the debt crisis. These factors added to the already high cost of doing business in Africa.

In addition, studies have shown (Kikeri *et al.* 1992) that the size of the parastatal sector is negatively correlated with the growth of the economy. Returns on investment in the sector are generally low, while its losses wipe out private sector savings. The combination of poor management, inadequate capital structures, bad investment decisions and the bureaucratisation of the decision-making process weakened most parastatals.

In outlining a positive theory of privatisation in sub-Saharan Africa, Laffont and Meleu (1997) have argued that bureaucrats and other powerful groups will not give up control structures from which they have benefited for altruistic motives. They may do so if they hope to benefit from privatisation by for instance making sure that some of the privatised companies or a portion of their shares accrue to them. When politically powerful groups also become entrenched in business, competition and efficiency are negatively affected.

THE DYNAMICS OF PRIVATISATION

Privatisation as policy lock-in

In recent evaluations the following have been included among the macro-economic goals of privatisation (Bhattacharay 1996, Due 1994, Due and Schmidd 1993): improvement of the efficiency of resource use via increased competition; increasing the tax base of the government as firms and transactions multiply; economic diversification as firms seek out new opportunities in traditional and new sectors; increased investment in infrastructure and utilities; expansion of the activities of the export sector; improving private access to credits and other forms of finance; and widening the ownership of key industries.

There are, however, a number of more specific ways in which privatisation can be beneficial to the operation of the economy. It increases the incentive of owners to monitor managers. It is, however, debatable whether the goal of privatisation should be to ensure as broad an ownership pattern for each individual firm as possible or whether it should ensure that privatised firms have 'real' owners. Widespread share ownership creates a powerful lobby for the private sector and becomes a guarantee against renationalisation. Gray (1996) has argued, however, that in light of the major restructuring and management problems facing newly privatised companies, it is necessary to make sure that the new owners have the power and incentive to monitor the activities of their managers. The case for privatisation could also be based on the need for governments to establish their reputation. In undertaking privatisation, governments signal to potential investors the course of future policies. It thus ties the hands of future governments, with policy-makers wary of undertaking policies that would have adverse impacts on the private sector. More predictable policies improve the planning horizon of economic agents, reducing the risks related to investment. However, while policy signalling is important for all countries, it has been even more crucial for those where nationalisation formed the thrust of economic policy in earlier years and where unsuccessful reform did serious harm to the credibility of governments. In this respect, privatisation marks a break with the past. The market becomes an agent of restraint, while the risk of bankruptcy enforces discipline. Subjecting firms to market discipline is thus the single most important outcome of privatisation.

Irrespective of the privatisation modalities, the 'new' industries will not grow or prosper in a vacuum. The size and assets of the privatised firms are often poor indicators of future performance, since they were acquired under a different market regime. Part of the government's responsibility is to create the conditions under which the 'new' firms can thrive after privatisation. This necessitates the removal of constraints on the business environment in areas such as taxation, property ownership, credit access and the law relating to bankruptcy. To improve the competitiveness of the privatised firms, cost-saving, quality-improving and energy-saving investments need to be undertaken. These have to be financed, which is another important factor to address. Measures that improve credit availability have a direct and positive impact on the success of privatisation. Finally, firm performance is also dependent on the availability of a functioning economic and social infrastructure.

Corruption and rent-seeking activities have been impediments to investment in Africa and are often cited as examples of a dysfunctional government apparatus, partly resulting from a poor incentive structure. As has been well explored in the literature (Wade 1985), corrupt activities demand real resources, not least in time and money, while they add little or nothing to total output. How can government deal with corruption without taking the economy back to the controls of the past? Market reforms such as those related to foreign exchange transactions have eliminated a number of discrepancies. But the culture of transparency takes time to build. In fact when public sector reforms imply costs or loss of income to influential groups they will be resisted (Schiavo-Campo 1996, Robinson 1990). The opposition to the introduction of value added tax (VAT) in many African countries is illustrative. Since VAT is incurred by the final consumer, it is less distortionary than other taxes. Nevertheless in many countries its loudest opponents have been urban producers and traders. One of the reasons for this has been that the administration of the tax demands the keeping of records, which in turn increases tax liability. The latter may fall more heavily on the poorer businesses than on the bigger and more influential ones.

To improve incentives in central government, many African countries have instituted specialised agencies for the performance of key tasks, such as tax collection, investment promotion and the undertaking of key projects in line Ministries. Revenue authorities have been set up in many countries, including Uganda, Tanzania, Ghana and Zambia, with support from the international financial institutions. They have in many cases been accompanied by one-stop investment agencies. Common for these institutions are much better wages for their workers than for comparable work in the civil service. These new initiatives have had dramatic impacts on tax collection and on the mobilisation of domestic and foreign investment. However, the exposure of a relatively small group of employees to a large and expanding private sector has taken its toll. There are reports of forgeries, bribery and collapsing morale. In the Uganda Revenue Authority, one of the first in the region, mass lay-offs are used frequently to 'unclog' the system.

While the pace of privatisation has been rapid in some countries, manufacturing output growth has remained weak. Part of the explanation is that the change of ownership has not removed the structural weaknesses of the former parastatals (Bigsten *et al.* 1994). Before privatisation, parastatals enjoyed credits and subsidies from the government, but since the private alternatives are still inadequate, and with equity markets too small to cater for the needs of the embryonic private sector, privatised companies still have poor access to capital. They have not been able to rehabilitate equipment or introduce new technologies as promised in the letters of intent. Governments have also been slow in instituting the appropriate legal framework to support the private sector, including the transfer and protection of property rights. On the other hand, the skill composition of the labour force was earlier disproportionately geared towards public sector work, and privatised enterprises now lack an adequate supply of managers, technicians and planners to run them in the changed market situation.

Economic impacts

With regard to fiscal outcomes, positive short-term impacts have been noted, especially those due to the reduction of subsidies and compensation to loss-making public firms (Naya 1990). However, Van de Walle (1989) has argued that there is a danger that any funds released via privatisation may instead go towards relieving debt repayments or to current expenditure and not necessarily into development. Another aspect of the fiscal impact relates to the trade-off between the prices at which parastatals are sold and the concessions the new owners wish to extract from the government – say, in terms of tax benefits. The latter amount to subsidies, implying potentially serious fiscal erosion even after privatisation.

Turning to efficiency, privatisation should improve allocative efficiency as relative prices better reflect the scarcity values of the factors of production. Improved use of inputs in the firm after the divestiture is also bound to raise productivity. However, many monopolies continue to exist after privatisation, and much time is spent lobbying the government for concessions, including higher tariffs to reduce competition. Since economic efficiency does not improve when a private monopoly replaces a public one, the state needs to establish a regulatory framework that can impose sanctions on excessive profiteering. Privatisation also relates to income distribution, since it changes ownership structures in favour of the private sector (Noll 1989). It has also been argued that the private sector sets a low premium on social goals such as poverty reduction and the reduction of unemployment. Indeed, following redundancies after privatisation the exercise is said by some to be labour-unfriendly (Davis 1991). However, the Eastern European experience has shown (Barberis *et al.* 1996, Nuti 1992) that the initial results and patterns from privatisation are rarely optimal. If the goal is a well performing market economy, it is inevitable that production structures will have to change.

In looking ahead, it is necessary to deal with two important issues. Apart from the larger economies such as South Africa, Nigeria and Egypt, and others that enjoy proximity to the European Union, individual domestic markets in Africa are small, and even after the privatisation process has been completed, will have a limited attraction to large foreign investment. It is necessary, therefore, to look at regional opportunities. Larger scale economies will enable the development of stock exchanges, transport networks and markets that can sustain an expanding private sector. Ultimately, a market that is unattractive to its domestic investors could not expect to attract great foreign interest, apart perhaps from the mining enclaves. There is need to examine closely the extent of indigenous participation in the privatisation process. There is a feeling that foreign investors have been attracted at the expense of creating incentives for domestic ones. Lessons from East Africa (Himbara 1994), and elsewhere (Elkan 1988) show that a sufficient indigenous stake in the economy is necessary to ensure policy stability and irreversibility.

SUPPORT STRUCTURES AND REGULATION

The state of the infrastructure has important implications for a firm's choice of production technique as well as that of its location. Firms will locate where certain conditional infrastructure thresholds are met. However, since firms cannot relocate frequently, they are forced to adjust inputs and outputs subject to infrastructure limitations once the choice of location has been made. The level and quality of infrastructure affect the factor intensities of the other private inputs. This implies that variations in the extent and quality of the infrastructure affect the marketing of the firm's products, as well as its ability to meet deadlines. Infrastructure impediments thus directly affect firm profitability, and regions that are well endowed with public capital will tend to attract firms with more modern production techniques.

A number of studies have tried to analyse the impact of infrastructural deficiencies on the performance of the manufacturing sector (Lee and Anas 1992, Baumol and Lee 1988). The poor performance of the infrastructure, in spite of high levels of investment, and the cost to the firm of finding alternative sources of supply, are the key obstacles. Though many African countries embarked on the construction of roads, electricity generating plants and other infrastructure after independence, the onset of economic crisis led to serious degeneration and the capacity to deliver services is now very low. This has meant higher private costs of production, eliminating the private sector's competitive edge. Firms have responded to these deficiencies in a number of ways. First, they have sought to relocate to regions with a better infrastructure. However, once the investment has been made, this is not an option that can easily be resorted to without incurring heavy costs. Moreover, in moving, the firm risks the loss of its clients and their associated goodwill.

281

There is also the danger of trading one set of deficiencies for another. Second, to minimise the impact of infrastructural disruptions on output, firms undertake factor substitution, making their production less infrastructure-intensive. However, even this is not an easy option, especially for huge companies whose production technique is more or less fixed in the short to medium run, where switches in techniques require substantial amounts of investment.

Third, given the frequent, and sometimes complete, breakdown of the infrastructure and public services, firms have resorted to self-provisioning. Still, the high cost per unit of installing equipment makes this option prohibitive for small companies. On the other hand, the bigger firms demand a considerable amount of services, and the cost of own production could be large. Thus, instead of full self-sufficiency, many firms resort to 'standby' measures, for example the installation of a diesel engine for the supply of electricity or a well for the supply of water. Firms that are completely dependent on the public sector for their services and production are forced to close down in their absence. Thus a poorly functioning infrastructure distorts production, hinders the adoption of new technologies and works against the goal of creating an efficient market economy. The worsening cost situation makes it difficult for local firms to compete on international markets.

How then should infrastructural impediments be alleviated? Two alternative approaches have been suggested. First, there should be changes in existing regulations in order to increase the capacity for private provision. The private sector could be encouraged – via taxation allowances, for example – to pool resources for the supply of key services. This would be most useful for firms located in the same area or those depending on the same defective source for service provision. To improve service provision, however, it may be necessary to introduce direct private sector participation. This makes the market for infrastructure contestable (Baumol and Lee 1988), thereby increasing efficiency in delivery. There are, however, many areas where the government will remain the main provider. Thus to reduce the financial burden on the government the pricing of social services has to be re-examined. To this end many African governments have set up pilot projects where communities defray some of the cost of the service. Lee and Jouravlev (1992) have even argued that user-fee financing of the infrastructure could well have a favourable distributive element. Still, the imposition of charges on public goods, such as roads, has been problematic. Moreover, while road tolls have been introduced in some countries the fiscal impact has been modest. More effective ways of collecting user fees still have to be devised.

Closely related to infrastructure provision is the nature of the regulatory environment. The latter environment imposes three burdens on firms: fiscal, bureaucratic and transitional. The fiscal burden is the amount of tax and other fees paid by individual firms. When these are huge, firms may try to circumvent them by becoming or remaining 'invisible' or by having recourse to 'lubricating' policy-makers. The bureaucratic burden involves all aspects of the firm-official transactions. Administrative overload, corruption and unnecessary delays could deter firms from entering the formal sector or, for those already there, from increasing investment. At a certain size, however, the benefits of informality – not paying taxes, for example – may be exceeded by those of formality, including access to credit facilities and modern services. Policy-makers should reduce the costs of transition by lowering the administrative overload and the high direct and indirect taxation on small firms. This would have beneficial effects on businesses at the tail end of the firm distribution, where indigenous business activities are concentrated in most African countries (Kimuyu and Kayizzi-Mugerwa 1993).

Encouraging the development of business associations could encourage self-regulation within branches of industry and trade. In many African countries the privatisation process has seen the strengthening of various business associations, notably those of manufacturers. This development has served a dual purpose. On the one hand, the associations now lobby governments on behalf of their members with respect to the business environment: that is, regarding regulation, taxes and services. On the other, a collective code of discipline ensures that members adhere to a modicum of standards in their business dealings, not least in meeting their tax obligations.

PRIVATISATION EXPERIENCES

In the above sections an attempt has been made to summarise the privatisation debate in Africa. In this section we present some privatisation experiences from a number of African countries, illustrating some of the issues discussed above. By end of 1995 the Uganda government had privatised assets worth about Sh.110 billion (about US$110 million), though only 40 per cent was paid in cash, while it planned that 85 per cent of the public enterprises would be in private hands by 1998. But as in other African countries, privatisation initially met with considerable political resistance. First, the government had wanted to sell only loss-making enterprises and those not considered strategic. However, such companies were not necessarily those that interested the private sector. Secondly, the government had no previous experience of mass privatisation, and the process was slow and initially riddled with political interference (Kayizzi-Mugerwa 1997).

Valuation of the companies to be privatised has been one of the most controversial issues. The public has little appreciation of the concept of 'sunk costs' and was outraged when companies were sold for a fraction of what had been spent earlier on their 'rehabilitation'. Another issue has been the lack of domestic capitalists. Following the expulsion of the Ugandan 'Asians' in the early 1970s by Idi Amin, few Africans had the resources and experience to fill the void created by their exodus. Twenty years later under Museveni's

283

government Asians were allowed to return and some have subsequently acquired a number of the businesses on sale, while African purchases have been confined to small businesses. To reverse this, a group of African businessmen have launched a venture capital fund to purchase shares on the newly introduced stock exchange. It is strongly felt that Africans need to take part in the privatisation process in order to ensure its success and reduce the risk of renationalisation.

The process of privatising five leading parastatals has been illustrative: Uganda Electricity Board, Uganda Posts and Telecommunications Corporation, Uganda Commercial Bank, Uganda Airlines and Coffee Marketing Board were in the past powerful extensions of the public sector, with boards composed of politicians and other influential people. They were also overloaded with non-commercial concerns such as facilitating rural credit supply, rural electrification, coffee rehabilitation, etc. Privatising these firms has demanded considerable resources, including, as in the case of the Uganda Commercial Bank, enlisting foreign expertise. To discourage private monopolies, the government has introduced legislation that allows the entry of more participants in the financial sector, telecommunications and utilities. For example, more than 100 exporters entered the coffee market in the early 1990s, the number of the private banks has increased, licences have been issued for the private generation of electricity and private airlines have been registered.

As noted above, privatisation is only a first step in efforts at establishing a dynamic market economy and takes place alongside the development of the private sector itself, via increased investment. To assist in investment mobilisation, a Uganda Investment Authority, where permits and other regulations are handled in the same place, was established. By 1996 up to a total of 2,000 investment licences had been issued to domestic and foreign firms, while land has been purchased for the erection of business premises. However, while a competitive atmosphere is part and parcel of market development, the bigger companies still possess considerable market power. It will be necessary in the future to put together a strong regulatory agency to monitor domestic competition.

With regard to investment incentives, the government has removed all non-neutral measures, such as tax holidays for foreign investors, which have tended to favour speculative investment. A new tax code, which incorporates all the incentives for both domestic and foreign investors, was presented to Parliament. It is hoped that the new code will address the private sector's demands for a simpler tax administration, expand the tax base (and thereby reduce the tax burden on individual businesses), and provide most of the investment and tax incentives.

Still, without the supportive role of a fully developed financial sector, efficient markets will not be able to develop in Uganda. Thus the reform of the financial sector is one of the most important interventions to be undertaken.

The banking sector still suffers from the overhang of a bad loan portfolio accumulated in the 1970s and 1980s. For example, the Uganda Commercial Bank lent huge amounts to politicians from successive regimes, and had huge non-performing assets by the late 1980s. In preparing it for privatisation, there has been retrenchment of employees, as well as branch closures. The non-performing assets of the bank were also placed in a 'bad' bank, and the properties of the debtors auctioned. At the end of 1997 49 per cent of the shares of the UCB were sold to Westmont Land of Malaysia.

In Francophone West Africa privatisation has been rapid in the past decade. Between 1988 and 1993 Benin reduced the number of its public enterprises by 75 per cent, from about sixty in 1988 to fifteen by 1993. Though initially most of the denationalised industries were small, and agri-based, many bigger companies were offered for sale beginning in 1995, including a government-owned hotel chain and mines. But, as has been the experience of many other countries, firms up for privatisation have been heavily indebted. For example, a sugar parastatal had accumulated debts of FCFA 16 billion (US$1=FCFA550), while a cement company, Onigbolo, had debts of FCFA 40 billion. It eventually proved impossible to sell the two companies. In the services sector, the government put the water and electricity parastatal, Sonede, under private management. Similarly, the oil parastatal, Sonacop, remained publicly owned, though the distribution of its products was privatised. Although used frequently in Francophone Africa, these 'partial privatisations' are rare in East Africa. Finally, and as in Uganda, the posts and telecommunications parastatal was divided into two separate entities to be considered separately for privatisation.

In Burkina Faso the privatisation drive, from 1995 and onwards, has led to the sale of banks, insurance companies and credit societies to the private sector. Also significant was the plan to sell the Abidjan–Ouagadougou–Kaya railway line by international tender. Indeed, a number of neighbouring countries are disposing of their national railways: in Cameroon a twenty-year management concession was being considered for the railways, while Gabon was planning to sell its network, covering some 648 km. Mali and Senegal put the Dakar–Bamako railway line up for sale in the mid-1990s. In East and southern Africa the railway systems remain largely in government ownership. The railway lines in Uganda and Tanzania are in relatively poor condition and would demand considerable rehabilitation before interesting private buyers.

In the 1960s African countries saw national airlines as important symbols of independence. However, except in a few countries, they became serious liabilities. In the past few years a number of airlines have been put on sale or simply liquidated. Air Mali, Air Chad and Air Zambia, for example, were declared bankrupt in the early 1990s, while the international routes of the Ugandan, Tanzanian and Rwandese national carriers were taken over by Alliance Air, a new airline jointly owned by a number of African countries, including South Africa. The recent privatisation of Kenya Airways has been illustrative. Though the airline had been ailing for over a decade and had accumulated huge debts domestically and abroad, the decision to privatise it, starting with a private management contract, was widely criticised. The deal was blamed for leading to loss of jobs to foreigners and even to the closure of profitable routes for ulterior motives on the part of the management consultants. Strikes and go-slow measures disrupted activities. Intervention at the highest political level was necessary for privatisation to go ahead. The first 26 per cent of the airline's shares was divested in 1995 and the public flotation of the rest was undertaken in 1996.

Compared with the rest of sub-Saharan Africa, foreign private investors have shown an unusually keen interest in the CFA franc zone countries, with a number of foreign firms acting as advisers and consultants. In the latter regard, Price Waterhouse was retained to supervise the sale of the companies related to the oil sector in the Congo. In Congo's telecommunications and electricity sectors there has been a considerable amount of international interest, among the bidders being American, French and South African companies. Côte d'Ivoire's CI-Télécom is partly owned by French interests, while the state retains 55 per cent of the shares with a view to selling off 20 per cent to company employees. In Gabon a management contract was agreed with a French and Canadian consortium, Socagi, to manage the water and electricity parastatal SEEG, while the London-based Mercer de Zurich undertook a feasibility study of the privatisation of the national railways. Furthermore, French aid assistance and funds from the World Bank have been instrumental in providing technical assistance to the privatisation effort.[2]

Among the lessons to be learnt is the importance of adequate preparation before privatisation begins. Countries in the CFA franc zone made rapid progress because they had adopted legal frameworks for privatisation at an early stage. The second lesson seems to be that there are no fixed formulas for privatisation. Governments have combined outright privatisation with franchises and private management, depending on their resources and political constraints. Thus flexibility is an important ingredient. Third, it has not been easy for countries to ameliorate the social costs, some due to retrenchment, of privatisation. However, while sometimes forcing policy-makers to abandon the privatisation plans, trade-union pressure to keep companies in government ownership in the face of limited finances invariably led to their collapse. Finally, a substantial degree of privatisation has been undertaken rapidly and with much less political opposition than anticipated. Lacking real alternatives, people seem to be willing to give privatisation a chance.

CONCLUSION

This chapter has looked at the public sector's changing role in the African economies. The transformation has been twofold: first, there has been a change in structure, with public enterprises sold outright or put under private management. Second, there has been a radical change in policy emphasis, with controls giving way to market promotion and private sector development. The transition from economies dominated by public enterprises to those functioning under private competition has, however, been made difficult by structural constraints, including poorly developed credit markets, inadequate economic infrastructure and even political opposition. But perhaps the most serious impediment to reform has been the public sector itself. Even after the retrenchment of the civil service, it has been difficult to improve conditions in the public sector by a great deal. Thus morale in the public sector remains low. This lethargy impacts on the private sector via inadequate services and poor regulation. Although recently created specialised agencies, such as those for tax collection, where employees receive enhanced wage packages, have led to remarkable productivity improvements, this cannot be replicated in the rest of government and the problem of wage harmonisation has arisen.

The success of privatisation will ultimately be judged by the extent to which it will contribute to sustainable economic growth via the fostering of institutions for market development and corporate governance. Gray (1996) has argued that 'although formal programmes may lay important ground rules, the tremendous economic, legal, political, and even moral uncertainty profoundly affects – and may even overwhelm – most formal efforts at privatisation, and it is beyond our ability or insight to know what the final results will be'. For Africa, however, it will be interesting to see whether privatisation was the spark that got the continent moving.

NOTES

Parts of the chapter are based on a background paper (Kayizzi-Mugerwa 1996) prepared for the African Development Bank's *African Development Report 1997*. A version of this paper was presented at a workshop on 'Globalisation and Private Sector Development in Africa' at the Centre for Development Research, Copenhagen, 16–18 January 1998. I thank participants for their comments.

1 When announcing his government's nationalisation of major foreign companies and banks in the early 1970s, President Milton Obote noted (Republic of Uganda 1970), 'Courage and boldness must be the essence in the consolidation of our independence.' This statement can be contrasted with that of President Frederick Chiluba when describing the rapid pace of privatisation in Zambia (Panafrican

News Agency, 2 December 1997), 'I don't care whether a cat is white or black as long as it catches mice.'

2 It is ironic that among the most aggressive buyers of public enterprises in Africa are public enterprises from developed countries. For example, France-Télécom has been a frequent buyer, as well as the Belgian parastatal Belgacom. The Swedish telephone parastatal, Telia, has bought shares in newly privatised telecommunication companies in a number of East and southern African countries. From the continent itself, South African parastatals such as Eskom and Sud-Africain Telkom have bought into a number of African utilities. This point was made to me in conversation by Thandika Mkandawire (see also Mkandawire 1998).

REFERENCES

African Development Bank (1997) *The African Development Report*, Oxford: Oxford University Press.

Bagachwa, M.S.D., Mbelle, A.V.Y. and Van Arkadie, B. (eds) (1992) *Market Reforms and Parastatal Restructuring in Tanzania*, Dar-es-Salaam: Economics Department and Economic Research Bureau, University of Dar-es-Salaam.

Barberis N., Boycko M., Shleifer A. and Tsukanova N. (1996) 'How does Privatisation Work? Evidence from Russian Shops', *Journal of Political Economy*, 104 (4): 764–90.

Baumol, W.J. and Lee, S.K. (1988) 'Contestable Markets, Trade and Development', *World Bank Research Observer*, 6 (1): 1–17.

Berg, E. (1992) 'Privatisation Strategies in Africa: the Need for a Reappraisal', mimeograph.

Bhattacharay, B.W. (1996) 'Trends in Privatisation in the Arab World and its Problems and Prospects', *Savings and Development*, XX (1): 5–32.

Bigsten, A., Aguilar, R., Hjalmarsson, L., Ikiara, G., Isaksson, A., Kimuyu, P., Manundu, M., Masai, W., Ndungu, N., Kayizzi-Mugerwa, S., Semboja, H. and Wihlborg C. (1994) *Limitations and Rewards in Kenya's Manufacturing Sector: A Study of Enterprise Development*, report to the World Bank, Washington DC: World Bank.

Chang, H. and Singh, A. (1993) 'Public Enterprises in Developing Countries and Economic Efficiency: a Critical Examination of Analytical, Empirical and Policy Issues', *UNCTAD Review 1993*: 45–82.

Davis, J.T. (1991) 'Institutional Impediments to Workforce Retrenchment and Restructuring in Ghana's State Enterprises', *World Development* 12 (7).

Due, J.M. (1994) 'Liberalization and Privatisation in Tanzania and Zambia', *World Development*, 21 (12): 1981–8.

Due, J.M. and Schmidd, S.C. (1993) 'Comparison of Privatisation of the Economies of Eastern Africa and Eastern Europe', *African Development Review*, 5 (12).

Elkan, W. (1988) 'Entrepreneurs and Entrepreneurship in Africa', *World Bank Research Observer*, 3 (2): 171–88.

Eriksson, G. (1991) *Economic Programmes and Systems Reform in Tanzania*, Macroeconomic Studies 19, Stockholm: Swedish International Development Co-operation Agency (Sida).

Forum Afrique Expansion (1996) *Privatisations dans les pays de la zone franc-stratégies et opportunités d'affaires*, Paris: Publications du Moniteur.

Gersovitz, M. and Paxson, C.H. (1996) 'The Revenues and Expenditures of African Governments: Modalities and Consequences', *Journal of African Economies*, 5 (2).

Gray, C.W. (1996) 'In Search of Owners: Privatisation and Corporate Governance in Transition Economies', *World Bank Research Observer*, 11 (2): 179–97.

Himbara, D. (1994) *Kenyan Capitalists, the State, and Development*, Nairobi: East African Educational Publishers.

Kanbur, R. (1995) 'Welfare Economics, Political Economy and Policy Reform in Ghana', *African Development Review*, 7 (1): 35–49.

Kayizzi-Mugerwa, S. (1996) 'The Public Sector's Changing Role in the Economy', background paper for the *African Development Report 1997*, Abidjan: African Development Bank.

Kayizzi-Mugerwa, S. (1997) *Uganda 1996: Security, Credibility, and Market Development*, Macroeconomic Report 1, Stockholm: Swedish International Development Co-operation Agency (Sida).

Kikeri, S., Nellis, J. and Shirley, M. (1992) *Privatisation: Lessons of Experience*, Washington DC: World Bank.

Killick, T. (1983) 'The Role of the Public Sector in the Industrialisation of African Developing Countries', *Industry and Development*, 7.

Killick, T. and Commander, S. (1988) 'State Divestiture as a Policy Instrument in Developing Countries', *World Development*, 16 (12): 1465–79.

Kimuyu, P. and Kayizzi-Mugerwa, S. (1993) 'Infrastructural Asymmetries in Kenya's Manufacturing Sector', background paper for the World Bank's Regional Programme for Enterprise Development, Washington DC: World Bank.

Laffont, J.-P. and Meleu, M. (1997), 'A Positive Theory of Privatisation for sub-Saharan Africa', paper presented to the African Economic Research Consortium bi-annual workshop, Harare, December.

Lee, S.K. and Anas, A. (1992) 'Costs of Deficient Infrastructure: the Case of Nigerian Manufacturing', *Urban Studies*, 29 (7): 1071–92.

Lee, T. and Jouravlev, A. (1992) 'Self-financing Water Supply and Sanitation Services', *Cepal Review*, 48: 117–28.

Mkandawire, T. (1998) 'Privatisation in Manufacturing Sector in Africa' paper presented at a workshop on Globalisation and Private Sector Development in Africa, Centre for Development Research, Copenhagen, 16–18 January.

Naya, S. (1990) *Private Sector Development and Enterprise Reforms in Growing Asian Economies*, San Francisco: Center for Economic Growth.

Noll, R.G. (1989) 'Economic Perspectives on the Politics of Regulation' in R. Schmalensee and R. Willig (eds), *Handbook of Industrial Organisation*, Amsterdam: North-Holland.

Nuti, D.M. (1992) *The Role of the Banking Sector in the Process of Privatisation*, Economic Papers, Brussels: Directorate-General of Economic Affairs, Commission of the European Communities.

Republic of Uganda (1970) *His Excellency the President's Communication from the Chair of the National Assembly on 20 April 1970*, Entebbe: Government Printer.

Robinson, D. (1990) 'Civil Service Remuneration in Africa', *International Labour Review*, 129 (3): 371–86.

Schiavo-Campo, S. (1996) 'Reforming the Civil Service', *Finance and Development*, September.

Van de Walle, N. (1989) 'Privatisation in Developing Countries: a Review of the Issues', *World Development*, 17 (5): 601–15.

Wade, R. (1985) 'The Market for Public Office: Why the Indian State is not Better at Development', *World Development*, 13 (4): 467–97.

Wangwe, S. (1992) 'The Nature and Extent of Parastatal Restructuring: Case of Industrial Parastatals in Tanzania' in M.S.D. Bagachwa, A.V.Y. Mbelle and B. Van Arkadie (eds) *Market Reforms and Parastatal Restructuring in Tanzania*, Dar-es-Salaam: Economics Department and Economic Research Bureau, University of Dar-es-Salaam.

World Bank (1994) *Adjustment in Africa: Results and the Road Ahead*, Washington DC: World Bank.

INDEX

Congress of South African Trade Unions
(COSATU) *see under* South Africa
Connor, W. 238–9
Consultative Group (CG) 54
contract enforcement 19
Co-operative Societies 129, 130
corruption 279
cost function estimates 159–61
Côte d'Ivoire 31, 162, 176, 266, 286
Crawford, E.W. 268
credibility 34, 38, 112
credit auctions 84; markets 19, 36,
255; rural 121, 128–32

Damus, S. 67
Davies, R. 102
Davis, J.T. 280
Ddumba-Ssentamu, J. 6, 126–35
De Long, J. 29
Deadman, D.F. 89
Deaton, A. 20
debt: external 3, 39–40, 204, 207–8,
234; overhang 38; relief 59
deforestation 266–7
de Klerk, F.W. 213–15
de la Torre, A. 235
Delgado, C. 256
De Long, J. 29
demand 86–8
demand-following hypothesis 110
Democratic Republic of the Congo 31,
36, 177, 181, 182, 267
democratisation 40–1
Denny, M. 166
Dervis, K. 70
Devarajan, S. 65
Diewert, W.E. 166
Djibouti 178, 180, 233–6, 237,
240
Dollar, D. 22, 53
Domovitz, I. 166
Donovan, W.G. 248
Dornbusch, R. 116, 217
Dowswell, C.R. 268
Dreze, J. 24
Due, J.M. 278
Durojaiye, B.O. 117

East African Community (EAC) 178–9,
182
Easterly, W. 20
economic adjustment 51, 53, 55
Economic Community of Central
African States 177
Economic Community of Countries in
the Great Lakes 177
Economic Community of West African
States (ECO-WAS) 177
economic growth: and agriculture 269;
constraints on 9; and
investment 28–32, 44–7;
kick-starting 216; latecomers 2, 16;
macroeconomic populism 217; record
of 16–18, 29–30; and regional
integration 174; shared 24; theory
28; *see also under individual countries*
economic liberalisation 4–5, 8
economic stability 43–4
education 21, 147–8, 178, 270
Edwards, S. 217
efficiency 19, 119, 280
Egypt 30, 31, 35, 177, 277
Eicher, C.K. 249, 257
Ekechi, A.O. 119
elasticities 80
Elbadawi, I.A. 33, 174–5
electrification 271–2
Elhiraika, A.B. 33, 37
Elkan, W. 281
employment 9
entrepreneurs versus rent-seekers 23–4
environment 135; business 41–2; and
population growth 250–1, 259, 271;
and poverty 10, 264–9;
regulatory 282
Equatorial Guinea 177
Ericksson, G. 277
Eritrea 178, 180, 233–7, 240–1, 244
Ethiopia 242–4; banking 138, 144;
civil war 237–8; Ethiopian People's
Revolutionary Democratic Front
(EPRDF) 233–4; ethnicity 240–2;
growth 15, 33; regional co-
operation 178, 180, 235–6
ethnonationalism 9, 237–42